*Nineteenth-Century*
*Literary Perspectives*

# Nineteenth-Century Literary Perspectives

## Essays in Honor of
## Lionel Stevenson

*Edited by*
Clyde de L. Ryals

*with the assistance of*
John Clubbe

*and*

Benjamin Franklin Fisher IV

Duke University Press
*Durham, N.C.*
*1974*

© 1974, Duke University Press
L.C.C. card no. 73–84842
I.S.B.N. 0–8223–0314–0
Printed in the United States of
America by Heritage Printers, Inc.
Charlotte, North Carolina

# Contents

# *Preface*

FOR OVER FORTY YEARS Lionel Stevenson taught English at various colleges and universities throughout the United States, literally from coast to coast. While his literary interests were wide and the courses he taught covered the whole range of English literature, as a scholar he is best known for the books and articles that he wrote about the nineteenth century, especially the Victorian period. Indeed it may be justly said that Professor Stevenson was one of the founders of Victorian studies. For at a time when Victorian literature was denigrated he demonstrated in his numerous publications that the literature of the period 1830–1900 was neither so sentimental nor so mindless as many of its detractors made it out to be. The popularity of Victorian prose and poetry today is surely owing to those like Mr. Stevenson whose pioneering efforts, both in their teaching and in their writings, cleared away the misconceptions concerning the era and revealed its vast body of literature to belong among the glories of the English language.

This volume gathers together essays written in his honor upon his retirement from Duke University, where he was James B. Duke Professor of English. While the book was in press, there came the sad news that Mr. Stevenson died on 21 December 1973 at Vancouver, where he was Distinguished Professor at the University of British Columbia for the academic year 1973–74. Because the volume was designed to honor him while alive, the introductory biographical essay has been allowed to remain as it was originally written. Appended to it are a bibliography of Mr. Stevenson's publications and a list of dissertations which he directed at Duke. The other essays reflect his special interest in the nineteenth century and provide new perspectives on the literature of the Romantic and Victorian periods.

January 1974                                                                 CLR

# Lionel Stevenson

John Clubbe

*Duke University*

WHEN Lionel Stevenson first began to study the Victorians early in the twenties, they were usually viewed with the ironic and slightly condescending smile of Lytton Strachey. Few deemed them serious subjects for graduate study. Today, nearly five decades later, the wheel has come full circle: hardly another period of English literature has had its major assumptions shaken and overturned with such frequency, its major figures studied and reevaluated so thoroughly, or can boast as distinguished an array of scholars working within it. Although Mr. Stevenson has ranged into other fields, the Victorian writers were his first love and his chief work has been done with them. Through his critical biographies and his essays he has taken a leading role in the reassessment of the Victorians which began hesitantly in the twenties, quietly gathered momentum in the thirties, but only after the second World War reached major proportions. Lionel Stevenson has been one of the most important pioneer scholars of his generation. Unlike some who have rested content with their initial discoveries, he has gone on to travel widely in the "realms of gold" he first explored. Today he is widely recognized as the doyen of America's Victorian scholars.

Arthur Lionel Stevenson was born in Edinburgh on 16 July 1902, and christened in St. Giles's Church. His father was Henry Stevenson; his mother, née Mabel Rose Cary, an aunt of the novelist Joyce Cary. It is an unusual fact of his ancestry that his grandfather was born in the last years of the eighteenth century; portraits of these Scottish forebears for five generations hang in the Stevenson home in Durham, North Carolina, today. When he was five, the family emigrated to Vancouver Island, British Columbia, where they settled in a small town forty miles above Victoria in an area then partly unexplored and uncharted. In 1922, at the age of nineteen, he received his B.A. from the University of British Columbia and the following year his M.A. from the University of Toronto. In August 1923 he moved to the United States to pursue his studies at the University of California at Berkeley and he has ever since made this country his home (he was naturalized an American citizen in 1930). Mr. Stevenson's excellence as a teacher owes much to the example of his own mentors. At the University of British Columbia Garnet Sedgewick left the deepest impression upon him, at Berkeley it was Benjamin Lehman. Both stimulated his interest in the Victorians. When he received his doctorate from Berkeley in 1925 with a dissertation later published as *Darwin Among the Poets*, he was not yet twenty-three years old.

An instructorship at Berkeley in 1925 was Mr. Stevenson's first full-time teaching appointment in an academic career now spanning nearly fifty years. He left it in 1930 to accept a position as professor and chairman of the English Department at Arizona State College (now University), then a school of 300 students, today of more than twenty thousand. Like Vancouver Island in the first decades of this century and the Bay area in the twenties, Tempe in the thirties had only half-emerged from its frontier days. Mr. Stevenson has prized memories of his early years in Canada and the United States and looks forward to the time when he can put them on paper. In 1933, the worst year of the Depression, the state of Arizona went bankrupt and for a while salaries were paid in warrants instead of cash. So disheartening was the academic situation at this time that Mr. Stevenson abruptly decided to withdraw his savings and fulfill a life-long wish by going to study at Oxford. This sudden decision—uncharacteristic on the surface—actually serves to reveal an underlying facet of his character: it must be seen as one of those impulses which have on occasion altered the career of a man whose way of life is rational action and whose scholarly hallmark is logicality of thought. In 1935 Mr. Stevenson received his B.Litt. from Oxford, where he was a student at St. Catherine's Society, with a thesis on Lady Morgan directed by D. Nichol Smith. Edmund Blunden and C. S. Lewis were his examiners, the latter on the threshold of his fame. Chapman & Hall published his thesis the next year as *The Wild Irish Girl: The Life of Sydney Owenson, Lady Morgan.* It remains the standard study of her life and career.

Upon his return from England, Mr. Stevenson spent two further years at Arizona State College before joining the University of Southern California in 1937 as assistant professor of English. He rose rapidly through the ranks, becoming associate professor in 1941, professor in 1944. He served as departmental chairman at Southern California from 1943 until 1955, when he accepted an appointment as James B. Duke Professor of English Literature at Duke University. Since then he has been a distinguished member of the Duke faculty, and from 1964 to 1967 he served the English Department as chairman. In addition to his regular appointments, Mr. Stevenson held a visiting professorship at the University of Illinois in 1952–53 and in 1967–68 was Berg Visiting Professor at New York University; in 1960–61 he was a visiting lecturer at Oxford and is now an honorary member of the Senior Common Room of St. Catherine's College. During 1972–73 he was a Visiting Professor at the University of Houston, and in 1973 was asked to hold the first Distinguished Professorship of English at the University of British Columbia, his alma mater. He has taught in the summer sessions at San Francisco State College, the University of British Columbia, New York University, and the University of Colorado. Few men in the academic profession today have had comparable breadth of experience as a teacher.

The many positions of responsibility within professional organizations which Mr. Stevenson has held and the many honors which he has received amply testify to the range of his activities and interests. Although they are noted elsewhere, two cannot pass without mention here: his election in 1951 as a Fellow of the Royal Society of Literature and his selection in 1960–61 as a John Simon Guggenheim Memorial Fellow. All his life he has shown interest in the creative endeavors of others, and, as chairman of the editorial committee of the Borestone Mountain Poetry awards since 1948, he reads each year hundreds of poems published during the preceding twelve months and helps to choose those that will be published in the annual volume *Best Poems of 19——*. A poet himself, with two published brochures to his credit, Mr. Stevenson takes pleasure in keeping up in this way with modern poetry. Every Christmas his cards greet his friends with a new poem of his own.

Apart from his verse, Mr. Stevenson has written ten books. They range from *Appraisals of Canadian Literature*, published in 1926, to *A History of the English Novel: Yesterday and After*, published in 1967, and written as the eleventh and concluding volume to Ernest Baker's *History of the English Novel*. The tenth book, *The Pre-Raphaelite Poets*, appeared late in 1972. Although the range of Mr. Stevenson's subject matter is impressive, it is his critical biographies of Victorian novelists that have secured his reputation. These include *Doctor Quicksilver: The Life of Charles Lever* (1939), *The Showman of Vanity Fair: The Life of William Makepeace Thackeray* (1947), and *The Ordeal of George Meredith: A Biography* (1953). In a front-page article in 1970 discussing modern scholarship on Meredith, the *Times Literary Supplement* singled out Mr. Stevenson's as one of "the most reliable and . . . readable books about Meredith" and commended him not only for mastering all the available sources but also for presenting "in straightforward, unprovocative form the known facts of Meredith's life and the opinions formed of him by those who knew him." It is perhaps the most perfectly conceived and sensitively written of Mr. Stevenson's biographies, though he himself will express no opinion as to his "favorite," believing each book the "best" as he was writing it. Between the Thackeray and the Meredith biographies came *English Literature of the Victorian Period* (1949), with John D. Cooke, still one of the best introductions to the field. His more recent studies show him encompassing larger subjects. *The English Novel: A Panorama* (1960) examines chronologically the varying fortunes of the novel in England as it developed over the course of three centuries, while the *History of the English Novel: Yesterday and After* surveys the novel in recent times. Mr. Stevenson's books reflect a mind that has never ceased to think about literature, one that envisages the scholar investigating different subjects over a lifetime instead of being content to remain *the* authority on one. He believes that the scholar, rather than learning more and more about less and less, should constantly seek to widen his knowledge so that each new project will build on the ones before. Mr. Stevenson's own work stands as a model of such cumulative endeavor: from studies of lesser-known figures to those on major writers like Thackeray and Meredith, finally the wider surveys of the novel.

The extent of Mr. Stevenson's other publications need only be hinted at here. He has edited *Victorian Fiction: A Guide to Research* (1964), also contributing the chapter on Thackeray; earlier he wrote a long bibliographical essay on "The Later Victorian Poets" for the companion volume *The Victorian Poets* (1956; 1968). He is the only scholar to have contributed to both volumes. Half-a-dozen reprints of Victorian novels bear introductions by Mr. Stevenson, while a listing of his contributions to reference works and his articles (several of which have been reprinted in books) fills several pages of the appended Bibliography. The articles range in time from "Overseas Literature from a Canadian Point of View" (1924) to a forthcoming paper on Meredith's poetry given as a lecture in the spring of 1971 before the Royal Society of Literature. Not only does the range of subjects testify to the breadth of Mr. Stevenson's intellectual interests, but it strongly suggests that his Scottish ancestry, Canadian upbringing, and American training have aided him in gaining the perspective needed to view the literature of the English-speaking world within a framework of cultural internationalism. Less evident on the surface perhaps but even more real, it also testifies to the joy which he finds in working with ideas and to his belief that only a scholar who writes as well as reads will continue to respond to the imaginative diversity of literature.

Mr. Stevenson views a biography as a work of art. Two books which came out in the late 1920's—Harold Nicolson's *The Development of Literary Biography* and especially André Maurois' *Aspects of Biography*—influenced his conception of the biographer's role. Like Maurois in his insistence upon the artistic qualities of a biography yet unlike him in his refusal to use fictionalizations and distorting irony, Mr. Stevenson values biography over fiction because, like Byron, he finds truth "stranger than fiction"—and intrinsically more interesting. He would agree with Maurois that no novelist can create a character that rivals the varied life and psychological depth of the real subject whose life the biographer must depict. Yet that life must have, in Maurois' words, a "hidden unity," and the biographer's challenge is to find it. He must also tell a good story well, discover the essential qualities which characterize his subject, and illuminate them by selecting the one detail which reveals rather than the ten which blur. "Biography," in Maurois' view, "does not consist in telling all one knows . . . but in taking stock of one's knowledge and choosing what is essential." A reading of any one of Mr. Stevenson's biographies will show how well he has mastered these techniques.

Mr. Stevenson has not only been a scholar but a begetter of scholars. Few of his students have left his classes without a finer understanding of literature. They are amazed that he can give perfectly organized lectures without notes and they speak with awe of the brilliance and the range of knowledge displayed in them. A Stevenson lecture can often be a dramatic performance, for he delights in graphic readings of poetry and strongly encourages students who intend to become teachers to act in plays to develop good voices. At Duke he has taught a wide variety of courses, undergraduate as well as graduate, in the nineteenth century. He has guided nearly forty doctoral dissertations in fields from the Romantics through contemporary literature, and though Victorian subjects have pride of place, his students have written on Wordsworth and Byron, Louis Mac-Neice and the development of Australian drama. They respect him as much for his wise guidance of their work as for the high but unobtrusive standard he set for them. Together they have honored him with letters testifying to his influence upon their scholarship and their lives.

The range of Lionel Stevenson's professional activities hardly begins to suggest the qualities of mind and character he displays daily with his colleagues and students. To speak at length about his character and personality would be inappropriate in a volume of this kind and would, moreover, be distasteful to him. But a few things must not be left unsaid. He is a man of unaffected modesty, whose reticence and self-control mask both sensitivity and tenderness. His keenness of mind is as conspicuous in his wit as it is in his scholarship. He is always alert and interested, whether listening to a scholarly paper or guiding the independent study of an undergraduate, always willing to help a student or colleague, whether by writing still another letter of recommendation or by giving advice that is as sensible as it is discreet. Only a man who possesses remarkable powers of self-discipline could handle such a staggering range of activities, yet his seriousness of purpose does not interfere with, but rather enhances, his constant enjoyment of life. The key to Mr. Stevenson's fine career may lie in his immense reserves of will power. His sense of responsibility to others is total. He will have everything ready on time, whether it is an examination to be typed, a dissertation to be read, a manuscript to be completed—"and all he did done perfectly." His mind immediately seizes the essence of a subject or problem and bodies it forth in lucid discourse or limpid prose. Rarely will there be hesitation, excess wordiness never. Yet even with such an impressive scholarly achievement, there remains a love of life and of humanity in the man, a realization that "the need for love" (the title of one of his recent essays) is a necessary and fulfilling part of every human being. Only a man who has lived with a full awareness of his own limitations could have written, as he did in his recent lecture on Meredith's poetry, that "the only possible means for attaining serenity and joy is submission to inexorable natural forces with a total rejection of fear and self-interest."

No tribute to Lionel Stevenson would be complete that does not include Lillian Stevenson, the former Lillian Sprague Jones whom he married in 1954. Mr. Stevenson has been fortunate in many things but in none more than in his wife, who, with her daughter Marietta, has enhanced his life with the privilege of parenthood and enlarged his circle of acquaintances through her winning hospitality. The longer one knows the Stevensons the more one recognizes how perfectly they complement one another. Since coming to Duke, they have participated actively in the life of their community and of their church, where Mr. Stevenson is a lay reader. He takes especial pride in the academic achievements of his stepdaughter, who was graduated from Radcliffe and then received a degree in architecture from M.I.T. Following her graduation in 1966 Marietta Stevenson became Mrs. David Millet.

Mr. Stevenson's long and active career suggests the possibilities open to those in the academic profession. It is, in every way, an exemplary career. As teacher, scholar, friend, his is a model of what a man's life can become.

Although his colleagues at Duke regret that his active involvement in the life of the English Department can be no more, they know that his professional activities will continue unabated. His friends await with expectation the volume of reminiscences which he has promised them of his youth and early life. Those of us who have been privileged to know and work with Mr. Stevenson wish him, in his turn, "serenity and joy" in the years to come. We delight to honor him with this gathering of studies in his spirit.

## Professional Affiliations

Fellow of the Royal Society of Literature, elected 1951.
Honorary member, Phi Beta Kappa, Phi Kappa Phi.
John Simon Guggenheim Memorial Fellow, 1960–61.

Vice-president, Western College Association, 1946–47,
Chairman, Southern Humanities Conference, 1959–60.

Chairman, Editorial Committee, Borestone Mountain Poetry Awards, 1948–73,
Associate Editor, *The Personalist*, 1948–59,
Member of Editorial Board, *The South Atlantic Quarterly*, 1956–72,
Member of Editorial Committee, *PMLA*, 1966–67,
Member of Advisory Board, *The Pacific Spectator*, 1948–55,
  *Nineteenth-Century Fiction*, 1949–73,
  *Victorian Studies*, 1959–62,
  *Studies in English Literature*, 1961–73,
  *College English*, 1962–63,
  *Victorian Poetry*, 1963–73,
  *Extrapolation*, 1971–73,
Editor, *Dickens Studies Newsletter*, 1972–73.

Secretary-treasurer, Philological Association of the Pacific Coast, 1928–32; president, 1948–50,
President, Men's Faculty Club, University of Southern California, 1942–43,
President, Southern California Branch, University of British Columbia Alumni Association, 1948–49.

Life member, Modern Humanities Research Association (American Chairman, 1968–72),
  Modern Language Association of America (member of book

publication committee, 1952–62; chairman of Victorian
literature section, 1959; English 10, Recent Developments
in Research in the English Novel, 1972; Seminar, English
Literature in Transition: The Short Story in Embryo, 1972),
California Writers' Club (president, 1928–30),
P.E.N. Club (president of Los Angeles center, 1943–53; dele-
gate to international congresses, Vienna, 1929, Edinburgh,
1934, Paris, 1937, Lausanne, 1951),
Oxford Society (California representative, 1938–55).

Member, College English Association (president of Southern California
region, 1950–51; national vice-president, 1953–54; member of
board of directors, 1954–56),
English-Speaking Union (president of Raleigh-Durham-Chapel
Hill branch, 1958–60),
Dickens Fellowship (president of East Bay branch, 1926–28, Los
Angeles branch, 1938–41, 1944–46),
South Atlantic Modern Language Association,
Poetry Society of America,
Canadian Authors' Association,
Authors' Club, London, England,
Arts and Letters Club, Toronto, Canada,
International Association of Professors of English (member of
advisory committee, 1965–73).

## Bibliography

### BOOKS

*Appraisals of Canadian Literature.* Toronto: The Macmillan Co., 1926.
*Darwin Among the Poets.* Chicago: University of Chicago Press, 1932;
New York: Russell & Russell, 1963.
*The Wild Irish Girl: The Life of Sydney Owenson, Lady Morgan (1776–
1859).* London: Chapman & Hall, 1936; New York: Russell & Russell,
1969.
*Doctor Quicksilver: The Life of Charles Lever.* London: Chapman & Hall,
1939; New York: Russell & Russell, 1969.
*The Showman of Vanity Fair: The Life of William Makepeace Thackeray.*
New York: Charles Scribner's Sons; London: Chapman & Hall, 1947;
New York: Russell & Russell, 1968.

*English Literature of the Victorian Period* (with John D. Cooke). New York: Appleton-Century-Crofts, 1949.

*The Ordeal of George Meredith: A Biography.* New York: Charles Scribner's Sons, 1953; London: Peter Owen, Ltd., 1954; New York: Russell & Russell, 1967.

*The English Novel: A Panorama.* Boston: Houghton Mifflin Co., 1960; London: Constable & Co., 1961.

*The History of the English Novel:* vol. XI. *Yesterday and After.* New York: Barnes & Noble; Guildford: Charles Traylen, 1967.

*The Pre-Raphaelite Poets.* Chapel Hill: University of North Carolina Press, 1972. N.Y.: W. W. Norton & Co. 1974. The Norton Library.

## POETRY

*A Pool of Stars.* Toronto: Ryerson Press, 1926.
*The Rose of the Sea.* Toronto: Ryerson Press, 1932.

## BOOK EDITED

*Victorian Fiction: A Guide to Research.* Cambridge, Mass.: Harvard University Press, 1964.

## INTRODUCTIONS

*The Man of Property,* by John Galsworthy. Modern Standard Authors. New York: Charles Scribner's Sons, 1949. Introduction, pp. vii–xviii.

*The History of Henry Esmond,* by W. M. Thackeray. Modern Classics. New York: Harper & Bros., 1950. Introduction, pp. v–xvii.

*The Ordeal of Richard Feverel,* by George Meredith. Modern Library College Editions. New York: Random House, 1950. Introduction, pp. ix–xxvii.

*The Egoist,* by George Meredith. Riverside Editions. Boston: Houghton Mifflin Co., 1958. Introduction, pp. v–xx.

*Vanity Fair,* by W. M. Thackeray. Pocket Library Editions. New York: Pocket Books, Inc., 1958. Introduction, pp. v–xiii.

*The History of Henry Esmond,* by W. M. Thackeray. Bantam Classics. New York: Bantam Books, Inc., 1961. Introduction, pp. v–xvii.

*Esther Waters,* by George Moore. Riverside Editions. Boston: Houghton Mifflin Co., 1963. Introduction, pp. v–xxiv. Appendix, pp. 335–54.

*A Thackeray Library,* by Henry Sayre Van Duzer. Port Washington, N. Y.: Kennikat Press, 1965. Introduction, pp. i–v.

ARTICLES REPRINTED IN BOOKS

Meredith and the Problem of Style in the Novel. *Stil- und Formprobleme in der Literatur*, ed. by Paul Böckmann. Heidelberg: Carl Winter Universitätsverlag, 1960. Pp. 339–43.

The "High-born Maiden" Symbol in Tennyson. *Critical Essays on the Poetry of Tennyson*, ed. by John Killham. London: Routledge & Kegan Paul, 1960. Pp. 126–36.

The Pertinacious Victorian Poets. *Victorian Literature: Modern Essays in Criticism*, ed. by Austin Wright. New York: Oxford University Press, 1961. Pp. 16–31.

The Artistic Problem: Science Fiction as Romance. *SF: The Other Side of Realism*, ed. by Thomas D. Clareson. Bowling Green, Ohio: Bowling Green University Popular Press, 1971. Pp. 96–104.

CONTRIBUTIONS TO REFERENCE WORKS

*The Victorian Poets: A Guide to Research*, ed. by Frederic E. Faverty. Cambridge, Mass.: Harvard University Press, 1956. Chapter 9, "The Later Victorian Poets," pp. 228–66. Second ed., revised, 1968, pp. 353–403.

*The Cambridge Bibliography of English Literature*, Vol. V: Supplement. Cambridge: The University Press, 1957. The Nineteenth Century: 3. Prose Fiction: "Bibliographies, Histories and Critical Studies," pp. 614–15; "George Meredith," pp. 636–37.

*Contemporary Literary Scholarship: A Critical Review*, ed. by Lewis Leary. New York: Appleton-Century-Crofts, Inc., 1958. Chapter 8, "The Victorian Period," pp. 139–56.

*Victorian Fiction: A Guide to Research*, ed. by Lionel Stevenson. Cambridge, Mass.: Harvard University Press, 1964. Chapter 4, "William Makepeace Thackeray," pp. 154–87.

*Collier's Encyclopedia*. New York: Crowell-Collier Publishing Co., 1962. "Thomas Hughes," XII, 342; "John Keble," XIV, 11; "George Meredith," XV, 721–22; "Sydney Smith," XXI, 97.

*Encyclopedia Americana*. New York: The Grolier Society, 1964. "Chronicles," VI, 636–37; "*Evelyn Innes*," X, 567f–g; "Holinshed's Chronicles," XIV, 317; "*The Light of Asia*," XVII, 495; "George Meredith," XVIII, 670–71; "Novelette," XX, 511a; "*Piers Plowman*," XXII, 77; "*Plain Tales from the Hills*," XX, 147.

*The New Cambridge Bibliography of English Literature,* Vol. III. Cambridge: The University Press, 1969. "William Makepeace Thackeray," pp. 855–64; "The Brontës," 864–73; "Charles Reade," 878–82; "Anthony Trollope," 882–89.

CRITICAL AND RESEARCH ARTICLES*

Overseas Literature from a Canadian Point of View. *English Review,* 39 (Dec. 1924), 876–86.

The Significance of Canadian Literature. *University of California Chronicle,* 27 (Jan. 1925), 32–42.

Canadian Literature and the New Universe. *Queen's Quarterly,* 33 (Dec. 1925), 143–55.

Barham and the Irresponsible Decade. *University of California Chronicle,* 28 (Oct. 1926), 400–18.

An Estimate of "The Strange Gentleman." *Dickensian,* 23 (Dec. 1926), 53–55.

A French Text Book by Robert Browning. *Modern Language Notes,* 42 (May 1927), 299–305.

Brooke's "Universal Beauty" and Modern Thought. *PMLA,* 43 (March 1928), 198–209.

A Source for Barrie's *Peter Pan. Philological Quarterly,* 8 (April 1929), 210–14.

Atherton vs. Grundy—the Forty Years' War. *Bookman,* 69 (July 1929), 464–72.

Masefield and the New Universe. *Sewanee Review,* 37 (July 1929), 336–48.

George Sterling's Place in Modern Poetry. *University of California Chronicle,* 31 (Oct. 1929), 404–21.

Stepfathers of Victorianism. *Virginia Quarterly Review,* 6 (April 1930), 251–67.

Dean of American Letters—Julian Hawthorne. *Bookman,* 73 (April 1931), 164–72.

Mute Inglorious Whitmans. *University of California Chronicle,* 33 (July 1931), 296–316.

The Ideas in Kipling's Poetry. *University of Toronto Quarterly,* 1 (July 1932), 467–89.

An Introduction to Young Mr. Dickens. *Dickensian,* 29 (March 1933), 111–14.

*Excludes reviews and short notes.

*Vanity Fair* and Lady Morgan. *PMLA*, 48 (June 1933), 547–51.

Romanticism Run to Seed. *Virginia Quarterly Review*, 9 (Oct. 1933), 510–25.

Names in *Pickwick*. *Dickensian*, 33 (Sept. 1936), 241–44.

Prude's Progress. *Virginia Quarterly Review*, 13 (April 1937), 257–70.

The Novelist as Fortune Hunter. *Virginia Quarterly Review*, 13 (July 1937), 376–90.

Dickens's Dark Novels, 1851–1857. *Sewanee Review*, 51 (Summer 1943), 398–409.

Tennyson, Browning, and a Romantic Fallacy. *University of Toronto Quarterly*, 13 (Jan. 1944), 175–95.

The Second Birth of the English Novel. *University of Toronto Quarterly*, 14 (July 1945), 366–74.

Miss Landon, "The Milk-and-Watery Moon of our Darkness," 1824–30. *Modern Language Quarterly*, 8 (Sept. 1947), 355–63.

Dickens and the Origin of *The Warden*. *Trollopian*, 2 (Sept. 1947), 83–89.

Who was Mr. Turveydrop? *Dickensian*, 44 (Dec. 1947), 39–41.

The "High-born Maiden" Symbol in Tennyson. *PMLA*, 63 (March 1948), 234–43.

Trollope as a Recorder of Verbal Usage. *Trollopian*, 3 (Sept. 1948), 119–25.

"The Ancient Mariner" as a Dramatic Monologue. *Personalist*, 30 (Winter 1949), 34–44.

The Antecedents of P. G. Wodehouse. *Arizona Quarterly*, 5 (Autumn 1949), 226–34.

The Intellectual Novel in the Nineteenth Century. *Personalist*, 31 (Winter Spring, 1950), 42–57, 157–66.

The Pertinacious Victorian Poets. *University of Toronto Quarterly*, 21 (April 1952), 232–45.

George Meredith's Birthplace. *Times Literary Supplement*, 5 June 1953, p. 365.

Meredith and the Interviewers. *Modern Philology*, 51 (Aug. 1953), 50–63.

Meredith's Atypical Novel, A Study of *Rhoda Fleming*. *The Image of the Work* (University of California English Studies) 9 (1955), 89–109.

An English Admirer of Walt Whitman. *American Literature*, 29 (Jan. 1958), 470–73.

Meredith and the Problem of Style in the Novel. *Zeitschrift für Anglistik und Amerikanistik*, 6 (Summer 1958), 181–89.

"My Last Duchess" and *Parisina*. *Modern Language Notes*, 74 (June 1959), 489–92.

1859: Year of Fulfillment. *Centennial Review*, 3 (Fall 1959), 337–56.

Matthew Arnold's Poetry: A Modern Appraisal. *Tennessee Studies in Literature*, 4 (1959), 31–41.

The Anthologist's Dilemma. *South Atlantic Quarterly*, 59 (Winter 1960), 82–87.

George du Maurier and the Romantic Novel. *Essays by Divers Hands* (Transactions of the Royal Society of Literature), ns, 30 (1960), 36–54.

Darwin and the Novel. *Nineteenth-Century Fiction*, 15 (June 1960), 29–38.

The Death of Love: A Touchstone of Poetic Realism. *Western Humanities Review*, 14 (Autumn 1960), 365–76.

The Modern Values of Victorian Fiction. *College Language Association Journal*, 4 (Sept. 1960), 1–7.

The Unfinished Gothic Cathedral: A Study of the Organic Unity of Wordsworth's Poetry. *University of Toronto Quarterly*, 32 (Jan. 1963), 170–83.

The Artistic Problem: Science Fiction as Romance. *Extrapolation*, 4 (May 1963), 17–22.

Joyce Cary and the Anglo-Irish Tradition. *Modern Fiction Studies*, 9 (Autumn 1963), 210–16.

Literature in an Emerging Nation. *South Atlantic Quarterly*, 64 (Summer 1965), 394–400.

American Poets and the Pre-Raphaelites. *English Studies Today*: Fourth series, ed. by Ilva Cellini and Giorgio Melchiori. Rome: Edizioni di Storia e Letteratura, 1966. Pp. 406–26.

The Relativity of Truth in Victorian Fiction. *Victorian Essays: A Symposium*, ed. by Warren D. Anderson and Thomas D. Clareson. Kent, Ohio: Kent State University Press, 1967. Pp. 71–86.

The Key Poem of the Victorian Age. *Essays in American and English Literature Presented to Bruce Robert McElderry*, ed. Max F. Schulz. Athens, Ohio: Ohio University Press, 1967. Pp. 260–89.

George Moore: Romantic, Naturalist, Aesthete. *Etudes Anglaises*, 21 (Dec. 1968), 362–66.

The Need for Love. *Virginia Quarterly Review*, 45 (Winter 1969), 168–72.

Hardy in Two Centuries. *Yale Review*, 60 (Autumn 1970), 126–30.

The Mystique of Romantic Narrative Poetry. *Romantic and Victorian: Studies in Memory of William H. Marshall*, ed. by W. Paul Elledge and Richard L. Hoffman. Rutherford, N.J.: Fairleigh Dickinson University Press, 1971. Pp. 26–42.

Varieties of the Novel. *Studies in Burke and His Time*, 13 (Spring 1972), 2251–59.

The Short Story in Embryo. *English Literature in Transition*, 25 (Fall 1972), 261–68.

The Rationale of Victorian Fiction. *Nineteenth-Century Fiction*, 27 (March 1973), 391–404.

The State of Victorian Studies, 1962–1972: Victorian Fiction. *Victorian Newsletter*, no. 43 (Spring 1973), pp. 11–15.

The Poets of the Nineties. *Victorian Poetry and Prose*, ed. Richard C. Tobias. Supplement to *Victorian Poetry*, 12 (Spring 1974), 72–76.

### Ph.D. Dissertations Directed at Duke University

1. Charles E. Edge. Jane Austen's Novels: The Theme of Isolation. 1958
2. Charles E. Johnson, Jr. The Dramatic Career of Robert Browning. 1958
3. Norman James. Oscar Wilde's Dramaturgy. 1959
4. Vereen M. Bell. Character and Point of View in Representative Victorian Novels. 1959
5. Caroline Herbert Smith. Journey, Ordeal, Recovery: Metaphoric Patterns in Meredith's Early Prose and Poetry, 1849–1859. 1960
6. Robert L. Zimmerman. Manuscript Revision in *Childe Harold's Pilgrimage*. 1960
7. Leslie F. Chard II. Wordsworth's Radical Career, 1791–1798. 1962
8. George E. McCelvey III. William Godwin's Novels: Theme and Craft. 1963
9. Max Keith Sutton. Shaping Forces in the Theory and Practice of Victorian Humor. 1964
10. William F. Halloran. William Sharp and Fiona Macleod. 1964
11. Richard Michael Kelly. Douglas Jerrold, Author and Journalist. 1964
12. Frank Jordan, Jr. "The Convenient Tribe": Scott's Narrators. 1965
13. Larry James Kirkpatrick. Elizabeth Bowen and Company. 1965
14. John J. Dunn. The Role of Macpherson's Ossian in the Development of British Romanticism. 1965
15. Mary Ruth Miller. The Crimean War in British Periodical Literature. 1966
16. Ralph Mandell Tutt. Charles Lamb: Author in Search of a Form. 1966
17. Arthur McA. Miller. The Last Man: The Eschatological Theme in English Poetry and Fiction, 1806–1839. 1966

*Nineteenth-Century*
*Literary Perspectives*

# A Nineteenth-Century Touchstone: Chapter XV
## of BIOGRAPHIA LITERARIA

U. C. Knoepflmacher

*University of California,*
*Berkeley*

THE NOTION THAT *Biographia Literaria* is a patch-work composed of unintegrated and unrelated disquisitions has best been discredited by those critics who have tried to show that the book is centered, not on Coleridge's own literary life and opinions, but rather on the work of William Wordsworth. In his essay on "The Integrity of 'Biographia Literaria,' " George Whalley first demonstrated how Coleridge's attack on Hartley simultaneously acts as a critique of Wordsworth's own theories of association and of the definitions of the imagination developed in the 1815 Preface.[1] Going one step further, Stephen Prickett has recently argued that "the early sections, up to the famous pronouncement on Imagination in chapter XIII have an even closer relationship to Wordsworth than Whalley suggests."[2]

In the essay which follows, I intend to provide further support for these views by taking a close look at chapter XV of *Biographia Literaria*, a chapter in which Coleridge draws heavily on material he had already used in one of his less successful Shakespeare lectures of 1811.[3] At first glance, chapter XV seems unduly digressive. Coleridge's remarks on Shakespeare's narrative poems "Venus and Adonis" and "The Rape of Lucrece" as well as his famous comparison between the creative modes of Milton and Shakespeare seem a diversion—a negation of the author's promise to explain "in as few words as possible" his ideas about poetry before returning to a sustained critique of Wordsworth's "poetic creed" ( ch. XIV).[4] It is my con-

---

1. *Essays and Studies* (London, 1953), pp. 87–101.
2. *Coleridge and Wordsworth: The Poetry of Growth* (Cambridge, 1970), p. 171.
3. See H. C. Robinson's record of Coleridge's fourth lecture: "He certainly might with a little exertion have collected matter enough for *one* lecture at least out of the poems of Shakespeare. But he utterly passed over the Sonnets and made no remark on the reception the poems have met with from modern critics" (in Thomas Middleton Raysor, *Coleridge's Shakespeare Criticism* [Cambridge, Massachusetts, 1930], II, 215).
4. Samuel Taylor Coleridge, *Biographia Literaria*, ed. George Watson (London, 1962), ch. XIV. Future references to this edition are given in the text.

tention, however, that the chapter must be read as a deliberate preparation for those later sections of the book in which Coleridge more openly catalogues Wordsworth's strengths and weaknesses. Far from postponing the discussion of Wordsworth's creed, chapter XV actually expresses, in the oblique and indirect manner so characteristic of Coleridge, his deep misgivings about the poetic course upon which his friend had embarked—a course he feared would be adopted by Wordsworth's successors.

Coleridge's reproduction, in 1817, of portions of his 1811 lecture was prompted by weightier considerations than the need to pad his book. He returned to this material because he discerned its relevance to key concerns of *Biographia Literaria*. His dicta on Shakespeare in chapter XV are as integral to the explanation of his reservations about Wordsworth's theories as they are to his wider efforts to reclaim Wordsworth from practicing forms of poetry unsuited to a peculiarly Miltonic genius. Moreover, Coleridge's attempts to confront Wordsworth and Wordsworth's admirers with the need to maintain the meditative wholeness of a Miltonic imagination are hardly unrelated to the plight of Coleridge's own diffusive and centripetal habits of mind.[5]

As the ensuing discussion should make evident, my interest in chapter XV goes beyond a mere desire to document the almost subliminal fashion in which Coleridge tried to urge Wordsworth to follow the Miltonic rather than a Shakesperean line. The Milton-Shakespeare polarity developed by Coleridge soon became a critical commonplace by which later writers tried to measure their own literary affinities and allegiances. As my occasional allusions to Victorian poetry and Victorian fiction ought to suggest, it is my belief that, in Wordsworth's move from *The Prelude* to *The Excursion*, Coleridge correctly foresaw a major shift in the poetic sensibilities of the century. His remarks thus are not only applicable to William Wordsworth but can also act as a valuable commentary on the aspirations and practices of those "young men of strong sensibility and meditative minds" who would become the successors of the Romantics.

I

The motives that prompted Coleridge to focus in chapter XV of *Biographia Literaria* on the narrative poems of a Shakespeare who has yet to

---

5. The extent of Coleridge's private use of Milton as a stabilizing element and idealized *alter ego* has been, I think, largely overlooked by students of both his poetry and criticism. From the exaggerated identification in "This Lime-Tree Bower My

find the proper outlet for his dramatic genius may be surmised if one re-
members the brunt of his objections to *The Excursion*. His reservations,
tactfully expressed in the letters he wrote to Wordsworth in 1815 and just
as tactfully reiterated in chapter XXII of *Biographia*, are centered on his
conviction that *The Excursion* exemplifies a pernicious return of that same
"undue predilection for the *dramatic* form" which had been evident in
some of the *Lyrical Ballads* but was kept in abeyance in poems like "Tintern Abbey," "Resolution and Independence," and *The Prelude*.

Coleridge correctly sees that the poet who provided *The Prelude* with a
fixed center has disappeared. In *The Excursion* Wordsworth's point of
view is parcelled out among the *personae* of those garrulous disputants,
the Wanderer, the Solitary, the Pastor. Although there still is an "I" who
retains a point of view of his own, this shadowy self is a far cry from the
sublimely egotistical self that dominated *The Prelude*. Unable to retain
this earlier Miltonic identity, temperamentally incapable of assuming the
dramatic strength and imagistic control of a Shakespeare, Wordsworth
has fallen back on the stance of a pseudo-historian. He records, not his
own epiphanies, the fleeting personal intimations of an interdependence
between Nature and the self, but rather the disappointments and mild triumphs experienced over the years by scores of humble men and women.
The narrator who spends half of the poem accounting for the lives of the
dead buried in the Pastor's valley thus becomes closer to the passive nar-
rator-historians of Victorian fiction[6] than to that self who, in *The Prelude*,
freed itself from history by retaining an active control over the imaginative
reality it recreated.

Coleridge's remarks on Shakespeare's dramatic narratives must therefore be read in light of his conviction that Wordsworth is squandering his
powers through a pseudo-dramatic and pseudo-narrative poem. Coleridge
argues that "the great instinct" which drew the young Shakespeare to
drama is already recognizable in the poet's early habit of placing "the
whole before our view, himself meanwhile unparticipating in the passions"
( ch. XV ). Shakespeare's powers are intellectual. In "Venus and Adonis"

---

Prison" with the older poet in his blindness to the echoes of *Paradise Lost* in "Kubla
Khan" and "The Ancient Mariner," Coleridge seems to have drawn on Milton as a
kind of moral correlative that he could rely upon in his own self-dialogue between a
Christian conscience and the unbridled powers of the imagination.

6. George Eliot's early fiction—her *Scenes of Clerical Life* and *Adam Bede*—owes
its conception directly to *The Excursion*. The novelist who began her career by pretending to be a chronicler of the tragedies of everyday life may be said to start at
precisely the point where Wordsworth left off.

and "The Rape of Lucrece" the poet reactivates the "pleasurable excitement" produced by a mind capable of exhibiting what it has already carefully assimilated, "accurately and profoundly contemplated." This quality —which led Coleridge to remark in his *Table-Talk* that "Shakespeare's poetry is characterless; that is, it does not reflect the individual Shakespeare,"[7]—cannot and should not be emulated by a poet whose talent lies precisely in his contrary ability to confer his own distinct character on his contemplations of man and nature.

Even Shakespeare's sonnets are instanced by Coleridge as examples of an assimilating mind striving to present reality in its fullest complexity through intricate associations of thought and images. Shakespeare's "intellectual energy," his unique capacity for accommodating contradiction and conflict, thus wrestles with his "creative power" (ch. XV). Only through drama could these two impulses be successfully reconciled and held in balance. The conclusion of chapter XV must be quoted in its totality:

> What then shall we say? Even this: that Shakespeare, no mere child of nature; no automaton of genius; no passive vehicle of inspiration possessed by the spirit, not possessing it; first studied patiently, meditated deeply, understood minutely, till knowledge become habitual and intuitive wedded itself to his habitual feelings, and at length gave birth to that stupendous power by which he stands alone, with no equal or second in his own class; to that power which seated him on one of the two glory-smitten summits of the poetic mountain, with Milton as his compeer not rival. While the former darts himself forth, and passes into all forms of human character and passion, the one Proteus of the fire and the flood; the other attracts all forms and things to himself, into the unity of his own ideal. All things and modes of action shape themselves anew in the being of Milton; while Shakespeare becomes all things, yet forever remaining himself. O what great men hast thou not produced, England! my country! Truly indeed,
>
>> Must *we* be free or die, who speak the tongue,
>> Which Shakespeare spake; the faith and morals hold,
>> Which Milton held. In every thing we are sprung
>> Of Earth's first blood, have titles manifold!
>>
>> WORDSWORTH.

7. *Specimens of the Table Talk of Samuel Taylor Coleridge* (Edinburgh, 1905), p. 71.

Coleridge's decision to end his examination of Shakespeare's early poems with this peroration—a peroration in which he so unexpectedly slips in a description of Milton's complementary genius and which he just as unexpectedly caps off with a quotation from "WORDSWORTH" (the name in capitals is the last word of the chapter)—is far more than a rhetorical flourish. Wordsworth has been his real target throughout chapter XV. Coleridge praises the young Shakespeare for exploiting a mode which he soon will fault Wordsworth for falsely pursuing. He refers to Milton in order to remind Wordsworth of the model so successfully pursued in *The Prelude*. And he alludes to Wordsworth's 1803 sonnet, "It Is Not To Be Thought Of,"[8] because that poem's concern with loss and discontinuity has become applicable to Coleridge's own concern about his friend's situation in 1817.

In his sonnet, one of many written before Wordsworth found himself able to resume his delayed work on *The Prelude*, the poet relies on an image used in the later poem by making a blocked stream stand for disruption and discontinuity. Fearful that "this most famous Stream in bogs and sands / Should perish" (ll. 7–8), he tries to find comfort by returning to England's antiquity, to Shakespeare's tongue and Milton's faith. Although concerned about a potential loss of liberty and independence, the poet is equally concerned with restrictions suffered by the imagination. He identifies the threatened "Flood of British freedom" with the curtailed flow of an imagination encumbered by the dark times on which it has fallen. In the more famous sonnets immediately preceding the one Coleridge quotes, Wordsworth is led to invoke a Milton who, by living at this hour, might prevent England from becoming "a fen / Of stagnant waters" and to wish that the great men of the past—"The later Sidney, Marvel, Harrington, / Young Vane, and others who called Milton friend"—might once again teach Englishmen "how genuine glory was put on." This notion of Milton the libertarian was soon to be replaced, in Wordsworth's mind, by the vatic Milton echoed in *The Prelude*—the seer who teaches the liberated speaker that "Poets, even as Prophets, each with each / Connected in a mighty scheme of truth, / Have each for his peculiar dower, a sense / By which he is enabled to perceive / Something unseen before."[9]

By placing an extract from "It Is Not To Be Thought Of" at the end of

---

8. The sonnet is the sixteenth in the first part of *Poems Dedicated to National Independence and Liberty*.

9. *The Prelude or Growth of A Poet's Mind (Text of 1805)*, ed. by Ernest de Selincourt, corrected by Stephen Gill (London, 1970), XII. 301–5.

chapter XV, Coleridge tries to provide Wordsworth with a reminder of that same impulse which finally helped "precipitate" *The Prelude*. In 1803, Wordsworth successfully overcame the impediments that seemed to have encumbered his creative imagination when he became able to transplant the personal note of urgency and immediacy of his political sonnets into his longer epic about the deliverance of a poet's mind. By 1817, however, the stream which had flowed in the poem he addressed and read aloud to his friend seemed once again to have run into bogs and sands.

It is no coincidence that the young Shakespeare discussed in chapter XV should be viewed at a stage in his poetic growth roughly analogous to that at which Wordsworth found himself in 1802–3. Shakespeare's conflicting strengths—his "creative power" and "intellectual energy"—led him away from narrative poetry and the sonnet to drama, where these two "streams" found a "wider channel and more yielding shores" and could blend, dilate, and "flow on in one current and with one voice" (ch. XV). Wordsworth, too, had begun to find a single voice when he rejected his "undue predilection for the *dramatic* form" by ascribing his sentiments to ineloquent rustics; moving beyond deceptively impersonal narratives, in which, as in "Venus and Adonis" you "seem to be told nothing" (ch. XV), he had come to realize his Miltonic ability to attract "all forms and things to himself, into the unity of his own Ideal." Coleridge thus implicitly juxtaposes a forward-looking Shakespeare to a Wordsworth who should look back at that crucial point of his career when his own "interrupted stream broke forth once more, / And flowed awhile in strength, then stopp'd for years."[10]

Coleridge makes it clear that Wordsworth "stands nearest of all modern writers to Shakespeare and Milton" (ch. XXII). Yet he also feels compelled to expose his friend's reversion to those dramatic and impersonal habits displayed in days in which he, like Coleridge himself, remained unsure of his poetic identity. Instead of progressing to the composition of that first genuine Philosophic Poem that Coleridge expects, Wordsworth has made "motions retrograde" like that river described in the opening of Book Nine of *The Prelude*:

> As oftentimes a River, it might seem
> Yielding in part to old remembrances,
> Part sway'd by fear to tread an onward road
> That leads direct to the devouring sea
> Turns, and will measure back his course, far back,

10. Ibid., VII. 10–11.

Towards the very regions which he cross'd
In his first outset; so have we long time
Made motions retrograde, in like pursuit
Detain'd.                                 (IX. 1–9)

Chapter XV must be read as an attempt to turn Wordsworth in a direction opposite to that taken by Shakespeare when he stood at a similar bifurcation in his own poetic progress. Shakespeare, according to Coleridge, could manipulate language in such a deft way that the reader of his poetry is necessarily reminded of the presence of a shaping intelligence; the reader therefore can perfectly well do without "that constant intervention and running comment by tone, look, and gesture" which in the plays was to be furnished by the actors. Wordsworth, on the other hand, Coleridge strongly implies, *should* intervene in his own voice, for, like Milton, he is needed as an interpreter or mediator. Wordsworth's strength lies in his presence—he feels *for*, but never *with*, the characters in his narratives just as he can feel for, but not with, natural objects. Whenever Wordsworth obscures that presence, he threatens to leave the reader bereft of these guiding feelings. It is when he pretends to adopt a different character than his own, when he pretends to write mere chronicles of rustic life, or when he pretends to render "local imagery" in and for itself, that his imaginative capacity to heighten reality and to infuse it with meaning—the hall-mark of all "philosophic" poets—is lost on his audience.

As early as 1798, Wordsworth had exhibited a tendency to displace his own feelings by attributing them to poetic personae. Moreover, like the Tennyson of *In Memoriam* who would protest that the "I" of that poem was not himself, he frequently tried to dissociate himself from the speakers of many of his poems. In his long note to "The Thorn" he hastily concocts a thumb-nail sketch of the "character which I have here introduced speaking" in order to make sure that the narrator's credulity and talkativeness should not be mistaken for his own.[11] Such devices, which prompted Byron

11. Wordsworth almost seems to invent the type needed to fit his poem: "The character which I have here introduced speaking is sufficiently common. The Reader will *perhaps* have a general notion of it, if he has ever known a man, a captain of a small trading vessel, *for example....*" There is a tentative, ex post facto quality to Wordsworth's justification which suggests his apparent need to furnish a naturalistic explanation for what remains a dramatization of an internal state of mind. The figure of the civilized observer moved and surprised by unaccountable events appears in the shape of Coleridge's Wedding Guest or the questioner of "La Belle Dame Sans Merci" without such realistic trappings. Soon, however, the very same type Wordsworth tries to concoct in a footnote would become transplanted into the fuller fictional world of the novel where he reappears as Emily Brontë's Lockwood, and, later, as-

to mock Wordsworth for his earnest efforts to make his readers "suppose" what should have been presented as a deliberate fiction,[12] nonetheless prefigure Browning's own displacement of his private attitudes or Tennyson's attribution of personal emotional conflicts to the "*supposed*" confessions of some second-rate sensitive mind. To Coleridge, that "species of ventriloquism, where two are represented as talking, while in truth one man only speaks" (ch. XXII) seemed particularly offensive if that one man was William Wordsworth. Though hardly averse to indirection in his own work, Coleridge felt that such tactics conspired against Wordsworth's particular genius. The excellences he cites in the early work of Shakespeare, a narrative poet about to become England's greatest dramatist, are therefore designed to set in relief the folly of a Miltonic poet who has given full vent to his "undue predilection" in the pseudo-dramatic narrative of *The Excursion.*

II

In 1815—the same year in which Coleridge first expressed his dissatisfaction with *The Excursion*—Wordsworth himself hinted his preference for that kind of imagination which "draws all things to one; which makes things animate or inanimate, beings with their attributes, subjects with their accessories, take one colour and serve to one effect."[13] Accordingly, Wordsworth directed his readers to the "grand store-houses of enthusiastic and meditative Imagination, of poetical, as contra-distinguished from human and *dramatic* Imagination" (italics added). These store-houses he located in "the prophetic and lyrical parts of the Holy Scriptures, and the works of Milton; to which I cannot forbear to add those of Spenser." He explains his preference of these writers over the Classics by arguing that Greco-Roman literature was made subservient to "the bondage of definite form" by the "anthropomorphitism" of Pagan religion. To Wordsworth, "our great epic Poet" Milton epitomizes this superiority: though imbued with classical literature, he always remained a "Hebrew in soul" to whom all things tended "towards the sublime." Significantly enough, after plac-

---

sumes the guise of those outside spectators brought in contact with a more elementary world of folklore and myth in the fictions of George Eliot, Hardy, and Conrad.
  12. "Preface," *Don Juan.*
  13. "Preface to the Edition of 1815," *Wordsworth: Poetical Works*, ed. Thomas Hutchinson, rev. Ernest de Selincourt (London, 1966), p. 755. Wordsworth is adapting Lamb's description of Hogarth's genius.

ing Spenser in Milton's category, Wordsworth quotes but two lines from *King Lear* to furnish a sample of that other form of imagination of which "the works of Shakespeare are an inexhaustible source," but which seems to interest him far less.[14]

In view of this avowed preference, Coleridge obviously felt entitled to redirect his friend along a course Wordsworth seems to have unwittingly forsaken. Lacking Shakespeare's profound ability to suggest a Protean omnipresence through language and symbol ("the picturesque in words," "the never broken chain of imagery"), Wordsworth would do well by continuing to emulate Milton's egotistical power of attracting all forms and things into the unity of his own being. In chapter XV of the *Biographia*, Coleridge praises the young Shakespeare for choosing "subjects remote from the private interests and circumstances of the writer himself"; elsewhere, he praises Milton for assimilating what is only seemingly remote and alien: "In the Paradise Lost—indeed, in every one of his poems— it is Milton himself whom you see; his Satan, his Adam, his Raphael, almost his Eve—are all John Milton; and it is a sense of this intense egotism that gives me the greatest pleasure in reading Milton's works. The egotism of such a man is a revelation of spirit."[15]

In the original plan of *The Lyrical Ballads*, the Coleridge who contributed "The Ancient Mariner" was assigned an essentially Shakesperean role: by relying on his indirect and intensely symbolical imagination, he was to make the remote seem accessible through the creation of a willing suspension of disbelief. Wordsworth, on the other hand, was given a task suited to his quite different talents. The "intense egotism" that Coleridge so admires in Milton was to be deployed in "Tintern Abbey" (Wordsworth's chief contribution to the 1798 *Lyrical Ballads*): there, landscape, the poet's past and his present selves, even his sister Dorothy, are all William Wordsworth. Wordsworth, then, was to look into his own mind and draw from it that same unity which Milton found through the impersonation of God's thunder "and the choir / Of shouting Angels" ("Preface," *The Excursion*, ll. 34–35). Instead of relying on myth, "a mere fiction of what never was" (l. 51), instead of converting God, Satan, Adam and Eve into elements of a psychomachia that would reconcile him and his readers to the temporal world, this new Milton could presumably go directly to that temporal world. By reshaping it into the unity of his ideal, he could transcend it and excite in the reader "a feeling analogous to the super-

14. Ibid., p. 755.  15. *Table Talk*, pp. 278–79.

natural, by awakening the mind's attention from the lethargy of custom."[16]

The aim was identical; the means, necessarily different. According to Coleridge, however, Wordsworth forsook the role he was assigned. In the absence of more productions from Coleridge's own pen about "persons and characters supernatural, or at least romantic," Wordsworth took it upon himself to write fictions—but fictions that were devoted to persons and characters natural. In so doing, he pursued—as far as Coleridge is concerned—a mode inimical to his assigned task as well as to his assimilative kind of imagination. To obscure the author's identity in a symbolic fiction such as "The Ancient Mariner" was perfectly feasible (as it would be, too, in a *Lamia* or *Prometheus Unbound*); however, to refine the author out of existence in poems such as "We Are Seven" or "The Thorn" was to create unforseen artistic problems (problems that would recur in a "Locksley Hall" or in some of Browning's more "realistic" monologues). In the first instance, the reader is aware of the consistently symbolic mode of representation and therefore accepts the mythical "reality" of the artistic construct as analogous yet also different from the actuality to which he belongs; in the second case, however, the reader may be fooled into thinking that he is beholding nothing more than a slice of life or, failing that, into feeling that the "reality" being represented has been left untouched by the mind and heart of a poet who has thought long and felt deeply before creating it.[17] Shakespeare, according to Coleridge, never abjures his role as creator but always manages to suggest that he is rearranging the polarities and contradictions of experience rather than merely reproducing them; by programmatically choosing simple life for his subject-matter, Wordsworth must signify to his readers his personal ability to infuse the meanest flower that lives with thoughts that do often lie too deep for tears.

Wordsworth, then, according to Coleridge, errs whenever he tries to rely on a Shakesperean or dramatic imagination to communicate his mind's perception of meaning in the commonplace. For one as rooted as Wordsworth in the material world and yet as committed to transcend it, Milton's

16. *Biographia Literaria*, ch. XIV.

17. Only in recent years have critics come to recognize the dramatic ironies at work in those poems by Wordsworth derided for their artless simplicity. See, for instance, J. L. Danby, *The Simple Wordsworth* (London, 1960), pp. 35–38, and Patricia M. Ball, *The Central Self: A Study in Romantic and Victorian Imagination* (London, 1968), pp. 66–71. Miss Ball is undoubtedly correct when she asserts that "Wordsworth opens up the chameleon sensibility in 1798 just as much as he pioneers the egotistical mode" (p. 71); unfortunately, her tendency to view the productions of poets as dissimilar as Keats, Wordsworth, Browning as specimens of the same "chameleon sensibility" makes her groupings seem unnecessarily reductive.

poetic line, literal yet highly emblematic, is far more appropriate. Coleridge's fear that Wordsworth's full-scale philosophic poem would resemble *The Excursion* rather than *The Prelude* led him to release the hitherto private "To William Wordsworth: Composed on the Night After His Recitation of a Poem on the Growth of an Individual Mind'" in the companion volume of *Biographia Literaria*. By publicly calling attention to a poem by Wordsworth that had hitherto been known only in manuscript by the most intimate members of the poet's circle, Coleridge hoped to remind Wordsworth of his blunted purpose. In his fulsome tribute, Coleridge hails the poet of *The Prelude* as a Miltonic bard whose "soul received / The light reflected, as a light bestowed" (ll. 18–19) and welcomes the poem on the progress of an individual mind as a kind of *Paradise Regained*, an "Orphic Song" heralding Glory and Futurity.

In chapter XX of *Biographia Literaria* Coleridge deplores that Wordsworth should suppress a style and diction which, "next to that of Shakespeare and Milton," are "the most *individualized* and characteristic." Just as an acquaintance with but a few of Shakespeare's plays permits a reader to identify a quotation from some other play by the dramatist, so, too, is Wordsworth's style identifiable:

> A similar peculiarity, though in a less degree, attends Mr. Wordworth's style, whenever he speaks in his own person, or whenever, though under a feigned name, it is clear that he is still speaking, as in the different *dramatis personae* of the *Recluse*. Even in the other poems in which he purports to be most dramatic there are few in which it does not occasionally burst forth. The reader might often address the poet in his own words with reference to the persons introduced:
>
> > It seems, as I retrace the ballad line by line,
> > That but half of it is theirs, and the better half is thine.[18]

Here, too, the comparison to Shakespeare is double-edged. Since Shakespeare can adopt all forms of human passion, each of *his* dramatic personae, though speaking in a fashion that is unmistakably Shakesperean, nonetheless speaks and acts in his own identity. Wordsworth, on the other hand, Coleridge rather playfully suggests, is most hampered in those poems in which he purports to record voices not his own: as soon as his personal voice bursts through, it exposes his puppets as the worst half of his poem.

18. *Biographia Literaria*, ch. XX; the lines Coleridge adapts are from Wordsworth's 1800 poem "The Pet Lamb."

Even in chapter XXII, the very last chapter of *Biographia Literaria*, Coleridge still uses subterfuge to suggest that his quarrel is primarily with *The Excursion*. But the reasons behind that quarrel now stand in full relief. Coleridge makes it clear that he attributes Wordsworth's stylistic "inconstancies" and "disharmonies" to his friend's passive desire to remain truthful to the multitudinousness of a reality composed of particulars. By photographically reproducing the most minute details of topography, by selecting incidents and characters seemingly at random and for their own sake, Wordsworth loses sight of the whole. In chapter XXII Coleridge pointedly contrasts the minuteness and fragmentation of *The Excursion* to Milton's ability to suggest a total design in each subordinate part. Wordsworth, in the name of verisimilitude, has chosen to tie himself down to the "accidentality" of life; instead of infusing life into chaos, he relinquishes his former role of synthesizer and yields to the "matter-of-fact." According to Coleridge, in its excessive devotion to an objective or factual "truth" composed of unintegrated particulars, *The Excursion* forsakes the higher pleasure that would attend the poet's attempts to reconstitute reality into the ideal and the universal, the Great and Whole desired by all human minds.

The religious awe he had so genuinely felt after the recital of *The Prelude* Coleridge could nowhere attach to the mere "eddying, instead of progression, of thought" that he found in *The Excursion*. He therefore relegated that work—as he would have relegated no doubt many of those spasmodic and fragmented productions by later poets in the nineteenth century—to the product, not of the imagination, but of fancy, that inferior quality of mind which leaves reality intact without interfering with its basic texture or shape. Coleridge all but declares that he regards the fictional fabric of a poem like *The Excursion* to be greatly inferior to those pleasing fictions in which the narrative poet or the novelist openly calls attention to the artifice of his work. By distinguishing between the manner of *Tom Jones* and the manner of Defoe's novels, "that were meant to pass for histories," Coleridge suggests that the poet of *The Excursion* should at least have shown Fielding's willingness to remind an audience of his authorial presence. The Wordsworth who rose above history in *The Prelude* has become a captive of time. Coleridge indicts Wordsworth for concealing his design in the name of verisimilitude and concludes that such excessive concessions to a factual reality can only thwart the balance needed for the full exercise of the creative imagination.

### III

The almost missionary zeal with which Coleridge set out to redeem Wordsworth from a course he so firmly believed to be mistaken was not destined to bear fruit: not only did *The Recluse* remain unfinished, a testimony to truncated ambitions, but even the changes which *The Prelude*—Wordsworth's "Poem to Coleridge"—underwent over the years prove that the criticism of *Biographia Literaria* was to go unheeded by his friend. Still, Coleridge's diagnosis of the break which separates the Miltonic Wordsworth of *The Prelude* from the pseudo-Shakesperean Wordsworth of *The Excursion* is valuable to us as literary historians—for the shift in Wordsworth is symptomatic of a much larger shift in sensibility that was to involve the younger generation of Romantics and eventually affect Tennyson, Browning, Clough, and Arnold, as well as novelists such as Thackeray and George Eliot. These novelists, by exploiting the indeterminateness of the events they profess to record objectively, can be said to have completed the movement from poetry to narrative fiction begun, in Wordsworth's own time, by writers such as Scott and Byron and recapitulated, in their own way, by poets such as Tennyson and Browning.

The shift in sensibility that Coleridge anticipated and tried to arrest was not from the Miltonic to the Shakesperean mode—or from the "egotistical sublime" to the "chameleon poet," to use the Keatsian terms preferred by Patricia M. Ball.[19] Instead, the shift he feared was from a unified poetic sensibility such as Milton *and* Shakespeare still possessed to quasi-dramatic, pseudo-Shakesperean dialogues of the mind with itself. The breakdown of his own shaping imagination had made Coleridge acutely aware of an external reality that could deny the mind's "beautiful and beauty-making power."[20] He dreaded the possibility that the one poet he had set up as a stable *alter ego*, a model for modern writers, might also have succumbed to the multitudinousness of an age incapable of reviving the systems of belief that had made possible Shakespeare's tongue and Milton's faith. The poets of the nineteenth century seemed in imminent danger of a mutilation of their artistic selves. Even "that *negative* faith which simply permits the images presented to work by their own force" (ch. XXII), that power

19. See note 17, above; Miss Ball's insufficient differentiation between the "egotistical" mode of, say, Wordsworth and Arnold, and the "chameleon" mode of writers as different as Keats and Tennyson makes her terminology too fixed and thus insufficiently flexible to discriminate between Romantic and Victorian modes.

20. "Dejection: An Ode," l. 63.

which Keats was to call a "negative capability," threatened to break down. Coleridge feared that a dispersion into unintegrated masks and partial posturings would no longer permit each poet to "remain himself" as the Protean Shakespeare and the all-assimilating Milton had managed to remain.

In later years, Coleridge continued to express his regret that Wordsworth did not give to the public his thirteen books on the growth of an individual mind—"superior, as I used to think, upon the whole, to the Excursion."[21] He also continued to derogate those "dialogues in verse" that were to become the staple of a kind of poetry which aspired toward drama and fiction: "I cannot help but think that a great philosophical poet ought always teach the reader himself as from himself."[22] The beliefs that Coleridge presented so elliptically in *Biographia Literaria* were finally voiced explicitly in his table-talk near the end of his life: "I think Wordsworth possessed more of the genius of a great philosophic poet than any man I ever knew, or, as I believe, has existed in England since Milton; but it seems to me that he ought never to have abandoned the contemplative position, which is peculiarly—perhaps I might say exclusively—fitted for him."[23]

Coleridge's remarks in *Biographia Literaria* should, however, not only be read as an exclusive commentary on the poet who, after 1807, found it so increasingly difficult to fit the external world to his inward mind. His observations deserve to be closely studied by those interested in the dilemma of the later poets who belonged to Carlyle's Age of Veracity. For Coleridge's criticism very definitely applies to the Browning who—through mask and indirection—believed he could best emulate Shakespeare by never unlocking his heart; to the Tennyson of *In Memoriam* who—though claiming that there was more of himself dramatized in "Ulysses"—discovered that he could chart the eddying progress of a poet's mind only by adapting the form of a Shakesperean sonnet-cycle; to the Arnold who—though blaming Shakespeare and "imitators" like Keats for the diffusion of modern poetry—had himself in *Empedocles* vainly tried to dramatize the doubts and discouragements of a self-divided Hamlet attired in Sicilian garb.

21. *Table Talk*, p. 185.                    22. Ibid., p. 184.
23. Ibid., p. 186.

# "The New Prometheus of New Men": Byron's 1816 Poems and MANFRED

## John Clubbe

*Duke University*

THE ROMANTIC ERA stirred men's latent energies in all spheres of activity. The Romantic poets responded vigorously to the Greek myths, and into none did they breathe more new life than the myth of Prometheus. "Prometheus," writes Harold Bloom, "is the mythic figure who best suits the uses of Romantic poetry, for no other traditional being has in him the full range of Romantic moral sensibility and the full Romantic capacity for creation and destruction."[1] Byron's interest in Prometheus developed early, chiefly through his reading at Harrow Aeschylus' *Prometheus Bound.* The enthusiasm the play aroused at that time proved lifelong. His allusions to it are especially significant in the poems he wrote in 1816, and in the character of Manfred he came closer than any other Romantic poet to capturing his age's conception of the Promethean hero. The 1816 poems include, besides *Manfred*, the third canto of *Childe Harold's Pilgrimage*, *The Prisoner of Chillon*, "A Fragment," "The Dream," "Churchill's Grave," "Darkness," the "Monody on Sheridan," and "Prometheus." In this year Byron came to understand better the essential character of the myth: that while Prometheus' fate was symbolic of the general human lot, it was still a fate ennobled by suffering and by a tremendous effort to maintain his mind's independence. Furthermore, the paradox of his existence—extraordinary mental energy driven within by enforced physical passivity—could only draw Byron to him. In the 1816 poems and in *Manfred* he tried to redefine the Prometheus myth in terms of his own crisis: he or his personae (sometimes they are indistinguishable) express the despair of a self-isolated man who now recognizes the limits of his mortality and who has abandoned hope of happiness within the human community.

Many works in the Romantic period and throughout the nineteenth century give evidence of the enormous appeal of the Prometheus myth. In

---

1. *The Ringers in the Tower: Studies in Romantic Tradition* (Chicago and London, 1971), p. 120.

German literature, it evoked Goethe's dramatic fragment on Prometheus (1773), his mocking lyric "Prometheus" (published in 1785 but written ten years before), and his culminating projection of Promethean individualism, *Faust* (1808); in English literature, to cite only the most famous work, Shelley's *Prometheus Unbound* (1820). In music, Beethoven's ballet score *The Creatures of Prometheus* (1801) stands at one end of the century, Fauré's opera *Prométhée* (1900) at the other. The *Prométhée mal enchaîné* of Gide, published late in the 1890's, heralds the disillusionment with which many creative artists of the twentieth century view heroic treatments of mythological figures. Yet Peter Brook's *Orghast* (1971), written in a new language composed by Ted Hughes, testifies that the myth retains its vitality into our own time. In this daring experimental drama the central theme which links the sequences together is the Prometheus myth. The lure of the myth has been, as David Grene perceives, not only the archetypal depiction of the "rebel versus tyrant conflict" but also the recognition that

> men have everywhere felt, some obscurely and some clearly, an opposition between the animal and the spirit in man, between violence and persuasion, between might and intellect. So when the Zeus . . . Prometheus . . . struggle is represented as another facet of the conflict between the two most powerful factors in human life—brute force and mind—the story has been invested with a new probability drawn from the community of man's experience. And men everywhere have known the torture of subjugation to a stronger force than themselves, have known the helplessness of persuasion against force, and yet have believed in the ultimate triumph of persuasion.[2]

It is one of the ironies of history that of Aeschylus' trilogy only his *Prometheus Bound* has survived complete. From this play the Romantic poets understood the myth of Prometheus to be full of the deepest pessimism, as much in the role it allots the gods as in that given man. Yet in their hands it could undergo transformation—as it did in Goethe's and Shelley's and ultimately in Byron's—into a defiant affirmation of the victory of the human spirit.

The age's renewed interest in the myth of Prometheus led, in turn, to renewed interest in the *Prometheus Bound* of Aeschylus. Eighteenth-

2. "Introduction to *Prometheus Bound*," in *Aeschylus II* (Chicago and London, 1956), pp. 133–34. Citations to Grene's translation of *Prometheus Bound* are given in the text by line number.

century critical theorists had followed Aristotle's *Poetics* and condemned the play, as Grene points out, for its "episodic" structure, its "extravagant and improbable" characters, and its "uncouth and wild" diction. "During the nineteenth century," he observes, "with the Romantic revival and the breakdown of the so-called 'classical' rules of the drama, the *Prometheus* was acclaimed by the critics as a great work of art. But they so acclaimed it entirely in terms of its theme or its poetry" (p. 132). At the dawn of European consciousness, Aeschylus had sufficient insight into the role of Zeus to embody in a living symbol his vision of the justice of the universe and the position of men under Zeus's reign. His Prometheus is indeed a symbol and, as is usual with symbols, we feel more about him than we can hope to understand. If we take him as as an emblem or prototype of the human condition, we see that the painful and lasting suffering necessary under Zeus's new system of justice is to be man's fate. "The meaning of the myths," C. Kerényi has observed in his illuminating Jungian study of Prometheus, "wherever they occur in a living state and not merely as works of literature, has to do with existence."[3] The suffering of Prometheus he later defines as "an existential suffering, not identified with any one person but inherent in existence" (p. 121). But we must remember that although Prometheus is depicted in literature preeminently as a symbolic sufferer he is other things as well: he is creator, destroyer, rebel, skeptic, supreme individualist, and a Greek. In the breadth and universality of his symbolic humanity lies his appeal for a poet like Byron.

The Prometheus theme in Byron undergoes variations and transformations from poem to poem. In significant ways, his use of it recalls Beethoven's. Beethoven reworked the exhilarating finale of *The Creatures of Prometheus* into the dominant theme of the last movement of the *Sinfonia Eroica*. There it is, as always, introduced in the bass and only reaches full melodic form after a superb series of variations. Beethoven uses the theme twice elsewhere besides, and every time he uses it he treats it in a different way. The theme had a special connotation for him, and his handling of it was deliberate and heavy with implication. As the *Eroica* was first intended to exalt Napoleon, the man whom Beethoven as well as Byron viewed as the age's greatest, so the Prometheus theme in Byron will often occur, to cite the symphony's subtitle, "To celebrate the memory of a great man." The "great man" may be Napoleon, he may be one of the titanic protagonists in Byron's poems, or he may be the artist as creator. He may

---

3. *Prometheus: Archetypal Image of Human Existence*, trans. R. Manheim (New York, 1963), p. xi.

even be Byron himself. As the *Eroica* also defines Beethoven's own heroic stature, so the Prometheus theme embodies one facet—an important one—of Byron's protean nature. Beethoven became disillusioned with Napoleon earlier than Byron, yet with neither—even measuring Napoleon against the ideal of Prometheus—was the disillusion total. Napoleon often stands behind Byron's understanding of greatness, and behind him stands Prometheus.

This essay, while not meant to be an exhaustive analysis either of the 1816 poems or of *Manfred*, does argue that the Prometheus myth and the ways Byron interpreted it significantly determined why these works came to assume their particular character and dimensions. They record his deepest response to the myth of Prometheus. They also come close in their revelation of self to assuming the character of a poetic journal for the summer months of 1816. In my reading of them, they have even more autobiographical relevance than much of the other poetry of this very autobiographical poet. *Manfred*, while occasionally recognized as an impressive achievement, has not yet found its just valuation within the Byron canon. It is Byron's most sustained effort to soar beyond a resigned acceptance of death and fate and mortality, a final wild burst of creative energy in which he hoped to "embody and unbosom" that which was within himself before accommodating to life on life's terms. In my view *Manfred* is the culmination and climax of the group of poems which Byron wrote on the shores of the Lake of Geneva in the summer of 1816. And in a reconsideration of Byron's romantic poetry—of which the 1816 poems and *Manfred* are by and large the finest flower—the theme of Prometheus looms large. I develop in this essay two main lines of argument: one takes up the history of Byron's response to the Prometheus myth, first as revealed in his "Ode to Napoleon Buonaparte," then as it appears in the third canto of *Childe Harold's Pilgrimage*, *The Prisoner of Chillon*, and the other 1816 poems; the other details the impact of Aeschylus' *Prometheus Bound* upon *Manfred*.

Many writers on Byron have made much of the fact that in August 1816 "Monk" Lewis "translate[d] verbally" for him scenes from Goethe's *Faust*. Far fewer have noted that earlier in the summer Shelley had translated for him Aeschylus' *Prometheus Bound*. " 'I have never read any of his plays since I left Harrow,' " Byron told Medwin in Pisa. " 'Shelley, when I was in Switzerland, translated the "Prometheus" to me before I wrote my ode.' "4

4. Medwin's *Conversations of Lord Byron*, ed. Ernest J. Lovell, Jr. (Princeton,

A fine Greek scholar and a translator of genius, Shelley no doubt translated the play for Byron in 1816 as fluently as he was later to translate it for Medwin in 1820. It may well have been the most important service he rendered the older poet that summer.

Without question Byron responded to the stimulus of Shelley's translation. But he had known *Prometheus Bound* since Harrow days when, as he told Murray in 1817, "it was one of the Greek plays we read thrice a year." [5] He had studied it intensely in the fifth form at the age of sixteen—old enough, certainly, to grasp some of the significance of what he was reading. His enthusiasm was kindled to the extent that, as he recalled in his "Detached Thoughts" (written in 1821), his "first Harrow verses (that is, English as exercises)" were "a translation of a chorus from the Prometheus of Aeschylus"; they were received, however, by Dr. Drury, his admired headmaster, "but cool[l]y." [6] Fragments of these verses survived the coolness to see publication in *Hours of Idleness* (1809). Carl Woodring finds this fragment "quite unlike his later uses of Prometheus," [7] but the contrast which Byron presents in it is one that will occur frequently in his poetry: a being superior to those who surround him, living by his own vision of the right, is set against those who live within the bounds of conventional attitudes. Though in later years Byron professed to scorn the classics he "hated so" and frequently asserted that he never read them after his schooldays, what he read then he did not forget easily. [8] He knew them, as he himself admitted, as well "as most school-boys after a discipline of thirteen years" (*LJ*, I, 172; cf. V, 136). The play he struggled through in the Greek in school, and of which he translated a part, gradually entered—not unwillingly—into the marrow of his bones. The myth of Prometheus, as rendered

---

1966), p. 156. Thanks to Professor Lovell, we now accept the general authenticity of Medwin's account and we read his *Conversations* in an edition that leaves little to be desired. Mary Shelley confirms that Shelley read *Prometheus Bound* in 1816 in her "Note on Poems of 1816" in *The Complete Works of Percy Bysshe Shelley* (London, 1905; rpt. 1956), p. 536. Cf. also Newman Ivey White, *Shelley*, 2 vols. (New York, 1940), II, 542.

5. *The Works of Lord Byron: Letters and Journals*, ed. Rowland E. Prothero, 6 vols. (London, 1898–1901; rpt. 1922), IV, 174. Hereafter cited parenthetically in the text as *LJ*. Also: *P: The Works of Lord Byron: Poetry*, ed. Ernest Hartley Coleridge, 7 vols. (London, 1898–1904; rpt. 1922). Citations from Byron's poetry are also given parenthetically.

6. *LJ*, V, 453. The Harrow verses on Prometheus are dated 1 December 1804. Samuel C. Chew lists many of Byron's subsequent references to Prometheus in ["Byroniana"], *Modern Language Notes*, 33 (March 1918), 308–9. One early reference he omits is in "The Girl of Cadiz" of 1809, in *P*, III, 1.

7. *Politics in English Romantic Poetry* (Cambridge, Mass., 1970), p. 149.

8. For the best-known instance of Byron's disdain for the classics, see *Childe Harold*, IV, 75–77.

by Aeschylus, struck a chord in his innermost being that would resonate through the poetry of a lifetime. His understanding of it grew and matured as he himself grew and matured. Significantly, his first major reference to the myth occurs in a poem on Napoleon.

Byron wrote his "Ode to Napoleon Buonaparte" in April 1814 immediately upon hearing that Napoleon had abdicated his throne and accepted exile to Elba. "His overthrow, from the beginning," he told Moore in 1821, "was a blow on the head to me" ( LJ, V, 336). It also catalyzed his thoughts about Prometheus, for neither the first two cantos of *Childe Harold* nor the oriental tales written before 1814 allude directly to the myth. John Cam Hobhouse, Byron's closest friend, must have played a part in leading him to see the Emperor's fall in the light of the Prometheus myth, for Hobhouse recorded in his diary for 10 March 1814 that he had "finished yesterday the 'Prometheus' of Aeschylus" and for 20 March that he had "copied a little of the 'Prometheus.'"9 Both the evening of the 10th and the two evenings following he spent in Byron's company (seeing him frequently as well in days after), and in all likelihood he would have told his friend of his having read *Prometheus Bound*. Perhaps under the stimulus of Hobhouse's conversation, Byron dipped into the favorite of his schooldays. The 1816 sale catalogue of his library indicates that he owned at this time two copies of Aeschylus in Greek: a two-volume Glasgow imprint (1806) of Porson's edition, and Schutz's edition published at Halle in 1798.10 It is true that he told Medwin in 1821 or 1822 that he had not read the play since Harrow, but the parallels between it and his Ode, written less than a month after Hobhouse had finished his reading of Aeschylus, are sufficiently precise that we may assume renewed familiarity with it.

The Ode's sixteenth stanza, heavily revised, compares Napoleon to "the thief of fire from heaven" and asks: "Wilt thou withstand the shock? / And share with him, the unforgiven, / His vulture and his rock!" (*P*, III, 312). In Byron's lifetime this stanza was the last published; it culminates the series of comparisons between Napoleon and deposed leaders of the past who had shown as much heroism in adversity as in triumph. The extent of the stanza's revisions reveals the difficulty that the poet—oscillating between reprimand and sympathy—had in resolving his always ambivalent feelings toward Napoleon.11 As mankind's champion Prometheus had opposed his

9. Lord Broughton [John Cam Hobhouse], *Recollections of a Long Life*, 6 vols. (New York, 1909–11), I, 94, 98.
10. William H. Marshall, "The Catalogue for the Sale of Byron's Books," *The Library Chronicle* (University of Pennsylvania), 34 (Winter 1968), 35.
11. I am grateful to the Humanities Research Center of the University of Texas at

mind against the brute force of oppression. He nobly accepted the fate to which the callings of his conscience had led him. Napoleon, in his turn, had chosen the dishonor of exile over the glory of death, and this decision Byron could not forgive. "Byron," G. Wilson Knight has observed perceptively, "saw Napoleon's *survival* of failure as a failure to assume Promethean stature."[12] In these years, too, Byron saw himself as "the grand Napoleon of the realms of rhyme" (*P*, VI, 444). Napoleon's failure to fulfill his destiny in the political sphere forced Byron, so greatly did it affect him, to ponder his own fate among men. Two years later Napoleon's crisis became *his* crisis.

The cluster of events that form the crisis of 1816 constitutes the central traumatic experience in Byron's life. In the spring of 1816 he felt that he had no other choice but to exile himself to the Continent. He had just agreed to a separation from his wife, and rumors raced about London that an incestuous relationship existed between him and his half-sister Augusta. Obloquy descended upon him from all quarters. The experience of the separation, the agony he felt over losing Augusta, and the distance now placed between him and the beings he loved most were a shock such as he had never before experienced. Nothing until then had equalled it in intensity of pain; nor would anything in after years leave him feeling quite so shattered and helpless. At no other time did his awareness of himself as a being within the human community ebb lower. When he arrived in Geneva at the end of May and rented the Villa Diodati nearby for six months, he was a traveler without a destination. He needed to think through what had happened to him, and the months he spent in Switzerland allowed him the time to try to put together once more the shards of his life.

The poems written in these months fuse autobiography, reading, conversation and landscape to a degree greater even than those he had written before. Only through incessant writing could he temporarily still the tur-

---

Austin for allowing me to examine the first draft of the manuscript of the "Ode to Napoleon Buonaparte." It reveals that the stanza comparing Napoleon to Prometheus was originally the twelfth, not the sixteenth. The Humanities Research Center has also acquired a fair copy in Byron's hand of stanzas 17–19 of the "Ode." Above them the poet has written "These three may be the last," indicating not only that he wished them added to the previous sixteen but that he may have contemplated writing still others. Not until 1832 were the three stanzas published with the poem.

12. *Lord Byron: Christian Virtues* (New York, 1953), p. 241. Cf. *His Very Self and Voice: Collected Conversations of Lord Byron*, ed. Ernest J. Lovell, Jr. (New York, 1954), p. 119.

moil within himself, and in this summer he concentrated more of his own feelings and thoughts into poetry than at any other time in his life. In 1821 he looked back upon the months in Switzerland as a time of unparalleled literary creativity—"*how I wrote there!*" (*LJ*, V, 376). The poems he wrote there stand apart from those before and after in their total lack of irony and in their unrelieved seriousness in probing the theme of death. Irony implies perspective, and perspective on what had happened to him is exactly what Byron did not possess as he looked back upon his chivvied existence in London and contemplated the future. Death occupied his thoughts constantly. The poems of this time probe the reality of death from different vantage-points, and in them Byron strives to resolve the conflict between his mortal being and his immortal mind, between, in the words of Manfred, his "half dust" and his "half deity" (I, ii, 40).

As Byron faced the problems of existence after the crisis, the Prometheus theme emerges from among many to dominant status in his poetry. The struggles of Prometheus, whose overleaping mind compensated in some measure for the impossibility of expending his energy in action, gave Byron a firmer consciousness of his situation and strengthened him to face it. Before 1816 his allusions to the myth are few; they are as few after. In that year, however, they chart the course of his tortured existence. His conception of Prometheus grew to encompass a vision of him as the chained martyr, even, in a symbolic sense, as man opposed to God. Prometheus served as a mythic model by which Byron learned to graft a new life upon the wreckage of the old.

The myth of Prometheus emerges at crucial points in *Childe Harold's Pilgrimage*, canto III, written in May and June 1816.[13] At Waterloo Harold sees the eagle—emblem of Napoleon and France—now wearing "the shattered links of the World's broken chain" (stanza 18). The chain is the world's, or mortality's, and it is meant to evoke Prometheus on the Caucasus as well as Napoleon on the isolated rock of St. Helena.[14] Prometheus' and

13. My discussion of *Childe Harold* is indebted to Robert F. Gleckner, *Byron and the Ruins of Paradise* (Baltimore, 1967), and to George M. Ridenhour, "Byron and the Romantic Pilgrimage: A Critical Examination of the Third and Fourth Cantos of Lord Byron's *Childe Harold's Pilgrimage*" (Ph.D. dissertation, Yale University, 1955).

14. The idea of a chain of mortality never left Byron. James Kennedy, in his *Conversations on Religion with Lord Byron . . .* (London, 1830), remembered the poet saying: "There is a chain which binds us all, high and low, and our inclination and will must bend to the circumstances of our situation" (p. 247). Byron talked with Kennedy on Cephallonia in the autumn of 1823. Lady Blessington recorded earlier in the same year that "misfortune was sacred in his eyes, and seemed to be the last link of the chain that connected him with his fellow-men" (*Conversations of Lord Byron*, ed. Ernest J. Lovell, Jr. [Princeton, 1969], p. 138).

Napoleon's chains have now become Harold's—and Byron's—as well. In 1816 the "invulnerable mind" (10) affords only the protection of a catatonic trance. Harold proceeds "worn with pain"; the invisible chain which clung round him "galled for ever, fettering though unseen, / And heavy though it clanked not" (9). Man's "clay" smothers the "spark immortal" (14); "ceaseless vultures" prey "on self-condemning bosoms" (59). Harold, bound to the rock of his mortality, cannot escape being "a link reluctant in a fleshly chain" (72). The limited acceptance of his mortality which Byron would reach in Italy was not yet his in Switzerland.

*The Prisoner of Chillon* and the "Sonnet to Chillon" both embody the Prometheus theme.[15] Byron had visited the Castle of Chillon on 25 June during his tour around the Lake of Geneva with Shelley, and he wrote *The Prisoner of Chillon* shortly afterwards. In the sonnet, written later, "Liberty"—the "Eternal Spirit of the chainless Mind"—refuses to bend before "tyranny." Chillon's vault, home of her most faithful "sons," has become a "holy place." But throughout *The Prisoner of Chillon*, only ostensibly about the Genevese Bonivard, Byron suffuses his own recent experience of isolation and the Prometheus myth serves him as an intellectual vehicle through which he can bare his personal ordeal. The poem's subtitle "A Fable" implies that in it (unlike in several of his previous narratives) Byron intended to exemplify a moral thesis.[16] The prisoner, molded as much in the image of Prometheus and of Byron as he is upon a historical Bonivard, is chained to a column in Chillon's dungeon, there to suffer a seemingly inescapable eternity of pain. Like his mythical double, the Prometheus of Chillon endures his rock and chain in an environment which totally isolates him from society: the vault in which Byron places him is by "a double dungeon wall and wave" (l. 113) isolated both by man and nature. Nor does the parallel in punishments end with chains or degree of seclusion. Bonivard holds no communication either with his jailors (as Promethus in Aeschylus' play remains mute with Hephaistos and Might) or with the Duke of Savoy, the Zeus figure who is not referred to by name in the poem. As Zeus could not bear the free spirit of Prometheus, so the reactionary Duke Charles of Savoy cannot bear the free spirit of Bonivard. Thus he has him imprisoned. Already the anonymity of Bonivard's tormentor evokes a sense of a force or power which it will be difficult

---

15. I wish to thank my former student Richard Harris for stimulating insights into the Promethean character of *The Prisoner of Chillon*.

16. E. H. Coleridge inexplicably omits the first edition's subtitle "A Fable" from his edition of the poem.

for the hero to grapple with. He is as helpless and cut off from society as Prometheus chained to a rock or Byron chained to his "clay." All three are linked in their physical isolation from society and in their metaphysical loneliness.

At the beginning Bonivard is "proud of Persecution's rage" (l. 20). But the "ceaseless vultures" which prey upon Childe Harold attack him with equal ferocity. His agony, like that of the hero of Byron's "Prometheus," becomes "a silent suffering, and intense" ("Prometheus," l. 6): "silent" in its seclusion, "intense" in his having to bear the torture of being unable to succor his brothers—"strangers in our sight" (l. 53)—or prevent their deaths. They are his brothers also in the broader conception of a brotherhood of man. They can die; he cannot. But he does die spiritually as their corpses are torn from him and relegated to "shallow" graves within the dungeon itself. For the mortal Bonivard as for the immortal Prometheus, death would loom as a welcome relief once isolation from humankind has become total: "I could have smiled to see / The death that would have set me free" (ll. 124–25). He endures mankind's pain and thus, in his martyrdom, symbolizes mankind's anguish. The unremitting nature of Bonivard's punishment also indelibly stamps his fate with overtones of the Prometheus myth. He, too, is refused the "boon to die" ("Prometheus," l. 23):

> I know not why
> I could not die,
> I had no earthly hope—but faith,
> And that forbade a selfish death.
>
> (ll. 227–30)

In the timeless imprisonment of his hero, Byron attempts to conceive what the sufferings of Prometheus must have been through eons of unrecorded time. Escape eventually comes to have no meaning for Bonivard, for "the whole earth would henceforth be / A wider prison unto me" (ll. 322–23). He now understands that his chains are, as Blake recognized, "mind-forg'd manacles." They admit of no bursting, as the human condition admits of no permanent escape, except through death. With Bonivard, as with Prometheus and Byron himself, it is acknowledgment of the fettered state that counts: he comes to see it as an inescapable part of the human condition. He is sentenced to perceive forever the reality of the living dead that Joyce portrayed in *Dubliners*. His is the recognition that the world is a prison of existential loneliness: "No child—no sire—no kin had I, / No partner in my misery" (ll. 324–25).[17] Solace may be found only in the retention of his vision. It is a vision which draws strength from the empathy learned in Promethean bondage:

> With spiders I had friendship made,
> And watched them in their sullen trade
> Had seen the mice by moonlight play,
> And why should I feel less than they?
> We were all inmates of one place.
>
> (ll. 381–85)

Momentarily, man's spirit may transcend his clay, but the clay ultimately triumphs. It was Bonivard's long defiance of human limitations under insuperable odds, not his having gained an illusory freedom, that drew Byron to him.

All the shorter, experimental poems which he wrote in July 1816—"A Fragment," "The Dream," "Churchill's Grave," "Darkness," the "Monody on Sheridan," "The Incantation," and "Prometheus"—meditate on the theme of death. They view the isolation of self as one of Promethean totality and may be read as objective correlatives for a spiritual state.[18] Communication between human beings, or between human beings and the natural world, has ceased. The persona retires into the solitude of his soul ("A Fragment"); or seeks to understand the present crisis by reviewing those of the past ("The Dream"[19]); or ponders the immutabilities of death before the forgotten grave of a fellow poet who also "blazed / The Comet of a season" ("Churchill's Grave"); or witnesses the extinction of the universe as he faces down his mortal enemy in a last confrontation and dies ("Darkness"[20]). In "Darkness," the most pessimistic of Byron's poems, we are

17. In the first draft of the poem this line reads: "No child—*no wife*—no kin had I" (italics mine). Quoted by permission of the Beineke Rare Book Library of Yale University. E. H. Coleridge consulted almost none of the first drafts of the 1816 poems in preparing his still standard edition of Byron's poetry. My examination of most of them has led me to conclude that these poems are even more closely interrelated in theme and in autobiographical significance than critics have generally assumed.

18. On these poems, see especially George M. Ridenhour, "Byron in 1816: Four Poems from Diodati," in *From Sensibility to Romanticism: Essays Presented to Frederick A. Pottle,* ed. Frederick W. Hilles and Harold Bloom (New York, 1965), pp. 453–65. It is not certain that all the poems were written in July. I reserve for discussion elsewhere the poems to Augusta.

19. The poem's original title seems to have been "The Destiny." I cite the manuscript of the first draft by permission of the Henry W. and Albert A. Berg Collection, The New York Public Library, Astor, Lenox and Tilden Foundations.

20. The manuscript of the first draft of the poem has the crossed-out subtitle "A

asked to envision a world void of light and of love, where "all earth was but one thought—and that was Death" (1. 42). Taken metaphorically, the image of the two enemies meeting "beside / The dying embers of an altar-place" (ll. 57–58) conveys the belief that man's Promethean capacity to realize and fulfill the goals of his imagination has become extinguished. His "flame"—the Promethean fire—has become "a mockery" (ll. 63–64). God has vanished from the scene, and man has not been able to take his place. "Darkness . . . was the Universe" (ll. 81–82).[21] In the "Monody on the Death of the Right Hon. R. B. Sheridan," Byron depicts his friend as an inspired creator and hails the plays of his young manhood as "bright with the hues of his Promethean heat" (1. 56). In "The Incantation," later used in *Manfred* but which first appeared with the other July poems and may have been composed at the same time, he voices the Promethean dilemma that will be Manfred's fate:

> Nor to slumber, nor to die
> Shall be in thy destiny;
> Though thy death shall still seem near
> To thy wish, but as a fear;
> Lo! the spell now works around thee,
> And the clankless chain hath bound thee;
> O'er thy heart and brain together
> Hath the word been passed—now wither!
>
> (I, i, 254–61)

Only "Prometheus" focuses exclusively on the myth. It offers the surest evidence for Byron's understanding of it. E. H. Coleridge has noted its many distinct echoes of Aeschylus' *Prometheus Bound* which Shelley had recently read to him. This reading stirred Byron's imagination to visualize the fate of the Titan Prometheus as his own writ large. No doubt he found tempting the thought that he could fling his poetry and his life against the world's opinion with the same vehemence that Prometheus had flung down his challenge to Zeus. But the immortal who casts his lot with mortals emerges in the first forty-four lines of Byron's poem as a patient and beneficient figure whose sufferings will endure forever: "the wretched gift

---

Dream" and the awkward first line "I had a vision—it was terrible." Cited from the Robert H. Taylor Collection, Princeton, N.J. The manuscript of "Churchill's Grave" is also in Mr. Taylor's collection on deposit at the Princeton Library.

21. Shelley perhaps mirrored this terrible scene in "Darkness" when in *Prometheus Unbound* he depicted the Promethean fire as having dwindled to "a glow-worm's lamp" around which "survivors . . . gather in dread" (I, 557–59).

Eternity / Was thine—and thou hast borne it well" (ll. 25–26). "What was thy pity's recompense," Byron (echoing Aeschylus) asks. And answers:

> A silent suffering, and intense;
> The rock, the vulture, and the chain,
> All that the proud can feel of pain,
> The agony they do not show.
>
> (ll. 5–9)

For mankind, he serves in the poem's last fifteen lines as "a symbol and a sign . . . of their fate and force" (ll. 45–46).

> Like thee, Man is in part divine,
>       A troubled stream from a pure source;
> And Man in portions can foresee
> His own funereal destiny.
>
> (ll. 47–50)

Man, confronting this grim destiny, can follow Prometheus' example and oppose "his Spirit . . . And a firm will, and a deep sense, / Which even in torture can descry / Its own concentered recompense" (ll. 53–57). Spirit and will, bolstered by what can only be called faith, together *can* triumph and make "Death a Victory" (ll. 58–59).[22] Yet Byron's Prometheus is a resigned hero, accepting his fate as inevitable and making no attempt to overthrow the order of things. He submits to a universe without plan, morality, or purpose; man's existence, mirroring his, is "sad unallied" (l. 52). Prometheus in Aeschylus' world order, Byron realizes, cannot succeed in his rebellion and must in the end submit to Zeus. Heroic as his defiance may be, ultimately it is futile. What *is* important is that he does act and that for his "crime" he is willing to suffer. This is the acceptance, more resigned than heroic but heroic too in being resigned, that Byron's Titan also reaches.

   In mid-September 1816 Byron began a twelve-day tour with Hobhouse of the Bernese Alps. It proved to be the most memorable experience of his

---

22. Two of the trial lines (both crossed-out) in the first draft of the ending are "For all may conquer who can die" and "To conquer—is to die." The number of false starts in "Prometheus," apparently written *currente calamo* and yet the most heavily revised of the 1816 poems, indicates the difficulty Byron had in finding effective phrasing to express his conception of Aeschylus' Titan. I quote the manuscript of "Prometheus" by permission of the Philip H. and A. S. W. Rosenbach Foundation Museum, Philadelphia.

stay in Switzerland. Only when Byron saw the rugged mountain vistas
of the Alps—he thought them "quite out of all mortal computation" (*LJ*,
IV, 96)—did the full dimensions of the Prometheus myth register upon
him. He tersely recorded in his "Journal to Augusta" the sights he saw
during his trip and their impact upon the tensions of his emotional state.
The "Journal," he told Murray, contained "the germs of *Manfred*" (*LJ*,
IV, 174; cf. V, 342). In the precision and brilliance with which concrete
particulars are seized, the descriptions of natural scenery in it often surpass,
to my mind, the vaguer, more rhetorical passages in *Childe Harold* III.
Many of them would find poetic reflection in *Manfred*.

Leaving Diodati, Byron went along the south shore of the Lake of Geneva, over the Jaman pass, along river valleys to Thun, and by boat up
the Lake of Thun to Interlaken. The alpine valley of Lauterbrunnen provided him with his first sight of the Alps at close range. He felt sufficiently
awed by the nearly thousand foot drop of the *Staubbach*, "neither mist nor
water," to compare it—in an image he would quarry for *Manfred*—to "the
*tail* of a white horse streaming in the wind, such as it might be conceived
would be that of the *'pale* horse' on which *Death* is mounted in the Apocalypse" (*LJ*, III, 358; II, ii, 1–8). From the Wengen Alp, the highest peak
he ascended, he had a dramatic view of the Jungfrau towering to the south
above its neighbors. He "heard the Avalanches falling every five minutes
nearly—as if God was pelting the Devil down from Heaven with snow
balls" (*LJ*, III, 359; cf. I, ii, 75–79). That same afternoon at twilight he
saw the glacier above Grindelwald—"very fine Glacier, like *a frozen hur-
ricane*" (*LJ*, III, 360; cf. II, iii, 4–8). On the way he "passed *whole woods
of withered pines, all withered*; trunks stripped and barkless, branches
lifeless; done by a single winter,—their appearance reminded me of me
and my family" (*LJ*, III, 360; cf. I, ii, 66–67, *Childe Harold* III, 78). The
next day he saw the Rosenlaui glacier—"said to be the largest and finest
in Switzerland" (361). At Meiringen he turned homewards. He had
experienced mountain scenery in all its grandeur and in insurpassable
weather. Yet overwhelmed as his senses were by the Alps, his emotional
turmoil remained unassuaged. The "Journal" concludes by recording the
failure of the natural world to console:

> But in all this—the recollections of bitterness, and more especially of
> recent and more home desolation, which must accompany me through
> life, have preyed upon me here; and neither the music of the Shepherd,
> the crashing of the Avalanche, nor the torrent, the mountain, the

Glacier, the Forest, nor the Cloud, have for one moment lightened the weight upon my heart, nor enabled me to lose my own wretched identity in the majesty, and the power, and the Glory, around, above, and beneath me (p. 364).

*Manfred* was written in the state of mind with which the "Journal" concludes. It is a poem unlike any that Byron had written before, emerging as an attempt—in large part successful—to resolve (or at least to express) the impact of the Alps upon his personal crisis. The crisis had brought his mythmaking powers to a new pitch of intensity, and once again he saw the Prometheus story mirroring his own dilemma. Over the course of the summer his comprehension of the plight of Aeschylus' tragic hero had deepened: as he became more aware of human limitations he became more aware of the Promethean dimensions of his own character. The Prometheus theme, present in *The Prisoner of Chillon* and in most of the July poems, now filled his mind even more and gave focus to his wild and whirling thoughts. In its structure and setting, but chiefly in the conception and sufferings of its hero, the *Prometheus Bound* of Aeschylus provided him with a model of epic proportions upon which he could form in *Manfred* his own vision of human helplessness in the face of an indifferent universe.

Aroused by the Alps to an eruption of creativity, Byron put on paper the first two acts of *Manfred* between his return to Diodati on 29 September and his departure for Italy on 5 October. "Byron could not then write the third act," Leslie A. Marchand has written, "for he did not know how to carry on from there."[23] Very likely he did not, but finishing *Manfred* may have been as much a question of time.[24] After all, Byron did write over nine hundred lines in less than five days—which, even allowing for his usual rapid rate of composition, remains an impressive achievement. In these days, too, he dined almost daily with Madame de Staël and had also to prepare his departure for Italy. Once travel interrupted the poem he found difficulty, as he admitted, in getting it going again. "I have not done a stitch of poetry since I left Switzerland," he wrote Murray from Venice on 2 January 1817, "and have not, at present, the *estro* upon me" (*LJ*, IV, 43). Not until late January or early February did he write the third act. Its composition must have caused him difficulties, for the first draft is melodramatic, unconvincing, at one point farcical. Byron found it temperamentally impossible to recapture his earlier mood. "The 2 first acts

23. *Byron: A Biography*, 3 vols. (New York, 1957), II, 659.
24. John Paul Mellon, "Byron's *Manfred* and the Critics: A Review of Sources and Ideas," (Ph.D. dissertation, University of Pittsburgh, 1964), makes this point on p. 53.

are the best," he told Murray on 9 April, "the third so so: but I was blown with the first and second heats" (ibid., 100). And five days later: "The third act is certainly dammed bad. . . . I will try and reform it, or re-write it altogether; but the impulse is gone, and I have no chance of making any thing out of it" (ibid., 110). Within a month he had rewritten it "altogether." Though it may succeed less well than the first two, it does bring the play's development to a natural, even logical, close.

Once in Venice, again in love and "in very good contentment" (ibid., 14), Byron emerged from the gloom and despair of Switzerland looking back upon the poem he wrote there with ironic detachment, even disdain. "I forgot to mention to you," he told Murray casually in mid-February, "that a kind of Poem in dialogue (in blank verse) or drama . . . begun last summer in Switzerland, is finished; it is in three acts; but of a very wild, metaphysical, and inexplicable kind" (ibid., 54–55). Elsewhere, he spoke of *Manfred* as "a sort of mad Drama" or "Bedlam tragedy" (ibid., 80). He regarded it as no more stageworthy than *Prometheus Bound* and insisted that Murray call it " 'a poem,' for it is *no drama*" (ibid., 100; cf. 55, 57, and V, 229). So involved was *Manfred* with Byron's deepest feelings that for a time he was without perspective on it and unable to judge its worth objectively. "I have really and truly no notion whether it is good or bad," he told Murray in March; "and as this was not the case with the principal of my former publications, I am, therefore, inclined to rank it but humbly" (ibid., IV, 68–69). Yet if in March he ranked it "but humbly," by July— after he had rewritten the third act—he deemed it "one of the best of my misbegotten, say what you will" (ibid., 147). The passing of years saw no diminution of the regard in which he held the poem.

Immediately upon *Manfred*'s publication, contemporary reviewers realized that it was a poem crucial to an understanding of Byron. But they, and subsequent critics during the next hundred years, sought chiefly to fathom it, not for its significance within Byron's development as a poet, but for its revelations regarding his alleged incest with Augusta. Recent writers, usually taking as proven the allegations of incest, shy away from biographical readings, but still reveal unease before the poem. Disliking its emotionalism, its misanthropy, its undeniable purple patches, they tend to dismiss it either as an imitative (and clumsy) Faustian drama or as tiresome autobiography.

*Manfred*'s first critic of note, John Wilson, suggested parallels between

the poem and Marlowe's *Tragical History of Doctor Faustus*.[25] Francis
Jeffrey took up the allegation in the August 1817 number of the *Edinburgh
Review*; he admitted "a certain resemblance, both in some of the topics
that are suggested, and in the cast of the diction in which they are expressed," but insisted upon the poem's "originality"—and superiority (pp.
430, 431). Wrong-headed as Jeffrey could be in his understanding of other
Romantic poets, few contemporary critics of Byron equal him for pene-
trating good sense. He saw immediately where lay the real influence in
*Manfred*:

> In the tone and pitch of the composition, as well as in the character
> of the diction in the more solemn parts, the piece before us reminds
> us much more of the Prometheus of Aeschylus, than of any more mod-
> ern performance. The tremendous solitude of the principal person—
> the supernatural beings with whom alone he holds communion—the
> guilt—the firmness—the misery—are all points of resemblance to which
> the grandeur of the poetic imagery only gives a more striking effect
> (p. 431).

The implication that he had plagiarized, even if unconsciously, from Marlowe disturbed Byron when he read Jeffrey's review (he may never have
seen Wilson's). He hardly appreciated Jeffrey's remonstrance in his favor.
In the past, wishing to avoid even the appearance of plagiarism, Byron had
usually made a point of acknowledging his literary sources to at least one
correspondent. For Murray, in his letter of 12 October 1817, he traced
*Manfred*'s evolution. "I *never read*," he wrote, "and do not know that I
ever saw, the *Faustus* of Marlow[e]. . . . I heard Mr. Lewis translate verbally some scenes from *Goethe's Faust* . . . last summer;—which is all I
know of the history of that magical personage" (*LJ*, IV, 174; cf. p. 177).

Byron clearly thought he knew what were *not* the literary sources for
*Manfred*. If sources must be found, however, he knew where to look. He
states in this same letter to Murray that it was "the *Prometheus* of Aeschylus" which he had in mind while composing *Manfred*—a play of which he
"was passionately fond as a boy." "The *Prometheus*," he insists, "if not
exactly in my plan, has always been so much in my head, that I can easily
conceive its influence over all or any thing that I have written;—but I deny

25. *Edinburgh Monthly Magazine*, 1 (June 1817), 289–95, especially p. 295; *Blackwood's Edinburgh Magazine*, 1 (July 1817), 389–94. The journal's name changed
between the June and the July numbers, which has caused some confusion in citations
of this two-part review.

Marlow[e] and his progeny, and beg that you will do the same" (ibid., 174–75). Byron here explicitly—and rightly—admits that Aeschylus' play is the major literary influence upon *Manfred*.[26] The major autobiographical influence, he is certain, is the Alpine tour with Hobhouse: "as to the germs of *Manfred*," he told Murray, "they may be found in the Journal which I sent to Mrs. Leigh . . . when I went over first the Dent de Jamont [Jaman], and then the Wengeren or Wengeberg [Wengen] Alp and S[c]heideck and made the giro of the Jungfrau, S[c]hreckhorn, etc. etc., shortly before I left Switzerland. I have the whole scene of *Manfred* before me, as if it was but yesterday, and could point it out, spot by spot, torrent and all" (ibid., 174).

The question of *Manfred*'s literary indebtedness continued to haunt Byron. Three years later, in 1820, Goethe in a review of the poem affirmed that "this singular intellectual poet has taken my *Faustus* to himself, and extracted from it the strangest nourishment for his hypochondriac humour" (*LJ*, V, 506). Once again Byron restated the facts as he saw them: "His *Faust* I never read, for I don't know German; but Matthew Monk Lewis, in 1816, at Coligny, translated most of it to me *vivâ voce*, and I was naturally much struck with it" (ibid., 37). He reiterated that "it was the *Staub[b]ach* and the *Jungfrau*, and something else, much more than Faustus, that made me write *Manfred*."[27] For Byron at least, seeing the Alps, reinforced by "something else" (the autobiographical background, presumably his feelings of guilt regarding the causes of his marital separa-

26. Few modern critics have taken him seriously. A notable exception is Samuel C. Chew, who in *The Dramas of Lord Byron* (1915) devotes several pages to the influence of *Prometheus Bound* on *Manfred*. None of the three doctoral dissertations on *Manfred*, written in the early sixties by William Neville, Gene Morokoff, and John Paul Mellon, regards the impact of the Prometheus myth as fundamental. Only Marchand in *Byron's Poetry: A Critical Study* (1965), pp. 18, 76, and David V. Erdman in *Shelley and his Circle 1773–1822* (1970), III, 312–13, insist that the Prometheus theme is an important and recurring one in Byron's poems. My essay has profited from the wider study of Prometheus by Raymond Trousson, *Le Thème de Prométhée dans la littérature européene*, 2 vols. (1964), from Gilbert Highet's *The Classical Tradition* (1949), G. Wilson Knight's *Lord Byron: Christian Virtues*, and Christian Kreutz, *Das Promethussymbol in der Dichtung der englischen Romantik* (1963), vol. 236 of *Palaestra*. Peter L. Thorslev's chapter "Satan and Prometheus" in *The Byronic Hero* (1962) sees Manfred "as representative of almost every one of the hero-types of the Romantic movement" (p. 167). While I do not deny this assertion, I think that it is Prometheus, rather than the Gothic hero or Faust or whoever, who dominates *Manfred*.

27. *LJ*, V, 37 and V, 342. Cf. Medwin, pp. 141–42, where Byron states: "All I know of that drama [*Faust*] is from a sorry French translation, from an occasional reading or two into English of parts of it by Monk Lewis when at Diodati." The "sorry French translation" of *Faust* was that of Madame de Staël in *De l'Allemagne*, which Byron read in 1813.

tion and his despair over losing Augusta), was what had brought *Manfred* into being.

The tie between *Manfred* and *Faust* is, then, as E. H. Coleridge observed, "formal, not spiritual" (*P*, IV, 82). It extends to similarities in temperament and circumstance between the two protagonists, to resemblances between the introductory scene of each play (which Byron noted, *LJ*, V, 37), to a number of verbal echoes, and, possibly, to structural parallels.[28] Andrew Rutherford has written: "Formally, *Manfred* is a new departure for Byron—an experiment in semi-lyrical romantic drama." He suggests that the form of the play derives from *Faust*.[29] No doubt *Manfred* is "a new departure"; it may even be "an experiment in semi-lyrical romantic drama"; but in my reading its structure follows that of *Prometheus Bound* more closely than it does that of *Faust*. The influence of *Faust* upon *Manfred* remained, for Byron, largely unconscious, one which he denied when it was proposed to him, and one which (though by no means negligible) pales into relative insignificance when set against that of Aeschylus' play. It does little good to attempt to second-guess Byron's thoughts beyond a certain point. Rather, we must acknowledge that the poet—though fond of paradox and what Scott called "mischief-making"—was fundamentally honest and that in this question of literary influence he wished to record the truth of the matter. Unconsciously he may well have remembered more of *Faust* than he realized, but we need not distrust him when he disclaims conscious imitation. The influence of *Prometheus Bound* was, on the other hand, largely conscious. Byron admitted it proudly. To him, it meant that he was vying with the finest play of the dramatist he considered classical Greece's greatest (cf. *LJ*, IV, 136, 491n.; V, 229).

My concern here will be to suggest some of the ways Byron responded in *Manfred* to the play which, "if not exactly in my plan," was by his own admission "always so much in my head, that I can easily conceive its influence over all or any thing that I have written." If critics have from the first perceived that *Manfred* owed a debt to Aeschylus' drama, they have never directed attention to the structural parallels between the two plays. Although *Prometheus Bound* disregards the Aristotelian "law of proba-

28. See especially Chew's Appendix II, "Manfred and Faust," pp. 174–78 of *The Dramas of Lord Byron*. One parallel between the two works Chew does not mention is that between the final scene of *Faust* and that of Act II of *Manfred*. While I do not deny that the parallels he finds, especially in the early parts of each work, are valid, it does seem that Byron's debt to Goethe is less than has often been suggested.

29. *Byron: A Critical Study* (Edinburgh and London, 1962), p. 76.

bility or necessity" (postulated, it is true, a century later), it still has a tighter structure than *Manfred*. In the Greek play, as H. D. F. Kitto has observed, "there is a law, but it is one of increasing tension, not of 'natural' or logical sequence."[30] Prometheus confronts, in successive scenes, the chorus of Oceanides, Oceanus, Io, Hermes. The Oceanides remain on stage throughout. At first sympathizing with, then becoming actively involved in, Prometheus' fate, they probably share it in the end. The encounters with Oceanus, Io, Hermes, each moving Prometheus a stage further toward his destiny, maintain and augment the tension. But from the time he is chained to the crag to the time he is hurled into the abyss Prometheus knows that he will eventually triumph, for he in effect possesses the secret of the universe which Manfred for all his magic has failed to seize. Without wishing to oversimplify each play's complex structure, or to reconcile the many differences between them, I find that the scenes in *Manfred* work (though less successfully) on a similar "law . . . of increasing tension."

No more than did Aeschylus does Byron follow the Aristotelian dictum of "probable or necessary sequence" in his presentation of scenes. The order of events in the first two acts of *Manfred*, though by no means as seemingly inevitable as that in *Prometheus Bound*, is certainly not arbitrary. The hero faces, in succession, the seven spirits, the Chamois Hunter, the Witch of the Alps, the Destinies, Nemesis and Arimanes, finally Astarte herself. He comes out of each encounter with a growing realization that his dilemma is insoluble; he is also unconsciously preparing himself for the climactic encounter with Astarte which closes Act II. The meeting with the spirits reveals Manfred's plight, his awareness of his human limitations; that with the Chamois Hunter—a figure usually viewed as representing common humanity—saves his life. He greets enthusiastically the Witch of the Alps, who symbolizes the beauty of the natural world, but when she insists he swear obedience to her will he refuses. Manfred's encounter with the henchmen of Arimanes, finally with Arimanes himself, reveals to him the strength of his position; that with Astarte which follows, its weakness. Failure to achieve reconciliation with the one being to whom above all others he is bound leaves Manfred without further hope of remaining in the human community.

*Manfred*'s third act reinforces the play's structural unity. After the encounter with Astarte the hero moves to a homeostatic state beyond

30. *Greek Tragedy: A Literary Study* (1952; rpt. Garden City, N.Y., 1954), p. 61. My discussion of *Prometheus Bound* is indebted to Kitto's chapter on the play.

hope. "There is a calm upon me," he exclaims, "inexplicable stillness! which till now / Did not belong to what I knew of life" (III, i, 6–8). He engages in a debate with the Abbot of St. Maurice, which soon becomes meaningless as he realizes that the conventional faith which the Abbot represents no more can suffice him than conventional knowledge. In this act Manfred utters two long soliloquies, one as he watches the sun set, the other as he recalls a time in his youth when he stood musing in the Colosseum. On a first reading they may seem extraneous to the movement of the poem, yet they fulfill a dramatic and psychological purpose in that they indicate Manfred's gradual acceptance of the inevitability of his own death. In the first soliloquy the sun's setting mirrors the increasing cold in Manfred's life, the disappearance (with Astarte's rejection) of the possibility of love, even of emotional response. In the second soliloquy Manfred dreams he stands in the moonlit Colosseum, overwhelmed by emotions which filled him "till the place / Became religion, and the heart ran o'er / With silent worship of the Great of old" (III, iv, 37–39). An existence devoid of human feeling leads to a state like Bonivard's in *The Prisoner of Chillon*, where "among the stones I stood a stone" (l. 236). Now Manfred is as cold as the Colosseum's stones, indeed he is one of them. The gigantic dimensions of the Colosseum correspond in the human world to the grandeur of the Alps in the natural world. In neither world can Manfred find fulfillment.

In both *Prometheus Bound* and *Manfred* the "action" resides in the speeches of the protagonist. "Action," as defined by Aristotle in the *Poetics*, "implies personal agents, who necessarily possess certain distinctive qualities both of character and thought; for it is by these we qualify actions themselves, and these—thought and character—are the two natural causes from which actions spring, and on actions again all success or failure depends."[31] Dante, in a key passage of the *Purgatorio*, presents a similar argument when he has Virgil tell Dante the pilgrim that every human being is guided by a *moto spiritale* ("movement of spirit") that determines his destiny.[32] God foreordains that destiny, but throughout his life man has the free will to make rational choices that cumulatively form his *moto spiritale*. "Action" or "movement of spirit" cannot then be viewed simply as the sum of a man's deeds, or as comprising the events he causes or participates in. Rather, it is as much the motivation from which the deeds

---

31. *Aristotle's Poetics*, trans. S. H. Butcher. Introduction by Francis Fergusson (New York, 1961), p. 62. For this paragraph I am indebted to the discussion in Fergusson's *Dante* (1966) as well as to his introduction to the *Poetics*.
32. See especially canto XVIII, ll. 31–33.

spring, the mental processes by which he comes to his decisions and makes his resolutions, as it is the deeds themselves. In both *Prometheus Bound* and *Manfred* the speeches of the protagonist serve to reveal the state of his soul, his "movement of spirit." The speeches of Prometheus address the elements, traverse vast reaches of time and space, and (if we include those of the chorus and Io) range over the whole known world. Those of Manfred, moving from early youth to and through death, from the Jungfrau's summit to the moonlit Colosseum, traverse equally vast reaches of time and space. Aeschylus wrote *Prometheus Bound* when drama had barely emerged as a literary form, Byron *Manfred* when the Romantic focus on the self reigned supreme. Yet, viewed in the perspective provided by Aristotle and Dante, no classical play embodies more "action" than *Prometheus Bound*, no Romantic poem more than *Manfred*. They are akin in that they are dramas of the mind's ordeal.

The awesome dimensions of Aeschylus' hero must have greatly impressed Byron. Jeffrey, in his review of *Manfred*, recognized that Byron had had "a grand and terrific vision of a being invested with superhuman attributes, in order that he may be capable of more than human sufferings, and be sustained under them by more than human force and pride."[33] Byron boldly faced in *Manfred* the problem of how to render a static situation dramatic. In this he learned from Aeschylus, for what Aeschylus does so well, Kitto observes, is to dramatize "the emotions and not the events. . . . The solitary hero is everything; and not what he does, but what he feels and is" (pp. 59, 66). Both plays concentrate on mental rather than on physical action: Prometheus literally does not move on stage, Manfred moves only to find new settings and beings to counterpoint his mind's conflict. Only he has a life of his own; the other characters hardly exist except as projections of his moods. Although Manfred, unlike Aeschylus' hero, does not remain physically stationary on stage, his chains gall him even more than Prometheus' in that they are those of his own human limitations. Through the intensity of his mental energy he attempts to divest himself of (or at least to transcend) his "clay." In *Childe Harold* III Byron had given this extraordinary intensity of being—"soul—heart—mind—passions—feelings"—its consummate expression in the "*one* word . . . Lightning" (stanza 97). There Harold yearned for the natural, elemental powers: he wished to speak as the thunderbolt, to roll his feelings and thoughts into "Lightning."

Aeschylus' Prometheus is a god, a Titan, an immortal. Byron's Manfred is a man and a mortal, but he believes he possesses that within him which is

33. *Edinburgh Review*, 28 (Aug. 1817), 419.

divine and immortal. His mortality he has transcended to the extent that, as he tells the Witch of the Alps, he has made his "eyes familiar with Eternity" (II, ii, 90). His mind has enabled him, like Prometheus, to dwell in his despair and to "live—and live for ever" (II, ii, 150). Manfred is fully aware of the extent of the divine within him when he affirms to the Seventh Spirit, his destiny and counterpart, that

> The Mind—the Spirit—the Promethean spark,
> The lightning of my being, is as bright
> Pervading, and far darting as your own,
> And shall not yield to yours, though cooped in clay![34]

"The con*crete* in nature nearest to the *abstract* of Death is Death by a Flash of Lightning," Samuel Taylor Coleridge remarked in 1806.[35] Byron wished both to embody Manfred's being in "lightning" and to have him taken off by it. Moments of greatest trial cause Prometheus and Manfred to display their "lightning": Prometheus when he learns his new punishment from "Zeus's footman" Hermes, Manfred when he confronts Arimanes, Zoroastrian prince of darkness who controls the forces of evil and destruction in the universe. Already the first Destiny has recognized kinship with Manfred:

> This man
> Is of no common order, as his port
> And presence here denote: his sufferings
> Have been of an immortal nature—like
> Our own; his knowledge, and his powers and will,
> . . . have been such
> As clay hath seldom borne; his aspirations
> Have been beyond the dwellers of the earth.
> (II, iv, 51–55, 57–59)

Paired with Prometheus in sufferings, knowledge, powers, will, aspirations, Manfred refuses to bow before Arimanes, for he knows that "above him"

---

34. I, i, 154–57. In the first draft of *Manfred*, written in Switzerland, these lines appear in different form and without mention either of the "Promethean spark" or of "lightning":

> The Mind which is within me—the high Soul—
> The Spirit of my being is as bright
> Pervading—grand [?]—and boundless as your own—
> It shall not yield to yours—though cooped in clay [.]

Quoted from the manuscript by permission of The Pierpont Morgan Library.

35. *Inquiring Spirit: A Coleridge Reader*, ed. Kathleen Coburn (1951; n.p., 1968), p. 39.

is the "overruling Infinite—the Maker" (II, iv, 46–47). Byron distinguishes, as Aeschylus and Homer did before him, between Zeus and a force (*moira*, or destiny)—austere, impersonal, indifferent—which stands apart from Zeus and to whose rule even he is subject. When the Oceanides ask Prometheus "Who then is the steersman of necessity?" he replies, "The triple-formed Fates and the remembering Furies." They ask again, "Is Zeus weaker than these?" He replies firmly, "Yes, for he, too, cannot escape what is fated" (ll. 514–18). Prometheus knows that the same destiny that rules him rules Zeus. Both immortal, they yet remain subject to laws of time and fate.

Differing in motivation, Prometheus has toiled for the good of mankind, Manfred for his own advantage and to escape human involvement. "From my youth upwards," he says, "My Spirit walked not with the souls of men, / Nor looked upon the earth with human eyes" (II, ii, 50–52). Manfred is, as Rutherford calls him, "a Prometheus *manqué*."[36] In his youth, he tells the Abbot of St. Maurice, he had had "noble aspirations" "to make my own the mind of other men, / The enlightener of nations" (III, i, 104–7). But his "Knowledge," as he observes and learns, has brought him nothing but "sorrow" (I, i, 10; II, iv, 61). Yet he affirms to the Chamois Hunter his capacity to "bear / In life what others could not brook to dream" (II, i, 76–77). Possession of Promethean knowledge, i.e., perception of cosmic truth, is at once the power of godlike ascendance and the damnation of eternal suffering. Manfred as well as Prometheus has the mind of a visionary: a mind that will not compromise its integrity. To *know* is to perceive on the human level the inadequacies of the human spiritual make-up. For Aeschylus' Prometheus, "Knowledge" is also "sorrow," but he accepts it knowing that it will bring him closer to suffering mankind. The Oceanides ask, "Is there no limit set for your pain?" He replies, "None save when it shall seem good to Zeus" (ll. 259, 260). Aeschylus here defines the human condition, as will Sophocles and Euripides after him, as one of irrational and potentially unlimited suffering.

Prometheus and Manfred each possess a fatal secret. Prometheus, whose name means "foreknowledge," knows that Zeus's long reign will end in his overthrow when he falls in love with Thetis and has a child by her, Heracles, who is destined to be mightier than his father. Manfred knows, though we never learn, what happened during the "all-nameless hour" (I, i, 24). Over the course of each poem the protagonist circles around his secret and gradually reveals more of it. Prometheus, in part goaded by pain and

36. *Byron: A Critical Study*, p. 89.

despair, tells his secret to the chorus but not to Hermes, for only by with-holding it from him can he resist Zeus effectively. Aeschylus makes its gradual disclosure a central dramatic motif. It becomes a driving force in the play, forcing the two polar figures—Prometheus and Zeus—to harden in their lines of resistance until the eruptive ending sends Prometheus hurtling to the depths. Manfred's secret, handled by Byron less adeptly, also serves as a structural device in that it focuses attention on his unde-fined guilt. As compelled to hint at his secret as Prometheus, he yet never quite divulges it. The encounter with Astarte, powerful as drama, ends ambiguously. We know neither Astarte's response to Manfred's plea for forgiveness nor what happened between them during the "all-nameless hour."

Secondary personages in *Prometheus Bound* and *Manfred* share simi-lar roles. The Oceanides, when they attempt to lighten Prometheus' burden of misery, only make him despond the more. The spirits of the universe, when summoned by Manfred in the hope that they will render him aid, only increase his frustration. The Chamois Hunter may correspond roughly to Oceanus, the friendly and obliging Titan who has made his peace with the new order. As Oceanus fails to move Prometheus toward reconciliation with Zeus, so the Chamois Hunter fails to persuade Manfred to return to the world of men. Elsewhere, the role of Oceanus may merge with that of the Witch of the Alps. He offers to intercede for Prometheus with Zeus; she offers to help Manfred if he submits to her will. As Prometheus rebuffs Oceanus, so Manfred abruptly spurns the Witch of the Alps. Neither Oceanus nor the Witch realizes that the being before them has values which transcend the practical and expedient.

*Manfred* has no Io, the maiden ravished by Zeus who wanders the world helpless before the jealousy of Hera. Constantly prodded on by the stings of Argos, tormenting but never fatal, she is allowed neither peace nor rest. In *Prometheus Bound* she is unforgettable, the living on-stage demonstra-tion of Zeus's caprice and cruelty. Now a girl, now a heifer, she represents the actual suffering of mankind, the human condition *in extremis*, for which Prometheus suffers. No scene in *Manfred* rivals in dramatic power those with Io in *Prometheus Bound*. Astarte could have provided the fillip that would have roused Manfred to new self-awareness; instead, the en-counter leaves him drained of the will to live. Io is intensely alive, trem-bling with outraged humanity; Astarte but a shadow and a voice.

The Alps stimulated Byron to place Manfred within a natural world that corresponded to the magnitude of his being. "No mind was ever so re-

ceptive as [Byron's] for the 'spirit of place,' as externally expressed," Ethel
C. Mayne wrote long ago. "The character of the scenes he saw, in every
country, coloured his imagination through and through: nothing in Byron
is more remarkable than his extreme sensibility to such influence, and the
inveterate victory of his 'Self' over it all." [37] This "mobility," as he insisted
in *Don Juan*, enabled him to respond truthfully to the perpetual diversity
of new impressions, and his writings of the moment accurately reflect his
changing moods. Earlier in the summer of 1816 Shelley had guided him to
a fairer understanding of Wordsworth's poetry, and for a while he shared
Wordsworth's belief that man could partake in a mystical communion with
the natural world. "I live not in myself," Harold believes, "but I become /
Portion of that around me; and to me / High mountains are a feeling"
(III, 72). But the solace which a transcendental nature afforded him at the
time he wrote *Childe Harold* III Byron found illusory by the time he came
to write *Manfred*. As the summer wore on, his belief in self-transcendence
within nature's bosom increasingly left him dissatisfied: it did not meet the
truth of his own impressions. Seeing the Alps helped restore his imaginative response to the natural world—"I have lately repeopled my mind
with Nature," he recorded in his "Journal to Augusta" (*LJ*, III, 355)—but
it also forced it to become more objective. Manfred, though he still finds
the natural world unendingly beautiful, feels cut off from it. Grandiose,
awe-inspiring are the mountains in the poem, but also indifferent, unfeel-
ing: as their skyward thrust corresponds to the aspirations of Manfred's
soul, so their rock and ice correspond to the emotional state of his being.

The setting of *Manfred* bears such obvious resemblance to that of *Prometheus Bound* that it is difficult to resist the conclusion that Byron learned
from Aeschylus. *Prometheus Bound* opens on "a bare and desolate crag in
the Caucasus." Might says to Hephaistos: "This is the world's limit that we
have come to; this is the Scythian country, an untrodden desolation." These
words bode ominously for Prometheus: he knows himself beyond the reach
of mankind, on the world's outermost edge. Later, Prometheus describes the
Caucasus range as "the highest mountains . . . the neighbors of the stars"
(ll. 720, 722). The crucial scenes in *Manfred* are set in the "Higher Alps":
the cliffs of the Jungfrau witness Manfred's attempt at suicide, the climactic
meeting with Arimanes and Astarte takes place on its summit. Queen of the
Bernese Alps, the Jungfrau stands dramatically apart from its neighboring
peaks, the Schreckhorn and the Eiger. Its summit, dazzling in its whiteness, Byron seems to have believed was yet unscaled. (It had, probably

37. *Byron*, 2 vols. (London, 1912), II, 110–11.

unknown to him, first been scaled in 1811.) Metaphorically at least, Manfred is as much chained to a mountain as Prometheus.

Might and Hephaistos depart leaving Prometheus in chains. "Everywhere below me, the inescapable earth. Above me, the inescapable sky"—he utters in Robert Lowell's free derivation of the play. He is at the midpoint between earth and heaven, yet in neither realm, helpless, totally exposed. Silence and solitude are an essential part of his punishment and have powerful dramatic effect, for the play is to a great degree about the loneliness of the human condition. After a long silence, Prometheus vents his outrage at earth and sky. He believes the elements do not sympathize with his plight, but he errs. The Oceanides, in the final antistrophe of their first chorus, tell him:

> The wave cries out as it breaks into surf;
> the depth cries out, lamenting you; the dark
> Hades, the hollow underneath the world,
> sullenly groans below; the springs
> of sacred flowing rivers all lament
> the pain and pity of your suffering.
>
> (ll. 431–36)

The Greeks saw man and the natural world as indissolubly one. Prometheus, though banished by Zeus to its outermost bounds, is still in harmony with natural forces. It is a harmony no longer possible for Byron's hero. Unlike Prometheus, he has lost touch with organic process.

Most striking of the parallel passages between *Prometheus Bound* and *Manfred* is Manfred's first apostrophe to nature:

> My Mother Earth!
> And thou fresh-breaking Day, and you, ye Mountains,
> Why are ye beautiful? I cannot love ye.
> And thou, the bright Eye of the Universe,
> Thou openest over all, and unto all
> Art a delight—thou shin'st not on my heart.
>
> (I, ii, 7–12)

E. H. Coleridge has noted that it echoes Prometheus' first words after being chained to the rock:

> Bright light, swift-winged winds, springs of the rivers, numberless
> laughter of the sea's waves, earth, mother of all, and the all-seeing

circle of the sun: I call upon you to see what I, a God, suffer at the
hands of Gods.                                              (ll. 89–92)

The desolate mountain vistas, geographically almost impossible to define,
in which each protagonist finds himself correspond to the overwhelming
sense of isolation he feels. Yet the natural world in Aeschylus, though
sympathetic, cannot alleviate the plight of Prometheus, and at the play's
end he descends into the bowels of the earth to begin his long wait for
justice. Manfred's expostulation falls unheard on "My Mother Earth": the
Alpine peaks remain icy and indifferent, the sun will not alleviate the
chill enveloping his heart.

Aeschylus in *Prometheus Bound* and Byron in *Manfred* contemplate an
abrupt end to earthly existence, yet reject death in favor of life, however
miserable the terms on which life must be endured. Io and Manfred, each
brought near to madness through suffering, face the temptation of an
easeful death. When Prometheus foretells to Io that in addition to endless
voyaging her existence will be "a wintry sea of agony and ruin," she cries
out:

> What good is life to me then? Why do I not throw myself at once from
> some rough crag, to strike the ground and win a quittance of all my
> troubles. It would be better to die once for all than suffer all one's
> days.                                                   (ll. 747–51)

Perhaps she recognizes that it is her fate to wander and suffer, for she does
not commit suicide. It is conceivable that Byron recalls this passage when
he has Manfred ponder his death upon the Jungfrau. Perplexed by the
mixed human condition and in despair over his own mortality, Manfred is
about to spring from the crag when the Chamois Hunter prevents him.
Realizing that though he wants to stop living he does not want to die, he
does not renew his dramatic attempt at suicide. He is tired of life, yet it is,
for a time, his "fatality to live" (I, ii, 24). His quest for knowledge leads
him to dive in his "lone wanderings, to the caves of Death, / Searching its
cause in its effect" (II, ii, 80–81). This journey symbolizes, through a
dream, the suicide of a mind desiring to escape the thoughts that torment
it. A moment afterwards, Manfred tells the Witch of the Alps: "My solitude
is solitude no more, / But peopled with the Furies" (II, ii, 130–31), and in
so doing echoes another of Aeschylus' creations, the tortured Orestes at the
end of *The Libation Bearers*. For both, "madness" would have been "a

blessing" (l. 134). Aeschylus with Io, Byron with Manfred, understand that a hard-fought existence is preferable to submission. This condition of survival plagued by suffering is labelled life.

The ending of each play develops inevitably from what has gone before. Hermes describes to Prometheus his fate: "First this rough crag / with thunder and the lightning bolt the Father / shall cleave asunder, and shall hide your body / wrapped in a rocky clasp within its depth" (ll. 1116–19). Obdurate and unyielding to the last, Prometheus shows no fear before Zeus's power. Nor does Manfred at the end flinch before death. The last scene shows him fiercely resisting demons and humbling them, unafraid though no longer able to shore up his spirits now that he has abandoned hope of Astarte. Recognizing that his time on earth is now over, he stands secure in the independence of his own mind and greets death as the undiscovered country. His final words to the Abbot of St. Maurice, "Old man! 'tis not so difficult to die," express resignation, not dismay, before his fate. When Murray, at Gifford's suggestion, left the line out of the first edition, Byron wrote him indignantly: "You have destroyed the whole effect and moral of the poem" (*LJ*, IV, 157). The moral, in terms of Byron's own development in 1816, is that it is extremely difficult to live, yet live he must.[38]

In the 1816 poems and in *Manfred* Byron created a new Prometheus, but he was a Prometheus *de nos jours*, a Prometheus arising from his own disillusioned, postwar generation. Another ominous hero—Mary Shelley's *Frankenstein: or, the New Prometheus*—also came into being in 1816, with Byron and Shelley as attendant godfathers. What Shelley himself learned from the animated conversations at Diodati that summer will never be fully ascertained. It is beyond question that his reading of Aeschylus' *Prometheus Bound* to Byron stimulated the writing of "Prometheus." Most critics agree that he came to find in Byron's lyric one of the inspirations for his *Prometheus Unbound*. I would argue that *Manfred*, itself stimulated by the reading of Aeschylus, had an even greater impact upon Shelley's poem.

Manfred evinces a dynamism which none of the other largely autobiographical personae in Byron's poetry of this summer possess. His movements around the Alps reflect the renewed momentum in the poet's life. Activity was always a sure sign of health in Byron's being, for it veered him

---

38. See the excellent discussion of the ending of *Manfred* in Edward E. Bostetter, *The Romantic Ventriloquists: Wordsworth, Coleridge, Keats, Shelley, Byron* (Seattle, 1963), p. 280.

away from introspective brooding and toward recovery of a more stable mental equilibrium. While the personae in *The Prisoner of Chillon* and the July poems look passively upon their destinies, Manfred dynamically confronts his existence. His "action," within the context of Byron's life, signifies hope: hope of which Byron was probably not conscious when he wrote *Manfred*, but which we, with the hindsight denied him, can see. Viewed within a life's perspective, the effect on Byron of writing *Manfred* was nothing less than cathartic. When he left for Italy on 5 October, having completed the first draft of the poem, he had completed a stage in his life. A new stage, unexpectedly bringing him more of real happiness than he could have foreseen that October day, now opened before him.

Never again did the Prometheus myth mean as much to Byron as it did in 1816. In Switzerland he had breathed Promethean defiance and endured Promethean pain. Once in Italy, it was the image of Prometheus as creator that more often inspired him. Following Shaftesbury who, a century earlier, had seen the poet as "a second *Maker*; a just Prometheus under Jove,"[39] Byron now conceived Prometheus not merely as the eternal sufferer but as the embodiment of the organic energies of creation. In the fourth canto of *Childe Harold*, written in 1817, he apostrophized the Apollo Belvedere as a Promethean image of "ideal Beauty" (stanza 162). Its sculptor had molded "an eternal Glory" (163). Even if Prometheus "stole from Heaven / The fire which we endure," the creative energy he brought man more than compensates him for the hell-flames of existence.[40] Later references to the Prometheus myth are few. Although Byron asserts in *Don Juan* that he was "born for opposition," the poem's chief allusion to the myth—to "Love" as the "Fire which Prometheus filched for us from Heaven" (XV, 22; I, 127)—is ironic, not disrespectful.[41] Still more revealing is a passage from *The Prophecy of Dante* (1819), in which Dante, speaking as the poet-prophet, records the distance which Byron had placed between himself and the myth which in Switzerland had given him such firm insight into his dilemma.

39. *Characteristics*, ed. J. M. Robertson, 2 vols. (New York, 1900), I, 136.
40. As E. H. Coleridge notes, Byron remembered this variant of the Prometheus legend from Horace (*P*, II, 448). Cf. the Promethean stanzas on Nemesis in *Childe Harold* IV, 132–37.
41. After irony, humor. See Trelawny's anecdote, upon his asking Byron one day (c. 28 Sept. 1823) how he felt: "Feel! why, just as that dammed obstreperous fellow felt chained to a rock, the vultures gnawing my midriff, and vitals too, for I have no liver." See his *Records of Shelley, Byron and the Author* (London, n.d.), p. 153. Cf. *P*, VI, 103, and *P*, IV, 586. The belief that Napoleon failed to measure up to the Promethean ideal remained with Byron to the last, for he couples the two names in *The Age of Bronze* (1823), V, 227–32 (*P*, V, 554).

Many are Poets but without the name;
   For what is Poesy but to create,
   From overfeeling, Good or Ill, and aim
At an external life beyond our fate,
   And be the new Prometheus of new men,
   Bestowing fire from Heaven, and then, too late,
Finding the pleasure given repaid with pain,
   And vultures to the heart of the bestower,
   Who, having lavished his high gift in vain,
Lies chained to his lone rock by the sea-shore?
   So be it: *we* can bear.[42]

42. IV, 10–20 (*P*, IV, 269–70). Italics mine.

In the preparation of this essay, I acknowledge here my gratitude to the National Endowment for the Humanities for awarding me a Younger Humanist Fellowship in 1971–72, to the Huntington Library for a summer grant in 1972, and to the Duke University Council on Research for providing me with supplemental assistance for travel and research.

# Shelley and KING LEAR

## Martin J. Svaglic

Loyola University of Chicago

IT WOULD NOT BE DIFFICULT, I think, to show that *King Lear* is the tragedy of Shakespeare that has most haunted the contemporary mind and for much the same reasons that have made a Conrad or a Sartre or a Hemingway one of the archetypes of that mind. Its picture of a world almost bereft of traditional values which man can at least partially redeem from absurdity by sheer willpower, human solidarity, and love is what makes *Lear* seem the most "existential" and the most contemporary of Shakespeare's plays. And so it is not surprising that *Lear* was also the play that most tenaciously gripped the minds of two great Romantics whose characteristic perceptions and attitudes were in their diverse ways peculiarly modern: Shelley and Keats.

This is not to deny that *King Lear* had a special attraction for most of the other Romantics, with the notable exception of Byron.[1] Wordsworth, for whom Shakespeare and Milton were the greatest of all poets, considered it a masterpiece of genius, echoed lines of it occasionally in his poetry, and drew upon it to a considerable degree for the moorland and storm scenes of *The Borderers* and for the characters of Herbert and Idonea, who bear some resemblance to Lear and Cordelia. *Othello*, however, was the principal Shakespearean source of *The Borderers*; and it was not *Lear* but *Macbeth* that Wordsworth considered the "best conducted" of Shakespeare's plays, the madness of Lear being for him, like the death of Julius Caesar, "too *overwhelming* an incident for *any* stage of the drama but the *last*. It is an incident to which the mind clings, and from which it will not be torn away to share in other sorrows."[2]

1. Byron professed no great admiration for Shakespeare and argued against him with Shelley. In Italy, according to Hunt, he was "anxious to show you that he possessed no Shakespeare and Milton" because "he had been accused of borrowing from them." (See Leslie A. Marchand, *Byron*, 3 vols. [New York, 1957], III, 991 and 1014.) According to Samuel C. Chew, however, "Byron distinguished Shakespeare the dramatist and Shakespeare the poet. He loved and admired the poet and his verse abounds in Shakespearean echoes; but the methods of the playwright were opposed to those for which Byron stood" (*The Dramas of Lord Byron* [Göttingen, 1915], p. 171).

2. From Conversations Recorded by the Bishop of Lincoln, *The Prose Works of William Wordsworth*, ed. A. B. Grosart, 3 vols. (London, 1876), III, 460.

Coleridge thought *Lear* "the most tremendous effort of Shakespeare as a poet; *Hamlet* as a philosopher or meditator; and *Othello* as the union of the two."[3] Although he has left us a keen analysis of both Edmund and Lear and took, as we shall see later, an interest like Shelley's in the character of the Fool, he eventually reached the conclusion that *Lear* was not quite in his critical line: "I have learnt," he wrote when considering the proposed lectures of 1819, "what I might easily have anticipated, that the *Lear* of Shakespeare is not a good subject for a whole lecture in *my* style."[4]

For Hazlitt, one of Keats's principal mentors, *Lear* was "the best of all Shakespeare's plays, for it is the one in which he was the most in earnest. The passion which he has taken as his subject is that which strikes its root deepest into the human heart; of which the bond is the hardest to be unloosed; and the cancelling and tearing to pieces of which gives the greatest revulsion to the frame."[5] Despite Hazlitt's great praise, however, *Lear* never apparently meant for him, much less for the religious Wordsworth and Coleridge, what it came to mean for Keats and Shelley. For the younger poets it was not so much a play as a paradigm, something to be pondered and contemplated as a guide to a better life.

What *Lear* meant to Keats we can pretty well know from his own words, some of which recall Hazlitt's. His underscorings of and occasional comments on passages in Hazlitt's chapter on *King Lear* make clear that for him as for Hazlitt, it was the intensity of the great passions expressed in the play that especially held him. Thus, he underlines Hazlitt's remark: "If there is anything in any author like this yearning of the heart, these throes of tenderness, this profound expression of all that can be thought and felt in the most heart-rending situations, we are glad of it; but it is in some author we have not read."[6]

When Keats echoes such passages, however, it is with an even greater emphasis than Hazlitt's on the cognitive value of *Lear*. Discussing Benjamin West's painting "Death on the Pale Horse" in the famous "Negative Capability" letter, he writes: "The excellence of every Art is its intensity, capable of making all disagreeables evaporate from their being in close relationship with Beauty & Truth—Examine King Lear & you will find this exemplified throughout; but in this picture we have unpleasantness

3. *Coleridge's Shakespearean Criticism*, ed. T. M. Raysor, 2 vols. (Cambridge, Mass., 1930), II, 351.

4. From a letter of 28 Feb. 1819, in Raysor, II, 327.

5. "Characters of Shakespeare's Plays," in the *Collected Works of William Hazlitt*, ed. A. R. Waller and Arnold Glover, 12 vols. (London, 1902), I, 257–58.

6. For Keats on Hazlitt's lecture, see Amy Lowell, *John Keats*, 2 vols. (Boston and New York, 1925), II, 587–90.

without any momentous depth of speculation excited, in which to bury its repulsiveness." This means, according to Professor Bate, that although the reality disclosed in *Lear* "may be distressing and even cruel to human nature . . . the harmony with truth will remain, and even deepen, to the extent that the emerging reality is being constantly matched at every stage by the 'depth of speculation excited'—by the corresponding release and extension, in other words, of human insight."[7]

*Lear* became the play "that was increasingly to haunt Keats's imagination more than any other."[8] He kept reading it again and again, he refers to it more than to any other, and he even wrote a sonnet, "On Sitting Down to Read *King Lear* Once Again," about its peremptory call back to the "fierce dispute / Betwixt damnation and impassion'd clay." For him it was another Moneta reminding him that if he were to be a true poet, the garden must be abandoned for the temple and ultimately the altar, the realm of Flora and old Pan for the agonies and strife of the vale of soul-making.

Of all the Romantics, however, it was for Shelley that *King Lear* had the greatest cognitive value and played the most central role in his thinking about poetry as an art. Yet what *Lear* meant to Shelley has not been discussed at any length, so far as I am aware. In his pioneering article "Shelley and Shakespeare," David Lee Clark cited some sixty-six passages in Shelley which in varying degrees echo Shakespeare in "thought, phrase, imagery, or symbolism"; but the echoes of *Lear* are relatively brief or slight except for two striking passages: Count Cenci's curse on his daughter (IV.i. 80–95), rather closely resembling Lear's curse on his daughters (II.iv.164–66, 167–70, 274–78, 281–85); and especially Prometheus's words to Asia (III.iii. 10–36), which were obviously inspired in part by Lear's beautiful words to Cordelia (V.iii. 8–19). John D. Margolis has more recently pointed out the distinct echo of *Lear* in the opening line of "England in 1819." A. C. Bradley, in considering *The Defence of Poetry*, which contains Shelley's key passage on the rank of *King Lear*, persuasively argues that since Shelley inclined to think it, in Bradley's words, "the greatest drama in the World,"

---

7. W. J. Bate, *John Keats* (Cambridge, Mass., 1963), p. 244. However, see S. R. Swaminathan, "Keats and Benjamin West's *King Lear*," *Keats-Shelley Journal*, 18 (1969), 15–16: "It has been generally held that Keats is here referring to Shakespeare's *King Lear* as an example of intensity. While no doubt it was one of his favorite plays, and the sonnet on *King Lear* is expressive of his response to its intensity, in this context, however, it is probable that Keats is referring not to Shakespeare's play but to Benjamin West's painting of the storm scene in *King Lear* for Boydell's *Shakespeare Gallery*. The painting shows Lear in the act of taking off his clothes, saying, 'Off, off, you lendings! Come, unbutton here.'" The painting is now in the Boston Museum of Fine Arts and is reproduced in this issue of the *Keats-Shelley Journal*.
8. Bate, p. 106.

and since it is not a direct portrait of perfection, we may conclude that
Shelley's concern with beautiful idealisms of moral excellence "did not
mean that the immediate subject of poetry must be perfection in some
form."[9] In general, such has been the tenor and almost the extent of the
discussion thus far of Shelley's relation to *King Lear*.

One reason that so relatively little has been written on the subject may
be that we do not have as much direct evidence about Shelley's view of
*Lear* as we do about Keats's. Neither Shelley nor Mary discusses the play
in the Letters, and there are very few references even to the reading of it
in either Letters or Journal. Furthermore, *Lear* was not the play Shelley
quoted from most often. That play, according to Bradley, was *Macbeth*.
His most obvious structural borrowings, as in *The Cenci*, were also from
*Macbeth*.

Counterbalancing this relative dearth of evidence, however, is the
weight of the evidence we do have. We may reasonably infer that the
reading of *Lear* in the Shelley circle was frequent, that it extended over a
long period of time, and that it was an experience taken very seriously
indeed. Thus in 1814 at Lucerne, Jane Clairmont suffered an attack of
"horrors" that delayed the departure of Shelley, Mary, and herself for
Dettingen; and to judge from her journal, the attack was caused, according
to White, "by a hypersensitive reading of *King Lear*."[10] We know from the
Journal that Mary was reading the play in March 1819, and may assume
that Shelley, who as we have seen borrows from it in parts of *The Cenci*,
was reading it, too, *The Cenci* having been written between May and
August 1819. We know that Shelley was reading it again late in February
1821, shortly before turning to Sidney's *Defence of Poetry*, both in apparent
preparation for his own *Defence of Poetry*, written in February and March
1821.[11] We know from Shelley's own words that *King Lear* was to be his
model for *Charles the First*, a never-completed play he began in 1821 but
had in mind since 1818, a play in which he hoped to "approach as near our
great dramatist as my feeble powers will permit."[12] And we also have

9. Clark, *PMLA*, 54 (1939), 261–87, passim; Margolis, "Shakespeare and Shelley's
Sonnet 'England in 1819,'" *English Language Notes*, 4 (1967), 276–77; and Bradley,
"Shelley's View of Poetry," The English Association Leaflet No. 4 (London, 1908),
p. 11. See also F. L. Jones, "Shelley and Shakespeare: A Supplement," *PMLA*, 59
(1944), 591–96, and Beach Langston, "Shelley and Shakespeare," *Huntington Library Quarterly*, 12 (1948–49), 163–90.

10. Newman Ivey White, *Shelley*, 2 vols. (New York, 1940), I, 359.

11. For the dates of Mary and Shelley's reading, see *Mary Shelley's Journal*, ed.
Frederick L. Jones (Norman, Okla., 1947), pp. 118, 148.

12. "*King Lear* is my model, for that is nearly perfect." See E. J. Trelawny, *Records
of Shelley, Byron, and the Author*, 2 vols. (London, 1879), I, 117, and N. I. White,

Shelley's words about *Lear* in the Preface to *The Cenci* as, along with "the two plays in which the tale of Oedipus is told, one of the "deepest and the sublimest tragic compositions."

Finally and above all we have the crucial passage in the essay setting down his maturest thoughts about his art, *A Defence of Poetry*, in which *King Lear* is by implication and virtually by explicit statement ranked above all other plays:

> On the modern stage a few only of the elements capable of expressing the image of the poet's conception are employed at once. We have tragedy without music and dancing; and music and dancing without the high impersonations of which they are the fit accompaniment, and both without religion and solemnity; religious institution has indeed been usually banished from the stage. . . . The modern practice of blending comedy with tragedy, though liable to great abuse in point of practice, is undoubtedly an extension of the dramatic circle; but the comedy should be as in *King Lear*, universal, ideal, and sublime. It is perhaps the intervention of this principle which determines the balance in favour of *King Lear* against the *Oedipus Tyrannus* or the *Agamemnon*, or, if you will with the trilogies with which they are connected; unless the intense power of the choral poetry, especially that of the latter, should be considered as restoring the equilibrium. *King Lear*, if it can sustain this comparison, may be judged to be the most perfect specimen of the dramatic art existing in the world; in spite of the narrow conditions to which the poet was subjected by the ignorance of the philosophy of the drama which has prevailed in modern Europe. Calderon, in his religious Autos, has attempted to fulfill some of the high conditions of dramatic representation neglected by Shakespeare; such as the establishing a relation between the drama and religion, and the accommodating them to music and dancing; but he omits the observation of conditions still more important, and more is lost than gained by a substitution of the rigidly-defined and ever-repeated idealisms of a distorted superstition for the living impersonations of the truth of human passion.[13]

Shelley's remarks about Calderón, whose influence on the poet was especially strong from 1819 to 1821, have already been elucidated at some

---

"Shelley's Charles the First," *Journal of English and Germanic Philology*, 21 (1922), 432.

13. *The Complete Works of Percy Bysshe Shelley*, ed. Roger Ingpen and W. E. Peck, 10 vols. (London and New York, 1926–30), VII, 119–20.

length.[14] It remains to be seen if any further light can be thrown on his words about *King Lear*. Why should this play have seemed to him quite probably "the most perfect specimen of the dramatic art existing in the world?" Why *Lear* rather than *Hamlet* or *Macbeth*, for instance? Shelley's praise of *Lear*, great as it is, does not really answer such questions, tantalizing as they are, surely, to anyone who thinks about the matter at all. One may attain at least highly probable answers to such questions, however, from the inferences that may legitimately be drawn from his remarks about the play in the *Defence*, and from the relation of these and other remarks in the essay to *Lear* itself and to other words of Shelley. Through such means we may come to see, in brief, that the affinity between Shelley and *King Lear* is very deep indeed and that it springs even more from his response to the plot, character, and thought of Shakespeare's play than to its diction.

The first thing that might be noted, before discussing the play in any detail, is something partly in *Lear's* disfavor, from Shelley's viewpoint, but also, considering the likely alternatives, probably even more to its credit. The reason that the art of the drama "never was understood or practiced according to the true philosophy of it, as at Athens," was that only the Athenians, according to Shelley in the *Defence*, "employed language, action, music, painting, the dance, and religious institutions, to produce a common effect in the representation of the highest idealisms of passion and of power." Since *King Lear* does not establish a relation between the drama and religion—at least in Shelley's view—nor accommodate them to music and dancing, it suffers for Shelley by comparison with the plays of the Greeks.

Such an attitude may seem surprising to a contemporary reader, particularly one still affected by the stereotype of the poet as an enemy of religion *tout court*. Yet Shelley was not the only Romantic who came to feel that Shakespeare's tragedies could have been enriched by a closer connection with religion. The later Wordsworth reached much the same conclusion, warning against speaking of Shakespeare "as if even he were perfect. He had serious defects," Wordsworth told Aubrey de Vere, "and not those only proceeding from carelessness. For instance, in his delineations of character he does not assign as large a place to religious sentiment as enters into the constitution of human nature under normal circum-

14. Salvador de Madariaga, "Shelley and Calderón," in *Transactions and Report of the Royal Society of Literature of the United Kingdom*, 37 (London, 1919), 137–76; and E. J. Gates, "Shelley and Calderón," *Philological Quarterly*, 16 (1937), 49–58.

stances. If his dramas had more religion in them, they would be truer representations of man, as well as more elevated, and of a more searching interest."[15]

Whereas *King Lear* may have been deficient for Shelley in this respect, however, as it would not have been for the more secular-minded Keats, to whom the near absence of religion might well have seemed a virtue, the play in its present form was at least preferable to the more likely alternative in Shakespeare's time: i.e., a Christian frame of reference such as pervades some of Shakespeare's other plays and especially those of the playwright whom, except for Shakespeare, Shelley most admired: Calderón. Shelley's growing other-worldliness or Platonism or whatever one wants to call it, did not imply any compromise with or tolerance of organized Christianity, particularly what he regarded as its most oppressive form, Roman Catholicism. Calderón, for all his excellence, was not only a Catholic but a priest; and whatever he gained by attempting to fulfill "some of the high conditions of dramatic representation neglected by Shakespeare," he lost still more in Shelley's view, "by a substitution" for beautiful idealisms of moral excellence "of the rigidly-defined and ever-repeated idealisms of a distorted superstition." *Lear*, then, if not involved with religious "institution," was at least not marred by crass superstition.[16]

If the Elizabethan theater had fewer sources of emotional appeal than the Greek, however, it had one which the Greeks lacked and which Shelley found of such importance in *King Lear* especially that it tipped the balance in favor of Shakespeare over the Greeks: the "modern practice of blending comedy with tragedy" was "undoubtedly an extension of the dramatic circle" as long as the comedy was "as in *King Lear*, universal, ideal, and sublime." It would be good to know from his own words just what Shelley meant by this: what the adjectives imply; whether the comedy in *Hamlet*, for instance, is equally deserving of such praise; and whether in *Lear* the words apply only to the comedy involving the Fool, as is likely, and not to that in the Kent-Oswald scene. However, Shelley has left us no discussion of the matter.

15. *Prose Works*, ed. Grosart, III, 488.

16. Actually *Lear* is much like *Oedipus the King* in that it is capable of being interpreted as implying an essentially sceptical or an essentially religious attitude about a divine harmony in the universe, the temperament of the critic being the decisive factor. For the view that *Lear* is, if not involved with the "institution" of religion, at least essentially religious in having a background "constructed by constant suggestions that the actions of all the characters are to be judged in relation to an ordered system of supernatural or divine activity," see Sandra Hale, "The Background of Divine Action in *King Lear*," *Studies in English Literature 1500–1900*, 8 (1968), 217–33.

We know that the praise of Shakespeare for employing comedy to heighten tragedy goes back at least as far as Dryden and Dr. Johnson. In this instance, however, one is tempted to surmise that if there was any outside influence operating, Shelley's view was more likely derived from Coleridge, who had earlier praised *Lear* for using comedy to enrich the tragedy, particularly in Act III, scene ii, where the Fool is unforgettably employed "to heighten and inflame the passion of the scene."[17] Coleridge was later to call the Fool "one of the profoundest and most astonishing" of Shakespeare's characters (II, 245). Shelley was at least as impressed as Coleridge. We have too little of the former's *Charles the First* to say just how *King Lear* was to be its model; but in the fragment we do have, the dominant figure is the jester Archy, and Archy is patterned almost too closely in character and speech after the Fool.[18]

Perhaps the most significant and inclusive reason why Shelley was drawn more to *Lear* than to any other of Shakespeare's plays, a reason which grows more obvious and compelling on reflection, can be stated very simply: the plot of *Lear* is the most Shelleyan plot in Shakespeare. More than *Hamlet* or *Macbeth*, it is an epitome of the one great preoccupation that dominated Shelley's thought from childhood to maturity and which in the Dedication of *The Cenci* to Leigh Hunt he thus characterizes: "In that patient and irreconcilable enmity with domestic and political tyranny and imposture, which the tenor of your life has illustrated and which, had I health and talents, should illustrate mine, let us, comforting each other in our task, live and die" (*Works*, II, 67–68). Lear is, in short, an unforgettably vivid

17. *Shakespearean Criticism*, ed. Raysor, II, 73–74. See also Coleridge on "The Origins of Modern Drama," I, 189ff., esp. pp. 194–95, 197–98; II, 266. Shelley had read a good deal of Coleridge, including the *Biographia Literaria* and the *Lay Sermons*. I have not found any evidence that he knew Coleridge's various lectures on Shakespeare even at second hand, and most of them were not published during Shelley's lifetime. On the other hand, the *Bristol Gazette* reported the lectures of 1813–14; and several of these reports were republished in London in the two papers Coleridge had friendly relations with through past contributions of prose and verse: the *Morning Post* and the *Courier*. The latter reprinted on 17 Dec. 1813 the report of the first lecture on the general characteristics of Shakespeare's plays, in which Shakespeare is praised for reinforcing tragedy with comedy, the example cited being *Lear* for the Fool's "wild wit" as contributory to the development of tragic passion. See Raysor, II, 253–54, 266.

18. According to White, the Fool also resembles Calderón's Fool in *Cisma de Inglaterra* (*JEGP*, 21 [1922], 436). In a letter to Peacock of 21 Sept. 1819, Shelley also praised Calderón highly for mingling comedy with tragedy: "He exceeds all modern dramatists, with the exception of Shakespeare, whom he resembles, however, in the depth of thought and subtlety of imagination of his writing, and in the rare power of interweaving delicate and powerful comic traits with the most tragical situation. . . ."

prototype of Shelley's tyrannical father-king who must be and is finally brought to terms.

According to Shelley, in the Preface to *The Cenci*, the "highest moral purpose aimed at in the highest species of the drama, is the teaching the human heart, through its sympathies and antipathies, the knowledge of itself; in proportion to the possession of which knowledge, every human being is wise, just, sincere, tolerant, and kind." *King Lear* is a play about a proud and inflexible ruler who has "ever but slenderly known himself" and who is brought painfully to self-knowledge, to wisdom, tolerance, and kindness, through his repudiation by Goneril and Regan, his sufferings on the heath, and the redemptive love and loyalty of Cordelia. It is Cordelia who acts as Beatrice Cenci should have acted if she had been "wiser and better": "Undoubtedly no person can be truly dishonored by the act of another; and the fit return to make to the most enormous injuries is kindness and forbearance, and a resolution to convert the injurer from his dark passions by peace and love. Revenge, retaliation, atonement, are pernicious mistakes" ( Preface to *The Cenci, Works*, II, 71 ). Cordelia is like Beatrice Cenci without her tragic flaw. To injury she returns kindness and forbearance; and she helps to convert her injurer by peace and love: "No blown ambition doth our arms incite, / But love, dear love, and our ag'd father's right" ( IV.iv. 27–28 ).

Shelley remained a moralist all his life, describing his own function in the image he applied in 1820 to the Skylark:

> a Poet hidden
> In the light of thought,
> Singing hymns unbidden,
> Till the world is wrought
> To sympathy with hopes and fears it heeded not.

As he grew older, however, he had come to emphasize the "hidden" nature of the poet: i.e., he should not directly obtrude his moral purpose on the audience, as he himself had done in *Queen Mab*; he should never be "didactic." "Those in whom the poetical faculty, though great, is less intense, as Euripides, Lucan, Tasso, Spenser, have frequently affected a moral aim, and the effect of their poetry is diminished in exact proportion to the degree in which they compel us to advert to this purpose" ( *Works*, VII, 118 ). Nevertheless, it remains true, he insists in the *Defence*, that poetry properly "acts to produce the moral improvement of man."

How is this end to be accomplished? Indirectly, through the instrumentality of the sympathetic imagination, which makes possible a union of the subject and object of contemplation. As we are told in one of the most impressive and deeply felt passages of the *Defence*:

> The great secret of morals is love; or a going out of our own nature, and an identification of ourselves with the beautiful which exists in thought, action, or person not our own. A man, to be greatly good, must imagine intensely and comprehensively; *he must put himself in the place of another and of many others; the pains and pleasures of his species must become his own.* The great instrument of moral good is the imagination; and poetry administers to the effect by acting upon the cause. . . . Poetry strengthens the faculty which is the organ of the moral nature of man, in the same manner as exercise strengthens a limb.[19]

Whether or not we agree that Shelley achieved his goal in *Prometheus Unbound*, which for all its beauties remains for many readers a heavily didactic poem, there can be no doubt at all that Shakespeare achieved it in *King Lear*, and in precisely the way Shelley insists that it should be achieved. As Lear undergoes the moral purgation that gradually turns him from egocentricity and vengeance to sympathy and love, we are led to identify with the morally beautiful in him just as he has learned to put himself in the place of many others, to make their pains and pleasures his own, and to care about them. In one of the profoundest speeches in the play, Lear, having urged the Fool to seek shelter in the hovel to which Kent had directed them, remains himself outside. Finding himself unexpectedly homeless, he begins to ponder at last the fate of all the dispossessed and his own responsibility for keeping them so:

> Poor naked wretches, whereso'er you are,
> That bide the pelting of this pitiless storm,
> How shall your houseless heads and unfed sides,
> Your looped and windowed raggedness, defend you
> From seasons such as these? O, I have ta'en

19. *Works*, VII, 118, italics mine. Shelley's ideas about the power of love owe much to Plato. Cf. his translation of the *Symposium*: ". . . Love is the divinity who creates peace among man, and calm upon the sea. . . . Love divests us of all alienation from each other, and fills our vacant hearts with overflowing sympathy . . . Love . . . showers benignity upon the world. . ." (*Works*, VII, 191–92). The idea of a sympathetic communion or identification with others made possible by the imagination is, of course, a commonplace in the Romantic Movement and may be seen in one form or another in Blake, Coleridge, Hazlitt, and Keats.

Too little care of this! Take physic, pomp;
Expose thyself to feel what wretches feel,
That thou mayst shake the superflux to them
And show the heavens more just.

( III.iv. 28–36. )

This great speech offers an epitome of the way in which true poetry acts to effect the moral improvement of man, not didactically but through the sympathetic imagination, according to the passage of the *Defence* just quoted. The resemblance to Shelley's thought is so close that it is not merely quite possible but even probable that Shelley had Lear's words somewhere in mind as he wrote.

This seems all the more probable considering that as we have seen, Shelley was reading *King Lear* again very shortly before or even during the writing of the *Defence*; and also that the blinded Gloucester later delivers another version of this same speech as he prepares to ask Edgar disguised as Tom o' Bedlam to lead him to the cliff from which he plans to jump:

Here, take this purse, thou whom the heav'ns plagues
Have humbled to all strokes: that I am wretched
Makes thee the happier: Heavens, deal so still!
Let the superfluous and lust-dieted man,
That slaves your ordinance, that will not see
Because he does not feel, feel your power quickly;
So distribution should undo excess,
And each man have enough.[20]

( IV.i. 64–71. )

No wonder, incidentally, that as David Lee Clark says in another connection, "Shelley found in Shakespeare what he thought was a confirmation of his own radicalism" (p. 287).

It cannot be disputed, in any event, that Shelley's "idea" of poetry, to use the word "idea" in the Coleridgean sense, is demonstrably inferrable from the redemption of King Lear; whereas it would be difficult or rather impossible to show just this empathetic process at work in what happens to Oedipus, Hamlet, Othello, or Macbeth. And by the ordinary laws of logic, this resemblance alone is therefore sufficient to create a probable explana-

---

20. Cf. the words of the Fury in *Prometheus Unbound*, I., 630ff.: "Many are strong and rich, and would be just, / But live among their suffering fellow-men / As if none felt; they know not what they do."

tion of why Shelley thought *King Lear*, rather than some other work of Shakespeare or the Greeks, "the most perfect specimen of the dramatic art existing in the world." [21]

Shelley, like so many of the world's moralists and prophets before him, had come to believe that an effective social reform was impossible without the spiritual regeneration of the individual members of society—the "great secret of morals" was "love." The greatest poetry was therefore poetry about the achievement and growth of love:

> Love, which found a worthy poet in Plato alone of all the antients, has been celebrated by a chorus of the greatest writers of the reno-vated world; and the music has penetrated the caverns of society, and its echoes still drown the dissonance of arms and superstition. At successive intervals, Ariosto, Tasso, Shakespeare, Spenser, Calderon, Rousseau, and the great writers of our own age, have celebrated the dominion of love, planting as it were trophies in the human mind of that sublimest victory over sensuality and force. (*Defence, Works*, VII, 128)

So it was that in his own most ambitious poem, *Prometheus Unbound*, Shelley had attempted a celebration of "the dominion of love" by making the third and the later added fourth act of that play what he had found in the Paradiso, for him the greatest book of Dante's *Comedy*, "a perpetual hymn of everlasting love" (*Works*, VII, 128). The regeneration and transformation of the world begins with the reunion of Prometheus and Asia, man and love, a reunion made possible by man's renunciation of hatred and vengeance.

> Henceforth we will not part. There is a cave,
> All overgrown with trailing odorous plants,
> Which curtain out the day with leaves and flowers
>
> .  .  .  .  .  .  .  .  .  .  .  .  .  .  .
>
> A simple dwelling, which shall be our own;

21. On this question (as indeed in most kinds of literary criticism), a probable conclusion is the most one can expect to arrive at since Shelley does not explain in so many words just what he meant. But a probable conclusion is surely better than no conclusion at all; and in this instance it is based not on any form of unwarranted mind-reading but on the external evidence of the dates of Shelley's reading of *Lear* and of the writing of the *Defense of Poetry*, and on the internal evidence of the close resemblance between key passages in the *Defence* and in *Lear* itself. If the conclusion here drawn is to be rejected as improbable, it must be on the basis of a demonstrable flaw in the present writer's logic or on comparably solid evidence that when Shelley praised *Lear* so singularly, he had something else in mind.

Where we will sit and talk of time and change,
As the world ebbs and flows, ourselves unchanged.
What can hide man from mutability?
And if ye sigh, then I will smile; and thou,
Ione, shalt chaunt fragments of sea-music,
Until I weep, when ye shall smile away
The tears she brought, which yet were sweet to shed.
We will entangle buds and flowers and beams
Which twinkle on the fountain's brim, and make
Strange combinations out of common things,
Like human babes in their brief innocence;
And we will search, with looks and words of love,
For hidden thoughts, each lovelier than the last,
Our unexhausted spirits; and like lutes
Touched by the skill of the enamoured wind,
Weave harmonies divine, yet ever new,
From difference sweet where discord cannot be;
And hither come, sped on the charmed winds,
Which meet from all the points of heaven, as bees
From every point aërial Enna feeds,
At their known island-homes in Himera,
The echoes of the human world, which tell
Of the low voice of love, almost unheard,
And dove-eyed pity's murmured pain, and music,
Itself the echo of the heart, and all
That tempers or improves man's life, now free.

(III.iii. 10–48, Works, II, 231–32)

Thus, at this triumphal moment of his greatest work, Shelley acknowledges his profound debt to *King Lear* by drawing heavily on one of the most moving speeches in all Shakespeare, Lear's reunion with Cordelia—Lear transfigured now by love:

> Come, let's away to prison;
> We two alone will sing like birds i' the cage:
> When thou dost ask me blessing, I'll kneel down,
> And ask of thee forgiveness: so we'll live,
> And pray, and sing, and tell old tales, and laugh
> At gilded butterflies, and hear poor rogues
> Talk of court news; and we'll talk with them too,

Who loses and who wins; who's in, who's out;
And take upon's the mystery of things,
As if we were God's spies: and we'll wear out,
In a wall'd prison, packs and sects of great ones
That ebb and flow by the moon.

(V.iii. 8–19)

Prometheus is a good deal wordier than Lear, but the resemblance in situation, thought, phrase, and cadence is as unmistakable as it is significant.

There is at least one other aspect of *King Lear* that might well have intensified Shelley's appreciation. I have already suggested that *Lear* would have strongly appealed to Shelley as demonstrating that a play can further a moral aim—and in this case a moral aim much like his own—without being in any way didactic. It is also true that in *King Lear* Shakespeare solved another problem that Shelley had not yet solved: the union of the abstract with the concrete, the ideal with the real. We know from Mrs. Shelley's note on *The Cenci* of Shelley's fear "that he was too metaphysical and abstract—too fond of the theoretical and the ideal, to succeed as a tragedian." She "shared this opinion with himself" (*Works*, II, 156); and she urged him to write *The Cenci*—he had first urged her to do it—in order to come down to earth, as it were, and make a more effective appeal to the ordinary man. If in *Prometheus Unbound* his characters tend to be ethereally abstract, in *The Cenci* they verge instead on melodrama, as Shelley apparently realized when he came to speak almost with contempt of the latter play as "written for the multitude," "dismal enough," and one "I don't think very much of" (*Letters, Works*, X, 148, 166). By contrast *King Lear* succeeds to a far greater degree than Shelley in combining both the abstract and the concrete. On the one hand, its characters are larger than life, verging indeed on myth, which may be what Coleridge meant in saying that *Lear* was not exactly in his line for an entire lecture; on the other, they are all to a considerable degree distinct individuals, it being possible to distinguish between Goneril and Regan and Cordelia, for instance, as few readers can do between Ione and Panthea and Asia. Lear himself is neither as crudely villainous as Count Cenci nor as sainted as the martyr Prometheus—he becomes indeed an intensely affecting human being.

That Shelley thought of this latter achievement of Shakespeare in connection with *King Lear*, we have no way of knowing except by an inference which cannot at least be termed unreasonable or unlikely. For the purpose of the present discussion, however, it does not really matter whether he did so or not; for it has already been shown that although Shelley himself never explained what he meant in judging *Lear* "the most perfect specimen of the dramatic art existing in the world," he had in fact many and excellent reasons for doing so. The double reward of reading criticism by a good poet is that usually it not only illuminates the work of the writers he is discussing but throws an even more revealing light on his own. One can hardly find a better key to the intentions and practice of T. S. Eliot, for instance, than his remarks on the Metaphysical Poets. In like manner, the more one thinks about Shelley's praise of *King Lear* in *The Defence of Poetry*, as well as about the play itself, the more vividly one realizes what the mature Shelley was trying to achieve in his poetry and might have achieved to an even greater degree had time permitted.

# *Keats's* LAMIA *as Dramatic Illusion*

## Richard Harter Fogle

*University of North Carolina, Chapel Hill*

KEATS'S BRILLIANT AND COMPLEX *Lamia* has evoked a large number of close and thoughtful analyses, and numerous interpretations. Many an essay has commenced like this, and I hasten to say that I do not formally claim that the definitive word on *Lamia* is about to be uttered—whatever unregenerate ambitions I may secretly entertain. The work in question, at any rate, is even more resistant than most substantial poems to subjugation by the critic.

Robert Penn Warren spoke wisely on the general problem, more than twenty-five years ago in his "Pure and Impure Poetry":

> the poem is like the monstrous Orillo in Boiardo's *Orlando Furioso*. When the sword lops off any member of the monster, that member is immediately rejoined to the body, and the monster is as formidable as ever. But the poem is even more formidable than the monster, for Orillo's adversary finally gained a victory by an astonishing feat of dexterity: he slashed off both the monster's arms and quick as a wink seized them and flung them into the river. The critic who vain-gloriously trusts his method to account for the poem, to exhaust the poem, is trying to emulate this dexterity: he thinks that he, too, can win by throwing the lopped-off arms into the river. But he is doomed to failure. Neither fire nor water will suffice to prevent the rejoining of the mutilated members to the monstrous torso. . . . So the monster will always win, and the critic knows this. He does not want to win. He knows that he must always play stooge to the monster. All he wants to do is to give the monster a chance to exhibit again its miraculous power.

As Warren says, no single method will defeat a poem. Yet it is hard to overcome the lust to "account" for it, to "exhaust" it, and perhaps especially hard for an academic critic. We know more than others about the poems we discuss, and what others have written about them. It is therefore natural for us to think that the final triumph lies within our grasp. This, however, cannot be, and *Lamia* is an exceptionally formidable monster besides. It will be quite enough, as Warren says, "to give the monster a chance to exhibit again its miraculous power."

For many years the key to *Lamia* appeared to be a passage at the end, which comments specifically upon the destruction of the beautiful apparition Lamia by the merciless gaze of "the sage, old Apollonius":

> Do not all charms fly
> At the mere touch of cold philosophy?
> There was an awful rainbow once in heaven:
> We know her woof, her texture; she is given
> In the dull catalogue of common things.
> Philosophy will clip an Angel's wings,
> Conquer all mysteries by rule and line,
> Empty the haunted air, and gnomed mine—
> Unweave a rainbow, as it erewhile made
> The tender-person'd Lamia melt into a shade.
>
> (II. 229–38)

But in 1935 C. D. Thorpe decisively disposed of simplistic readings of the poem: "An error that most critics of *Lamia* have made is to assume that Keats meant either Lamia or Apollonius to be in the right. The facts rather seem to be that Keats was here dealing with two falsities." [1]

All subsequent readings of the poem have had to reckon with this statement. Naturally and properly enough, most readers have tried to sum up their conclusions in a single conceptual proposition. This is the way the mind works, and the basic process of interpretation: we try to assimilate our material, then organize it in one point. The difficulty is, however, the problem of distinguishing between a poem and a logical discourse in prose. We have all been told about this problem many times, frequently in a manner that irritates us, since we still have the basic human instinct to find out "what it means." One does not necessarily take kindly to Archibald MacLeish's famous dictum that a poem must not mean but be. It is a little too much like Gertrude Stein's great truism that a rose is a rose is a rose. Somehow it tends to cut off discussion.

In the case of *Lamia*, the poem, like *Endymion*, appears to lend itself to allegorical interpretation. Lamia herself, for instance, can be taken to

1. John Keats, *Complete Poems and Selected Letters* (Garden City, N.Y., 1935), p. xliii. I do not attempt to acknowledge individually the considerable number of noteworthy essays on *Lamia* that have appeared in journals and books between 1935 and the present.

represent the poetic imagination, in accordance with the "awful rainbow" passage earlier quoted. She has the power of self-projection, or of freeing the individual from selfish limitations, that the romantic poets so highly prized:

> But first 'tis fit to tell how she could muse
> And dream, when in the serpent prison-house,
> Of all she list, strange or magnificent:
> How, ever, where she will'd, her spirit went.
>
> ( I. 202–5 )

There are complications, however, since Lamia *is* a lamia, a serpent, and hardly a fit representative of the divine faculty of imaginative creation. The poem is immensely fertile in ideas and associations, but it is unsafe to pursue any one of them to its logical extremity. If one presses for consistency and reality, the path trails out rapidly.

What, for example, is Lamia's precise state of being? What is her origin? Appearing at the outset as a remarkably lovely serpent, she tells the god Hermes,

> "I was a woman, let me have once more
> A woman's shape, and charming as before."
>
> ( I. 117–18 )

Yet when her wish is granted, she is clearly not a human female. Does she come from Ovid's story of Tiresias and the snakes in the *Metamorphoses,* which so engaged T. S. Eliot in his notes to *The Waste Land?* Through the snake-theme she has her resemblances to Coleridge's Geraldine in *Christabel,* and this reflection opens up an almost boundless vista of possibilities. Is Lamia supernatural, or in Coleridge's terms merely praeternatural? One thinks of all the haunting fairy ladies, including Keats's own Belle Dame, who are both above human nature and somehow below it. ( If one goes on thinking, the *lais* of Marie de France will come to mind, and eventually Chinese fox-spirits, not to mention Montague Summers at all.)

Again, in her serpenthood Lamia raises the question of evil, and yet the poem does not make her evil except to Apollonius, who says to Lycius, " 'And shall I see thee made a serpent's prey?' " At the crisis of the poem it is Lycius who is "fierce and sanguineous":

> Against his better self, he took delight
> Luxurious in her sorrows, soft and new.
> His passion, cruel grown, took on a hue

> Fierce and sanguineous as 'twas possible
> In one whose brow had no dark veins to swell.
> Fine was the mitigated fury, like
> Apollo's presence when in act to strike
> The serpent—Ha, the serpent! certes, she
> Was none.
>
> (II. 73–81)

Our text is Lamia, but it might be noted of Lycius that his badness is not very bad, at worst a "mitigated fury" that is even "fine." Further, the Apollo-simile is interesting, when one thinks of the Lycian Apollo—Lycius—and in turn of Apollonius. Yet in Keats's source, Burton, the name is Menippus Lycius, and in Burton's source as well. More complications!

Another effect of the snake-motif is to suggest the ramifications of sexual love, with its mingled attractions and repulsions. Lamia on the one hand is a vision of ideal beauty; yet there is still that serpent in her dubious lineage. Perhaps the opposite of uncritical adoration is revulsion and horrible jealousy. Some have suggested that Keats idealized too quickly and was likewise all too quickly disillusioned, and have turned to his agonized letters and verses to Fanny Brawne to illuminate poems like *Lamia* and "La Belle Dame Sans Merci." If we look at Lamia herself, however, we find little to verify this dark possibility. Her own approach to love is straightforward and wholesome, perhaps healthily selfish at the outset. As a serpent, she laments, and is overheard by Hermes, who has his own simple wants:

> There, as he stood, he heard a mournful voice,
> Such as once heard, in gentle heart, destroys
> All pain but pity: thus the lone voice spake:
> "When from this wreathed tomb shall I awake!
> When move in a sweet body fit for life,
> And love, and pleasure, and the ruddy strife
> Of hearts and lips! Ah, miserable me!"
>
> (I. 35–41)

Here is a girl (or snake) who is unabashedly in love with love. A bit later she is equally direct:

> "I love a youth of Corinth—O the bliss!
> Give me my woman's form, and place me where he is."
>
> (I. 119–20)

As in *Isabella, The Eve of St. Agnes,* and the "Ode to Psyche," there is the unreserved assumption that love is enough. We are placed firmly and instantly on the side of the lovers. There is little need to ask what Lamia sees in Lycius, but one may speculate that he seems complete in himself. Lacking and apparently desiring nothing, he is desirable:

> And once, while among mortals dreaming thus,
> She saw the young Corinthian Lycius
> Charioting foremost in the envious race,
> Like a young Jove with calm uneager face,
> And fell into a swooning love of him.
>
> (I. 215–19)

The poem raises no doubts about the quality of Lamia's love for Lycius. When trouble comes she is wise, self-sacrificing, and compassionate. Facing death, her only concern is to save her lover from disillusionment:

> Then Lamia breath'd death breath; the sophist's eye,
> Like a sharp spear, went through her utterly,
> Keen, cruel, perceant, stinging; she, as well
> As her weak hand could any meaning tell,
> Motion'd him to be silent; vainly so,
> He look'd and look'd again a level—No!
> "A serpent!" echoed he; no sooner said,
> Than with a frightful scream she vanished.
>
> (II. 299–306)

One final complication yet remains. Is Lamia's "vanishing" equivalent to death? The quoted passage refers to death, but considering her mysterious origins and her proven aptitude for transformations, may she not reappear in Crete, where she started, at this same moment, back in her serpent's form once more? This is doubtless a question that should not be asked, just as one should not consider too curiously what happened to Madeline and Porphyro when they "fled away into the storm" at the end of *The Eve of St. Agnes.* But I have been raising a series of questions that should not be asked about *Lamia,* for the purpose of showing that most solutions to the poem's problems would have to take this sort of querying into account to deal faithfully with it. In for a penny, in for a pound; or, as Warren says of the critic and the poem, "There is only one way to conquer the monster: you must eat it, bones, blood, skin, pelt, and gristle."

In relation to the reality that a fixed conceptual interpretation presupposes, both *Lamia* and Lamia are illusions. What both require is sufficient belief in them to make them acceptable for what they are. At the end of Part I, as Lamia and Lycius enter their enchanted palace, the poet tells us:

> none knew where
> They could inhabit; the most curious
> Were foil'd, who watch'd to trace them to their house:
> And but the flitter-winged verse must tell,
> For truth's sake, what woe afterwards befel,
> 'Twould humour many a heart to leave them thus,
> Shut from the busy world of more incredulous.
>
> (I. 391–97)

It is his business, however, to "Shut from the busy world of more incredulous," and the passage too is an illusion, with the truth that it invokes. Briefly, I am arguing that the "ruin" (II. 16) of Lamia and Lycius belongs to the structure and framework of the poem, and that it functions to enhance the ideal and supernatural experience that the poem centrally emphasizes. Just as (in my opinion) the theme of "transience" in the Great Odes is an element of contrast that brings out the fullness of their imaginative utterance, and not an expression of disillusion, Lamia is in poetry triumphant.

The argument is poised as it were on a knife-edge. Ultimately it would have to depend upon a theory of the "ontology" itself of the poem, and the degree of autonomy one allows it. To illustrate my notion of it, I adduce Coleridge's theory of dramatic illusion, which is basically the same as the famous "willing suspension of disbelief" and the "poetic faith" of *Biographia Literaria*, chapter XIV. It is a comprehensive theory of imaginative literature, pervasive in Coleridge's thought. The total effect of a work is a collaboration between the poet and his reader. What is most important here is the skill of the poet in stimulating his reader to bring fully into life what he (the poet) has partially provided, or has been able to suggest. Here one may think of Keats's comment about *Lamia*: "I am certain there is that sort of fire in it which must take hold of people in some way—give them either pleasant or unpleasant sensation. What they want is a sensation of some sort." He has readers in mind, and a conception of the effect he has intended.

For Coleridge an imaginative work is an illusion in relation to any truth obtainable through the discursive reason, or understanding. Literature *can* convey the truths of the transcendental reason by the mediation in symbol of the imagination, but these truths are in themselves immediate and unsusceptible of analysis. Insofar as a poem or play or prose-fiction is an imitation of literal reality it is obviously an illusion, although its power depends upon its seeming real to us. It has its own laws and conventions, different from actual laws, which the poet by his artistry causes us to accept. Thus Coleridge speaks of "the logic of passion," of a probability and naturalness, a truth of art which come from harmony, unity, continuity. These enable a reader or an audience to rise above their ordinary prepossessions and limitations, and to sympathize with the poetry or the dramatic action presented to them.

Coleridge's "dramatic illusion" is analogous to sleep and dream, but with a difference: "In sleep we pass at once by a sudden collapse into this suspension of will and the comparative power; whereas in an interesting play, read or represented, we are brought up to this point, as far as it is requisite or desirable, gradually, by the art of the poet and the actors; and with the consent and positive aidance of our own will. We *choose* to be deceived."[2] Keats in his last letter makes a profoundly significant statement, characteristically brief, very sad, most revelatory: "There is one thought enough to kill me; I have been well, healthy, alert, etc., walking with her [Fanny Brawne], and now—the knowledge of contrast, feeling for light and shade, all that information (primitive sense) necessary for a poem, are great enemies to the recovery of the stomach." The making of an illusion is no light thing.

In Coleridge's sense, then, both Lamia and *Lamia* are illusions. The poem lures us on to extract from it propositions and generalizations about life which exist in it merely as suggestions, and to give its characters the illusion of life. On his own evidence Keats meant to write the richest, the most intense, the most complex poem he could encompass. "I have," he says, "great hopes of success." He wished to furnish a sensation, to provide a fire, and to achieve the greatest possible complexity. *Lamia* is an apt illustration of his famous words to Shelley. "There is only one part of it [*The Cenci*] I am judge of—the poetry and dramatic effect, which by many spirits now-a-days is considered the Mammon. . . . An artist must serve

2. *Coleridge's Shakespearean Criticism*, ed. T. M. Raysor (Cambridge, Mass., 1930), I, 129. Cf. my *Idea of Coleridge's Criticism* (Berkeley and Los Angeles, Calif., 1962), pp. 115–24.

Mammon; he must have 'self-concentration'—selfishness, perhaps." He goes
on to advise Shelley, of course, to "be more of an artist, and load every rift
of your subject with ore."

*Lamia*, indeed, is so heavily loaded with ore that, as I have been main-
taining, no single interpretation of it can be sustained. What emerges as its
dominant meaning will inevitably be colored by its critics' own dominant
interests and presuppositions. My sense of the poem rests upon its ontology, or its status as illusion, along with reflections about the total
meanings of the Great Odes, especially of the "Ode to a Nightingale":
their use of "framing," of contrast, of harmony. That is, artistically Lamia
as ideal, or as the heart's desire, is inseparable from her transiency, and
inseparable from the manner of her presentation.

From this point of view Lamia is the poem, the illusion, who needs belief
in her to exist—the qualified, forebearing belief of the instructed reader,
motivated by the skill of the poet. Years ago it was suggested that Apollonius represented Keats's reviewers; perhaps it could be more broadly
put that he is the insensitive reader, impervious to artistry. When he has
identified Lamia as a serpent he is satisfied. He is, to put it mildly, unre-
ceptive to dramatic illusion:

> So in they hurried all, maz'd, curious, and keen:
> Save one, who look'd thereon with eye severe,
> And with calm-planted steps walked in austere;
> 'Twas Apollonius: something too he laugh'd,
> As though some knotty problem, that had daft
> His patient thought, had now begun to thaw,
> And solve and melt:—'twas just as he foresaw.
>
> (II. 156–62)

Nathaniel Hawthorne, who as his Prefaces attest was greatly concerned
with artistic illusion and credibility, has a passage in his "Main Street"
that strongly suggests the case of Lamia and Apollonius. A "showman"
presenting an historical panorama is bedevilled by a matter-of-fact spectator. He defends his illusion: " 'But, sir, you have not the proper point of
view. . . .You sit altogether too near to get the best effect of my pictorial
exhibition. Pray, oblige me by removing to this other bench, and I venture
to assure you the proper light and shadow will transform the spectacle into
quite another thing.' " But the critic replies, " 'I want no other light and
shade. I have already told you that it is my business to see things just as

they are.'" A little later the showman again protests, "'you break the illusion of the scene.'" So it is with Lamia, whose life and beauty gradually vanish under Apollonius' eye:

> Now no azure vein
> Wander'd on fair-spaced temples; no soft bloom
> Misted the cheek; no passion to illume
> The deep-recessed vision:—all was blight;
> Lamia, no longer fair, there sat a deadly white.
>
> (II. 272–76)

Poor Lycius, the devotee, is not strong enough to withstand the dreadful power of skepticism, but the loss of the illusion kills him. We may believe that a more skillful interpreter would have survived the test.

Confessedly this interpretation is a tour de force, which is not a serious battle with the monster and is very far from eating it, "bones, blood, skin, pelt, and gristle." (Warren does not mention the problem of regurgitating it in critical discourse.) Many things contribute to the grand illusion of *Lamia*. There are all kinds of chimings and niceties of structure in the poem. The opening passage, for instance, derives both from Chaucer's *Wife of Bath's Tale* and Dryden's redaction of it, but remains thoroughly Keatsian too. The metamorphosis of Lamia from serpent to woman strongly suggests the deification of Apollo in the earlier *Hyperion*, with its "dying into life," or less vividly the translation to Olympus of *Endymion*, or the apotheosis of Porphyro in Madeline's chamber in the castle:

> Beyond a mortal man impassion'd far
> At these voluptuous accents, he arose,
> Ethereal, flush'd, and like a throbbing star
> Seen mid the sapphire heaven's deep repose. . . .

The question would be here, what are the differences as well as the likeness? W. J. Bate suggests that the *Lamia* passage is a parody of *Hyperion*, and clearly it has comic elements. The issue is complex enough, however, to warrant caution in accepting the implications of "parody," since it would affect one's sense of the poem as a whole.

Something of the unity of *Lamia's* illusion depends upon a constant play on dissolving and melting away, commencing with the serpent Lamia's "silver moons, that, as she breathed, / Dissolv'd, or brighter shone" (I. 51–52). In her transformation she

Melted and disappear'd as suddenly;
And, in the air, her new voice luting soft,
Cried, "Lycius! gentle Lycius!" —Borne aloft
With the bright mists about the mountains hoar
These words dissolv'd: Crete's forests heard no more.

(I. 166–70)

One thinks of the "Ode to a Nightingale"—"Fade far away, dissolve, and quite forget."

Lycius, when Lamia finds him, is himself focussed upon intangibility: "His phantasy was lost, where reason fades, / In the calm'd twilight of Platonic shades." He seems "shut up in mysteries." Captured by Lamia's beauty, and significantly looking "Orpheus-like at an Eurydice," he is "afraid / Lest we should vanish." " 'For pity do not this sad heart belie,' " he pleads, " 'Even as thou vanishest so shall I die' "; and yet again, finally,

If thou shouldst fade
Thy memory will waste me to a shade:—
For pity do not melt!"

(I. 269–71)

Upon the first ominous appearance a little later of the sage Apollonius, Lycius anxiously asks Lamia, " 'Why does your tender palm dissolve in dew?' " All this unquestionably contributes to the effect of the famous unweaving of the rainbow by philosophy, "as it erewhile made / The tender-person'd Lamia melt into a shade."

These dissolutions appear in various contexts throughout the poem, and have much to do with our total impression of it. Its illusion is based on a unity that is composed of many levels—planes, they might be called, of atmosphere or even of being. Space is wanting here for a full analysis, which with *Lamia* would be extraordinarily difficult. The way to it might be opened through the slightly simpler world of *The Eve of St. Agnes* and its contrasts and harmonies: the careful entrance into the illusion of the castle from the outside cold and the austerities of the beadsman; the distancing by means of "the argent revelry . . . Numerous as shadows"; the still greater isolation of Madeline among "Agnes' dreams, the sweetest of the year"; the intrusion of Porphyro into them, his discordance and final harmonizing with them; the setting of "St. Agnes' moon"; the lovers' emergence "into the storm," which is yet complexly "an elfin-storm from faery land"; and the abrupt and difficult balances of the conclusion, which evokes not only the lovers but the jarring associations of malice, triviality, and sad old age.

In *Lamia* there are even more various distances and perspectives, heralded by the beginning with its doubly imaginary past of Greek myth and the fairyland of Oberon and Titania, and followed by the problem of reconciling the supernatural Hermes with the preternatural and fabulous Lamia. Correspondingly one must consider the immortal loves of Hermes and the nymph, in which "Real are the dreams of Gods," and the different relationship of Lamia with the mortal Lycius. There is, too, the modulation between their atmosphere and the atmosphere of ancient Corinth, already distanced in the imagination, dreamlike, and yet a chosen norm for everyday reality.

> As men talk in a dream, so Corinth all,
> Throughout her palaces imperial,
> And all her populous streets and temples lewd,
> Mutter'd, like tempest in the distance brew'd,
> To the wide-spreaded night above her towers.
>
> (I. 350–54)

This evocation of Corinth points in opposite directions: toward the larger dream of the poem and toward the "dreadful guests," "the gossip rant," the "common eyes" who come to destroy it. And Apollonius as destroyer is on still another plane from these trivial visitants from the outside world. Such are the facets of this many-sided poem, elements of harmony and illusion, the light and shade, the contrast, the "information necessary for a poem."

# "Tennyson, we cannot live in art"

## A. Dwight Culler

*Yale University*

"TENNYSON, WE CANNOT LIVE IN ART." Such is the remark which Richard
Chenevix Trench is said to have made to Tennyson when they were young
men at Cambridge together and which, according to Tennyson, prompted
the writing of "The Palace of Art." There is apparently no doubt about the
fact. It is asserted in the notes to the Eversley edition, for which Tennyson
was responsible, and in the *Memoir*[1] on the basis of a note which Tennyson
made in 1890. The original of this note is apparently to be found in a brown
notebook now in the Tennyson Research Centre at Lincoln: "The Palace of
Art. 'Tennyson we cannot live in art' Trench (afterwards Archbishop) said
to me when we were at Trinity Cambridge together. This Poem is the embodiment of my own belief that the godlike life is with & for man." No one,
however, seems to have asked the question when and under what circumstances the remark was made, and hence what it meant to the original
speaker and hearer. The usual assumption is that the future Archbishop of
Dublin was rebuking Tennyson for the apparent aestheticism of poems in
the 1830 volume and that Tennyson, accepting the rebuke, sharply altered
his course in "The Palace of Art." It should be noted, however, that this
interpretation is based partly on a presumed sequence which we construct
of "The Lady of Shalott," "Oenone," and "The Palace of Art," all of which
actually appeared together in the *Poems* of December 1832 (dated 1833)
and partly on a presumed relation between the future Archbishop and the
future Laureate. Aubrey de Vere, building on these assumptions, tells the
following "legend. . . , whether authentic or not," which he remembered
hearing: "Alfred Tennyson and Richard Chenevix Trench had been friends
at Cambridge, and had a common love of poetry. Soon after his ordination
the future Archbishop paid a visit to the future Laureate. He spoke about
the new heresy which substituted Art for Faith and Beauty for Sanctity.
His brother-poet, it is said, contested nothing, but simply listened, occasionally replenishing his pipe. When Trench had taken his departure the
auditor took up his pen, and the single thought became a poem" (*Memoir*,

1. Hallam Tennyson, *Alfred Lord Tennyson: A Memoir* (London, 1897), I, 118–19.

I, 505–6). Apart from the fact that this anecdote has all the marks upon it of an incident that did not occur, one may note that Trench and Tennyson were not acquainted while the former was an undergraduate and that Trench was ordained on 5 July 1835, two and a half years after "The Palace of Art" was published.[2] When we look into the matter it appears that Trench made the remark to Tennyson in late May or June 1830, under very unusual circumstances, and that it referred as much to Trench as to Tennyson.

For the facts are that the future Archbishop of Dublin was himself in his undergraduate days quite an aesthete. The second son of a member of the Anglo-Irish aristocracy and of a distinguished literary mother, Melesina Trench, Richard profited very little from the regular studies of his undergraduate days and was almost exclusively concerned with poetry and particularly the study of Spanish literature. He had written a tragedy, *Bernardo del Carpio*, which was handed round in manuscript and received some praise from Macready but was never acted or published. But his chief interest was in translating the dramas of Calderón into verse. Calderón had been rediscovered by A. W. Schlegel in his *Lectures on Dramatic Art and Literature* (tr. 1815), had been brought to the fore in England by Shelley's translation of the *Magico Prodigioso*, and was now one of the heroes of that remarkable group of undergraduates to which Trench belonged, the Cambridge Apostles. There can be no question but that the appearance of Calderón among the artists and poets enshrined in the first version of "The Palace of Art" was due to his high standing with this group. Not only Trench but also John Kemble and Edward FitzGerald were translating him, and to provide an outlet for their efforts Trench founded and edited a small family periodical entitled the *Translator*. He also contributed articles on Spanish literature to the *Athenaeum*,[3] which John Sterling and Frederick Denison Maurice, the two leading spirits of the Apostles, had purchased as an organ of Apostolic opinion. It was among this "gallant band of Platonico-Wordsworthian-Coleridgean-anti-Utilitarians,"[4] with their wide-ranging literary, philosophical, and social interests, that

2. This was to the priesthood. He was ordained deacon on 7 October 1832, still too late to have been the occasion of the poem. (R. C. Trench, *Letters and Memorials* [London, 1888], I, 123, 200; J. Bromley, *The Man of Ten Talents* [London, 1959], pp. 47, 58.)

3. *Athenaeum*, 30 July 1828, p. 632; 20 Aug. 1828, p. 681; 29 Oct. 1828, pp. 840–43.

4. Trench, *Letters and Memorials*, I, 10. All quotations from letters to or from Trench are from this source unless otherwise indicated. Page references may be inferred from the date of the letter or, if no date is assigned, will be given in parentheses at the end of the quotation.

Trench found his life—with Sterling, Maurice, Kemble, J. W. Blakesley, W. D. Donne, and Arthur Hallam. "I should look back upon my Cambridge career," he wrote near the end of his days at the University, "with un-mingled regret for wasted time, etc., were it not for the friendships I have formed, and opinions I have imbibed (but for these I owe the University nothing). . ." (I, 14). Being a poor mathematician, he took an undistin-guished degree and left the University about 1 February 1829—without, it should be noted, having met Alfred Tennyson. Tennyson had come into residence at Trinity in November 1827,[5] and therefore he and Trench over-lapped by a year and three months, but in February 1829 they were not yet acquainted. Tennyson did not meet Hallam until April of that year, and he did not become a member of the Apostles until May.

After taking his degree Trench went immediately to his father's house in Southampton and then left on a hunting and fishing trip to Scotland. Not having settled on a vocation and being under no necessity of earning a living, he thought to indulge his interest in Spanish literature and history and also in the present condition of Spain by a trip to that country. By May he was writing his father from Burgos, reporting initially on the rough travelling conditions, but then more and more on the dangerous and unsettled political situation. His attention had already been drawn to this by the plight of the Spanish constitutional exiles in London, whose cause was being championed by Sterling in the *Athenaeum*. These pa-thetic people, some two hundred families in all, had fled Spain in 1823, when the French army had entered their country and reimposed the ab-solute authority of Ferdinand VII. Carlyle gave a vivid picture of them in the *Life of Sterling*: "Daily in the cold spring air, under skies so unlike their own, you could see a group of fifty or a hundred stately tragic figures, in proud threadbare cloaks; perambulating, mostly with closed lips, the broad pavements of Euston Square and the regions about St. Pancras new Church . . . [with] dusky look of suppressed fire, in general their tragic condition as of caged Numidian lions." These people, as the *Athenaeum* reminded its readers in November 1828, "are now, in the most literal acceptation of the word, STARVING." It urged that literary men con-tribute to a volume of miscellaneous writings to be sold to defray their expenses, and it was probably for this purpose that Trench wrote, in 1829, his two sonnets "To the Constitutional Exiles of 1823." As he arrived in Spain he initially thought the King was attempting to hold a balance be-

5. Edgar F. Shannon, Jr., "Alfred Tennyson's Admission to Cambridge," *TLS*, 6 March 1959, p. 136.

tween the constitutionalists and the clerical reactionaries who would bring
in the Inquisition again. But as the summer wore on he became more and
more depressed. "The great and perplexing problem which presents itself
to me at every moment and in every shape is, how does the present concern
hang together? how the State coach runs, except that it has got with age
into such deep ruts that it cannot overturn if it would?" (I, 31). By the
end of August he declares, "I do not think there is any chance of a political
redemption for Spain," and although he immediately repudiates this letter
as having been written in "a fit of disgust," by mid-October he is again
declaring, "I do not think Spain has any chance of escaping a bloody and
terrible revolution."

Horrible as the political conditions were, it is apparent that part of
Trench's difficulty was personal. The heat, the bad food, the desolateness
of the landscape, and probably a touch of fever debilitated him, and for
a time he was driven to the seashore to recover. Beyond that, he was
"sometimes very homesick," and in his lack of companions he brooded
too much on what he ought to do, or could do, to help. The purpose of his
tour, as his father reminded him, was primarily literary, and he had been
collecting books, unearthing little-known Spanish authors, and continuing
his translations. But who can do this amidst a suffering people and be sure
of its value? The very nation which had produced the literature he loved
was suffering under a despotism he hated. Worn and exhausted, he tried
to summon up energy to go home, but just then came a letter from his
father and brother that they were on their way south and hoped to meet
him in Avignon. Avignon he could or would not make, but on a second
plea from his brother he finally bestirred himself and joined them in Italy.
There, sometime in the winter or early spring he suffered his version of
the Victorian spiritual crisis.

To understand it we must go back a little and explore some of the other
matters that had been occupying Trench's mind. Though as an undergraduate his interests had been primarily literary, he was not unaware of
the dangers of relativism and solipsism in a purely philosophical culture.
Sterling, for instance, had come back from a trip to France alarmed at the
miserable condition of religion and the arts in that country. "The most
melancholy circumstance of all," he wrote to Trench on 21 November
1828, "is that the best school of French thinkers . . . are not at all inclined
to do more than treat Christianity as a highly respectable form of the
'religious idea,' without having in general a notion that it should be made
a matter of personal concern to every man. The continental philosophy of

the eighteenth century undervalued Christianity because it looked at all religions with equal contempt. The continental philosophy of the nineteenth century undervalues it because it looks at all with equal respect, and is as far in the one case as in the other from comprehending rightly the wants of the individual mind. Cousin makes it the peculiar glory of our epoch that it endeavours to comprehend the mind of all other ages. And I fear it must be the tendency of his philosophy, while it examines what all other philosophies were, to prevent us being anything ourselves." The following July, writing to Trench in Spain, he added, "I am more and more convinced that Goethe rescues the individual from contending passions, not to animate it with new life, but to bury it amid the pomps and beneath the mausoleum of art." Trench was so impressed by Sterling's remarks that, more than a year later, when he was writing to Kemble from Florence and inquiring about his plans to go to Germany to study, he asked, "Is German literature good for the inner man? You are not cosmopolitizing, I am sure; if as Englishmen we include anything, we must exclude much more. They seem rather to look on Christianity as the best form of the religious idea, than as having anything to do with the individual's wants. They would receive Christianity somewhat after the fashion that the Roman emperor proposed to receive the statue of its founder—as one among the gods of a peopled Pantheon." We recall that in "The Palace of Art" Christianity was simply one among the "legends fair" that adorned the Palace, and that the inhabitant of the Palace dwelt apart, "holding no form of creed / But contemplating all." In this same letter Trench alludes to his own crisis: "For myself, I have been but a recreant knight from Poesy and all good. Ill health, and low spirits, partly its consequence and partly that of solitude, were strong against me during much of my residence in Spain. However, when I had been almost driven to the extreme edge, I took heart, and turning on my pursuers, stood at bay, and they fled directly; 'and I again am strong,' and, almost for the first time in my life, earnest." Despite the quotation from Wordsworth, Trench's turning on his pursuers was more like Carlyle's Protest in his perambulation of Leith Walk than like the Everlasting Yea itself. For he had more to learn in Rome, whither he now proceeded with his brother and father.

In Rome he made a pious pilgrimage to the graves of Keats and Shelley and met Joseph Severn, the friend of Keats. Severn told him about Keats's end. "His sufferings were terrible and prolonged. Shelley and Hunt had deprived him of his belief in Christianity. . . , and he endeavoured to fight back to it, saying if Severn would get him a Jeremy Taylor, he thought he could believe; but it was not to be found in Rome" (I, 51). Most of his time Trench spent with a group of artists who had come to Rome from all over Europe to study. They were "certainly the most interesting body of men" he had found in the city, and he "endeavoured as far as lay in [his] power to live with them." But he was rather disappointed. "I do not think they recognize, and certainly not with an overwhelming conviction, the ultimate object of theirs, as of all other arts, namely, the incarnation of Beauty. They seldom marry, and their morality regarding women is rather below par" (I, 51). He wrote a sonnet on the subject, beginning, "What is thy worship but a vain pretence, / Spirit of Beauty, and a servile trade," if those who tend thy altars remain selfish and find in their ministrations no defence from "Life's sordid stain." He is "Vexed that my soul should ever moved have been / By that which has such feigning at the heart."[6]

As a result, though in the very city of art he has no appetite for its treasures. Five years later, after he was ordained, married, and completely happy, he returned to Rome and spent a delightful spring which he could not help contrasting, in a poem "Addressed on Leaving Rome to a Friend Residing in that City," with the "dreary sickness of the soul" that he had known before. He says that although nature and art were not indifferent to him—nay, were the sole source from which he drew "whatever lightened . . . the burden of our life and weary load," he had no interest in viewing their marvels, but either withdrew into some ruin or else—alluding to his artist friends—

>                                          I loved,
> With others whom the like disquietude,
> At the like crisis of their lives, now kept
> Restless, with them to question to and fro
> And to debate the evil of the world,
> As tho' we bore no portion of that ill,
> As tho' with subtle phrases we could spin
> A woof to screen us from its undelight:
> Such talk sometimes prolonging into night,
> As being loth to separate, and find
> Each in his solitude how vain are words,
> When that which is opposed to them is more.[7]

6. R. C. Trench, *The Story of Justin Martyr, and Other Poems* (London, 1835), p. 166.

7. Ibid., p. 100.

In the same letter of 18 February 1830, in which he had spoken of Keats and the Roman artists, Trench declared,

> I will not return to England till I have done a little to put on the other side of the balance against twenty-three years of existence squandered away. There are two ways of finding happiness and moral elevation—either to be surely supported on the actual reality of things, or to raise oneself into the regions of pure art or of intuition. I have lost my footing in the first without having gained the second and far nobler, being, as it is, a region of perfect freedom; and herein I find the solution of all my misery, which is not worth attempting to cast off. . . . Of one thing I am sure, that he who has never felt the riddle of existence pressing upon him with an almost overwhelming weight has little chance of ever solving it; but, alas! to attempt it and fail is fatal, as is so magnificently symbolled forth in the story of the Sphinx.

Again, one recalls that as the Soul in "The Palace of Art" began to experience the Nemesis of her situation, "Full oft the riddle of the painful earth / Flashed through her as she sat alone," an image which Trench elaborated more fully in another poem, "To Poetry," which refers to this time. In youth, he says, poetry was his bliss,

> But years went on, and thoughts which slept before,
> Over the horizon of my soul arose—
> Thoughts which perplexed me ever more and more;
> As though a Sphinx should meet one, and propose
> Enigmas hard, and which whoso not knows
> To interpret, must her prey and victim be;
> And I, round whom thick darkness seemed to close,
> Knew only this one thing, that misery
> Remained, if none could solve this riddle unto me.

He then remembered the large promises which poetry had made and asked it "to read / The riddle that was baffling me," but its answer was unsatisfying, "So that I counted thee an idle thing."

> And I turned from thee, and I left thee quite,
> And of thy name to hear had little care.

But finally, "inquiring everywhere, / I won an answer from another shrine, / An holier oracle, a temple more divine."[8]

8. R. C. Trench, *Sabbation; Honor Neale; and Other Poems* (London, 1838), pp. 2–3.

It seems likely that this conversion experience occurred, or at least culminated, at a particular time and place, for Trench has given us a vivid account of it in his first published poem, "The Story of Justin Martyr." There it is doubtless mingled with fictitious details, but its essential truth is witnessed by the autobiographical poems "On Leaving Rome" and "To Poetry." "The Story of Justin Martyr" is set in a classical ruin by the sea, and as Trench and his brother left Rome to travel south through Naples and then around Sicily, it is likely that Argrigentum or Selinute[9] on the south coast of Sicily was the site of the experience, mingled perhaps with memories of the ruins of Rome, where Trench, as we already know, delighted to sit. One morning, says the speaker in the poem, he wandered forth upon the shore and wished this life was over, "for all that fed / The dream of my proud youth had fled, / My dream of youth, that I would be / Happy and glorious, wise and free, / In mine own right," repelling the heavy load that crushed "the servile multitude." "The purpose of my life had failed, / The heavenly heights I would have scaled, / Seemed more than ever out of sight." He only wanted rest and the ocean seemed to offer it: sweet seemed death.

But though he loathed to live, he feared to die, so he went forward till he stood amid an ancient ruin where two solitary pillars stood on a hillside and a little distance away another was fallen. He thought, this pillar the hand of man might raise again, but who will raise the fallen spirit? As he wept, he heard a voice and, looking up, saw an aged man (rather like Wordsworth's Leech-gatherer) to whom he told his sorrow.

> I told him how, when I began
> First to verge upward to a man,
> These thoughts were mine—to dwell alone,
> My spirit on its lordly throne,
> Hating the vain stir, fierce and loud,
> The din of the tumultuous crowd;
> And how I thought to arm my soul,
> And stablish it in self-controul;
> And said I would obey the right,
> And would be strong in wisdom's might,
> And bow unto my own heart's law,
> And keep my heart from speck or flaw,

9. Trench's brother, Francis, gives a delightful account of their visit to these ruins in late April 1830, in *A Few Notes from Past Life: 1818–1832* (Oxford, 1862), pp. 175–88. Paestum in Italy would also be a possibility.

That in its mirror I might find
A reflex of the Eternal mind,
A glass to give me back the truth—
And how before me from my youth
A phantom ever on the wing,
Appearing now, now vanishing,
Had flitted, looking out from shrine,
From painting, or from work divine
Of poet's, or of sculptor's art;
And how I feared it might depart,
That beauty which alone could shed
Light on my life—and then I said,
I would beneath its shadow dwell,
And would all lovely things compel,
All that was beautiful or fair
In art or nature, earth or air,
To be as ministers to me,
To keep me pure, to keep me free
From worldly service, from the chain
Of custom, and from earthly stain;
And how they kept me for awhile,
And did my foolish heart beguile;
Yet all at last did faithless prove.

The old man declared that he was not opposed to the youth's setting for himself a higher aim than the blind lives of most men—he was rather glad that a spiritual Presence had stirred his heart. His error was that he had thought to find the root of good in his own heart and mind.

But, thanks to heaven, it is not so,
That root a richer soil doth know
Than our poor hearts could e'er supply,
That stream is from a source more high;
From God it came, to God returns. . . .[10]

The old man then spoke more explicitly of the Christian dispensation, and the youth, filled with hope, walked home through the evening, the ruined temples so transfigured by the setting sun that they seemed all perfect as before, or rather the very image of the Heavenly City. The title of the poem,

10. Trench, *The Story of Justin Martyr*, pp. 17–18, 20–22. The theme is also developed in other poems by Trench, e.g., "Anti-Gnosticus."

as a note indicates, refers to Justin Martyr's first dialogue with Trypho, in which he tells how, when he was a pagan infatuated with Platonism, he had gone apart hoping to see God face to face and had met with an old man, who had converted him to Christianity.

Trench's illness, his desolation, and his travels in Italy and Sicily remind us very much of Newman's Sicilian experience just three years later, and just as Newman was very eager to get home because, as he cried out in his illness, "I have a work to do," so too was Trench. He had been receiving letters from his friends at home telling him about the flourishing state of the Apostles. On 24 January 1830, J. W. Blakesly had written:

> You ought to come home. . . . We have a handful of men in Cambridge who will continue the race of the Maurices and Sterlings, and cherish an untiring faith in the undefeated energies of man. The majority of the Apostolics are decidedly of the proper way of thinking, and the society is in a flourishing state. We are now twelve in number, and those whom we shall lose this Christmas are by no means the best. I think that we are now in a better state, and that the tone of our debates is higher than it ever has been since the giants were on the earth.

A little later in the same letter he adds, "The Society has received a great addition in Hallam and in Alfred Tennyson, the author of the last prize poem, 'Timbuctoo' (of which Landor, whom, I dare say, you will see at Rome, will give you an account)—truly one of the mighty of the earth. You will be delighted with him when you see him." On 1 April Kemble wrote, "Hallam you already know, and, I hope, like. He is an excellent man, full of high and noble qualities, and is young enough to become a greater and better man even than he is. But you do not know either Charles or Alfred Tennyson, both of whom are dying to know you. The first opportunity, therefore, that you have of making their acquaintance, neglect it not. They are poets of the highest class. In Alfred's mind the materials of the very greatest works are heaped in an abundance which is almost confusion. Charles has just published a small volume of superb sonnets; and his brother and Hallam are about to edit their poems conjointly. One day these men will be great indeed." This would obviously have whetted Trench's appetite to meet Tennyson, and the thought that all his friends were taking orders, winning fellowships, and otherwise finding their niche in life made him very eager to return. By 7 May he was back in Milan and "thirsting for England." He hoped to arrive before the end of May. "If I am in time I shall pay a visit to Cambridge immediately." There is no information about the exact date of his return, but it must have been late May or early June (I, 65), and therefore it was between that date and 2 July, when Tennyson and Hallam left for the Pyrenees, that Trench must have made his famous remark. For on 11 July he too left again for Spain and did not see Tennyson again for nearly a year, by which time his mind was on other things. The important point is that although he doubtless considered that Tennyson and all the Apostles could use the advice, the remark grew directly out of his own experience and primarily had reference to himself. It is, indeed, doubtful whether, when he made it, he had ever read any of the poems of Tennyson that might have convicted him of aestheticism. Tennyson's first volume was published in this very month of June, and it is not until 23 June, by which time he had gone to Southampton, that he evidences a knowledge of it. Writing to Donne, he says, "You have probably long ere this received the volumes of both the Tennysons—. . . . I think his brother [Alfred] may be a much greater poet even than he [Charles] is, but his friends at Cambridge will materially injure him if he does not beware; no young man under any circumstances should believe that he *has* done anything, but still be forward looking." It is clear that he thought Tennyson was being too much lionized, and there may be a touch of jealousy in his remark, for it was he who had hitherto been the poet of the Apostles. But there is no hint that he thought Tennyson guilty of aestheticism, and "The Lady of Shalott," of course, was still in the future.

In view of the close relation of several details in "The Palace of Art" to images and ideas in Trench's letters, one feels that Trench must have come straight to Cambridge and there, and possibly also in London, poured out to the Apostles, in long evening sessions, all that he had been thinking and suffering during the preceding year. It may be also that his letters to Donne, Kemble, Blakesley, and Hallam were passed around the group, or read aloud, so that Tennyson would have been familiar with his ideas and phrases even before he arrived. Clearly, he would have been as eager to meet Trench as Trench was to meet him. Of course, one should note that Trench's *Story of Justin Martyr, and Other Poems* was not published, and perhaps much of it not written, until 1835, two years after the publication of "The Palace of Art," so that his poems may have been influenced by Tennyson, as well as vice versa. Both of them embodied impulses from Hallam and Sterling, and this is why the Apostles found "The Palace of

Art" a poem to "talk out of,"[11] because it arose so directly from their own communal life.

Had Trench merely made his remark, however, and then gone away without backing it up by his own life, the poem would never have taken the form that it did. For he arrived in England to find his friends engaged in a fantastic scheme to overthrow the Spanish government. Sterling had become intimate with General Torrijos, the leader of the Constitutional exiles, and had persuaded himself that if a small band of patriots, well-armed and resolute, were to land on the Spanish coast the whole country would rise in sympathy and the monarchy be toppled. He involved his friends and particularly his cousin, Robert Boyd, just back from service in the Indian army. Hallam and Tennyson were to take money to rebel leaders in the north, whose rising would effect a diversion. The rest were to embark in an armed brig which Sterling and Maurice had purchased and make a simultaneous landing on the south coast. Unfortunately, the English government got wind of the scheme and seized the brig, but the adventurers, nothing daunted, arranged for alternative passage. Hallam and Tennyson left on 2 July, Kemble on 7 July, Trench with the main body of exiles on the 11th. Sterling did not go. His health was not good, and at the last moment his fiancée persuaded him to stay home and get married instead.

It is clear that Trench, at least, set out on this expedition with a kind of restless despair, well aware (though perhaps not really believing it) that they might all be killed, yet thinking that any fate was preferable to doing nothing. "The possibilities are that we shall be both hanged. . . ," Trench wrote to Donne on 23 June. "You will say that all this is very foolish, but it is action, action, action that we want, and I would willingly go did I only find in the enterprise a pledge of my own earnestness." His letters are full of Hamletic and other mock-heroic phrases. Sterling, he says, "has no hope. For myself, I believe I wear the aspect and the form of living men, and as I manage to get through the shows of society with sufficient dexterity, do not excite much attention. But the future, the future—who shall question that? What will one be? What will this age be? Must one end in a worldling; and our age, will it prove the decrepitude of the world? Are we not gathering up the knowledge of past generations, because we are adding nothing ourselves? Do we not place the glory of our century in the understanding of past ages, because our individual energy is extinct, and we are

11. So Spedding writes in *Tennyson and his Friends*, ed. Hallam Tennyson (London, 1911), p. 395.

ourselves nothing?" He is deeply concerned lest, after one or two revolutions of opinion, all the poetry of Keats, Shelley, Wordsworth, and Byron will become unintelligible, because it is founded on purely subjective emotions. And with this highly pertinent reflection he went off to the land of Don Quixote to tilt against the King of Spain.

The sequel of the story is well known. The risings in the north did not occur, the sympathizers in the south never materialized. Cooped up in Gibraltar, bored and inactive, the exiles were unable even to land in Spain because they were watched by the Spanish gunboats. Trench finally returned home in March 1831, and Kemble in May. The rest lingered on until December, when they were finally told by the British authorities, whose patience was naturally exhausted by the presence of a group planning a hostile act against a country with which England was ostensibly at peace, that they would have to leave. Their ship was run aground by the Spanish boats at Malaga, and all, including Boyd, were executed. So ended this Victorian version of the Bay of Pigs.

Only Tennyson and Hallam had a good time. As Hallam wrote to Trench on 2 December 1830, "Alfred went . . . with me to the south of France, and a wild bustling time we had of it. I played my part as a conspirator in a small way, and made friends with two or three gallant men, who have been since trying their luck with Valdes. . . ." When they returned they found their own country in flames. Writing ebulliently from Cambridge in the same letter of 2 December, Hallam exclaimed, "The game is lost in Spain; but how much good remains to be done here! The country is in a more awful state than you can well conceive. While I write, Maddingley, or some adjoining village,[12] is in a state of conflagration, and the sky above is coloured flame-red. This is one of a thousand such actions committed daily throughout England. The laws are almost suspended; the money of foreign factions is at work with a population exasperated into reckless fury. I do not, however, apprehend a revolution, as the intelligent part of the community are tolerably united, and the present ministers seem prepared to meet the emergency." All through the fall and the spring these disturbances continued, the work of a mysterious "Captain Swing," who exhorted the desperate peasants to burn ricks, pillage barns, and write threatening let-

---

12. It was actually Coton, two miles to the west of Cambridge, as is evident from the Journal of Henry Alford, a Trinity undergraduate who, at this date, had just met Tennyson: "Dec. 3 [1830]—Dreadful state of the country. Fearful fire at Coton last night, went there and worked engines. Peacock assembled the men in the cloisters and organized us in bodies of ten or eleven, in case of an attack on Cambridge which is meditated." (*Life, Journals, and Letters of Henry Alford* [London, 1873], p. 61.)

ters to the landlords.[13] Tennyson himself was one of the undergraduates organized by the Dean into a bucket brigade to put out the blazing ricks, and he has recorded his opinion, in language not unknown today, that he sympathized with the aims of rioters but did not approve their methods.

Trench got back to England the first week in March and must have gone immediately to Cambridge, for he reports that he saw Tennyson there "for a few hours . . . and heard recited some of his poems, which were at least as remarkable as any in his book" (I, 85, 91). It is, of course, barely conceivable that Trench could have made his famous remark on this occasion, but it would have been the most crashing anti-climax in history, for after Spain neither he nor anyone else was even thinking of living in art. Moreover, Tennyson had just received the news of his father's death and had to leave immediately for Somersby. He and Trench probably did not meet again until fall[14] and, indeed, they never became very well acquainted. "I regret, with you," wrote Hallam to Trench in March 1832, "that you have never had the opportunity of knowing more of him [A. T.] His nervous temperament and habits of solitude give an appearance of affectation to his manner, which is no true interpreter of the man, and wears off on further knowledge. Perhaps you could never become very intimate, for certainly your bents of mind are not the same, and at some points they intersect; yet I think you could hardly fail to see much for love, as well as for admiration." One wonders, then, whether the lines "To ————," prefixed to "The Palace of Art," really were addressed to Trench, as is usually assumed, or to some closer friend such as Hallam. Perhaps Tennyson assumed that the friendship would ripen, for the wording of the 1832 text, "I send you, Friend, a sort of allegory, / (You are an artist and will understand / Its many lesser meanings)," though perfectly applicable to Hallam, would perhaps be more appropriate to Trench. The 1842 version, "I send you here a sort of allegory— / For you will understand it—" (presumably because you, as a result of your experience, are in a position to do so) is almost pointedly personal, and perhaps the omission of "Friend" acknowledges their more casual relationship.

One should say, then, that "The Palace of Art" is not a palinode, not a *mea culpa*,[15] but neither, of course, is it directed especially at Trench. All

13. E. J. Hobsbawn and George Rudé, *Captain Swing* (London, 1969), p. 165.
14. Francis Trench, *A Few Notes from Past Life*, p. 286.
15. One does not mean to exculpate Tennyson entirely. On 26 July 1831, Hallam wrote to Tennyson, "You say pathetically, 'Alas for me! I have more of the Beautiful than the Good!' Remember to your comfort that God has given you to see the difference. Many a poet has gone on blindly in his artistic pride" (*Memoir*, I, 81).

the Apostles, all of England, all of Europe is included. Many readers have commented on the general resemblance between the Palace of Art and the Cambridge colleges, particularly Trinity,[16] and there is also a resemblance to the great country houses which were being destroyed in France and seriously threatened in England. On another level, the terraces and ramparts of the Palace of Art are clearly related to those of Nineveh, Babylon, and the other great cities of the ancient world which, in so many of Tennyson's early poems, are threatened with apocalyptic destruction. As to Trinity, it is clear from Tennyson's "Lines on Cambridge of 1830" that he regarded the college, at least so far as the dons were concerned, as a place of selfish leisure, leading to intellectual pride. "There was no *love* in the system," he said.[17] There was also one Sunderland, an undergraduate, unfortunately a member of the Apostles, who gave himself great airs and was accustomed to prate about the "rational intuition," which it seems that he alone could understand.[18] He was a great trial to all his fellows, was satirized by Tennyson in "A Character," and probably contributed as much as anyone to the ethical temper of the Soul in "The Palace of Art."

As to the country houses, we must remember that before the days of the National Gallery, when there was only the Dulwich and the as yet unhoused Fitzwilliam, these were the great art palaces of England. Fonthill Abbey, Beckford's fantastic vanity, may have contributed to the poem both directly and through *Vathek*, but there were also others which Tennyson may have visited and which he had certainly read about in William Hazlitt's *Sketches of the Principal Picture Galleries in England* (1824). Tennyson possessed a copy of this work (now at the Tennyson Research Centre), and we know that he read it, for it is the source of "The Lord of Burleigh." It gives descriptions of eleven galleries, most of them private or semi-private, and each description follows the pattern of Tennyson's poem in beginning with a tour of the building itself and then going on to describe its treasures. Moreover, it mingles a rather extravagant aestheticism with Hazlitt's well-known republican sentiments. Of Mr. Angerstein's collection: "Here is the mind's true home. The contemplation of truth and beauty is the proper object for which we were created, which calls forth the most intense desires of the soul, and of which it never tires."

16. A. C. Howell works out some of the details in "Tennyson's 'Palace of Art'— an Interpretation," *Studies in Philology*, 33 (1936), 507–22; but his view that the poem expresses Tennyson's resentment at not being able to take a degree seems to me groundless.
17. *Tennyson and his Friends*, pp. 212–13.
18. Trench, *Letters and Memorials*, I, 50, 58, 63.

Of Dulwich: "It is like a palace of thought—another universe, built of air, of shadows, of colours." Of the Marquis of Stafford's: "Oh! thou, whoever thou art, that dost seek happiness in thyself, independent on others . . . seek it (if thou art wise) in books, in pictures, and the face of nature, for these alone we may count upon as friends for life!"

On the other hand, Hazlitt is not without resentment against the wealthy owners of these pictures. As he leaves Lord Grosvenor's mansion he comments on the difficulty of returning to humble scenes and tries to "abstract the idea of exclusive property" from his mind and concentrate on the beauty of the pictures. "Fonthill-Abbey," he notes, "which was formerly hermetically sealed against all intrusion, is at present open to the whole world; and Wilton-House, and Longford-Castle, which were formerly open to every one, are at present shut, except to *petitioners*, and a favoured few. Why is this greater degree of strictness in the latter instances resorted to? In proportion as the taste for works of art becomes more general, do these Noble Persons wish to set bounds to and disappoint public curiosity? Do they think that the admiration bestowed on fine pictures or rare sculpture lessens their value, or divides the property, as well as the pleasure with the possessor?" In the frame to *The Princess* Tennyson has Sir Walter Vivian, the type of a fine English gentleman, open up his park one day a year to the Mechanics Institute, and he implies that it is this English condescension which "keeps our Britain, whole within herself," whereas the French overseas are constantly going to the extremes of tyranny and revolution. "Why," he cries, "should not these great sirs / Give up their parks some dozen times a year / To let the people breathe?" Thus, whereas in the early apocalyptic poems Nineveh and Babylon are destroyed in their pride, Tennyson hesitates to invoke this doom on England. The doom will befall it if the great of the land do not take heed and if the Universities do not come abreast of the times and speak to the hearts as well as the minds of the young. Tennyson gives them warning in "The Palace of Art," and it is because he has faith, in this year of reform 1832, that England will take the warning, that he concludes,

> 'Yet pull not down my palace towers, that are
>     So lightly, beautifully built;
> Perchance I may return with others there
>     When I have purged my guilt.'

The "I" who is speaking here is not Tennyson, but England, Europe, modern civilization.

# The "Voyages" of Tennyson
# and Baudelaire

G. Robert Stange

*Tufts University*

*"It is bitter knowledge that one acquires from a voyage."*

*Baudelaire*

OF THAT SMALL GROUP of conventional literary images which recur so frequently that we are justified in calling them archetypes, the image of the
voyage is perhaps the most resonant. A critic who set out to trace its appearance and variant meanings from the story of Jason to the wandering
tales of our own time would find himself dealing with almost every major
writer in the Western tradition. Conrad, in saying that some voyages
"seem ordered for the illustration of life . . . . [and] might stand for a symbol of existence,"[1] makes a definition conclusive enough to discourage any
general discussion of this theme or any attempt to trace its "development."
If it is indeed for so vast a thing as life that the voyage stands, any example
of a serious writer's use of the archetype would necessarily be worth our
study, and we might justifiably assume that his treatment of the image
reflected in an especially vivid way his apprehension of reality.

In respect to voyage imagery the case of Tennyson is, as always, an odd
one. In none of his major works is a voyage employed as a unifying motif,
and though the image recurs often enough to claim attention as a basic
theme of Tennyson's poetry, it seems always to present itself as an unarticu-
lated preoccupation, rather than as a consciously manipulated object of
the imagination. In reading the several voyage poems—"Ulysses," "Recollections of the Arabian Nights," "The Sea-Fairies," "The Lotos-Eaters"—
one is impressed by a certain obliquity, by a sense of conflicting impulses
that work uneasily beneath the surface of the poem, of ambiguities felt but
not controlled. The critical essays on "Ulysses" and the occasionally tiresome disagreements about the implications of that poem bear witness to
these uncertainties.

I propose to look closely at one of the less famous poems, "The Voyage"
of 1865, to argue that it is an especially clear example of Tennysonian

1. *Youth* (London, 1923), pp. 3-4.

contradictions and, by considering it alongside its great companion work, "Le Voyage" of Baudelaire, to see if it can lead us to some finer sense of that puzzling but consistent complex which is Tennyson's total work.

Though "The Voyage" was not published until 1865, its position in the *Trinity Notebook* leads Professor Ricks to suppose that it was composed around 1836.[2] Sir Charles Tennyson merely says of it that it is "an allegorical ballad which [the poet] liked to read aloud."[3] Tennyson's own remark is interesting but ultimately unhelpful: "Life," he noted, "is the search after the ideal."[4] It would seem at first that "The Voyage," with its light and almost breezy tone, might have been conceived as a pendant to the sombre plangencies of "Ulysses," and those few critics who have taken note of the poem tend to pursue a hearty line. Tennyson's friend, F. T. Palgrave, said of it, "Life as Energy, in the great ethical sense of the word, —Life as the pursuit of the Ideal,—is figured in this brilliantly descriptive allegory."[5] And a twentieth-century commentator, Professor Buckley, calls it "the proud chant of mariners who sail forever in pursuit of 'one fair vision.'"[6] These remarks are somewhat misleading. In the first place, the poem is an allegory only in the loosest sense of the term; but more important, the surface tone is, I would suggest, quite deceptive.

The pleasant texture of "The Voyage" is apparent in the first stanza:

> We left behind the painted buoy
>     That tosses at the harbour-mouth;
> And madly danced our hearts with joy,
>     As fast we fleeted to the South:
> How fresh was every sight and sound
>     On open main or winding shore!
> We knew the merry world was round,
>     And we might sail for evermore.

---

2. *The Poems of Tennyson*, ed. Christopher Ricks (London, 1969), p. 653. All quotations from the poem will be from this edition.

3. Sir Charles Tennyson, *Alfred Tennyson* (London, 1949), p. 343.

4. Quoted in Ricks, p. 654.

5. Quoted in *The Poems of Alfred Lord Tennyson*, ed. W. J. Rolfe (Boston, 1898), p. 108.

6. Jerome Buckley, *Tennyson: The Growth of a Poet* (Cambridge, Mass., 1960), p. 152. Two exceptions to this view should, however, be noted. In an essay on "Crossing the Bar" (*VP*, 8 [1970], 55–60) David Soenstrom devotes a fine paragraph to "The Voyage." Though he reads it as a poem which "celebrates questing," he refines certain contrary implications in the poem. Many of the "negative" elements of "The Voyage" were suggested in the notes on the poem in *Victorian Poetry and Poetics*, ed. W. E. Houghton and G. R. Stange (2nd ed.; Boston, 1968), pp. 107–8.

It is to be remarked that this voyage is directed *away* from home and haven; the mariners' "mad" joy is the result of their having left the shelter of the harbor and passed the painted buoy, the last sign of the directing vigilance of society. They set their course for the genial south. Everything is fresh and promising, and the voyage need never end.

In a first reading of the poem one does not dwell on the implications of the last two lines of the first stanza. The possibility of sailing "for ever-more" round and round the world is provocative and delightful. In retro-spect, however, one receives an ominous intimation of an endless—and goalless—journey, a sense which Tennyson develops explicitly by repeating the lines in another context at the very end of the poem.

The note of enterprise and joyous determination is sustained through the second stanza. The ship sails clean and unaffected through both the warm winds and the gale. From the south their course takes them to the west:— "We seemed to sail into the Sun!" And in the third stanza the images begin to effect a change of mood:

> How oft we saw the Sun retire,
>   And burn the threshold of the night,
> Fall from his Ocean-lane of fire,
>   And sleep beneath his pillared light!
> How oft the purple-skirted robe
>   Of twilight slowly downward drawn,
> As through the slumber of the globe
>   Again we dashed into the dawn!

The repetition of "how oft" suggests weariness; nature is no longer fresh and brisk, but burning, falling, sleeping and "downward drawn." Suddenly the ship's course, so clearly directed up to this point, becomes erratic: the mariners had been sailing to the west, but now, "again," they dash into the dawn. The attentive reader must by now have begun to alter his responses to this proud pursuit.

In the next four stanzas, which continue the description of the wild voyage, there is a growing sense of the isolation of the sailors. The ship moves so quickly that the stars change every moment, and a "naked moon" runs across "The houseless ocean's heaving field"—a curiously grotesque metaphor which becomes charged with the associations that Tennyson often attaches to barren solitudes, to ice fields (as in "Come down, O maid") or to estranging heights of the sort to which Tithonus is condemned. The tension is between the vacant and lonely sea and the inhabited land the mariners have joyfully forsaken. When the ship does pass close to shore the towns are only "dimly seen," and though the familiar temptations of the Eden isle are evoked they seem remote and perfunctory:

> At times a carven craft would shoot
> From havens hid in fairy bowers,
> With naked limbs and flowers and fruit,
> But we nor paused for fruit nor flowers.
>
> (ll. 53–56)

Weak as it is, this temptation is the strongest one the mariners meet, and the stanza that follows offers the first explanation of the motives that make it possible to resist the offered delights of the land and to sail on forever:

> For one fair Vision ever fled
> Down the waste waters day and night,
> And still we followed where she led,
> In hope to gain upon her flight.
> Her face was evermore unseen,
> And fixt upon the far sea-line;
> But each man murmur'd, "O my Queen,
> I follow till I make thee mine."
>
> (ll. 57–64)

The elusive vision (imaged in the poem, perhaps significantly, as the female principle) is a symbol of all the abstract goals which men set themselves. She appears (in stanza nine) sometimes as Fancy and at others as Virtue, Knowledge, Heavenly Hope or Liberty—as, in short, the intellectual and social ends of life. Up to this point the mariners themselves have not been identifiable; now we must take it that the crew represents those men, of different interests and activities, who give their lives to the pursuit of an ideal. The ship's company cannot stand for all mankind, since the lands they pass are inhabited by races of less adventurous men, but rather for the moral elite, those who live an active and dedicated life.

Only one mariner is characterized, the malcontent: "he saw not far: his eyes were dim: / But ours he swore were all diseased" (ll. 76–77). After denouncing the whole enterprise as a ship of fools he throws himself overboard. The figure is distantly related to some other Tennysonian characters; not able to rest in the security of the mainland, he is nevertheless contemptuous of the voyage, and makes his final solution suicide. The morbid young men of "Supposed Confessions of a Second-Rate Sensitive Mind" and "The Two Voices" are like him in being manifestations of the "divided will" that can neither stay at home nor last the journey out.

In the two concluding stanzas of "The Voyage" the intimations of futility and even suffering become more evident. The mariners ignore the normal rhythms of life, and in seeking their earthly ideals reject the order of nature: "We loved the glories of the world,/ But laws of nature were our scorn" (ll. 84–85). And at the end of the poem the voyage is seen in purely negative terms:

> Again to colder climes we came,
>   For still we followed where she led:
> Now mate is blind and captain lame,
>   And half the crew are sick or dead,
> But, blind or lame or sick or sound,
>   We follow that which flies before:
> We know the merry world is round,
>   And we may sail for evermore.

The mariners' goal, we must assume, is unattainable; their hopeful quest has turned into a futile and endless circling of the globe. The adventurous and resolute spirit, of which so strong a sense is given in the earlier stanzas, is undercut by the repetition—now in an ironic context—of the last two lines of the first stanza. The voyage, it appears, is meaningless and absurd and the poem which seemed at first so high-spirited and affirmative, turns into an almost harsh rejection of the conduct of men who give themselves totally to the pursuit of an ideal.

It might be apposite here to quote the comment the philosopher Henry Sidgwick made on the poem. Discussing, in a letter of 1864, the *Enoch Arden* volume, he wrote:

> what growth there is in the man mentally! How he has caught the spirit of the age in 'The Voyage'! I thought he had fallen into the didactic-dramatic mood that grows on poetic souls with advancing years; but how wonderful—to me—is the lyricised thought of verse 9. . . . How sad—but a chastened sadness, our sadness—that of the second half of the 19th century—no 'Verzweiflung.'[7]

Sidgwick, at least, is not deceived by the light, ballad-like tone of the poem. "Chastened sadness" is very good; and the assertion that there is no

---

7. *Henry Sidgwick: A Memoir*, ed., Arthur and E. M. Sidgwick (London, 1906), pp. 119–20.

despair is not inconsistent with the sense of cold disillusion which I perceive in the poem.

The peculiarity of the feeling "The Voyage" leaves with us is illustrated by a comparison with "Ulysses," where the sense of despair is strong, but the voyage never conceived as entirely futile. Ulysses and his friends, after all, were to seek "a newer world," perhaps be reunited with the great Achilles, and at least achieve a restful death. Their course was set straight into the west; there was to be no errant and endless circling. Ulysses, too, is the man of experience; his resolution "To strive, to seek, to find, and not to yield" is tempered by a knowledge of suffering and a minimal expectation. The mariners of "The Voyage" are innocents; their boisterous resolution is perhaps deluded; their course is confused, they find no rest. Both poems involve a rejection of domestic life, but there is a critical difference in the attitudes the poet takes toward that rejection. Ulysses, the spiritual adventurer, is marked out for the highest things, and the reader ultimately approves his decision to renounce the claims of an unsympathetic people and the humble duties of the home. "The Voyage" leaves us with a stranger mix of attitudes; man is apparently driven to pursue "the ideal," to shun the satisfactions of ordinary life; but is the life of the mainland not more satisfactory and more purposive than the frantic voyage?

II

It is not often that two major poets publish in the space of a few years poems with identical titles, making use of similar metaphorical schemes, and expressing points of view that are not dissimilar. "Le Voyage" of Baudelaire appeared in the second edition of Les Fleurs du mal in 1861.[8] There is no reason to believe that Tennyson had read the poem, though he did at some point read Les Fleurs du mal.[9] Baudelaire, however, knew Tennyson's work very well and considered him, along with Byron and Poe, "a star of the first magnitude."[10] "Le Voyage" contains a kind of tribute to Tennyson: an allusion to the land "In which it seemed always afternoon" in "The Lotos-Eaters," and an echo of Ulysses' summoning of his mariners.[11]

8. The poem was first published as a pamphlet in 1859, then in the Revue française for 10 April of that year. In its final version it was placed last in the second edition of Les Fleurs du mal (1861). See Charles Baudelaire, Oeuvres complètes (Bibliotheque de la Pléiade; Paris 1961), p. 1561. My quotations from the poem are from this edition.
    9. See Alfred Tennyson, p. 460.          10. Oeuvres, p. 805.
    11. Baudelaire's lines are (Oeuvres, pp. 126, 127):

> Le Lotus parfumé! c'est ici qu'on vendange
> Les fruits miraculeux dont votre coeur a faim;

Even without such parallels "Le Voyage" is, for the twentieth-century reader, inevitably part of the critical context of Tennyson's poem, but Baudelaire's achievement is so assured that in comparing it with "The Voyage" one runs the risk of merely affirming Baudelaire's powers and depreciating Tennyson's. There is not, after all, much to learn from a comparison of Ambrose Philips's pastorals to those of Pope, or of *The Purple Island* to *The Faerie Queene*. The differences in the case of the nineteenth-century poets arise from the facts that Baudelaire thought Tennyson a great poet and one worth imitating, and that Tennyson himself liked "The Voyage" well enough to read it aloud frequently. What we can hope to gain from a consideration of Baudelaire's work is a sense, first, of that ability—which Tennyson so often lacked—to make poetry of one's own ambivalences, and secondly, of the French poet's good fortune in being able to work naturally with some fruitful poetic conventions which Tennyson's literary background had simply not made available to him.

In its immense complexity "Le Voyage" is totally coherent. The poem moves from a fixed point, develops, reaches conclusions, but leaves us with a mystery. Its several unifying patterns are drawn from different areas of experience, but continually reinforce each other. The form of the poem is partly determined by the convention of the pastoral day; it begins with morning, progresses to an afternoon land, and ends in evening and darkness. As is traditional, the poetic day is also a lifetime—the opening lines evoke the world of childhood:

> Pour l'enfant, amoureux de cartes et d'estampes,
> L'univers est égal à son vaste appétit.
> Ah! que le monde est grande à la clarté des lampes!
> Aux yeux du souvenir que le monde est petit![12]

After this follow the voyages of youth and of disenchanted maturity. The poem ends:

> O Mort, vieux capitaine, il est temps! levons l'ancre!
> Ce pays nous ennuie, ô Mort! Appareillons!
> Si le ciel et la mer sont noirs comme de l'encre,
> Nos coeurs que tu connais sont remplis de rayons!

> Venez vous enivrer de la douceur étrange
> De cette après-midi qui n'a jamais de fin!

And,

> O Mort, vieux capitaine, il est temps! levons l'ancre!

12. For the child in love with maps and prints, the universe is equal to his enormous appetite. Ah, how large the world is by the light of a lamp, how small in the eyes of memory!

Verse-nous ton poison pour qu'il nous réconforte!
Nous voulons, tant ce feu nous brûle le cerveau,
Plonger au fond du gouffre, Enfer ou Ciel, qu'importe?
Au fond de l'Inconnu pour trouver du *nouveau!*[13]

The conclusion suggests that the innumerable voyages which make up
life itself are, like Tennyson's voyage, endless, that in unknown ways the
quest continues beyond the depths of the unknown. However, this conclusion is a final stage of awareness for which the poem has prepared us,
and we arrive at it—not with perplexity, as in the case of "The Voyage"—
but with satisfied awareness. The reader's vision is modified as the poem
develops: in the beginning we look through a child's eyes at small familiar
things—maps and prints, an imaginary voyage traced under the cozy light
of lamps. This joyful fantasy gives way to the "real" setting forth of the
adventurous youthful spirits:

Un matin nous partons, le cerveau plein de flamme,
Le coeur gros de rancune et de désirs amers,
Et nous allons, suivant le rhythme de la lame,
Berçant notre infini sur le fini des mers . . . .[14]

Then in the monologue of one of the "étonnants voyageurs" we hear a
"noble tale" of voyages of the middle years and of jaded age. From innocent curiosity the poem moves to contemplation of *Curiositas*, a sin to
which the mature man (such as Dante's Ulysses) is especially subject; of
insatiable lust ("Désir, vieil arbre à qui le plaisir sert d'engrais"); of the
"boring spectacle of immortal sin." The "désirs amers," in the context *keen*
desires, which swell the heart of youth, are replaced by "Amer savoir, celui
qu'on tire du voyage," a bitter knowledge.[15] Death (so strangely omitted
from Tennyson's poem) is hailed as the captain of the final voyage, as the
traveller yearns with a kind of eager despair to journey further into the
pit itself.

The program of Baudelaire's poem sounds mechanical when briefly

13. O Death, old captain, it is time! Let us raise the anchor. This country bores us,
O Death. Let us set sail. Though the sky and the sea are black as ink, our hearts, which
you know, are filled with rays of light.
Pour us your poison so that it might comfort us. This fire so burns our brains that we
want to plunge to the bottom of the pit—Hell or Heaven, what does it matter? To the
depths of the unknown to find somehing *new!*
14. One morning we leave, our minds full of flame, our hearts swollen with rancor
and with keen desires, and we go, following the rhythm of the wave, cradling our
infinity on the finiteness of the seas (ll. 5–8).
15. L. 110.

summarized, but the development is actually accomplished by a scheme of modulations that resembles a musical pattern. The motif of innocence, for example, imaged by the pictures, maps and childish dreams, is expressed at the beginning of the second strophe by a complex emblem which transforms children's toys into objects of horror; "we"—poet and reader—are said to twirl like tops and bound like balls while Curiosity whips us into our dance as a cruel angel might whip the whirling suns:

> Nous imitons, horreur! la toupie et la boule
> Dans leur valse et leurs bonds; même dans nos sommeils
> La Curiosité nous tourmente et nous roule,
> Comme un Ange cruel qui fouette des soleils.

In succeeding strophes innocence takes the form of naive admiration for travellers' tales and idealism about the charms of remote places—fancies which the experienced voyager reproves as the products of a childish mind. For one who has experienced it the "eternal news of the whole globe" is of nothing but the ennui of sin, "babbling humanity, drunk with its own genius, and mad now as it was in the past."[16] The word *"nouveau,"* with which the poem ends, represents a final modulation by which childish illusion and invincible self-deception fuse with a kind of hope that may be found in the very bottom of the unknown.

In contrast to Tennyson's "Voyage," in which so little dramatic use is made of the speaker within the poem, "Le Voyage" gains strength from a dramatic organization by which the poet assumes the role of learner. He first speaks in tones of ingenuous lyricism, but after the "amazing traveller" has told his tale, the poet's speech is chastened, slowed, tinged with the sadness of experience. The viewpoint of Tennyson's mariner shows no change, and though a principal subject of "The Voyage" is the nature of those illusions that draw men through life, the experiences of the poem do not lead to knowledge. What the reader learns from Tennyson's poem is in the interpretation of an attitude expressed, an awareness—indirectly communicated—that the quest is without meaning. Our sense of the ennui of the voyagers, caught in eternal movement, is perhaps stronger in "The Voyage" than in Baudelaire's poem, but one feels that in Tennyson's case the effect is achieved almost inadvertently. By means of a single extended image he has communicated a mood of despair; the method is as restrictive —and as purely expressionistic—as that of some twentieth-century "experimental" dramatists.

16. Ll. 102–3.

Illusion might be considered the subject of "Le Voyage," but Baudelaire's treatment of it is charged with moral passion. For him that painfully
gained knowledge which replaces illusion is the end to which the poem
must lead. It is notable that even when he uses almost the same materials
as Tennyson his intentions are quite different. In one section of his poem
the soul is compared to a three-masted ship searching its Icaria; a voice
from the bridge calls, "Watch out!", and from the crow's nest another voice
"ardente et folle" cries, "Amour . . . gloire . . . bonheur!" But though this
pursuit of abstract ideals seems identical to that of Tennyson's mariners,
Baudelaire is concerned to distance his material by irony, to reveal and
judge it:

> Chaque îlot signalé par l'homme de vigie
> Est un Eldorado promis par le Destin;
> L'Imagination qui dresse son orgie
> Ne trouve qu'un récif aux clartés du matin.[17]

It is Baudelaire who is the more traditional, the more "moral" poet.
Though his work has an air of modernity which Tennyson's is often thought
to lack, though he expresses, among other things, the peculiar emotional
restlessness of post-Romantic man, the contemporaneity of "Le Voyage"
rests on a network of mythical and religious allusions: the wanderings of
Odysseus, the paradigm of the voyager, are evoked in its opening stanzas;
later other eternal travellers are set beside him. The Wandering Jew and
the Apostles represent those who incessantly flee our vigilant and deadly
enemy, Time,[18] and at the end of the seventh strophe the ambiguity of all
our journeys is suggested by a parallel with Orestes, whose wanderings
are at once a search and a flight. All of us, embarked on the sea of darkness, at first resemble those simple voyagers who are beguiled by the
relatively easy temptations of Circe's palace or a lotos-land. But as we
penetrate more deeply into the underworld, ghosts speaking in familiar
tones stretch out their arms to us. We recognize our own Pylades, while
in the distance Electra calls to us:

> A l'accent familier nous devinons le spectre;
> Nos Pylades là-bas tendent leurs bras vers nous.

___

17. Each island announced by the lookout is an Eldorado promised by Destiny. The
imagination which prepares its orgy finds nothing but a reef in the morning light
(ll. 37–40).
    18. See ll. 114–21.

"Pour rafraîchir ton coeur nage vers ton Electre!"
Dit celle dont jadis nous baisions les genoux.[19]

Baudelaire's poem evokes from us a fullness of response which we deny to "The Voyage." Both works have a definable "tone," but while in Tennyson's case tone can conduce to our confusion, it is for Baudelaire a unifying medium. All the elements of "Le Voyage" are under control; there are none of those *attitudes irréfléchies* that so often erupt in a poem of Tennyson's. To say this is not to suggest that as a poet Tennyson is generally inferior to Baudelaire; one is reminded that an account of the best qualities of "Le Voyage" might apply equally well to "Tithonus": there we find the same poignant ennui, the painful transition from illusion to knowledge, and the paradoxical sense of a vital death which offers the last temptation and the ultimate joy. There, too, Tennyson can be said to have given extension to his limited, personal vision by a deftly handled mythological parallel. Finally, of course, the triumph of "Tithonus" is, like that of "Le Voyage," a triumph of *tone*.

"The Voyage," must be characterized as an interesting failure, a work which is not greatly appealing, but which exerts a stubborn, low-keyed attraction. So grand a motif in the hands of so fine a poet will always yield us something: I am tempted to see the poem as an image of Tennyson's own imaginative journey, almost an epitome of his career. The disparity between his external success, the seeming assurance of his public voice, and his inner melancholy is curiously matched by the tension between the brisk, active surface of "The Voyage" and its weary, despairing depths.

---

19. The figure of Electra in this context shows Baudelaire's method of enriching the texture of his verse by conflating allusions. This apparition is both the Electra of the *Oresteia* and the mysterious ideal girl De Quincey seeks in the murk of London.

# The Structural Logic of THE RING

## AND THE BOOK

Boyd Litzinger

*St. Bonaventure University*

WHAT STRUCTURAL LOGIC underlies *The Ring and the Book?* The problem, in one or another of its forms, has fascinated critics for a century now, from some of the earliest reviewers to the recent centennial writers. Frederick Greenwood marvelled at "the intricacies of fact, argument, and character through which the poet moves with the light of his genius . . . ,"[1] and Robert Buchanan at the "wondrous beauty of the workmanship" which he found in "the *opus magnum* of our generation."[2] Henry James commemorated the centenary of Browning's birth with a long address, frequently reprinted thereafter, explaining how a novelist would have approached the materials.[3] In 1943, Professor Bruce R. McElderry, Jr., demonstrated how skilfully Browning avoided needless repetition in the poem by distributing the narrative emphases among the several monologists,[4] Robert Langbaum in 1956 contributed importantly to the subject by analyzing the "relativist" features of the poem,[5] and in their recent *Browning's Roman Murder Story*, Richard D. Altick and James F. Loucks, II, suggested a triadic arrangement to explain parts of the poem's design which will be discussed later in this essay.[6] Despite this variety of partial approaches, there is room for speculation on what Browning intended to accomplish by his organization of *The Ring and the Book* and how he went about designing a structure to fit his concepts.

1. *The Cornhill Magazine*, 19 (Feb. 1869), 252.
2. *The Athenaeum*, 20 March 1869, p. 399.
3. "The Novel in *The Ring and the Book*: Address Delivered Before the Academic Committee of the Royal Society of Literature in Commemoration of the Centenary of Robert Browning, May 7, 1912," *Transactions of the Royal Society of Literature*, 2nd series, XXXI, 269–98.
4. "The Narrative Structure of Browning's *The Ring and the Book*," *Research Studies of the State College of Washington*, 11 (Sept. 1943), 193–233.
5. "*The Ring and the Book*: A Relativist Poem," *PMLA*, 71 (March 1956), 131–54.
6. See the chapter titled "The Poem's Design," *Browning's Roman Murder Story: A Reading of "The Ring and the Book*," (Chicago, 1968).

The story of how Browning discovered the "Old Yellow Book" is told in Book I and this tale, together with his own accounts of researching and planning the work, has been too often recounted to bear repeating here. Confronted with a mass of source-materials, willing to seek out still others, Browning felt immediately, instinctively, that he had penetrated the body of conflicting arguments and had reached the heart of the matter: Pompilia was perfectly innocent, Guido was thoroughly guilty. But the problem of presenting the facts in poetic fashion was still formidable and complex. Other writers might very well have narrated the poem,[7] but this would have gone against the grain of habit: over a long period he had developed and cultivated the dramatic monologue. Appropriately, the materials themselves—the legal procedure, the written arguments of the adversaries, the conflicting testimonies—helped Browning to determine to let a series of characters tell the story each in his own way. Because it was a complicated and, for him, an important story, he decided to make it epic in scope. It can be argued that this fact, and little else, accounts for the twelve-book division.

It is quite possible to treat *The Ring and the Book* as a nineteenth-century version of the literary epic, and one can find most, if not all, of the devices traditionally associated with epic poetry. Like the epic poets, Browning has not invented his story but has recovered it from the (very obscure) literature of the past. His theme is an important one, evil besetting a good which is finally triumphant, and is stated in a number of places in the poem. The action (which gets underway in Book II) begins *in medias res*, with the crimes already committed but with the climaxes still to come. The muse—in this case, the poet's dead wife—is invoked in the famous "O Lyric Love" passage which closes Book I. The rollcall of principals is recorded in the first book, long set speeches are the very manner of the poem, and narratives of past events leading to the present situation abound. Without pressing the thesis too hard, one can find a descent into a figurative Hades in Book XI, where we discover the hellish truth from the condemned Guido's lips. If the language of the poem is not always dignified, if the speech is colloquial and informal, if certain characters are ludicrous, these are simply modifications which every reader ought to expect from a Robert Browning whose muse never quibbles at a descent to the comic or the grotesque.

It may be argued that, unlike most epics, this poem has no great and

---

7. Indeed, Browning twice offered the materials to novelists for their use, but neither accepted.

significant action, no epic-scale hero, no grand human significance; but Browning could have countered each argument. The significance of the action extends far beyond a sordid trial-for-murder in an Italian setting now forgotten. The struggle is that of truth and innocence, beset by lies, rumor, and evil. If the Victorian Age was one of uncertain faith and darkening doubt, of rising science and declining belief—the time between Arnold's "two worlds"—this struggle was a central concern. The condition portrayed is the universal human one and transcends time and place. If a villain, Guido, seems to dominate much of *The Ring and the Book*, so does Satan dominate much of *Paradise Lost*. In Guido we see the terrible depths to which a human being can descend. In Caponsacchi, the Pope, and Pompilia we see the heights to which the human spirit can rise. In the gossiping Romans, the grasping Comparini, and the faithless lawyers, we see the ordinary, the petty, and the cunning minor fools of the world. In short, *The Ring and the Book* is nothing less than a microcosm of the world as Browning views it—a struggle between God and Satan, truth and falsehood —and therefore an appropriate subject for epic poetry.

In order to discuss the structure of the poem, it is not necessary, of course, to subscribe to the theory that Browning had an epic intention. His twelve books are a fact, and we must ask whether they form an organic whole, whether every book is justified, and why they were arranged in their final order.

Browning's story, first, hinges upon the dispute between Guido and Pompilia. Their claims are utterly contradictory: one is right, one is wrong. Given Browning's decision to use the monologue form, then Books V (Count Guido Franceschini) and VII (Pompilia) are necessary. Since, in Browning's view, the question of murder or justifiable homicide hangs upon the question of Pompilia's innocence, and since this question hangs in turn upon the nature of her relationship with the young priest, Book VI (Giuseppe Caponsacchi) is also necessary. Because the triangle came to Browning in the form of a trial-report, complete with legal arguments and precedents, the pro-Guido and anti-Guido lawyers must be heard, and Browning was therefore committed to Books VIII (Archangelis) and IX (Bottini). Because in fact a decision was rendered in the case, it is necessary that the voice of judgment be heard; and, because Guido had appealed beyond the secular court to the church, the Pope rather than the civil magistrate is chosen to pass judgment in Book X.

Thus six books have been accounted for, but six remain. Books I and XII are Browning's own. He calls them a rising to a plateau and a descent

from it, an introduction and a conclusion. In one sense, because the poet
intrudes *in propria persona*,[8] it can be argued that they are not organically
necessary, but these books can be defended. Browning argues that truth
can seldom be known and is often lost; he must recreate for us a moment
now lost in time. Book I presents the "facts" and introduces us to the
*dramatis personae*. The poet must bring us up to the level of a moment
when, as he says, "hearts beat hard and blood ran hot." To bring us out of
the ordinary events of every day and to raise us to a pitch of passionate
life by such means as Browning here employs is quite legitimate and is not
unknown in other poems.[9] Book XII ties up the loose ends by showing us
the immediate aftermath of the trial and by bringing us back to the reality
of the present.

Of the four remaining books, three are not absolutely necessary to the
story, but they are to the poet's purpose. In a work devoted to the search
for truth, Books II (Half-Rome), III (Other Half-Rome), and IV (Tertium
Quid) are purely relativistic; portraying three uninformed but possible
attitudes, they are not only admissible but also artistically valuable and
organic to Browning's conception.

Which leaves us with the most difficult problem of all: the place of
Guido's second monologue, Book XI. The presence of this monologue has
disturbed some critical readers from the time of its publication. In her
letters to the poet, Julia Wedgwood complained repeatedly that Guido's
blackness dominated Pompilia's whiteness and that Browning emphasized
the world's evil too strongly for goodness to overcome it. Browning, of
course, disagreed, defending himself upon the ground of fact: the blackness existed in his source-materials and, were he to have lightened the
picture, he would have falsified. Still, he admitted that he perhaps enjoyed
portraying evil better than he should have enjoyed it, and he recognized
his penchant as a possible character-flaw.[10]

---

8. In her *Browning's Voices in "The Ring and the Book": A Study of Method and
Meaning* (Toronto, 1969), Mary Rose Sullivan treats Books I and XII as true dramatic,
rather than personal, monologues, but the argument is not quite convincing.

9. This technique is used with notable success and with similar intent in Wordsworth's *Michael*.

10. The Browning-Wedgwood correspondence, as it touches *The Ring and the
Book*, begins 17 May 1867 with Browning's offer to submit the proofs to her for
criticism, and ends effectively on 8 March 1869 with Browning's flat "I think you are
in the wrong about the proper treatment of facts.... They want explaining, not al-
tering." Between the two dates lie a number of fascinating insights into Browning's
creative method (and perhaps into his professional pride). See Richard Curle, ed.,
*Robert Browning and Julia Wedgwood: A Broken Friendship as Revealed by Their
Letters* (New York, 1937).

Nevertheless, why is it that the villain of *The Ring and the Book* is given two opportunities to speak—in two of the longest monologues at that? Is it only that Browning enjoyed the portrayal of villainy or that the facts as he found them forced him into writing Book XI? I think not. It seems to me that for two reasons this book is organically necessary to the whole. First, there is the matter of truth-telling. In this relativistic poem, it is necessary that each character tell the truth as he sees it, so that the reader can make the necessary judgments. And to this point, every monologist has done precisely that: prejudiced, stupid, well-meaning, self-serving, or ill-informed, each speaker has given us his version of the truth. In Book V, however, Guido lies from beginning to end in an effort to avoid condemnation. Browning's consistency demands, therefore, that Guido speak again, and finally, to tell the truth as he sees it. Secondly, we must understand that, believing in Pompilia's innocence, and faced with source materials which obviously admit of other conclusions, Browning wanted to prove his case for Pompilia beyond shadow of doubt. After all—as Browning well knew— witnesses have in the past lied and been mistaken, lawyers have been overly persuasive, magistrates and popes have erred, innocent men have been convicted. In order to eliminate every possible doubt, it was for Browning necessary that the guilty man confess his guilt. Thus Guido undergoes a triple condemnation: the court has judged him guilty; the Pope has found him thoroughly reprehensible; and finally in Book XI he himself confesses his unrelieved wickedness.

Thus the *raison d'être* for each of the twelve monologues. The question of their order remains, however, and this question also admits of a logical explanation. In general, it can be said that the poem is so ordered that truth is approached gradually and with increasing intensity, pointing to significant poetic and emotional climaxes.

Browning's introductory book is intended to be objective, confidential, and indeed almost light-hearted. Distant more than a century and a half from the tragedy, knowing it only from written records, the poet is an interpreter of events at third-hand. He can give us a cast of characters and the "facts" as he has found them, but he can also speak playfully to his British public, secure in the belief that the public will judge as he has judged once all the "human testimony" has been heard. And because in Book I we are at a considerable chronological and psychological distance from the actual events, the poetic and emotional intensity is quite low.

The next nine books (II–X) can be treated in groups of three. "Half-Rome," "Other Half-Rome," and "Tertium Quid" are contemporary commentators on the tragedy, but not one of them has first-hand knowledge of the events which constitute the central facts or of the persons who acted them out. The observers speak in a carefully-arranged sequence which represents a trial in miniature: "Half-Rome" speaks on 3 January 1698 in defense of Guido, "Other Half-Rome" on 4 January in defense of Pompilia, and "Tertium Quid" a little later in what he thinks are objective terms. Were we to believe either of the first two speakers, "Tertium Quid" would again cast all into doubt. The emotional level of these three books, however, is quite low, and Browning leaves us in no doubt as to the prejudices of each speaker. It is in the next three books (V–VII) that we approach the heart of the matter—the testimony of the three principal actors in this drama.

It will be noted that these three books, organically central, are also as nearly physically central as is possible in a twelve-part arrangement. As the accused, Guido is allowed the first opportunity to speak. He defends himself brilliantly, admitting that he has killed but denying that he has murdered, drawing skilfully upon every rhetorical device imaginable. But the defense is entirely self-centered—far, as we shall be made to see, from the kind of outgoing, human concern which will characterize the other principals. Despite his years of marriage to Pompilia, Guido does not know her and gives a distorted view of their relationship.

It is, therefore, significant that the next speaker is Caponsacchi rather than Pompilia. Browning will not permit, even in his poem, Guido to be near Pompilia. Just as in their fleeting lives they were psychologically separated, so too in the permanence of poetry they must be physically separated; and just as in life Caponsacchi placed himself as a shield before Pompilia, so too in the poem his monologue must be interposed between husband's and wife's. Caponsacchi is even more impassioned than Guido; his love for Pompilia, his hatred of Guido, and his sense of outrage are powerful enough to offset the cool defense presented in Book V, but are also so strong as to disqualify him as an objective witness.

Thus are we prepared for the high poetry of Book VII and the pure white light of Pompilia's monologue. Here the sense of love is strong—a human but pure love of the priest, a mother's natural love for her son, and a very simple love of God—but there is no sign of hate for her tormentor and murderer, only forgiveness and the inability of radical innocence to grasp the reality of radical evil. With her "And I rise" all but the most cynical readers must be convinced of the truth and where it lies. And it is at this point that we realize the skill with which Browning has solved a

difficult problem: how to treat a heroine who has the terrible disadvantage
of being perfectly pure. Flawless, young, inexperienced, and quite simple,
Pompilia could very well have been a thorough bore. As Browning wrote
in *Bishop Blougram's Apology*:

> Our interest's on the dangerous edge of things.
> The honest thief, the tender murderer,
> The superstitious atheist, demirep
> That loves and saves her soul in new French books—
> We watch while these in equilibrium keep
> The giddy line midway: one step aside,
> They're classed and done with.[11]
>
> (ll. 395–401)

Pompilia keeps no "giddy line." Her character is so plain, so uncomplex,
that she cannot bear the light of prolonged and intense scrutiny. Therefore
Browning approaches her very gradually and by indirection: first through
the reports of three gossiping Romans who know of her only through
rumor; next through her husband, who, though he lived with her, never
actually knew her; then through Caponsacchi, who knew her better than
any other person. Finally, for a relatively brief moment (Book VII is the
shortest of the monologues delivered by the major characters), we meet
her first-hand and hear her voice. This gradual approach allows her to
occupy a growing and finally a central position in our consciousness without subjecting her for very long to our direct judgment, and it prevents us
from being bored by her fragile goodness.[12]

Books VII, VIII, and IX come logically together as the process of trial
and judgment unfolds. A close student of Shakespeare, Browning was
fully aware of the uses of comic relief. Having placed three emotionally-
charged monologues together, it was now necessary for the poet to allow
the reader some psychological relaxation. That Browning was acting quite
deliberately is made clear to Julia Wedgwood in a letter of 21 January
1869: "The buffoon lawyers (not a bit intellectually and morally beneath
lawyers I have known) serve an artistic purpose, and let you breathe a
little before the last vial is poured out. . . ." Because Innocent's judgment

11. All line references are to *The Works of Robert Browning*, 10 vols. (London,
1912), edited by F. G. Kenyon.
12. Close student of Browning and careful reader of *The Ring and the Book* that
he was, Henry James may very well have borrowed this technique when he came to
portray Millie Theale, that most fragile of heroines, in *The Wings of the Dove*. The
final word has yet to be said regarding the literary debt James owes to Browning.

and Guido's confession are to be full of poetic and human intensity, the
books of the lawyers—one too jolly to care, the other incapable of emotion,
—are a kind of trough between two emotional waves. And for this reason
the monologue of Archangelis (Book VIII) is relaxed, informal, and nearly
comic, centering as much upon the preparations for Giacinto's birthday
dinner as upon the preparations for Guido's legal defense. Despite this
interlude, the idea of progress towards an inevitable end is maintained
through an interesting device: in Book VIII Archangeli prepares only a
first draft of his defense:

> Done! I' the rough, i' the rough . . . .
> . . . to-morrow I review my piece
> Tame here and there undue floridity.
>
> (ll. 1737, 1743–44)

In Book IX, however, Bottinius has completed his final draft and plays the
game of wish-fulfillment, pretending to read his speech before an expec-
tant court:

> I rise, I bend, I look about me, pause
> O'er the hushed multitude: I count—One, two—
>
> (ll. 15–16)

There is no joking, no macaronic verse, no straying from the subject. The
trial of Guido Franceschini is on in earnest, and we are being prepared for
an emotional rise in the sober judgment of a solemn Pope, delivered in
Book X not upon legal grounds open to debate but upon moral grounds
which can admit of no argument. Because Innocent is a passionate seeker
of truth, and because his judgment must settle the case—establish Pompilia's innocence and Guido's guilt,—it is not surprising that his monologue
is filled with emotion and high poetry.

As Altick and Loucks have shown, Books II through X form three triads,
an elaborate exercise in dialectics: the "two halves" of Rome contradict
each other and are judged by the "objective" Tertium Quid; Guido and
Caponsacchi contradict each other and are placed in moral perspective by
the dying Pompilia; the opposing arguments of the lawyers are risen above
and resolved in Pope Innocent's judgment.[13]

Beyond this design so well described by the authors of *Browning's
Roman Murder Story* lies still a larger design, which I have elsewhere
described briefly:

13.This outline does not do justice to Altick and Louck's sophisticated argument,
and the reader must be referred to their chapter on "The Poem's Design."

. . . Half-Rome presents a thesis, Guido's innocence, Other Half-Rome presents the antithesis, Pompilia's innocence, and Tertium Quid presents a synthesis, one which of course turns out to be false. In the second triad, then, Guido and Caponsacchi present thesis and antithesis, with the innocent Pompilia, who refuses to recognize fully the unutterable evil of Guido, presenting an emotional synthesis on a higher level. These two triads then are both thesis and antithesis themselves, to be resolved in a synthesis which is the third triad. In this the lawyers argue, one for Guido, one for Pompilia, and their thesis and antithesis are resolved in the Pope's final synthesis at the highest plane of human thought.[14]

Thus the Triad of Rumor (Books II–IV) has been opposed by the Triad of Testimony (Books V–VII), and these have been resolved in the Triad of Judgment (Books VIII–X). And it is at this point that Guido, speaking his second monologue while awaiting execution, admits his guilt, thereby assenting to the justice of the judgment arrived at through the dialectic process. In this impassioned plea for life, the intensity of Guido's emotion rises until, in a moment of fear and despair, he exonerates Pompilia entirely by praying to her.[15]

Following the low-keyed books devoted to the lawyers, one a personable and family-centered defender, the other a calculating and cold-blooded prosecutor, we have been raised again to pitches of poetic intensity in Books X and XI. It remains only for Browning to return us to the level of everyday, modern experience—and this he does by gradations in Book XII. There he presents us with "documents" relating to the post-trial events: letters from a gentleman who has lost his bet that Guido would be pardoned and from the two lawyers who now have other fish to fry, and finally an account of Fra Celestine's sermon on the tragic events. Reported, rather than recorded as monologues, this melange lets us gently and gradually down and away from the high dramatics of Book XI. Having thus led us

---

14. Review of *Browning's Roman Murder Story, JEGP*, 68 (July 1969), 549.

15. The question has often been raised as to whether or not Guido "repents and is saved." It seems to me not. Firstly, Guido's cry is "Pompilia, will you let them *murder* me?" (emphasis added), from which I infer that his cry is for mercy, not forgiveness. Secondly, when Julia Wedgwood argued that "Shame and pain and humiliation need the irradiation of hope to be endurable as objects of contemplation" (*Browning-Wedgwood*, pp. 149–50), Browning replied, "Guido 'hope?'—do you bid me turn him into that sort of thing? No, indeed!" (p. 153). Ironically, however, Guido will not be damned eternally; for, according to the Pope's remarkable theology (Book X, ll. 2127–32), if worst comes to worst and Guido does not repent, God will have to "re-make" the villain's soul "He else made first in vain; which must not be."

back, Browning in his own voice and person returns us to the present, in which he links the end and the beginning of the poem with his ring image and a final reference to his "Lyric Love."

As a structural entity, *The Ring and the Book* is then logically and psychologically sound. If the ring metaphor can still arouse debate, it is because Browning and his critics disagree over the uses of "fancy and fact," "ore and alloy"; but in terms of structure—the number and the arrangement of parts, the gradual approach to Pompilia and the truth, the placement of poetic climaxes and emotional relaxations, the variety of emphases within the monologues, the subtle impressions given of the passage of time, and the inexorable progress from rumor to fact to judgment—the poem is tightly organized. *The Athenaeum* may have overstated the case by calling it "beyond all parallel the supremest poetical achievement . . . since the days of Shakespeare,"[16] and no poem of epic length is without its flaws. But in structuring his *magnum opus,* Browning had every reason to believe that his "justifiably golden" ring had been fully and satisfyingly rounded.

16. 20 March 1869, p. 399.

# Prince Hohenstiel-Schwangau: *Browning's* "Ghostly Dialogue"

### Clyde de L. Ryals

*Duke University*

MOST OF BROWNING'S POEMS after *The Ring and the Book* are unpopular. It may well be that *Prince Hohenstiel-Schwangau* is the most unpopular of all. G. K. Chesterton is a minority of one in praising it as "one of the finest and most picturesque of all Browning's apologetic monologues." More typical are critics who find it "wordy" and "boring": George Saintsbury, who could and apparently did read everything, allowed that he would much rather peruse the worst of Southey's epics and Dryden's plays than *Prince Hohenstiel-Schwangau*. William Clyde DeVane sums up critical opinon when he says that the poem is one of those works "not pleasing to any but confirmed and determined Browningites." [1]

The poet himself was originally enthusiastic about his monologue. In the midst of composition Browning confided to his friend Isa Blagden: "I have written about 1800 absolutely new lines or more, and shall have the whole thing out of hand by the early winter,—that I can't help thinking a sample of my very best work. . . ." [2] Yet when the poem was printed, he told Edith Story: "I expect you not to care three straws for what, in the nature of things, is uninteresting enough, even compared with other poems of mine which you have been only too good to." [3]

Perhaps critics' lack of regard for the poem is largely owing to its diffi-

1. G. K. Chesterton, *Robert Browning* (London, 1903), p. 121; George Saintsbury, "Browning," reprinted in *The Browning Critics*, ed. Boyd Litzinger and K. L. Knickerbocker (Lexington, Ky., 1967), p. 34; William Clyde DeVane, *A Browning Handbook*, 2nd ed. (New York, 1955), p. 32. The critical literature on *Prince Hohenstiel-Schwangau* is slight. No periodical essay devoted to the monologue has, to my knowledge, been published within the past fifty years. Books on Browning allude to it in passing. Only Philip Drew in his *The Poetry of Browning: A Critical Introduction* (London, 1970) has in recent years given the poem more than brief attention; his concern is focused mainly on the topicality of the monologue (pp. 291–303).

2. *Dearest Isa: Robert Browning's Letters to Isabella Blagden*, ed. Edward C. McAleer (Austin, Texas, 1951), p. 367.

3. *Browning to his American Friends*, ed. Gertrude Reese Hudson (London, 1965), p. 166.

culty of interpretation. J. M. Cohen, for example, objects: "At first he [the Prince] appears to be no more than a seedy political adventurer; only as the poem progresses does it become clear that Browning has endowed him too with some of his own qualities. But the passages in which the poet speaks with his own voice are much outweighed by the poem's inconsistencies, its casuistries and tangled argument."[4] But why did Browning so drastically revise his estimate of the poem when it was completed? An answer to such a question must necessarily be speculative, but an attempt to provide one might illuminate some of the problems of the monologue. In taking account of the author's altered opinion of his work this essay proposes to show (1) that whatever inconsistencies there are in *Prince Hohenstiel-Schwangau* stem not from the poet's inability to control his material but from the character of the speaker himself and (2) that the poem is a product of Browning's further experimentation with the dramatic monologue and manifests his increasing awareness of the limitations of that mode.

On the manuscript of *Prince Hohenstiel-Schwangau* Browning wrote at the conclusion that a "few lines of the rough draft [were] written at Rome, 1860";[5] and soon after its publication he confirmed, in a letter, that he "conceived the poem, twelve years ago in the Via del Tritone—in a little hand-breadth of prose."[6] The idea of a monologue spoken by a character representing Napoleon III was, then, not new.[7] So during a holiday in Scotland in the late summer of 1871, *Balaustion's Adventure* published and apparently having no other idea for a poem, Browning took up his discarded monologue based on Louis Napoleon and began "perpetrating 'Hohenstiel Schwangau' at the rate of so many lines a day, neither more nor less."[8]

Evidently the original conception of a poem written in the name of the French Emperor had been of a dramatic monologue more or less along the

4. J. M. Cohen, *Robert Browning* (London, 1952), p. 129. Mrs. Sutherland Orr in her *Handbook to the Works of Robert Browning*, 6th ed. (London, 1927), p. 163, makes more or less the same observation: "the imaginary speaker so resembles Mr. Browning himself, that we forget for the moment that we are not dealing with him."

5. Quoted by DeVane, p. 358.

6. *Browning to his American Friends*, p. 167.

7. Early in 1871 Browning said: "I wrote, myself, a monologue in his [Louis Napoleon's] name twelve years ago, and never could bring the printing to my mind as yet." *Letters of Robert Browning, Collected by Thomas J. Wise*, ed. Thurman L. Hood (New Haven, 1933), p. 145.

8. The recorder of this fact was a guest of Benjamin Jowett's who was in the neighborhood at the time. Quoted by DeVane, p. 360.

lines of those in the *Men and Women* volume of 1855. Yet in the decade or
so since Browning first attempted a poem modelled on Louis Napoleon,
the shape of his work had altered a great deal, though continuing in the
direction begun many years previously. From the time that he abandoned
his early poetry of disguised autobiography and turned to poetry "always
Dramatic in principle, and so many utterances of so many imaginary persons, not mine" (Preface to *Dramatic Lyrics*), Browning's constant quest
was for a poetry of greater and greater objectivity. In the *Essay on
Shelley*, while discussing "the subjective poet of modern classification," he
wrote:

> There may be no end of the poets who communicate to us what they
> see in an object with reference to their own individuality; what it was
> before they saw it, in reference to the aggregate human mind, will be
> as desirable to know as ever. Nor is there any reason why these two
> modes of poetic faculty may not issue hereafter from the same poet. . . .[9]

The poetic strategy by which he sought to combine the two was of course
the dramatic monologue.

The method of the dramatic monologue was, however, an interior one,
for it was the expression of a particular point of view. But since every object has many sides, the dramatic monologue was a window opening on to
only one aspect. How then to see the object in its fullness? In *The Ring and
the Book* Browning aimed for wholeness by grouping twelve monologues,
representing varying points of view, around a single episode. Yet even here
he was still confined for the length of the individual monologue to one
perspective, though this particular view could be immediately dropped
and another assumed. So his problem remained unsolved, for in *The Ring
and the Book* the poet was at the mercy of a sequential structure.

In *Balaustion's Adventure* (1871), the first poem published after *The
Ring and the Book*, Browning sought to widen the scope of the dramatic
monologue by combining a purely objective form of literature, Euripidean
drama, with the more internal monologue by having the drama filtered
through the eyes and mouth of a young girl from Rhodes. Yet innovative
though *Balaustion's Adventure* was in form, it remained nothing more than
a dramatic monologue expressive of but one point of view. Was it feasible

9. All citations of Browning's published works are from the Florentine Edition,
*The Complete Works of Robert Browning*, ed. Charlotte Porter and Helen A. Clarke
(New York, 1910). The quotation here is from XII, 288. The text of *Prince Hohenstiel-
Schwangau* may be found in volume IX.

to experiment further in this mode which Browning had always found
most congenial?

One other possiblity lay in the combination of the dramatic monologue
with the internal dialogue such as employed in *Christmas-Eve and Easter-
Day*. After all, in a certain sense the monologues are what the speaker in
"Christmas-Eve" calls "talking with my mind" (1132). What if he now ex-
perimented with an internal dialogue, in which the different voices are
clearly not the speaker himself, set within the confines of a dramatic monologue? It would be basically the method of *Balaustion's Adventure*—that is,
monologue *in propria persona* plus interpolated material with a return in
the final lines to the speaker's own voice.

During this period of experimentation with the dramatic monologue
which began with *The Ring and the Book* Browning was not content to
repeat his previous efforts. If this were to be a poem somewhat like *Balaustion's Adventure* in form, it would nevertheless have to be different. It
would not suffice that interior dialogue serve in lieu of a play. Rather the
dialogue would provide another point of view so that, somewhat like the
later *Parleyings*, the vision of the poem would be almost double. Presumably with such a strategy in mind Browning set out in writing *Prince
Hohenstiel-Schwangau* to test whether he could achieve greater objectivity
by using a form which would present differing points of view, not sequen-
tially but almost simultaneously, within one poem.

Aside from purely experimental considerations of form it was also quite
necessary that Browning not be restricted to one point of view when writing about Napoleon III. For the poet had highly ambivalent and constantly
changing feelings about the Emperor. During his wife's lifetime he and
Mrs. Browning did not often agree on the stature and sincerity of the
French ruler, and this division in their opinions was a source of some pain
to him. In the 1850's and until her death in 1861 Mrs. Browning regarded
Napoleon as the one hope for the liberation of Italy. Browning, however,
"thought badly of him at the beginning of his career . . . ; better afterward,
on the strength of promises he made, and gave indications of intending to
redeem,—I think him very weak in the last miserable year [1870–71]."[10]
Further, he wrote to another correspondent several days later, "I don't
think so much worse of the character as shown us in the last few years,
because I suppose there to be a physical and intellectual decline of faculty,
brought about by the man's own thoughts, no doubt—but I think he strug-

10. *Dearest Isa*, p. 371.

gles against these. . . ."[11] In brief, the poet saw in Napoleon III the man who is constantly pulled first one way and then the other by the contradictory thrusts of his personality: "he meant to do what I say," Browning wrote to Isa Blagden, "and, but for the weakness . . . could have done what I say he did not."[12] This is to say that for Browning the Emperor was a complex personality whose ideals and actions were frequently antithetical.

In his youthful poetry Browning had written of the romantic desire for the ideal untethered to the real and had portrayed characters, like Paracelsus and the lover of Pauline, who sought the infinite without regard to physical and psychological limitations and thus failed. But by and large the poet had, in his middle years, ceased to be interested in these conflicting forces. He focussed instead on those personages who, if idealistic by bent, achieved their goals without compromising with the world's claims, or who, if material-minded, fought for their desiderata without reference to an ideal conception of the way the world might be. In short, he pictured individuals either unbothered by or not subject to contending demands of personality. This is admittedly only a partially accurate generalization, but we have only to recall the Grammarian, the coda to "The Statue and the Bust," Pompilia, and Guido to see its partial truth.

Yet in 1871 Browning began once again to examine individuals whose actions were to some degree paralyzed by an unhappy blending in their temperaments of these conflicting desires.[13] It was, then, all the more important that he discover a form which would allow expression of the various sides of man's nature. The solution as to which form would best serve apparently came to him while he was vacationing in Perthshire in the summer of 1871.[14] And he was so pleased with the solution that he declared to Miss

11. *Browning to his American Friends*, p. 167.
12. *Dearest Isa*, p. 371.
13. The reason for this renewed interest, which continued with the writing of *Fifine at the Fair* and *Red Cotton Night-Cap Country* in 1872 and 1873, may not be far to find if we remember one particular biographical fact: namely, Browning's proposal of marriage to Louisa Lady Ashburton in September 1869. Browning made his proposal in the frankest terms and on the most practical grounds, telling the lady that his son needed a mother but that as far as his heart was concerned it was buried with his dead wife in Florence. Naturally the offer was rejected. The ensuing guilt on the poet's part for his unfaithfulness to the spirit of his beloved wife may well have contributed to the conception and composition of *Prince Hohenstiel-Schwangau*. Here in this story of a man torn between his highest ideals and the practicalities of life which sully those ideals Browning may have recognized some of his own shortcomings. For the Ashburton affair as it may have informed *Fifine at the Fair* see W. O. Raymond, *The Infinite Moment and Other Essays in Robert Browning*, 2nd ed. (Toronto, 1965), ch. 7, pp. 105–28.
14. Although he wrote Edith Story on 1 Jan. 1872, that he "conceived the poem,

Blagden: "I never at any time in my life turned a holiday into such an occasion of work." [15] It was evidently his pleasure with the form which made
him hold so high an opinion of the poem which critics have almost universally dispraised and which he himself came later to misprize.

The poem implicitly asks this question: why do men with good intentions
fail to attain to what they aspire? And the answer provided is that the
human personality is never adequate to the demands made upon it. For
with imperfect eyes and imperfect speech man never can properly visualize
or verbalize the promptings of his soul. Once those aspirations are brought
up from the depths of the self into the light of external reality they are, by
the very nature of the world, deflected from their true intent. And it is this
truth which the speaker of the poem learns from his attempted multifaceted
examination of himself.

Yet to ask and answer a question about the nature of man and the world
is not the purpose of the Prince's speech. In so far as it has any motivation at
all it is simply that which he provides—"Revealment of myself!" (22),
talking for the sheer love of it. Commentators have called the monologue
"a defence of the doctrine of expediency" [16] and have spoken of the Prince
as one of Browning's great casuists. [17] Yet in so far as casuistry implies de-
ception the Prince is no casuist at all. For though there is an initial pretence
of an auditor—and this mainly to provide a dramatic context in which the
monologue might occur—the Prince is speaking solely to himself. Only as
the monologue progresses does it become clear that the revelation is to
himself, which means justification of himself to himself. As it begins
the monologue evidently has no strategic purpose at all. If Hohenstiel-
Schwangau is an unreliable narrator, it is not by design but from lack of
self-understanding.

The first part of his monologue is spoken *in propria persona*. Here the
Prince attempts to justify his conservative rule:

> To save society was well: the means
> Whereby to save it,—there begins the doubt
> Permitted you, imperative on me;

---

twelve years ago in the Via del Tritone," he evidently meant that he had thought of
writing a monologue about Napoleon III. It was only in Perthshire that "a little hand-
breadth of prose" was "breathed out into this full-blown bubble in a couple of months
this autumn that is gone." *Browning to his American Friends*, p. 167.

15. *Dearest Isa*, p. 367.                    16. Mrs. Sutherland Orr, p. 161.

17. See especially Raymond's chapter on "Browning's Casuists" in *The Infinite
Moment*, pp. 129-55.

Were mine the best means? Did I work aright
With powers appointed me?—since powers denied
Concern me nothing.

(701–6)

His defense is that he has acted in a practical manner: if he has not done all
that social visionaries would have him do, it is because he has first had to
devote himself to the immediate needs of his people. He recognized the
importance of idealism in politics, but he was also aware that he had to
assure his people sufficient material sustenance:

No, my brave thinkers, whom I recognize,
Gladly, myself the first, as, in a sense,
All that our world's worth, flower and fruit of man!
Such minds myself award supremacy
Over the common insignificance,
When only Mind's in question,—Body bows
To quite another government, you know.

(1101–7)

But the more he talks the less convincing he finds himself to be, and he
commences to perceive that his career may not have been quite so al-
truistic or even so successful as in the beginning he made claims to. For in
speaking he half realizes that what he consciously thought himself to be
may not be what in fact he is:

you know the thing I tried to do!
All, so far, to my praise and glory—all
Told as befits the self-apologist,—
Who ever promises a candid sweep
And clearance of those errors miscalled crimes
None knows more, none laments so much as he,
And ever rises from confession, proved
A god whose fault was—trying to be man.
Just so, fair judge,—if I read smile aright—
I condescend to figure in your eyes
As biggest heart and best of Europe's friends,
And hence my failure. God will estimate
Success one day; and, in the mean time—you!

(1201–13)

The insight is evanescent but it is signified by the Prince's semijocular admission that he is a "failure" (1212) and one of life's "losers" (1217). Having so confessed, he immediately shifts perspective from "Autobiography" (1220) to biography, from a first- to a third-person narrative. Human kind can bear only so much reality.

The second part of the poem is what Hohenstiel-Schwangau terms "pure blame, history / And falsehood"—"what I never was, but might have been" (1221–22, 1224). It is offered as a counterbalance to what has already been recounted of "my praise and glory . . . as befits the self-apologist" (1202–3). But we soon see that the second half, which is told from two points of view—the Head Servant, the idealized ruler, and Sagacity, the shrewd opportunist—is but yet another strategy in self-apology. For the speaker claims always to have acted as the Head Servant and to have turned a deaf ear to the unprincipled pleas of Sagacity.

Yet here the speaker has as much difficulty in convincing himself that he has followed the highest ideals as he had in the first part in pretending that he acted practically but altruistically:

> (Veracious and imaginary Thiers,
> Who map out thus the life I might have led,
> But did not,—all the worse for earth and me—
> Doff spectacles, wipe pen, shut book, decamp!)
>                                        (2084–87)

For the truth is that he has been both idealistic and opportunistic. In other words Hohenstiel-Schwangau has had no consistent political philosophy: he has acted as it suited him at the moment. This does not mean that he has been an evil ruler; it signifies only that he is a man who has been aware of the right steps to take but has frequently not taken them. This is but one aspect of the Prince's personality that he and we discover. There are sill others.

The speaker begins by claiming to be a man of boundless energy, one who must always be doing: "Better to draw than leave undrawn, I think, / Fitter to do than let alone, I hold" (39–40), for "it is my nature . . . to put a thought . . . Into an act" (80–84). Moreover, it is his "mission" to act (277). We begin to suspect a bit of self-delusion when we learn that all his alleged energy in action was directed towards "sustainment" (710)—this because, he claims, a man has not sufficient time in one life span to put to right the ills of the world. Therefore his enemies, far from accusing him of reckless action, charge him with "indolence, / Apathy, hesitation" (1179–80).

No, his is not the gift to make "what is absolutely new"; rather, his talent lies in turning "to best account the thing that's half-made": "I make the best of the old, nor try for new. / Such will to act... Constitute[s] ... my own / Particular faculty of serving God" (268–73). If things are not better than one could wish, they might well be worse. If he has not followed the visionary and socially dislocating schemes of Comte and Fourier, the Prince at least has kept society together. In sum, he has "held the balance straight" (473) by meeting the people's immediate needs.

It is here that the Prince begins to defend himself against the charge of expediency. His justification of his unwillingness or his inability to reform social evils is that he did what, at the time, it was possible to do. Yet what he does not allow or perhaps even comprehend is that the feebleness of his actions stemmed, in large part, from his incapacity to make up his mind what he should be undertaking. For the longer he talks the more we see in him an uneasy combination of good and ill, of democratic sympathies and imperial designs.[18]

In many cases there can be no doubt that he wants to do the right thing. Yet it is difficult for him to act in accordance with his nobler aspirations because "I found earth was not air" (903): while Mind might advance in one direction, "Body bows / To quite another government" (1106–7). Every time he would follow his nobler impulses he feels forced by immediate practical necessity to take a different course. In short, Hohenstiel-Schwangau argues that his ideals have had to yield to realities—the descendental, in Carlylean terms, ever triumphing over the transcendental.[19] If the world were different, he would act differently. But imperfect nature is ever a bar to the realization of nobler hopes. Hence he must discourage the Comtes, Fouriers, and Proudhons who would give his people only beautiful dreams instead of the bread they need to feed their hungry stomachs:

18. Maisie Ward wisely observes: "Perhaps one reason which makes it so difficult to understand Browning's *Prince Hohenstiel-Schwangau Saviour of Society* is that it is almost impossible to understand Napoleon III." *Robert Browning and His World: The Private Face (1812–1861)* (London, 1968), p. 278.

19. The name sounds as though it were borrowed from *Sartor Resartus*. If Browning took the name from the eccentric King Ludwig's beautiful palace Hohenschwangau, he might have intended it to suggest the polarities of the Prince's personality and the frequently antithetical nature of his actions. Browning said that Napoleon III "wants ... to serve God & the Devil, and will succeed no better than anybody else." *Dearest Isa*, p. 302.

> Mankind i' the main have little wants, not large:
> I, being of will and power to help, i' the main,
> Mankind, must help the least wants first.
>
> $$(1057-59)$$

But the truth is that, neither "creator nor destroyer" (299), the Prince has revealed himself akin to Milton's Belial, content with eking out a little life from dried tubers. Better to be, he seems to claim, no matter what the condition, than cease to be.

Though he is sarcastic about the Thiers-Hugo version of his life which forms more than a third of the poem, this heroic history is a perfect analogue not only of the Prince's self-justification in the preceding 1200 lines but also of his whole existence. The vacillation between high ideals and the demands of practicality has made him impotent to act. Though he claims to possess abundant energy, he has led a life of constant frustration because, torn by the conflicting claims of his nature, he has not known how to channel that energy in a proper direction.

What we have, then, is an indecisive ruler whose only claim to decent rule has been "sustainment"—and this, given his nature, because he could not do otherwise. Of course like Fourier he has had his visions, but they have always met with revisions. Between the conception and the creation there fell the shadow of indecisiveness. Thus the monologue ends with what is to be his last great moment of indecision—and incidentally the great irony of the poem. Should he foreswear the imperialistic idea or not? "Double or quits! The letter goes! Or stays?"[20]

Yet for whatever he did or did not do Hohenstiel-Schwangau refuses to be held accountable. He has acted only in accordance with the "law" enjoined upon him. He tells his fictitious listener that in order to reveal himself he must make plain "the law by which I lived" (26). This is, he says, the only means by which a man's life can be understood, how all the "facts" of one's existence can be connected: "Rays from all round converge to any point: / Study the point then ere you track the rays" (65–66).

His "law" has been to act independently in the service of God—that is, to do God's bidding. Other men, of course, may have "Another law" (171). God imposed a duty upon him and he has tried to discharge it in every way possible, even if at times the commission seemed contrary to what his own better nature urged: "Such is the reason why I acquiesced / In doing

---

20. As Browning says in a letter, the decision to commence the war was made by the Emperor's wife, not by the man himself: he "engaged in this awful war because his wife plagued him." *Dearest Isa*, p. 371.

what seemed best for me to do" (231–32). Therefore he did not only what "head and heart / Prescribed my hand" but also used "every sort of helpful circumstance, / Some problematic and some nondescript" (235–40). In short it was his "law" to be what he is and to do what he has done (246–50). His "mission" was "to rule men—men within my reach" and to "order, influence and dispose them so / As render solid and stabilify / Mankind in particles" (277–80). If he is pleased to act in a certain way, it is because he takes pleasure in doing God's will; thus he rules men "For their good and my pleasure in the act" (282). Hence all is excused by this "law" divinely mandated.

The circularity of his views is exemplified throughout the poem by the Prince's frequent appeals to law for justification of himself and of the *status quo*. Just as his "Particular faculty of serving God" is to "make the best of the old, nor try for new" (268–73), so to conserve the present order is to work with God. God had a plan in making things as they are, and "my task was to co-operate / Rather than play the rival, chop and change / The order whence comes all the good we know" (620–22). Further, only in an imperfect world—"this same society I save"—can a man prove his devotion to God; and for that reason Hohenstiel-Schwangau has rapped the tampering knuckles of the idealistic reformers for twenty years to prevent them from setting up a society in which pity, courage, and hope could not be experienced. Yes, "Such was the task imposed me, such my end" (639–48).

It would be tedious to point out all the instances in which the speaker justifies himself by appeal to law and too obvious to examine the contradictions of his various appeals. It is sufficient simply to say that the word "law" occurs with greater frequency in *Prince Hohenstiel-Schwangau* than in any other of Browning's poems, as a glance at the Broughton and Stelter Concordance will indicate. In each case the "law" of which the Prince speaks is his interpretation of what he feels God has enjoined upon him. To ask how he knows what God wishes for him is to ask a question which the Prince himself does not pose.

Such rationalization for his lack of deeds is carried on at the conscious level. This is not to say that his design is to deceive, only to state that in excusing himself for inaction he is aware of what he is doing. Yet on a less conscious plane Hohenstiel-Schwangau reveals another aspect of his nature which, if understood by the speaker, is never openly expressed. In this connection it is instructive to inquire why he chooses such an imaginary auditor for his revelation. Mrs. Sutherland Orr suggests that "his choice of a *confidante* suits the nature of what he has to tell, as well as the circum-stances in which he tells it. Politically, he has lived from hand to mouth. So in a different way has she."[21] But it is not that Hohenstiel-Schwangau finds a fitting analogue for his political prostitution in the imaginary lady of the streets. Rather it is that his choice of listener reflects more than a little about himself.

For the Prince is by nature a voluptuary. We have hints in the opening lines, where the "bud-mouth" is fancied to be an Oedipus who lurks "Under a pork-pie hat and crinoline, / And, lateish, pounce on Sphinx in Leicester Square" and who "finds me hardly gray, and likes my nose, / And thinks a man of sixty at the prime." We have further intimations when throughout he dwells on the delights of cigar-smoking, and at the close of the mono-logue spoken in his own (rather than imagined) voice when he sends "this final puff . . . / To die up yonder in the ceiling-rose" (1215–16). And finally our suspicions tend to be confirmed when we are told that the speaker is not in a London cafe with a prostitute but is day-dreaming in the Resi-dency: "Alone,—no such congenial intercourse!" (2145). It would be a mistake to label the poem an erotic reverie, yet the sensual and specifically sexual elements should not be overlooked.[22] For they all point to the Prince as *homme sensuel* instead of man of action as he initially thinks himself.

Through his monologue the speaker reveals himself to the imaginary Lais (and to the reader) as a different kind of man from that whom he believes himself presenting. She and we learn that he is an indecisive volup-tuary. But what does he reveal to himself? At the start he had promised "Revealment of myself" (22) to Lais and, by implication, to himself. Does he achieve his goal? does he learn anything at all?

What Hohenstiel-Schwangau learns is what the poet himself learns: namely, that no matter how truthful one wishes to be—whether he speak from his own point of view or whether he attempt to gain another perspec-tive on himself—one ultimately is forced to lie. For no matter how objective one tries to be, all ratiocination is but rationalization: "Yes, forced to speak, one stoops to say—one's aim / Was—what it peradventure should have been" (2113–14). In the "ghostly dialogue" (2092) which takes place with-

21. *Handbook*, pp. 161–62. J. M. Cohen says: "The lady seems hardly a fitting listener to play Gigadibs to his Blougram. Indeed the personality of his curiously chosen interviewer . . . casts a preliminary aura of doubt on the value of the 'once redoubted Sphynx's' confession." *Robert Browning*, p. 129. But why this should necessarily be so I fail to comprehend.

22. Browning said of Napoleon III that "when the mask fell . . . we found a lazy and worn-out voluptuary." *Dearest Isa*, p. 356.

in the self without verbal language there is no need to justify or defend one's self and one's motives, because all claims are put "to insignificance / Beside one intimatest fact—myself / Am first to be considered" (2101–3). But try to express one's aims in words, the result is special pleading: "Somehow the motives, that did well enough / I' the darkness, when you bring them into light / Are found, like those famed cave-fish, to lack eye / And organ for the upper magnitudes" (2106–9). The result is, as the speaker discovers at the end of this monologue, that "one lies oneself / Even in the stating that one's end was truth, / Truth only, if one states as much in words" (2123–25). Yet "Words have to come"; language is man's only means for dealing with the world, even though "words deflect / As the best cannon ever rifled will" (2133–34). The only truthful statement about oneself that one can make in words is that language is inadequate for apprehension of the self. "Revealment of myself"? Impossible if one aims to tell what one is and does. If the revelation comes, it will be only by indirection, by clues that one had no notion of.

The disappointment which the Prince expresses was doubtless shared by his creator. In his quest for greater objectivity Browning had sought to overcome the most serious limitation of the dramatic monologue by combining the mode with internal dialogue. But the result was the same: the exercise of the dialogue ended in special pleading, with the speaker rationalizing his motives and actions in the same way as in the monologue *in propria persona*. No wonder then that Browning's enthusiasm for the poem flagged with its completion. For *Prince Hohenstiel-Schwangau* proved once again that the dramatic monologue was at best a very partial means by which to explore the world. It would require a good many more years of experimentation before the poet arrived at the double vision of the *Parleyings*.

But though *Prince Hohenstiel-Schwangau* did not prove to be the formal break–through that Browning had hoped, it nevertheless paints an excellent picture of a man who, for the most part knowing and wanting to do right, failed to act in accordance with his noblest aspirations. In his portrait of the character modelled on Napoleon III, Browning showed that it is in the nature of things for one's best intentions frequently to be frustrated. Hopes are born in air; their realization must take place on ground. "Once pedestalled on earth," says the Prince, "I found earth was not air" (902–3). Whatever his situation, a man is always at the mercy of the world, the devil, and the flesh—of all, in short, which constitutes phenomenal reality. Remembering this, Browning could create a verbal portrait of a complex man whom he did not admire but of whom he could charitably say when the picture was finished: "I think in the main, he meant to do what I say, and, but for the weakness,—grown more apparent in these last years than formerly,—would have done what I say he did not."[23] The "inconsistencies," "casuistries," and "tangled arguments" are owing then not to the poet's lack of control of his material but to the character of the speaker and ultimately, perhaps, to Browning's conception of human nature.

23. *Dearest Isa*, p. 371.

# A Background for Arnold's "Shakespeare"

## David J. DeLaura

*The University of Texas
at Austin*

### Shakespeare

Others abide our question. Thou art free.
We ask and ask—Thou smilest and art still,
Out-topping knowledge. For the loftiest hill,
Who to the stars uncrowns his majesty,

Planting his steadfast footsteps in the sea,
Making the heaven of heavens his dwelling-place,
Spares but the cloudy border of his base
To the foil'd searching of mortality;

And thou, who didst the stars and sunbeams know,
Self-school'd, self-scann'd, self-honour'd, self-secure,
Didst tread on earth unguess'd at.—Better so!

All pains the immortal spirit must endure,
All weakness which impairs, all griefs which bow,
Find their sole speech in that victorious brow.

MATTHEW ARNOLD's most famous sonnet is, paradoxically, a tissue of nineteenth-century commonplaces about Shakespeare and one of the most disputed of Arnold's poems. An attempt has been made to interpret the poem by a kind of "criticism by parallel," elaborating the use of cognate themes and images in other early poems by Arnold.[1] The present essay

1. By Robert A. Greenberg, in "Patterns of Imagery: Arnold's 'Shakespeare,'" *SEL*, 5 (Autumn 1965), 723–33. Apart from Greenberg and the readings by Baum and Culler mentioned below, there is a short but telling commentary in W. Stacy Johnson, *The Voices of Matthew Arnold* (New Haven, 1961), pp. 21–23. An unnoted parallel to the sonnet occurs in *Merope*, ll. 622–43, essentially about the difficulty of discovering the sources of the buried life. But the topographical imagery is a con-

explores the range of attitudes held by Arnold's contemporaries and his Romantic predecessors concerning the topics raised in the sonnet. Beyond the possibility of establishing "sources" for Arnold's ideas and phrasing, the method employed here, no doubt not beyond dispute, implies that for a "lofty" but rather obscure short poem on a familiar topic (like Arnold's) the range of allowable interpretation may plausibly be set by its "moment" in critical history.

I

The manuscript of Arnold's sonnet, one of his earliest poems, is dated 1 August 1844. A. Dwight Culler notes that this was a period of intensive research in Shakespearean biography—but with extremely meager results.[2] The "questions" put to Shakespeare by the nineteenth century were of very different orders of seriousness. The plays were generally regarded as enigmatically if "divinely" impersonal; the sonnets seemed to promise much more in the way of biographical detail and yet they too somehow withheld their secret. Where Wordsworth, defending the sonnet form, declared, "with this key / Shakespeare unlocked his heart," an indignant Browning replied, "Did Shakespeare? If so, the less Shakespeare he!"—but he was thinking of tobacco and separate bedrooms. At this level, as one later critic puts it, "When we say that we do not know Shakespeare we mean that we do not know his opinions."[3] Browning, himself a very mixed case of "dramatic" impersonality, moved to a somewhat deeper level in speaking of the "objective poet" in his 1852 "Essay on Shelley." "We are ignorant," he says, "what the inventor of 'Othello' conceived of that fact as he beheld it in completeness. . . . We are ignorant, and would fain be otherwise." This "objective" poet, who "hides himself behind his work," is a legacy from the highly influential discussion of "naive" and "sentimental" poetry set afloat for the Romantics by Schiller. It was also Schiller who complained that he "could not bear that the poet in Shakespeare could never be seized and would never give me an account of himself."[4] But there is no evidence

---

fusing mélange of "plumbing" the depths, exploring the "narrow world" of one's own heart, and scaling a "region in perpetual cloud."

2. *Imaginative Reason: The Poetry of Matthew Arnold* (New Haven and London, 1966), pp. 63ff. His own most interesting discovery is the Memoir of Shakespeare (1843) by Barry Cornwall, who not only spoke of our baffled inquiries about Shakespeare the man, but found that he "held commerce with the stars." See *Poetry and Criticism of Matthew Arnold*, ed. A. Dwight Culler (Boston, 1961), pp. 538–39.

3. Augustus Ralli, *Later Critiques* (London, 1933), p. 7.

4. First noted in Paull F. Baum, *Ten Studies in the Poetry of Matthew Arnold*

that Arnold had read Schiller by 1844; and apparently Carlyle, Arnold's chief source for his knowledge of the Germans, did not give the passage.

Carlyle's own lecture on Dante and Shakespeare in *Heroes and Hero-Worship* (1841) is plainly the chief direct source of the sonnet, and even perhaps its occasion. Kathleen Tillotson first suggested the parallels:

> To Carlyle Shakespeare was 'great, quiet, complete, *self-sufficing*', 'placid', and 'victorious' in his strength (Arnold's 'that victorious brow'), his works growing (according to Carlyle's principle of 'unconsciousness') 'as the mountains and waters shape themselves'; Carlyle emphasized the enigma of his life, 'how much in Shakespeare lies hid', 'we did not account him a god—while he dwelt among us' (Arnold's 'Did'st walk the earth unguessed at').5

To these Kenneth Allott added further parallels: "I call Shakespeare greater than Dante, in that he fought truly, and did conquer. Doubt it not, he had his own sorrows [referring to the sonnets]. . . . how could a man delineate a Hamlet, a Coriolanus, a Macbeth . . . if his own heroic heart had never suffered?"6 On the basis of this evidence, I suggest that the still puzzling and elliptical final tercet must mean: all human sorrows and struggles find their sole *adequate* expression in Shakespeare's plays because their author, beyond even a Dante, had fought through his personal sorrows and struggles and had achieved serene illumination and spiritual sovereignty (symbolized by the high smooth brow of Shakespeare's portrait or bust). The primary reference, then, in "pains," etc., is to the plays, and the "victorious brow" is a metonymy for the spiritual state of their author. The sonnets, with their direct evidence of personal sorrow, simply corroborate our intuition that a certain course of purification is required to achieve Shakespeare's otherwise "placid" and "tranquil" impersonality, his "calm creative perspicacity."7

Carlyle also provides the logical link between Shakespeare's earthly "unguess'd at" condition and the "royal solitude" where he "dwell[s] apart" (V, 85). The answer lies in Carlyle's doctrine of creative "unconsciousness." For the state achieved by Shakespeare requires that his quality of spirit be

(Durham, N.C., 1958), p. 7n. This is supplemented by Kenneth Allott in *The Poems of Matthew Arnold* (London, 1965), p. 49. Hereafter cited as *Poems*. Baum, pp. 10–11n., usefully surveys past interpretations of the final tercet.

5. *Mid-Victorian Studies* (London, 1965), p. 227.

6. *Poems*, p. 50.

7. *The Works of Thomas Carlyle*, Centenary Edition (1897–1901; rpt. New York, 1969), V, 103–4. Hereafter cited by volume and page number only.

not only unrecognized by his contemporaries ("Priceless Shakespeare was the free gift of Nature; given altogether silently;—received altogether silently as if it had been a thing of little account"; p. 103), but in a crucial sense not fully apparent to Shakespeare himself: Shakespeare's is "the greatest of Intellects," but his is also "an unconscious intellect; there is more virtue in it than he himself is aware of" (p. 107).

> Such a man's works, whatsoever he with utmost conscious exertion and forethought shall accomplish, grow withal *un*consciously, from the unknown deeps in him. . . . How much in Shakspeare lies hid; his sorrows, his silent struggles known to himself; much that was not known at all, not speakable at all: like *roots*, like sap and forces working underground! Speech is great; but Silence is greater. (p. 108)

Better so! Shakespeare became the supremely creative artist of the final tercet and "a voice of Nature," precisely *because* he not only consciously struggled against personal pain and sorrow, but also "silently" opened himself to an unconscious process below the level of mere personality. His works thus "grow up . . . *un*consciously, . . . with a symmetry grounded on Nature's own laws, conformable to all Truth whatsoever" (p. 108). The essential unity of the poem is apparent: Shakespeare's doubly unguessed-at state, his "silence" that baffles our inquiries, is the very basis of his supreme and luminous insight into nature and the human condition. He is silent in two senses: he is "victorious" in his conscious but silent triumph over personal "obstructions" (p. 104); he triumphs in a more passive and obscure way by submitting to a process of spiritual clarification sponsored by Nature itself. Carlyle puts the basis of the doctrine more abstractly elsewhere: "The uttered part of a man's life . . . bears to the unuttered unconscious part a small unknown proportion; he himself never knows it, much less do others. . . . our greatest, being also by nature our *quietest*, are perhaps those that remain unknown!"[8]

In the *Heroes* lecture, Carlyle finds Shakespeare's pattern of silence and "victorious strength and greatness" duplicated in modern times only in Goethe (V, 104, 105). Indeed, the larger background of the lecture itself is the elaborate (and highly questionable) portrait of Goethe, as the greatest of modern spiritual guides, presented in Carlyle's early essays. Goethe, we hear in 1828, "has not only suffered and mourned in bitter agony under the spiritual perplexities of his time; but he has also mastered these, he is

8. "Sir Walter Scott" (1838), XXIX, 49. The entire passage is worth study in connection with the sonnet.

above them, and has shown others how to rise above them" (XXVI, 210).
Moreover, it is hard to discover in Goethe's writings "what sort of spiritual
construction he has, what are his temper, his affections, his individual
specialities. . . . he is of no sect or caste: he seems not this man, or that
man, but a man." Here, as frequently in the essays on Goethe, Carlyle turns
to Shakespeare for an analogy, finding this quality the characteristic of "all
great Poets":

> How true it is of Shakspeare and Homer! Who knows, or can figure
> what the Man Shakspeare was, by the first, by the twentieth, perusal
> of his works? He is a Voice coming to us from the Land of Melody:
> his old brick dwellingplace . . . offers us the most inexplicable enigma.[9]

Arnold of course paid the closest attention to Carlyle's writings on Goethe.
Some have seen that the Shakespeare sonnet is connected with the view
of the lofty, impassive poet of "Resignation" who sees not deep but wide,
and with Arnold's numerous references to clarity of vision and elevated
station.[10] In effect, not only Homer, but Shakespeare and Goethe also,
stand with clear souls scanning "The Wide Prospect" ("To a Friend").[11]
Carlyle's essays on Goethe and other Germans provided a rich quarry for
the imagery of triumphant serenity and elevated impartiality.

As early as *The Life of Friedrich Schiller* (1825), Carlyle presented
Shakespeare (and then Goethe) in the very stance of the carefully disillusioned but sublimely illuminated poet of "Resignation":

> [Shakespeare] is endowed with an all-comprehending spirit; skilled,
> as if by personal experience, in all the modes of human passion and
> opinion; therefore, tolerant of all; peaceful, collected; fighting for no
> class of men or principles; rather looking on the world, and the various
> battles waging in it, with the quiet eye of one already reconciled to
> the futility of their issues; but pouring over all the forms of many-
> coloured life the light of a deep and subtle intellect, and the decora-
> tions of an overflowing fancy; and allowing men and things of every
> shape and hue to have their own free scope in his conception, as they
> have it in the world where Providence has placed them. (XXV,
> 90–91)[12]

9. XXVI, 245. Mrs. Tillotson, p. 227n., mentions this passage.
10. See Greenberg, n. 1 above, and Baum, p. 13.
11. In the "Goethe" essay (XXVI, 245), after speaking of Goethe and Shakespeare,
Carlyle continues: "And what is Homer in the *Ilias*? He is THE WITNESS; he has seen,
and he reveals it."
12. There is an anticipation of the tone and imagery of "Resignation" (and perhaps

The linkage of Goethe and Shakespeare as equally "victorious" over contradiction and suffering and as showing "others how to rise above them,"
as universally tolerant and philosophically comprehensive ("In [Shake-
speare's as in Goethe's] mind the world is a whole; he figures it as Providence governs it"; XXIII, 27), as men of "utmost Clearness" for whom the
Natural and the Supernatural "become one" (XXVII, 437), as "Prometheus-
like" men who were "open to the Universe and its influences" but not
anxious to "open" themselves to view (XXVII, 439)—all of these often-
repeated themes are central to Carlyle's early conception of the ideal artist
and his function, as they are also keys to Arnold's most "aesthetic" aspirations up through "The Scholar-Gipsy." [13] Finally, Arnold may even possibly
have found in Carlyle the inspiration for his controlling image of the brow
containing universal experience, and in connection with Shakespeare. In
"Goethe's Portrait" (1832), Carlyle speaks of Goethe's head, "the brow,
the temples, royally arched, a very palace of thought," and explains: "it is
no wonder the head should be royal and a palace; for the most royal work
was appointed to be done therein. Reader! within that head the whole
world lies mirrored, in such clear ethereal harmony as it has done in none
since Shakspeare left us" (XXVII, 372).

Others besides Arnold were speculating in the early forties on this
cluster of topics, no doubt under Carlyle's influence, since the *Critical and
Miscellaneous Essays* had been collected in 1839. In a remarkable passage
in an essay on Goethe published a year before Arnold's sonnet, G. H.
Lewes brought together several of these Carlylean themes and in doing so
anticipated Arnold with startling exactness:

> His [Goethe's] picture is before us now, the calm dominion which
> reigns there contrasting strongly with the passionate and intense ex-

---

of "Shakespeare") in the conclusion to Carlyle's 1831 "Schiller" essay: "Schiller can
seem higher than Goethe only because he is narrower. Thus to unpractised eyes, a
Peak of Teneriffe ... may seem higher than a Chimborazo; because the former rises
abruptly ... ; the latter rises gradually, carrying half a world aloft with it; only the
deeper azure of the heavens, the widened horizon, . . . disclose to the Geographer
that the 'region of Change' lies far below him" (XXVII, 214). Allott (*Poems*, p. 49)
quotes Emerson on the great poet, who "will stand out of our low limitations, like a
Chimborazo"; but since Emerson's *Essays, Second Series* did not appear until October
1844, the Carlyle essay is a far more likely source.

13. Carlyle seems at times aware of how questionable is his grouping of Shakespeare
and Goethe under a single mode of creativity. In 1832, for example, he remarks
(XXVII, 440): "What Shakspeare's thoughts on 'God, Nature, Art,' would have been,
especially had he lived to number fourscore years, were curious to know; Goethe's,
delivered in many-toned melody, as the apocalypse of our era, are here for us to
know."

pression of his great countryman, Beethoven. . . . The brow immense, lofty, wide, solid as marble and as smooth, indicates the large and well-balanced faculties, which, as in Shakespeare, puzzle you with their separate greatness, and prevent a prominence being assigned to any one. . . . The deep lines traced by time across the lower part of the face are evidences of the struggle, as the smooth and lofty brow is of the victory.[14]

II

If what has been suggested here is true about the importance of Carlyle's view of a "Shakespearean" creative mode, not only in the Shakespeare sonnet but in much of Arnold's early poetry, the still continuing neglect of Arnold's response to Carlyle noted by Mrs. Tillotson (*Mid-Victorian Studies*, p. 216n.) prevents us from adequately defining the intent of Arnold's early poetry. Still, the suggestion that Arnold expressed admiration, in the sonnet and elsewhere, for Shakespeare's "objective" and impartial treatment of universal human experience after a successful struggle to transcend his own obstructions, should not be taken to mean that Arnold's own most congenial mode was that of Schiller's "naive" or classical poet. A. Dwight Culler shrewdly observes[15] that Arnold belongs to the type of the Wordsworthian or Miltonic "Egotistical Sublime," which transmutes all of experience into a mode of the poet's self. But it is hard to accept Culler's view that Arnold's "solid and unchanging" Shakespeare is *also* of the party of the Egotistical Sublime. The problem is one of the inadequacy of categories to fit the case. One agrees with Culler that Arnold's Shakespeare is not merely Keats's "chameleon poet," who by Negative Capability loses his "identity" and enters into, and is transformed into, all other kinds of experience.[16] The fact is that the Shakespeare presented in Carlyle and in Arnold's sonnet escapes the Keatsian disjunctions by combining the two modes in a third, paradoxical, and unique union. For the Shakespeare of the sonnet, Carlyle's Shakespeare, is indeed the "protean" artist capable of sympathetic identification with all of human experience ("all things imaged in that great soul of his," V, 103; "All pains, . . . All weakness, . . . all griefs")[17] The problem comes with the other thrust of the

14. "Character and Works of Göthe," *British and Foreign Review*, 14 (1843), 85.
15. *Imaginative Reason*, p. 67.     16. Ibid.
17. The view of Shakespeare as the "unlimited" genius of course long antedates Coleridge, Hazlitt, or Keats. Near the beginning there is Dryden's ringing statement, cited below. Coming nearer, William Richardson, in 1774, said: "Possessing extreme

Keatsian ideal, the attempt to eliminate "the egoistic assertion of one's own identity."[18]

The answer is that the majestic and assured poise of Arnold's and Carlyle's hill-like and "self-secure" Shakespeare is not egotistical in the familiar sense. In Carlyle, as we saw, Shakespeare actively shapes experience, but, more importantly, he also passively opens himself to experience; in the dual process, he becomes virtually a voice of Nature itself. In Arnoldian terms, Shakespeare has risen beyond the ordinary self, the mere ego, into the universality (where "we are united, impersonal, at harmony")[19] of the real or central self, the "best self" of the later religious writings. Carlyle's and Arnold's Shakespeare had achieved a unique and higher mode of being and knowledge. He eschews all "irritable reaching after fact & reason," as he does with Keats, but he nevertheless becomes "a calmly *seeing* eye; a great intellect" (V, 104), one who *knows* the stars and sunbeams as well as human experience.

Elizabeth Barrett, not yet Mrs. Browning, was struggling in these very years with a similar set of ideas that anticipate Arnold and may throw light on his meaning. In "The Book of the Poets," a series of articles that appeared in the *Athenaeum* in June and August 1842, she came very close to Arnold's creative concerns.[20] Despite her characteristic indistinctness and a certain juggling of categories, she was exploring precisely the "third" mode, won through personal struggle, that Arnold was attempting to describe.

> the poetic temperament, halfway between the light of the ideal and the darkness of the real, and rendered by each more sensitive to the other, and unable, without a struggle, to pass out clear and calm

---

sensibility, and uncommonly susceptible, he is the Proteus of Drama: he changes himself into every character, and enters easily into every condition of human nature." Cited in Earl R. Wasserman, "Shakespeare and the Romantic Movement," in *The Persistence of Shakespeare Idolatry*, ed. Herbert M. Schueller (Detroit, 1964), p. 85.

18. The phrase is Walter Jackson Bate's, in *John Keats* (1963; rpt. New York, 1966), p. 243. The whole of ch. X, "Negative Capability," deserves the closest attention with regard to the matters raised here.

19. *The Complete Prose Works of Matthew Arnold*, ed. R. H. Super (Ann Arbor, 1960– ), V, 134. Hereafter cited as *CPW*.

20. I refer in my text to the pages of her *Essays on the English Poets and the Greek Christian Poets* (New York, 1889). She also in "A Vision of Poets" (*Poems*, 1844) suggested Arnold's Shakespeare of pains and griefs:

> There Shakespeare, on whose forehead climb
> The crowns o' the world: O eyes sublime
> With tears and laughter for all time. (ll. 298–300)

Her two volumes did not appear until 13 August, however, probably too late to have influenced Arnold, never one of her enthusiastic admirers anyway.

into either, fears the impress of the necessary conflict in dust and blood. The philosophy may be, that only the stronger spirits do accomplish this victory, having lordship over their own genius. . . . (p. 39)

After exploring other possibilities, she ends with "the highest vision of the idealist, which is subjectivity turned outward into an actual objectivity" (p. 39). "To the last triumph, Shakespeare attained" (p. 39). She attempts a formula for the self-knowledge which is universal knowledge, in these terms: "we scarcely can guess that the man Shakespeare is grave or gay, because he interposes between ourselves and his personality the whole breadth and length of his ideality. . . . He was wise in the world, having studied it in his heart; what is called 'the knowledge of the world' being just the knowledge of one heart, and certain exterior symbols" (p. 59). "Shakespeare," she concludes, "wrote from within—the beautiful; and we recognize from within—the true. He is universal, because he is individual" (p. 60).

Although he too yearned for the loftiness and the special mode of impersonality exhibited by Shakespeare, Arnold knew how greatly his own poetic tendencies diverged from Shakespeare's. We are not surprised that Arnold was agitated by the "confused multitudinousness" he saw in Keats's poetry and letters—in effect, the ideal of the chameleon poet—and that to it he opposed his own need for "an Idea of the world."[21] But the more complex Shakespearean mode also disturbed him. As he told Clough in December 1847,

> to *solve* the Universe as you try to do is as irritating as Tennyson's dawdling with its painted shell is fatiguing to me to witness: and yet I own that to *re-construct* the Universe is not a satisfactory attempt either—I keep saying, Shakspeare, Shakspeare, you are as obscure as life is: yet this unsatisfactoriness goes against the poetic office in general: for this must I think certainly be its end. But have I been inside you or Shakespeare? Never. (*LC*, p. 63)

Though the grammar is rather uncertain, Arnold seems to be ascribing the "re-constructive" mode to Shakespeare: he is unhappy in his own dissatisfaction with a mode he admits is the proper "end" of poetry. A chief reason for his uneasiness is his finding Shakespeare as "obscure" as the life he reshapes. This is again the paradoxical Shakespeare of Carlyle and of the

---

21. *The Letters of Matthew Arnold to Arthur Hugh Clough*, ed. Howard Foster Lowry (London and New York, 1932), pp. 96–97; after Sept. 1848–49. Hereafter cited as *LC*.

sonnet: infinitely penetrative and comprehensive, but working from a self above "self," not apprehensible to the reader. That reconstructive power was linked by Carlyle with the high poet's special mode of "Insight" and "Spiritual Wisdom": "The true Sovereign of the World, who moulds the world like soft wax, according to his pleasure, is he who lovingly *sees* into the world; the 'inspired thinker,' whom in these days we name Poet" (XXVII, 377). Or again: "For Goethe, as for Shakspeare, the world lies all translucent, all *fusible* we might call it, encircled with WONDER"—a quality then linked with their "majestic Calmness" and "their perfect tolerance for all men and all things" (XXVII, 437–38).

At the center of Shakespeare's distressing obscurity was this morally ambiguous universal tolerance—somehow like that of Providence itself (as Carlyle and the Romantics had said) but also baffling all our usual moral and intellectual categories ("We ask and ask—Thou smilest and art still"). Arnold tried hard to give this admittedly highest mode its due. That is the significance of the note in the Yale MS:

> The easy tone of a Shakspeare suits the immoral-vulgar: the moralist conscious of his own imperfection & strain, admires it: but what does the poet's own conscience say to it—what would he say at seeing his easy morality erected by Germans & others into a system of life, & a thing to be held in view as an object for inward disciplining of oneself towards. He would say—You fools—I have walked thro: life $\epsilon\pi\iota$ $\xi\upsilon\rho\upsilon$ $\alpha\kappa\mu\eta\varsigma$ God knows how—if you mistake my razor edge, you damned pedants, for a bridge, a nice mess you will make of your own & others' walk & conversation.[22]

This is the high and almost indifferent Shakespeare, shorn even of the exemplary role assigned to him (by association with Goethe) in Carlyle. A number of Arnold's early poetic experiments must be seen as attempts,

22. C. B. Tinker and H. F. Lowry, *The Poetry of Matthew Arnold: A Commentary* (London, 1940), p. 25. Thomas Arnold, it should be noted, "was troubled by Shakespeare's apparent inability to create good men." See Arnold Whitridge, *Arnold of Rugby* (London, 1928), p. 42. Earlier "moralists," too, had by no means always admired Shakespeare's "easy morality." Johnson, above all, was disturbed that Shakespeare "sacrifices virtue to convenience, and is so much more careful to please than to instruct, that he seems to write without any moral purpose. . . . his precepts and axioms drop casually from him; he makes no just distribution of good and evil, nor is always careful to shew in the virtuous a disapprobation of the wicked; he carries his persons indifferently through right and wrong, and at the close dismisses them without further care, and leaves their examples to operate by chance." Johnson's Preface to Shakespeare, 1765, in *Johnson on Shakespeare*, ed. Arthur Sherbo, 2 vols. (New Haven and London, 1968), I, 71; vol. VII of *The Yale Edition of the Works of Samuel Johnson*.

in this Shakespearean mode, to "see" rather than "solve" the Universe. In May 1848 he had denounced Clough as 'a mere d——d depth hunter in poetry and therefore exclusive furiously" ( *LC*, p. 81). But by July a surprisingly abashed Arnold admits that something is going wrong; he tells Clough:

> The spectacle of a writer [like Clough] striving evidently to get breast to breast with reality is always full of instruction and very invigorating —and here I always feel you have the advantage of me: 'much may be seen, tho: nothing can be solved'—weighs upon me in writing. However it must be continued to tread the wine press alone. ( *LC*, p. 86)

The detached mode went increasingly wrong, as Arnold's distressful poems of 1849 and 1850 testify, until he gave up the task in favor of getting breast to breast with reality himself.[23] A minor symptom is Arnold's lifelong avoidance of extended critical encounter with Shakespeare, usually mentioned only cursorily or in formulas. The culmination comes in an article of 1884, when Arnold had long since abandoned the balance of the Shakespeare sonnet or the moral detachment of the Yale MS note. The "master-thought" and "governing motive" of Shakespeare's work, we are told, lies in the maxim, " 'Let the good prevail' "—though he hedges by defining "the morality of Shakspeare" as his dealing with "the life of all of us—the life of man in its fulness and greatness."[24]

III

The problems presented by Shakespeare, especially that of the role of the self in poetry, are at the heart of Romantic poetics. More specifically, behind the Shakespeare of Carlyle and Arnold rises the small mountain of eighteenth-century and Romantic Shakespeare criticism. It seems evident that Carlyle knew the Shakespeare commentary of Hazlitt and Coleridge,

23. See Kenneth Allott, "A Background for Arnold's 'Empedocles on Etna,' " *Essays and Studies*, ns 21 (1968), 80–100, for the most convincing brief treatment of the breakdown of Arnold's poetic struggles.

24. "George Sand," *The Works of Matthew Arnold* (London, 1904), IV, 246–47. The best, if rather severe, account of Arnold's "fumbling and uncertain" handling of Shakespeare occurs in John Shepard Eells, Jr., *The Touchstones of Matthew Arnold* (New Haven, n.d.), chs. VII and VIII, and p. 170. He concludes (p. 220) that "Shakespeare eluded Arnold's theories, and offended his principles of morality and style." E. K. Brown ("Matthew Arnold and the Elizabethans," *UTQ*, 1 [April 1932], 333–51) finds that Shakespeare, who was not "modern" in the way Sophocles and Goethe were, "does not seem to have meant much to Matthew Arnold" (p. 346). The topic cries out for fuller development.

and that he probably read them again not long before composing the
Shakespeare lecture in *Heroes* in the spring of 1840. Arnold's is a different
case. Despite his evident wide reading in the Romantic poets, and his lifelong if variable interest in them, he left remarkably few traces of any
reading in the major Romantic prose writers. Of Lamb, Hazlitt, and De
Quincey, there is virtually no mention;[25] and even his reading of Coleridge
has to be reconstructed out of scanty external evidence. I have discussed
elsewhere the possibility of Arnold's having read in Hazlitt.[26] Here, I
want to suggest that Arnold may have read—as Carlyle almost certainly
did read—Hazlitt's Shakespeare criticism, and that the closest parallels to
the sonnet are precisely in the area of Shakespeare's problematic and paradoxical "selfhood."

   Hazlitt's too frequent references to Shakespeare's comprehensiveness
("the most universal genius that ever lived") have a background in a view
he himself cites from Pope: "he is not so much an imitator, as an instrument
of nature; and it is not so just to say that he speaks from her, as that she
speaks through him." [27] Behind both men is Dryden's view of Shakespeare's
paradoxical *inward* universality. Shakespeare, he said,

> was the man who of all modern, and perhaps ancient poets, had the
> largest and most comprehensive soul. All the images of nature were
> still [i.e., always] present to him, and he drew them, not laboriously,
> but luckily. . . . he needed not the spectacles of books to read nature;
> he looked inwards, and found her there.[28]

In Dryden's "lucky" inwardness is a hint of the conscious-unconsciousness
that Hazlitt dwells upon and bequeathed to Carlyle—and perhaps Arnold.
Obviously Carlyle took note of Hazlitt's emphasis on Shakespeare's "unconscious power of mind which is as true to nature as itself" and his view
that the "peculiar property" of Shakespeare's imagination was his ability
to keep men and women "distinct" as they would be in reality, "accompanied with the unconsciousness of nature: indeed, imagination to be
perfect must be unconscious . . . ; for nature is so" (Howe, V, 49; IV, 294).
This theme reaches its most paradoxical state (and suggests the topography

   25. There is a fleeting reference to Lamb's Shakespeare criticism in 1864: see *CPW*,
III, 250.
   26. "Arnold and Hazlitt," *English Language Notes*, 9 (June 1972), 277–83.
   27. *The Complete Works of William Hazlitt*, ed. P. P. Howe (London, 1930–34),
IV, 238, 171. Hereafter cited as Howe.
   28. John Dryden, "An Essay of Dramatic Poesy," *Dramatic Essays*, Everyman's
Library (London, 1912), p. 40.

of Arnold's sonnet) when, in a passage translated from Schlegel, it is combined with images of height and depth, with a "Coleridgean" reconciliation of opposites, and with the special mode of childlike passivity later emphasized by Carlyle:

> He unites in his genius the utmost elevation and the utmost depth; and the most foreign, and even apparently irreconcileable properties subsist in him peaceably together. The world of spirits and nature have all laid their treasures at his feet. In strength a demi-god, in profundity of view a prophet, in all-seeing wisdom a protecting spirit of a higher order, he lowers himself to mortals, as if unconscious of his superiority: and is as open and unassuming as a child. (Howe, IV, 174)

Arnold's awkward image of Shakespeare "Planting his steadfast footsteps," the Shakespeare who "didst tread" (1849: walk) on earth, and who expressed all human pains, weakness, and grief, is anticipated in a striking passage in Hazlitt's *Lectures on the English Comic Writers*:

> [Shakespeare] is the only tragic poet in the world in the highest sense, as being on a par with, and the same as Nature, in her greatest heights and depths of action and suffering. There is but one who durst walk within that mighty circle, treading the utmost bound of nature and passion, shewing us the dread abyss of woe in all its ghastly shapes and colours, and laying open all the faculties of the human soul to act, to think, and suffer, in direct extremities. . . . (Howe, VI, 30–31)

At the bottom of such hyperboles is Hazlitt's attempt to define Shakespeare's special mode of working, in a self above the biographical self or an ego above egoism. Arnold would have been attracted to Hazlitt's discussion of Shakespeare's own self-discovery. In the poems and sonnets Shakespeare

> was a mere author, though not a common author. It was only by representing others, that he became himself. . . . There was . . . something of modesty, and a painful sense of personal propriety at the bottom of this. Shakespear's imagination, by identifying itself with the strongest characters in the most trying circumstances, grappled at once with nature, and trampled the littleness of art under his feet. . . . (Howe, IV, 357–58)

A related theme is Shakespeare's almost divine moral impartiality which at once attracted Arnold (as in the Yale MS note) and troubled him (as in the letter to Clough of 1848–49). Even the rhythm of the final tercet of Arnold's sonnet is anticipated in the conclusion of this passage from *Lectures on the English Poets* (1818):

> The striking peculiarity of Shakspeare's mind was its generic quality, its power of communication with all other minds—so that it contained a universe of thought and feeling within itself and no one peculiar bias, or exclusive excellence more than another. He was just like any other man, but that he was like all other men. He was the least of an egotist that it was possible to be. He was nothing in himself; but he was all that others were, or that they could become. (Howe, V, 47)

Like Keats, the Arnold of the MS note was drawn to the almost Providential tolerance of Shakespeare described by Hazlitt: "His genius shone equally on the evil and on the good, on the wise and the foolish" (Howe, V, 47).29 Even closer to Arnold in the 1853 Preface is Hazlitt's contrast of Shakespeare with "a modern school of poetry," that of the Romantics, which he defines as an "experiment to reduce poetry to a mere effusion of natural sensibility; or what is worse, to divest it both of imaginary splendour and human passion, to surround the meanest objects with the morbid feelings and devouring egotism of the writers' own minds" (Howe, V, 53). The extremity of paradox is reached in a more out of the way passage in *Table Talk* (1821):

> Shakespear (almost alone) seems to have been a man of genius, raised above the definition of genius. 'Born universal heir to all humanity,' he was 'as one, in suffering all who suffered nothing;' [*Ham.* III. ii. 71] with a perfect sympathy for all things, yet alike indifferent to all: who did not tamper with nature or warp her to his own purposes; who 'knew all qualities with a learned spirit,' [*Othello* III. iii. 353] instead of judging of them by his own predilections; and was rather 'a pipe for the Muse's finger to play what stop she pleased,' [*Ham.* III. ii. 75] than anxious to set up any character or pretensions of his own. (Howe, VIII, 42)

---

29. "Shakespear," we hear, "never committed himself to his characters. . . . He has no prejudices for or against them; and it seems a matter of perfect indifference whether he shall be in jest or earnest" (Howe, IV, 225).

I think it clear that Hamlet's description of Horatio "as one in suffering all who suffered nothing," difficult as it is to paraphrase, brings us close to the paradox attempted in the conclusion of Arnold's sonnet. In any event, Horatio, "A man that fortune's buffets and rewards / Hast ta'en with equal thanks," a "man / That is not passion's slave," is not very different from the "poet" in Arnold's "Resignation." And always in Hazlitt, as in the sonnet, Shakespeare remains "free," somehow above even his own self-transcending activities: "Shakespear's genius was . . . greater than any thing he has done, because it still soared free and unconfined beyond whatever he undertook —ran over, and could not be 'constrained by mastery' of his subject" (Howe, XII, 197).[30]

IV

And there is Coleridge's Shakespeare criticism, as it may lie behind Hazlitt and Carlyle, a topic too complex to be developed here. We must concentrate on what of Coleridge's views of Shakespeare Arnold might have known, in the four main sources: *Biographia Literaria, The Friend, Table Talk*, and *Literary Remains*.[31] Coleridge established, in a more philosophical way, most of the points elaborated by Hazlitt and Carlyle.[32] In chapter XIV of the *Biographia*, we are told that a sign of genius is "the choice of subjects very remote from the private interests and circumstances of the writer himself," the poet "himself meanwhile unparticipating in the passions."[33] The reader's closest attention is required in "Venus and Adonis"

30. And in the lecture on Shakespeare and Ben Jonson: Shakespeare's "imagination was the leading and master-quality of his mind, which was always ready to soar into its native element" (VI, 32).

31. Thomas Arnold knew and admired both *Table Talk* and the first two volumes of *Literary Remains*, and owned at least the latter. See letters of 12 Oct. 1835 and 16 Nov. 1836, in Arthur Penrhyn Stanley, *The Life and Correspondence of Thomas Arnold*, 7th ed. (London, 1852), pp. 347, 394. Matthew Arnold himself acquired, at an unknown date, both the *Literary Remains*, 4 vols. (1836–39) and the *Biographia Literaria*—the latter, surprisingly, uncut. See Roger L. Brooks, "Some Additions to Matthew Arnold's Library," *PBSA*, 65 (First Quarter 1971), 69–70. Arnold refers familiarly to *The Friend* in 1848: see *LC*, p. 80. There is a casual reference to Coleridge's Shakespeare criticism in the Preface to *Merope* (written 1857): *CPW*, I, 61. I have elsewhere suggested that Coleridge's portrait of Hamlet may have influenced Arnold's "Empedocles on Etna": see "Coleridge, Hamlet, and Arnold's Empedocles," in *Papers on Language and Literature*, 8, supplement (Fall 1972), 17–25.

32. René Wellek, *A History of Modern Criticism: 1750–1950*, vol. II: *The Romantic Age* (New Haven, 1955), p. 188, nevertheless stresses not only the "very different" philosophical assumptions of Coleridge and Hazlitt, but their "utterly different" critical methods—Coleridge being "primarily a theorist handling general ideas," Hazlitt "a practical critic."

33. *Biographia Literaria*, ed. J. Shawcross (London, 1907), II, 14, 15. Hereafter cited as *BL*.

because of "the alienation, and, if I may hazard such an expression, the utter *aloofness* of the poet's own feelings from those of which he is at once the painter and the analyst" (*BL*, II, 15–16). The clear-but-obscure Shakespeare that so troubled Arnold is neatly formulated: "You seem to be told nothing, but to see and hear everything" (II, 15). And finally, Shakespeare on the summit of the mountain: Shakespeare, "no passive vehicle of inspiration," who "meditated deeply" until intuitive knowledge "wedded itself to his habitual feelings" and

> gave birth to that stupendous power, by which he stands alone, with no equal or second in his own class; to that power which seated him on one of the two glory-smitten summits of the poetic mountain, with Milton as his compeer, not rival. While the former darts himself forth, and passes into all the forms of human character and passion, the one Proteus of the fire and the flood; the other attracts all forms and things to himself, into the unity of his own IDEAL. All things and modes of action shape themselves anew in the being of MILTON; while SHAKESPEARE becomes all things, yet for ever remaining himself. (*BL*, II, 19–20)

This is essentially Arnold's version of the protean Shakespeare, who expresses all human passion out of a higher and special unity of self.[34] The contrast between the "egoistic" Milton and the protean Shakespeare becomes of course a commonplace of Romantic poetics. But Coleridge's Shakespeare, like Arnold's, is not merely the "chameleon" poet. For Coleridge, Shakespeare is not simply passive or a "mere child of nature," but a deeply meditative spirit, who, though he becomes all things, nevertheless retains a tall and "aloof" integrity of self. Similarly, Arnold presents Shakespeare's lofty and inexplicable integrity ("Self-school'd, self-scann'd, . . . self-secure") as the very source of his ability to express all human suffering.

*Table Talk* includes a number of remarks that explain the special Shake-

34. Coleridge also stresses the "calm and tranquil temper" of Shakespeare, his "evenness and sweetness of temper," and his indifference and resignation regarding "immediate reputation," though he was not ignorant of "his own comparative greatness" (*BL*, I, 21). Despite T. S. Eliot's reiterated scorn for Coleridge's Hamlet criticism (*Selected Essays*, 3rd ed., [London, 1951], pp. 33, 141), his own "impersonal" theory of poetry is frequently developed in terms that recall the Romantic view of Shakespeare as the "aloof" and impersonal poet. The following, from "Shakespeare and the Stoicism of Seneca" (*Selected Essays*, p. 137), approaches the tone and point of Carlyle's lecture and Arnold's sonnet: "Shakespeare . . . was occupied with the struggle—which alone constitutes life for a poet—to transmute his personal and private agonies into something rich and strange, something universal and impersonal."

spearean mode. First, the poetry does not proceed from "the individual Shakspeare": "Shakspeare is the Spinozistic deity—an omnipresent creativeness. Milton is the deity of prescience; he stands *ab extra*. . . . Shakspeare's poetry is characterless; that is, it does not reflect the individual Shakspeare; but John Milton himself is in every line of the Paradise Lost."[35] This special kind of "subjectivity" is explained in another entry: "There is no subjectivity whatever in the Homeric poetry. There is a subjectivity of the poet, as of Milton, who is himself before himself in everything he writes; and there is a subjectivity of the *persona*, or dramatic character, as in all Shakspeare's great creations, Hamlet, Lear &c."[36] Coleridge's distinction-between the "individual" I and the "*I* representative" is also the subject of an important passage in *Literary Remains*:

Shakspeare shaped his characters out of the nature within; but we cannot so safely say, out of his own nature as an individual person. No! this latter is itself but a *natura naturata*—an effect, a product, not a power. It was Shakspeare's prerogative to have the universal, which is potentially in each particular, opened out to him, the *homo generalis*, not as an abstraction from observation of a variety of men, but as the substance capable of endless modifications, of which his own personal existence was but one, and to use this one as the eye that beheld the other, and as the tongue that could convey the discovery. There is no greater or more common vice in dramatic writers than to draw out of themselves. . . . Shakspeare, in composing, had no *I*, but the *I* representative.[37]

35. *Table Talk* (1835 ed.), 12 May 1830; cited in *Coleridge's Shakespearean Criticism*, ed. Thomas Middleton Raysor (Cambridge, Mass., 1930), II, 352–53. Hereafter cited as *SC*.

36. 21 May 1830; cited in *Coleridge's Miscellaneous Criticism*, ed. Thomas Middleton Raysor (Cambridge, Mass. 1936), p. 405. Hereafter cited as *MC*.

37. *Literary Remains* (1836–39; rpt. New York, 1967), I, 105–6. Hereafter cited as *LR*. Raysor corrected most of the texts in *Literary Remains*, but I have given the passage as Arnold would have read it. The difficult concept in this passage is partly explained in one of Collier's reports of the lectures of 1811–12 (which Arnold could not have seen until 1856): Shakespeare's being "out of time" enabled him "to paint truly, and according to the colouring of nature, a vast number of personages by the simple force of meditation: he had only to imitate certain parts of his own character, or to exaggerate such as existed in possibility, and they were at once true to nature, and fragments of the divine mind that drew them. . . . the characters of our great poet . . . are still nature, still Shakespeare, and the creatures of his meditation" (*SC*, II, 117). Or from the lectures of 1808: "Shakespeare describes feelings which no observation could teach. Shakespeare made himself all characters; he left out parts of himself, and supplied what might have been in himself" (*SC*, II, 17). Raysor notes the similarity of this latter to a passage in A. W. Schlegel.

Behind all this, we may say briefly, is Coleridge's larger philosophical defense of the "method" of Shakespeare's works, in *The Friend*, as consisting in "that just proportion, that union and interpenetration of the individual and the particular, which must ever pervade all works of decided genius and true science."[38]


V


Some may think that Arnold's fourteen lines have sunk out of sight in a sea of conjectural sources and "background." But the advantage of the method employed here is to place Arnold's sonnet firmly in the context of Romantic literary speculation, especially the attempt by Coleridge, Hazlitt, and Carlyle to define a paradoxical Shakespearean mode of impersonal subjectivity. At the head stands Coleridge, speculating philosophically on the relationship of Shakespeare's personal experience and the universal experience he expressed. Shakespeare "worked in the spirit of nature, by evolving the germ from within by the imaginative power according to an idea" (*LR*, I, 103–4). In the middle distance is Hazlitt, providing usable images for the protean and chameleon poet. The immediate, and essential, context is provided by Carlyle, who defines Shakespeare's special qualification for expressing universal experience by adding the notion of a "victorious" process of interior purification. Most importantly, the unity of the poem—the relationship of Shakespeare's anonymity,[39] his victorious brow, and his capacity for expressing human suffering—is more coherently established within this tradition of speculation than in any other reading of the poem I know. Put differently, this reading frees us from the either/or of most readings, in which the sufferings in the final tercet are *either* personal to Shakespeare *or* those of men generally. They are instead, and paradoxically, both.[40] Considered as a problem in the methodology of

38. *The Friend* (1818), ed. Barbara E. Rourke (London and Princeton, 1969), I, 457: *The Complete Works of Samuel Taylor Coleridge 4*. This, one of Coleridge's "Essays on the Principles of Method," appeared in an earlier form as the Introduction to the *Encyclopaedia Metropolitana*; the Shakespeare passages are gathered in SC, II, 342–50. Roberta Morgan, in "The Philosophical Basis of Coleridge's *Hamlet* Criticism," *ELH*, 6 (Dec. 1939), 256–70, illuminatingly reads Coleridge's discussion of Hamlet's "overbalance" of mind as against action as "a specific application of the distinction between Reason and Understanding which Coleridge took over from Kant, and which is paralleled by his famous distinction between Imagination and Fancy."

39. Coleridge is as emphatic on this point as any later critic: "How well we seem to know Chaucer! How absolutely nothing do we know of Shakspeare!" *Table Talk*, 15 March 1834; *MC*, p. 433.

40. Baum, pp. 12–13, is the reader who most emphatically attributes the sufferings to Shakespeare personally: "the sufferings of his immortal spirit here among mortal

literary history and interpretation, I would argue that so rich and immediate a context of speculation can legitimately set a limit to the range of inference as to Arnold's probable meaning. Arnold's poem is short, and "impressive" in tone; he unquestionably would have (directly and indirectly) some apprehension of the crucial questions of Romantic Shakespeare criticism; the poem is unlikely to wander far from that context. More intrinsically, and as a further check, this context "explains" all elements of the poem, which cohere in an elliptical but integral unity.

What such a reading cannot do, admittedly, is to quite save the sonnet from F. R. Leavis's devastating attack on the poem's "general debility" and "dead conventionality of phrasing," its "lack of any vital organization among the words."[41] His touchstone is line 5, which he finds "ludicrous." The sonnet in fact is "an orotund exercise in thuriferous phrases and generalities, without one touch of particularity or distinction," and it "has nothing worth calling a theme." A mountain could never stand for Shakespeare's greatness or inscrutability: "There is nothing remote or austerely and inhumanly exalted about Shakespeare, whose genius is awe-inspiring by the inwardness and completeness of its humanity."[42] Beyond the overstatement, Leavis simply throws over one kind of exaggeration, that of the "divine" and lofty poet, and substitutes another, that of the intensely inward and "human" Shakespeare. Arnold does have a theme, vaguely expressed perhaps, as he strives for a more complex Shakespeare than Leavis allows.

Leavis of course has a point: Arnold's tone is oracular and the phrasing indistinct; and the poem leans on "the work of other poets"—or more accurately, of other critics. But he is quite wrong to say that the poem does not embody "a personally felt theme." The persistent admiration felt for the poem, and the place it continues to hold in the anthologies,[43] testify to its obscure but genuine impressiveness. It is a Miltonic-Wordsworthian

---

men and his victory over them are known to us only from his serene countenance." Though the drift of his reading of the final lines is sound enough, the context provided here offers an escape from the incomplete and contradictory notion that "the conflict between his humanity and the immortal spirit within him is visible *only* in his features, i.e., not in his plays." True to a point (the purely "personal" Shakespeare is refined out of his plays), this misses the vital connection between Shakespeare's special inwardness and his universality.

41. *Education & the University: A Sketch for an 'English School'* (1943; rpt. New York, 1948), p. 76.

42. Ibid., p. 75.

43. There are surprisingly few cavilers in the tradition; even Saintsbury admired it. A rare dissenter is Herbert Paul (*Matthew Arnold* [London, 1902], p. 23), who judges that line 10 ("Self-school'd," etc.) "is but fine writing after all."

incantatory tribute to a "Shakespearean" ideal toward which Arnold yearned and which he rarely achieved. The tone and the theme, as we have suggested, are very like those mysterious best passages in "Resignation." Unfortunately, by the time of the 1853 Preface, Arnold's praise for the ideal of the poet "effacing himself" (*CPW*, I, 8) represented a less complex view of the relationship of "self" and external action.

# A Key Poem of the Pre-Raphaelite Movement: W. M. Rossetti's "Mrs. Holmes Grey"

William E. Fredeman

*University of British Columbia*

THE QUESTION "What is Pre-Raphaelitism in Poetry," posed so long ago, has by now become almost rhetorical.[1] The materials for a considered answer may be found in three recent anthologies.[2] Yet none includes the one poem composed with the specific intention of demonstrating in poetry the principles of Pre-Raphaelite painting, William Michael Rossetti's "Mrs. Holmes Grey." Written for inclusion in *The Germ*, but not published there, "Mrs. Holmes Grey" is characterized by the same intense realism evident in many of the early PRB paintings. The poem is almost directly antithetical in subject and treatment to a work such as "The Blessed Damozel," often taken to be the Pre-Raphaelite poem *par excellence*. Where the latter is dreamy, vague and nebulous, "Mrs. Holmes Grey" is ultra-realistic, concrete and stark, almost to the point of grotesqueness; but it underscores a prominent concern of the early Pre-Raphaelites with actuality and the present, what F. G. Stephens in *The Germ* called "the poetry of the things around us."[3] "Mrs. Holmes Grey" is no masterpiece, but it is useful critically in the same way that John Ferguson MacLennan's lost collection of *Poems on the Pre-Raphaelite Principle* would be were it rediscovered[4] because it provides an insight into those principles of Pre-Raphaelitism that have tended to be disregarded owing to the paucity of critical comment by the Brotherhood. Had Rossetti's poem appeared as planned in *The Germ*, it might perhaps have helped to clarify some of the vagueness evinced in

1. See the article of this title by Anna Janney De Armond in *Delaware Notes*, 19th series (1946), pp. 67–88.
2. James B. Merritt, *The Pre-Raphaelite Poem* (New York, 1966); Cecil Y. Lang, *The Pre-Raphaelites and Their Circle with 'The Rubáiyát of Omar Khayyam'* (Boston, 1968); Jerome H. Buckley, *The Pre-Raphaelites* (New York, 1968).
3. In the essay "Modern Giants," *Germ*, no. 4 (April 1850), p. 170. A similar concept is espoused in J. L. Tupper's article, "The Subject in Art. No II," *Germ*, no. 3 (March 1850), p. 118. Lionel Stevenson in *The Pre-Raphaelite Poets* (Chapel Hill, 1972), which appeared after this paper was written, says of the poem that it was W. M. Rossetti's "most ambitious effort to practice Pre-Raphaelite realism" (p. 254).
4. For details of this work, see William E. Fredeman, *Pre-Raphaelitism: A Bibliocritical Study* (Cambridge, Mass., 1965), 85.1.

that manifesto, in which the word Pre-Raphaelite hardly appears.[5] Certainly the poem offers an alternative to the ordinary assumptions made about Pre-Raphaelitism that are based on a poem such as "The Blessed Damozel."

I

William Rossetti's own account of the genesis, development, intent, publication, and reception of "Mrs. Holmes Grey" in *Some Reminiscences*[6] provides a convenient introduction to the poem, but it requires some elaboration. The composition of the poem can be traced fully through entries in the *PRB Journal*, the diary that William Michael was commissioned to keep in his capacity as Secretary.[7]

On 12 September 1849, while on the Isle of Wight, William entered in the *PRB Journal*:

> After writing a letter to Woolner, I sat down to think for a subject for a poem, &, without much trouble, invented one, but which is as yet very incomplete & meagre. I composed 21 lines of it in blank verse.[8]

Over the next fortnight he completed the first draft of the poem, writing as many as 146 lines in a single day. In early October, after he had returned to London, he sent his manuscript, now some 700 lines long and entitled "An Exchange of News," to Dante Gabriel, who was then in Paris with Holman Hunt, and who had been clamoring to see it.[9] His brother responded at once and enthusiastically, sending William his own and Hunt's joint observations. Both felt that the title could be improved; and, *inter alia*, objections were raised to lines that were too "common," "trivial," "abrupt," "crackjaw," "metaphysical," "melodramatic," "violent," and "Tennysonian." On the credit side, other passages were "good," "very fine,"

5. In fact, the term never appears in reference to the PRB.
6. 2 vols. (London, 1906), I, 80–82.
7. *The PRB Journal* was partially published by W. M. Rossetti in *Præraphaelite Diaries and Letters* (London, 1900); the complete manuscript (of the surviving mutilated fragment) is in the Angeli Papers at the University of British Columbia. Later references to the published portion are to *PRDL*, to the unpublished portion, AP. A critical edition of the full text of *The PRB Journal*, ed. W. E. Fredeman, will be published in 1974 by The Clarendon Press. "Mrs. Holmes Grey" will appear in an Appendix.
8. *PRDL*, p. 220.
9. See *Letters of Dante Gabriel Rossetti*, ed. Oswald Doughty and J. R. Wahl, 4 vols. (Oxford, 1965–67), Letters 43, 44, 47. Subsequent references to the letters are to *DW* with the letter number.

"excellent," "powerful," and, of course, "really stunning"—the *sine qua non* of Pre-Raphaelite criticism. Summing up, Rossetti said:

> I think your poem is very remarkable, and altogether certainly the best thing you have done. It is a painful story, told without compromise, and with very little moral, I believe, beyond commonplaces. Perhaps it is more like Crabbe than any other poet I know of; not lacking no small share of his harsh reality—less healthy, and at times more poetical. I would advise you, if practicable, to show it to any medical man at hand . . . . He might discover some absurdity which escapes us, or suggest something of value to the story.[10]

William Michael took his brother's advice in many of the details of revision, soliciting from John Lucas Tupper, to whom he read the poem on 13 October, some medical corroboration.[11] The poem was read to virtually all the PRB's including Millais, who heard it on the 9th of November, by which date the title had been altered to "A Plain Story of Life."[12] Outside the Brotherhood but within the circle, Rossetti passed the manuscript to Coventry Patmore, who found in it "a most objectionable absence of moral dignity, all the characters being puny & destitute of elevation. He means, nevertheless," William added, "to read it thro' again, that he may be able to judge of it in detail without looking so much to the scope,—or want of scope. These are very much the objections that we had foreseen & acquiesce in."[13] In mid-December, Tupper reported that he had "spoken to a medical man about the scientific requirements for the death of the woman in my 'Plain Story of Life,' & that 'congestion & effusion of the ventricle' is the right term."[14] Though William noted that "this will adapt itself to rhythm with all ease," the poetic parallel is not unlike finding a rhyme word for Hepzibah. A month later, William sent the manuscript to W.B. Scott, "begging for his opinion and suggestions." Scott retorted in a testy letter on 26 January 1850, which William only summarizes: "He evidently looks on it as a curiosity out of his line of thought & poetic faith, not wanting in good description, but *exceptional* & wrong in delineation of character."[15] In all, the reception was insufficiently favorable to encourage William to include the poem in *The Germ*, and the last entry in the *Journal* pertaining to it ( on 27 February) reports the reaction of Joseph Wrightson,

10. *DW* 48.          11. AP.
12. AP.
13. *PRDL*, p. 230; Patmore's comments were reported to Rossetti by Woolner.
14. AP, 15 Dec.
15. AP, 16 and 26 Jan. 1850. Scott's letter is in the Durham University Library.

the editor of *The Weekly Dispatch*, who looked on it "as more than half intentionally comic, & advised me to send it to Bentley's magazine, where he thinks it would have a very fair chance of insertion."[16] According to William, he never sought to place the poem, even when, around 1861, he was encouraged to publish it by George Meredith. The next reference to "Mrs. Holmes Grey" is in William's diary for November 1867, and concerns the arrangements for the poem's publication in *The Broadway*. It appeared in that magazine on 28 January 1868.[17]

II

"Mrs. Holmes Grey" consists of 810 lines of blank verse divided into 87 irregular verse paragraphs varying in length from a single line to forty or more. Structurally, it falls into three distinct parts: an introductory narrative and dialogue which establishes the setting, character relationships, and general situation (ll. 1–397);[18] the newspaper account of the Coroner's Inquest into the circumstances surrounding the death of Mary Grey (ll. 398–731); and a denouement concluding with the theme of revenge (ll. 732–810). An epigraph from Poe's "The Imp of the Perverse" establishes one of the central themes of the poem: "Perverseness is one of the primitive impulses of the human heart; one of the indivisible primary faculties or sentiments which give direction to the character of man."

Because "Mrs. Holmes Grey" is little known, it is necessary to introduce the poem with a précis of the narrative. On a grey, wet October day, towards evening, in an English seaside resort, John Harling, who has been living in Italy and France for the past eight years, is walking alone when he suddenly sees in an upstairs window of a house "with close-drawn blinds" the face of his old friend, the Oxford surgeon, Holmes Grey, with whom he has corresponded during his absence. When Harling speaks, Grey disappears with no sign of recognition. As Harling goes to the door, Grey admits him with an unbecoming formality, addressing him as "Sir." Without further conversation, he invites Harling upstairs, where, even in the darkness, Harling can see that a great change has come over his friend.

16. AP.

17. The poem actually appeared in *The Broadway Annual*, 1 (Feb. 1868), 449–59, with an illustration by Arthur Boyd Houghton. See *Rossetti Papers, 1862–1870*, ed. W. M. Rossetti (London, 1903), pp. 243–44, 284–85, 296.

18. The poem is unlined in *The Broadway Annual*; all subsequent line numbers are documented internally.

Harling, however, has no knowledge of his friend's tragedy, as his enquiry about Grey's wife reveals. The narrative is interrupted by several false starts as each man encourages the other to commence his story first. Finally, Harling outlines for Grey his activities since his last letter; how he was caught up in the French Revolution of 1848, in which his former sweetheart was shot to death and he himself was taken for an Orleanist, "an English spy, or something." As Harling concludes, Grey invites him into an adjoining room in which there stands a coffin, "not yet closed." Inside lies Grey's wife, her mouth contorted in anguish; her "head was laid / Upon a prayer-book open at the rite / Of solemnizing holy matrimony. / Her marriage-ring was stitched into the page" (ll. 243–46). Leaving the room, Grey informs Harling, "It is not merely death would make me feel / Like this—no, there is something more behind / Harder than death, more cruel" (ll. 269–71). He then commences his narrative, beginning two months before with his meeting, in this same city, of a surgeon named Edward Luton, whom he had invited to spend a fortnight in his Oxford home. Grey's narrative is more allusive than factual, recounting first the change that came over his wife, which he attributed to grief over the loss of their little daughter, or to reminders of this loss carelessly made by a visiting cousin. In any event, after Luton had cut short his visit, for business reasons as he explained, Mary continued to be plagued by fits of tears. Finally, she proposed visiting her two sisters, and with Grey's permission she left the house, exacting from him an agreement that neither should communicate by letter with the other. For three weeks he heard nothing; then, he received a "letter on black-bordered paper" from Luton, informing him that he must come immediately, that he was to prepare himself, and that Luton "dared not trust his pen to tell me more" (l. 385). At this point, Grey cannot continue, and hands Harling a newspaper containing the report of the "Coroner's Inquest—A Distressing Case," in which "Public interest was widely excited."

In contrast with the preliminaries to this point, this section of the poem moves swiftly to the details of the central narrative, through the sworn testimony of six witnesses: Holmes Grey, husband of the deceased; Jane Langley, a lodging-house keeper in whose house Mary resided under the name Mrs. Grange; Edward Luton, who gives the fullest account of the events leading to Mary's death; Mrs. Gwyllt, Mary's cousin; Anne Gorman, Luton's servant; and Dr. Wallinger, the attending physician. Interspersed are comments and questions by the Coroner and at least one of the jurors.

Throughout, verisimilitude is heightened by the terseness and perfunctori-
ness of the reporting, in which the emotional reactions of both the principals and the court auditors are presented.

Merging the testimony, the story is as follows: Holmes and Mary Grey
had been married for upwards of three years when Luton went to visit
them in Oxford. When Luton, who had known Mary previous to her marriage, found that she gave no sign of knowing him, he "seemed a stranger"
until, on the sixth day, she acknowledged their former acquaintance. Two
days later, she "spoke of love," overheard by her cousin Mrs. Gwyllt. Not
seeing Mary after this, Luton heard from Grey that his wife was unwell,
and a day or so later Luton left the house. Two weeks later, Mary, who had
left Oxford and found lodgings at Jane Langley's, arrived at Luton's house,
professed her love, "and conjured me much / Not to desert her" (ll. 500–
1). Luton succeeded in convincing her to leave by promising to write her
a letter. Five days later, when he still had not written, he saw her standing
before his house at dusk; accordingly, he "wrote at once / She absolutely
must return to her home" (ll. 517–18). He also informed her that he was
engaged to be married. Over the next few days, Mary presents herself daily
at Luton's, where she sits silently for an hour. On the sixth day, perceiving
that they are being watched, Luton writes her again to advise that she will
no longer be admitted to his house. That afternoon, however, the door being
left ajar, she breaks into his room protesting that it "was impossible / She
should return to live with Mr. Grey / Again" (ll. 552–54):

> 'Because' (I recollect her words) 'this flame
> All eats me up while I am here with you;
> I hate it, but it eats me—eats me up,
> Till I have now no will to wish it quenched.'
>
> (ll. 556–59)

When Luton threatens to write to her husband, Mary stands up, screams
twice, and dies. The physician who is called concurs with Luton's diagnosis
that "instant death must have ensued / Upon the rupture of a blood-vessel"
(ll. 582–83). Under cross-examination, Luton denies any physical familiarity with the deceased—though "She would clasp / Her arms around me in
speaking tenderly, / And kiss me. She has often kissed my hands. / Nothing
beyond that" (ll. 611–14); gives the court a letter written by Mary declaring her undying love, which is read into the record; and answers
candidly questions regarding their relationship previous to her marriage.
His evidence is corroborated by others. Dr. Wallinger concludes the testi-

mony by identifying the cause of death as "congestion and effusion of the ventricle" (l. 713); and the jury brings in a verdict of "Died by the visitation of God" (l. 728).

The last eighty lines of the poem introduce the husband's irrational commitment to revenge himself on Luton, whom he intends to ruin professionally and thereby prevent his marriage. He refuses to return to Oxford, even though Harling offers to accompany him. When Harling takes Luton's side and says, "Why, he . . . never did / One hair's-breadth wrong to you: his hands are clean / Of all offence to you and yours. For shame!" (ll. 768–70), Grey perversely answers that he blames Luton for rejecting Mary—"What a heart he must have had!" (l. 780). Harling prefers to leave rather than "harass him with argument and blame" (l. 790), and as he makes to go, Grey takes him to the window and points out Luton's house, saying that one day Luton shall pay in full: "John, I can wait; but when the moment comes . . !" (l. 808).

III

In his note appended to "Mrs. Holmes Grey" in *The Broadway*, Rossetti explained the Pre-Raphaelite genesis of the poem:

> I . . . entertained the idea that the like principles of Pre-Raphaelite painting might be carried out in poetry; and that it would be possible, without losing the poetical, dramatic, or even tragic tone or impression, to approach nearer to the actualization of dialogue and narration than had ever yet been done.

It was this "actualization of dialogue and narration"—what Rossetti elsewhere called the "principle of strict naturalism" in Pre-Raphaelite art, that in literature excluded "exalted descriptive matter from any speech which professed to be a speech uttered in ordinary real life"[19]—that was most acutely criticized in the one formal notice of the poem to appear. For H. Buxton Forman, who published his critique as the last of a three-part examination of "The Rossettis" in *Tinsley's Magazine*,[20] it was, however, less the "innocuous approach to the actualities" that was to be censured than the

19. *Some Reminiscences*, I, 81.
20. Published anonymously in *Tinsley's*, 5 (Oct. 1869), 276–81. The quotations immediately following may be found on pp. 276, 278. Forman's articles on D. G. and Christina were reprinted in *Our Living Poets* (London, 1871); the essay on William Michael was not. For D. G. Rossetti's reaction to Forman's critique of "Mrs. Holmes Grey," see *DW*, 874 and 875.

absence of any redeeming *poetic* quality in Rossetti's poem. "The most decided prose we have had to deal with for some time," "Mrs. Holmes Grey" was, Forman felt, a failure, but it was the treatment rather than the subject that was unpoetic; and he referred to the "dry scansion" of the iambification of a language that was essentially prosaic. Swinburne, attracted by the most innovative section of the poem—the Coroner's Inquest —wrote shortly after its publication to Rossetti that it beats everything but Balzac.[21] More than a year later, he reaffirmed his initial reaction following three consecutive readings, saying that "it seems to me not only good but great in quality," and adding, "that both in conception and execution it is worthy of Balzac—only *he* would not have given it that flavour of tragic poetry which *I* feel throughout" (*Letters*, II, 28). Neither of these extremes of response, however—and Rossetti always felt that Forman "came nearer the mark than Mr. Swinburne"[22]—reflects the avowed experimental quality of "Mrs. Holmes Grey," which for the critic of Pre-Raphaelitism must be its primary interest.

It is the Pre-Raphaelite penchant for ultra-realism in the depiction of detail that is most apparent in "Mrs. Holmes Grey"—what the Pre-Raphaelites with too little precision chose to label "Truth to Nature." But the Ruskinian formula of "selecting nothing—rejecting nothing"[23] is really no more applicable to Pre-Raphaelite methods than the attribution to them of a kind of photographic realism which merely records what the eye (or the camera) sees. Nor is Pre-Raphaelite realism concerned solely with the subject; rather, it affects the relationship between the whole and its constituent parts, insisting on the same care in the particularization of the trivial as of the consequential, of minute details as of principal subjects, of background as of foreground, of inanimate as of animate objects. It was this indiscriminate, total realism in Pre-Raphaelite pictures—the chips on the floor of the carpenter's shop—that generated such a chorus of initial abuse, this and their rejection of idealized models, which Dickens and others interpreted as a morbid and perverse preference for ugliness over beauty.[24] "Truth to Nature" and "fidelity to inner experience" are not simply empty terms in the vocabulary of Pre-Raphaelite criticism, but they must be applied within specific contexts.

21. *The Swinburne Letters*, ed. Cecil Y. Lang, (New Haven, 1959–62), I, 289.
22. *Some Reminiscences*, I, 82.
23. See Ruskin's *Pre-Raphaelitism* (London, 1851).
24. See Charles Dickens' "Old Lamps for New Ones," *Household Words*, 1 (15 June 1850), 265–67.

On the most obvious level, Rossetti's poem follows the principles of Pre-Raphaelite realism in its descriptive sections, largely in the beginning where the setting, both literal and tonal, is established:

> Rain-washed for hours, the streets at last were dried.
> Profuse and pulpy sea-weed on the beach,
> Pushed by the latest heavy tide some way
> Across the jostled shingle, was too far
> For washing back, now that the sea at ebb
> Left an each time retreating track of foam.
> There were the wonted tetchy and sidelong crabs,
> With fishes silvery in distended death.
>
> No want of blue now in the upper sky: —
> But also many piled-up flat grey clouds,
> Threatening a stormy night-time; and the sun
> Sank, a red glare, between two lengthened streaks,
> Hot dun, that stretched to southward; and at whiles
> The wind over the water swept and swept.
>
> (ll. 1–14)

But in his note to the poem Rossetti specifically refers to the application of these principles to the dialogue and the narrative, both of which are more prominent than the descriptive sections of the poem. After the first nine verse paragraphs, which continue the tonal description to the actual meeting of Harling and Grey, the remainder of the first part is taken up almost exclusively with dialogue, with only sufficient narrative interruption to further the story. Throughout, there is a cold, almost clinical objectivity in the language, whatever suspense there is deriving from the sometimes too intense forestalling of narrative advancement. Even the absence of any real *action* in the poem—at least so far as this relates to the account of Mrs. Holmes Grey, which is entirely retrospective—tends to decelerate the pace; and the indirectness of the narrative emphasizes, at least in the first part, the inconsequentiality of much that passes between the two men. Much of their discourse is trivial and contrived, but in part this is necessitated by the demand that their relationship, distanced first by separation and now accentuated by Grey's recent tragedy and the mental strain accompaning it, be re-established. The whole episode has made Grey suspicious of friend and foe alike, and his loss, compounded by what he clearly regards as a disgrace, has brought him to the point of madness.

'Harling,' said Grey, after a pause, 'you think
No doubt that this is all — her death is all.
Harling, when first I saw you in the street,
I feared you meant to come and speak to me;
So hid myself and waited till you knocked,
Waited behind the door until you knocked,
Longing that you, perhaps would go. When I
Had opened it, I think I called you *Sir* —
Did you not chide me? Do you know it seemed
So strange to me that any one I knew
Before this happened should be here the same,
And know me for the same that once I was,
I could not quite imagine we were friends.'

(ll. 255–68)

Grey's anguish, which makes him unable to finish his tale to Harling, also allows for the introduction of the main structural device in the poem—the story within the story as presented in the newspaper account of the Coroner's Inquest. This section is without a doubt Rossetti's most singular achievement in the poem. The language, stripped of any emotional tension associated with the speaker, is merely perfunctory in the narrative passages that supply the continuity. And even though direct evidence, within quotation marks, is given in the report of each witness's testimony, the facts recounted, by this time three times removed from the event, have something of the matter-of-fact, dispassionate literalism of any ordinary newspaper account of a sensational episode. Only because the reader is familiar with one of the principals does the story have an impact beyond the journalistic resumé of the coroner's hearing. However, the newspaper account does affect the reader in a subtle and important way by dramatizing the contrast between private and public involvement; and because Grey alone of all the principals has any other than a second-hand reality, it is with his transformation that the reader is concerned. By its very nature, the Coroner's Inquest adds to the verisimilitude of the story. Through successive testimony, the exact chronological sequence becomes apparent, and it is possible to fill in the narrative continuity with precise dates, places, and events, culminating in the death of Mrs. Grey. The burden of the narrative at the inquest is, of course, carried by Luton, who, apart from Mrs. Grey herself, was the only person privy to the complete curcumstances. But though Luton was as much a victim of Mrs. Grey's obsession as she herself, and though he is by his testimony exonerated from any culpability in her death, he has not at the end been absolved. The dénouement of the story is, in fact, unrealized, and Grey's revenge on Luton is left open; but Grey's final words to Harling, and the night "equal, unknown, and desolate of stars" (l. 810) into which Harling stares, carry ominous overtones of a doom that will pursue Grey and Luton as persistently and with the same success as that which has already triumphed over Mary.

"Mrs. Holmes Grey" is very much within the tradition of the domestic tragedy, gothicized in the manner of Poe, under whose influence the poem was so demonstrably written. Grey and his wife are both victims of and studies in perverseness and in the inscrutability of human emotions and motivations. The theme, admittedly adolescent and a popular one in Victorian literature, is here a clever variation on the triangle relationship in love and marriage, heightened by grotesqueness and the mystery of the unexplained. Its importance as a Pre-Raphaelite poem, however, lies mainly in its technique, and in this regard it is more successful than Forman would allow. His limited praise, couched wholly in negative terms, was that, written "under strong convictions," the poem betrayed "no weakness such as flabbiness of texture, or meagreness of imagination or expression." (p. 279). Viewed more positively, the poem, for all its limitations, employs a stark, flat, prosaic style and language in both dialogue and narration to achieve a particular, and unusual, realistic effect. In this it parallels, intentionally, one of the principal techniques of the earliest paintings of the Pre-Raphaelite Brotherhood. There is no attempt to introduce purely pictorial elements—and in this regard it differs markedly from many poems by D. G. Rossetti, Morris and others that are more conventionally acknowledged as Pre-Raphaelite—but Rossetti's use of both external and psychological detail and the intensity of his overall surface realism, even to the point of belaboring the commonplace, is integral to the experimental aspect of the poem. Written explicitly for *The Germ*, under the impress of early Pre-Raphaelite theories, "Mrs. Holmes Grey" has a documentary significance that overshadows its literary shortcomings.

# The Carlyles and Thackeray

## Charles Richard Sanders

### Duke University

THE RELATION of Carlyle to Thackeray, like that of Carlyle to most of his other major contemporaries, is complex. Temperamentally and in many matters concerning art and literary taste extremely different, Carlyle was an untamed, almost savage Thor among writers, working in the tradition of Biblical, seventeenth-century, and German models, while Thackeray with supreme aplomb sought for and to a considerable degree achieved the urbanity and surface brilliance of a Horace or a Pope. Both had highly social natures, but Carlyle's friendships were based in the main on the picturesqueness and even the rough edges of a rugged and pronounced individualism, whereas Thackeray's ways were the accepted ways of the world, which usually kept the paths smooth for those who would come to him as friends. Despite important differences and philosophies of life, however, Carlyle and Thackeray found much to admire in one another and a considerable amount of common ground to stand on.[1]

As early as August 1831, in a letter to Ottilie von Goethe, the poet's daughter-in-law, Thackeray asked for the identity of the person who had written Carlyle's song beginning "Now yarely soft my boys," which he understood had appeared in Frau von Goethe's magazine *Chaos* but which he had found in *Fraser's Magazine*.[2] On 25 January 1832 he wrote again to her to say, "The bearer of this letter [Henry Reeve] comes recommended

---

1. For a helpful summary of the relationship, see Gordon N. Ray's Introduction to his edition of *The Letters and Private Papers of William Makepeace Thackeray* (Cambridge, Mass., 1946), I, cvi–cix (hereafter referred to as Ray, *Letters*); and his *Thackeray: The Uses of Adversity (1811–1846)* (New York, Toronto, London, 1955), pp. 215, 382.

2. *Chaos* ran from 28 August 1829 to the middle of February 1832. Carlyle's poem mentioned by Thackeray was "The Sower's Song," which appeared in the 37th number of the journal, 25 April 1830, and in *Fraser's Magazine*, 3 (April 1831), 390. He later altered the first line of the poem to read "Now hands to seedsheet, boys." See his *Works*, Centenary Edition (London, 1896–99), XXVI, 472–73. Carlyle made other contributions to *Chaos*, namely, "What Is Hope," "Faust's Curse," "Tragedy of the Night-Moth," and "All Mute." Thackeray, who became an intimate friend of Ottilie von Goethe, also made contributions to *Chaos*, beginning in 1830. See Trevor D. Jones, "English Contributors to Ottilie von Goethe's 'Chaos, X'" *Publications of the English Goethe Society*, ns, 9 (1931–33; rpt. 1966), 68–91.

to your father-in-law by Mr. Carlyle." [3] Although Carlyle, like Thackeray, was still an obscure writer at this time, quite clearly Thackeray knew of him and even of his correspondence with Goethe. Furthermore, one of Thackeray's best friends, Charles Buller, whom he had known at Cambridge, had been tutored many years before by Carlyle and was still Carlyle's intimate friend. Buller had always admired Carlyle greatly, and it appears that Thackeray too had come to share this admiration. He wrote in his diary for 29 and 30 April 1832, "I wish to God, I could take advantage of my time & opportunities as C Buller has done— It is very well to possess talents but using them is better still. . . . To be sure as to advancement & society & talent he has had greater than most men, not the least of them that Carlyle was his tutor." [4]

Just when Carlyle and Thackeray first met has not been precisely determined. Both wrote for *Fraser's Magazine* in the early years of its existence, and their pictures appear in Maclise's well-known picture "The Fraserians," published in the magazine for January 1835. Carlyle contributed to the very first issue, February 1830; and Thackeray may have contributed to the magazine as early as February 1831, certainly as early as May 1834. Furthermore, another of Thackeray's old Cambridge friends, John Sterling, was the friend of Carlyle, and Carlyle himself states that he had seen Thackeray at both the Bullers' home and the Sterlings' before he finished *The French Revolution* and went to Scotland for a vacation in late June 1837. [5]

That Jane Carlyle, later to establish for herself a high reputation not merely as a letter-writer but as a reader of novels and an authority as to their merits, also knew Thackeray and had won his confidence by this time is attested by the following passage from an undated letter to her husband of late July or early August. It deals, scarcely with justice, with Thackeray's review of Carlyle's *The French Revolution*, which would appear in the *Times* on 3 August and which she had read in proof.

Apropos of the *French Revolution*; I have read Thacker[a]y's article in proof—, and as Tommy Burns said of Eliza Stodart's leg—"It's nae great tings"! so small a *ting* indeed that *one* barrel of the Inevitable-Gun may be decidedly said to have missed fire— He cannot boast of having, in any good sense, "*served Thacker[a]y*" however he may have "*served Carlyle*." When you consider that this is Thacker[a]y's *coup*

---

3. Ray, *Letters*, I, 184.          4. Ibid., I, 196.
5. Ray says that Thackeray first met Carlyle soon after leaving Paris and settling in London in March 1837 (ibid., I, cvi).

*d'essai*, in his new part of political renegade, you will however, make some allowance for the strange mixture of bluster and platitude which you will find in his two Columns, and rather pity the poor white man, wishing with Mrs Sterling so often as his name comes up that "he would but stick to his sketchings."[6]

Carlyle, however, was at least moderately pleased with Thackeray's review, a copy of which Jane sent to him in Scotland. To his brother John he wrote on 12 August: "I understand there have been many reviews of a very mixed character. I got one in the 'Times' last week. The writer is one Thackeray, a half-monstrous Cornish giant, kind of painter, Cambridge man, and Paris newspaper correspondent, who is now writing for his life in London. I have seen him at the Bullers' and at Sterling's. His article is rather like him, and I suppose calculated to do the book good."[7] On 18 August he wrote to Jane with less restraint and gave in full detail an account of how much he and two of his other brothers enjoyed reading Thackeray's review together:

> He [John Stuart Mill in a recent letter] says in reference to Thackeray's Article, which he attributes to Sterling, it will get me many new readers: *esto*! By the by this Article did us all some good here. It was a sunny Monday morning; Alick had been up here, Jamie and I were escorting him homewards: daily for above a week had the little messenger flown to the Post Office without any effect at all; what was Goody about, why was there no tidings or token? Lo, on the top of Potter's Knowe (the height immediately behind Middlebie), Betty Smeal unfastening her luggage; presenting two Newspapers with their strokes in Goody's hand; one of which was this *Times!* They made me take place under the shade of the head [hill] and beechtrees, and read it all over to them, amid considerable laughter and applause. One is obliged to men in these circumstances who say even with bluster and platitude greater than Thackeray's, Behold this man is not an ass.[8]

6. From the MS letter in the Pierpont Morgan Library. "Pity the poor white man" is coterie speech deriving from Mungo Park's *Travels in the Interior Districts of Africa* (London, 1799). Cf. *The Collected Letters of Thomas and Jane Welsh Carlyle*, Duke-Edinburgh Edition (Durham, N.C., 1970), III, 390.
7. MS, National Library of Scotland (hereafter NLS), 523–51.
8. MS, NLS, 610.34. Edward FitzGerald's comment in a letter to Thackeray of 1 Sept. was not so favorable: "As to Carlyle's book [*The French Revolution*] I looked into it, but I did not desire to read it—I do not admire the German school of English." Ray, *Letters*, I, 347.

Many years later, after Jane's death in 1866, Carlyle touched on the subject of Thackeray's review once more, this time with mixed feelings intensified by his memory of the great encouragement his wife had given him at the time and by his deep sense of loss now that she was gone:

> Thackeray's laudation, in the *Times*, I also recollect the arrival of (how pathetic now Her mirth over it to me!)—but neither did Thackeray inspire me with any emotion [any more than the hostile review in the *Athenaeum*], still less with any ray of exultation: "One other poor judge voting," I said to myself; "but what is he, or such as he? The fate of that thing is *fixed*! I *have* written it; that is all my result." Nothing now strikes me as affecting in all this, but *Her* noble attempt to cheer me on my return home to her, still sick and sad; and how she poured out on me her melodious joy, and all her bits of confirmatory anecdotes and narratives; "O, it has had a great success, Dear!"—and not even she could irradiate my darkness, beautifully as she tried for a long time, as I sat at her feet again by our own parlor-fire. "Ah, you are an unbelieving creature!" said she at last, starting up, probably to give me some tea. There was, and is, in all this something heavenly;— the rest is all of it smoke, and has gone up the chimney, inferior in benefit and quality to what my pipe yielded me. I was rich once, had I known it, very rich; and now I am become poor to the end.[9]

In spite of Jane's satirical comments on it, Thackeray's long review, coming at a time when it could be extremely helpful in furthering Carlyle's career, was well calculated to produce the feeling of jubilation which Carlyle and his two brothers felt when they read it at Potter's Knowe. It was a friendly, well-intentioned, but at the same time well-balanced piece of criticism. In the main, it defends Carlyle and calls attention to his great merits as a writer and historian. "Never did a book sin so grievously from outward appearance," Thackeray wrote, "or man's style so mar his subject and dim his genius. It is stiff, short, and rugged, it abounds with Germanisms and Latinisms, strange epithets, and choking double words, astonishing to the admirers of simple Addisonian English, to those who love history as it gracefully runs in Hume, or struts pompously in Gibbon—no such style is Mr. Carlyle's." But the reader, Thackeray said, "speedily learns to admire and sympathize; just as he would admire a Gothic cathedral in spite of the quaint carvings and hideous images on door and but-

9. *Reminiscences*, ed. C. E. Norton (London and New York, 1887), II, 288.

tress." Carlyle's nonpartisan point of view is highly praised: "He, is not a party historian like Scott, who could not, in his benevolent respect for rank and royalty, see duly the faults of either: he is impartial as Thiers, but with a far loftier and nobler impartiality. . . . It is better to view it [history] loftily from afar, like our mystic poetic Mr. Carlyle, than too nearly with sharp-sighted and prosaic Thiers. Thiers is the *valet de chambre* of this history, he is too familiar with its dishabille and off-scourings: it can never be a hero to him." Lazy readers, repelled by Carlyle's strange style or merely amused by his grotesqueness, would never be able to understand or appreciate Carlyle's philosophy or his remarkable power of description. Thackeray quoted with admiration Carlyle's account of the charge upon the Bastille, which, he said, is given "with an uncouth Orson-like shout," and passages dealing with Mirabeau and Charlotte Corday. "The reader, we think, will not fail to observe the real beauty which lurks among all these odd words and twisted sentences, living, as it were, in spite of the weeds; but we repeat, that no mere extracts can do justice to the book; it requires time and study." Finally, after giving long extracts from Carlyle's account of the deaths of Danton and Robespierre, Thackeray concluded in a vein which permitted his own philosophy and his own penchant for satire to creep in (here at the expense of Carlyle's critics):

The reader will see in the above extracts most of the faults, and a few of the merits, of this book. He need not be told that it is written in an eccentric prose, here and there disfigured by grotesque conceits and images; but, for all this, it betrays most extraordinary powers —learning, observation, and humor. Above all, it has no CANT. It teems with sound, hearty philosophy (besides certain transcendentalisms which we do not pretend to understand), it possesses genius, if any book ever did. It wanted no more for keen critics to cry fie upon it! Clever critics who have such an eye for genius, that when Mr. Bulwer published his forgotten book concerning Athens, they discovered that no historian was like to him; that he, on his Athenian hobby, had quite out-trotted stately Mr. Gibbon; and with the same creditable unanimity cried down Mr. Carlyle's history, opening upon it a hundred little piddling sluices of small wit, destined to wash the book sheer away; and lo! the book remains, it is only the poor wit which has run dry. . . . The hottest Radical in England may learn by it that there is something more necessary for him even than his mad liberty—the authority, namely, by which he retains his head on his shoulders and his money in his pocket.[10]

Early in 1838 some papers entitled "Old England" written in imitation of Carlyle appeared in the *Times* which he believed were written by Thackeray. On 10 January he wrote to his brother Alexander:

> By the bye, a man in the *Times* Newspaper, for the last ten days, is writing diligently a series of Papers called "Old England" extravagantly in my manner; so that several friends actually thought it was I! I did not see them till last night; and had a loud laugh over them then. It is that dog Thackeray (my Reviewer in the Times); you remember the Potter Knowe; he, I am persuaded, and no other: I take it as a help and compliment in these circumstances; and bid it welcome so far as it will go.

The papers, however, signed "Coeur de Lion," were written not by Thackeray but by Disraeli.[11]

From 27 April to 11 June 1838 Carlyle gave his second series of lectures, *On the History of Literature.* It is highly probable that Thackeray attended some of these and that two of the reviews of them in the *Times* are by him. In the review of 1 May the reporter states that he was struck by "the look of strong and ardent individual character" in the lecturer, "such as fashion and outward advantages never can form, and sometimes tend to stifle. And in harmony with this was the whole discourse which he delivered—often rough, broken, wavering, and sometimes almost weak and abortive; but full throughout of earnest purpose, abundant knowledge, and a half-suppressed struggling fire of zeal and conviction, which gave a flash of headlong impulse to faltering sentences, and lighted up and clothed in dignity, meanings half obscure, and undeveloped images." Unquestionably, the speaker was motivated by "an insatiable thirst for truth" and had attained "a devout faith in reason and conscience, . . . a large and pure humanity, . . . [and] a comprehensive and guiding knowledge as to the whole progress and all the achievements of man's nature." The forthcoming lectures promised much, especially to those who were already familiar with Carlyle's "generous, imaginative, and soul-fraught writings."

---

10. Thackeray's review was reprinted in his *Sultan Stork and Other Stories and Sketches,* ed. R. H. Shepherd (London, 1887).

11. For Carlyle's letter and evidence of Disraeli's authorship, see Edwin W. Marrs, *The Letters of Thomas Carlyle to his Brother Alexander* (Cambridge, Mass., 1968), pp. 434–35.

The second review, that of 22 May, covered three of Carlyle's lectures and dealt delightfully with Carlyle's comments on the German race in the Middle Ages, on Dante, and on Cervantes:

> The three last lectures have presented to us in bold forms and star-tling light the great spectacle of the Middle Ages. We have seen the grey and huge ruins of the Roman world as their background, with the energetic masses of the German race swelling up and bursting across these, while hymns and shrines have been noticed as arising slowly above the tumult, and Gothic life and Christian faith have been painted in all their grave depth and rich variety of aspect. In the midst of this noble and stirring world, the lecturer evoked for us with a hand of quiet power the great singer of old Christian Europe, "that deep voice from the innermost heart of man"—Dante, the exiled Florentine. His three visionary kingdoms, the Inferno, Purgatorio, and Paradiso, were laid open as embodying on the mysterious stage of an extra-mundane eternity the three essential conditions of man's existence, such as we know it here on earth—its penal agonies, its hopeful prog-ress, and its assured and peaceful triumph. The lecture which fol-lowed on the disclosure of this gigantic scenery, and which is the last delivered, transferred us into superstitious, chivalrous, and loyal Spain, and after a description, to which we can only allude, of the various elements of race and faith which entered into the formation of the old Castilian mind, it introduced us to the presence of the maimed and destitute soldier, "Naked Adam," as he called himself, of "Spanish posts [poets?]"—the genial and heroic Cervantes, author of *Don Quix-ote*. This man has never, we are persuaded, been made so thoroughly and delightfully intelligible to Englishmen as by Mr. Carlyle's descrip-tion, which presented him as completely realizing both the old Teu-tonic courage and daring, and the purely Christian element, unknown to the Pagan world, of meek generosity and affectionate self-sacrifice. This lofty and idealizing character, united with a profound sense of the hindrances which it must needs meet with in practical life, and which through all his days entangled Cervantes, was animated and brightened by the truest, kindliest humour, which was the proper genius of the man, and stamped itself for all ages and nations in the imperishable and exquisite creation of *Don Quixote*. The few words we have here set down can at best give no conception of the inimitable earnestness and humane glowing sincerity of the lecturer's discourse,

which perpetually break out in touches of high eloquence and the deepest pathos, and would, in our estimate, amply excuse far more than his imperfections in the purely technical part of oratory.[12]

On 20 August 1836 Thackeray had married Miss Isabella Shawe in Paris. After the Thackerays settled in London in 1837 the social relationship soon established with the Carlyles was made more felicitous not merely by common friends like Sterling and Buller but also by the honest criticism and words of encouragement for Carlyle contained in Thackeray's reviews in the *Times*. The pleasant nature of the situation is reflected in a letter from Mrs. Thackeray to Mrs. Carmichael-Smyth, 15 May 1839, in which she wrote: "Besides there was a report that Charles Buller was to be a cabinet minister. . . . We met Charles Buller at Mr. Carlyle's yesterday he laughed and joked about it but of course neither said yea or nay."[13] In late December of the same year Thackeray wrote to his mother: "We were to have gone to Carlyle's tonight, but 4 good dinners last week were too much for my poor dear insides and I was compelled last night to dosify."[14] He wrote to her again on 18 January 1840 that he had recently paid a visit to Chelsea "to see Carlyle and Mrs. C.—pleasanter more high-minded people I don't know."[15] Carlyle, on his side, encouraged Thackeray in his efforts to write fiction. After the last numbers of *Catherine*, Thackeray's novel to show what criminals really are, appeared in *Frazer's Magazine* in early 1840, Thackeray proudly wrote to his mother: "The judges stand [up] for me: Carlyle says Catherine is wonderful, and many more laud it highly, but it is a disgusting subject & no mistake."[16] Clearly by the middle of 1840 Carlyle had for Thackeray become an extremely important part of the London scene. On 29 June of this year he proposed writing for *Blackwood's* a light humorous sketch of London life which would include such things as "the London Library, Tom Carlyle and the 'Times,'" as well as other matters.[17]

The tremendous admiration which Thackery had for Carlyle in this period is reflected particularly in the generous and even striking praise

---

12. For evidence of Thackeray's authorship and a full text of the two reviews, see Harold Strong Gulliver, *Thackeray's Literary Apprenticeship* (Valdosta, Ga., 1934), pp. 92, 198–200.

13. Ray, *Letters*, I, 382. The State University of Iowa possesses a very friendly letter from Thackeray to Mrs. Carlyle, undated, but since it was written from 13 Great Coram Street, Brunswick Square, it belongs to the period from May 1838 to April 1843, when Thackeray lived there.

14. Ray, *Letters*, I, 404.          15. Ibid., I, 413.

16. From a letter dated 11–15 Feb., Ray, *Letters*, I, 421.

17. Ibid., I, 451.

which he gave to his *Miscellanies* in four volumes (1838–39), first appearing like *Sartor Resartus* in an American edition. In late 1839 Thackeray
wrote to his mother: "I wish you could get Carlyle's Miscellaneous Criti-
cisms, now just published in America. I have read a little in the book, a
nobler one does not live in our language, I am sure, and one that will have
such an effect on our ways of thought and prejudices. Criticism has been
a party matter with us till now, and literature a poor political lacquey—
please God we shall begin ere long to love art for art's sake. It is Carlyle
who has worked more than any other to give it its independence."[18]
Twentieth-century scholars and critics may be astonished to find the phrase
"art for art's sake" in such an early English context, though Gautier, who
would become Thackeray's friend and visit him in England some years
later, had used it earlier; but they may be even more astonished to find
Thackeray applying the phrase with considerable emphasis to the writings
of Thomas Carlyle. But if Carlyle himself had been called on to defend
Thackeray's application of the phrase to his writings, he would probably
have made some remark about what he owed to old Samuel Johnson and
Johnson's great respect for the dignity and independence of the man of
letters.

Thackeray's confidence in Carlyle's scholarship and faith in his authenticity as a historian as evidenced by *The French Revolution* caused
him to come to his defense when Carlyle was attacked by some newspapers
in 1839–40 in what came to be known as the *Vengeur* controversy, a controversy in which the press of both Great Britain and France engaged.
In giving an account of a naval battle near Brest between the British and
the French which took place on 1 June 1794, Carlyle in the first edition of
*The French Revolution* had described in glowing colors and with dramatic
vividness the heroism displayed by many members of the crew of the
French ship *Vengeur*, which even when the ship was sinking stayed with
it, firing from the upper deck when the lower one was under water, refusing to strike but keeping the Tricolor proudly aloft, and shouting *Vive la
République* until the ship completely disappeared under water. Some
months after his book was published Carlyle discovered evidence which
convinced him that virtually the whole story of the heroism of some members of the crew of the *Vengeur* was a fabrication put in circulation soon
after the battle by a French journalist and historian named Barère[19] for
purposes of patriotism and propaganda and soon accepted as truth and

18. Ibid., I, 396.
19. Bertrand Barère de Vieuzac (1755–1841).

handed down through the years as traditional by both the French and British press. Particularly telling as evidence against the accepted story was a letter printed in the *Sun* in November 1838 from Rear-Admiral A. J. Griffiths, who had been on board the British ship *Culloden* during the battle, had seen the whole action, and had helped to rescue and receive as prisoners on the *Culloden* many members of the *Vengeur*'s crew, including its captain Renaudin. Griffiths refuted practically every article of the story which would exemplify French *gloire* and said that the crew of the sinking *Vengeur* acted as members of a sinking ship usually do act: they took to their boats and did what they could to save their lives. In *Fraser's Magazine* for July 1839 Carlyle published an article on the sinking of the *Vengeur* in which he examined the evidence provided by Griffiths and other evidence and concluded that the heroic version which he and others had accepted was based on a hoax perpetrated by Barère. In addition in the second edition of *The French Revolution* (1839), after retaining his stirring account of the glorious behavior of the French crew when the *Vengeur* sank, he followed it by a paragraph which emphatically denied it all and compared Barère with other tellers of tall tales. "Mendez Pinto, Munchhausen, Cagliostro, Psalmanazar," and declared that this story "may be regarded as Barrère's [*sic*] masterpiece; the largest, most inspiring piece of *blague* manufactured, for some centuries, by any man or nation."[20]

The controversy continued to rage in the press, however, even though new evidence appeared to support Carlyle's conclusions. Thackeray more and more took an interest in the question, entirely convinced that Carlyle was right. In an undated letter of probably late 1839 Carlyle wrote to his friend Mrs. Mary Rich, eldest daughter of Sir James Macintosh: "It appears, a certain official man has discovered in the French Naval Archives the original dispatch of Rénaudin [*sic*] the *Vengeur* Captain, entirely confirming our old Admiral's account; and moreover has been so honest as publish it in the *Revue Britanique* some months ago;—of which publication the *National* Newspaper has *not* taken any notice! I am inquiring for the thing, but have not yet got it. Thackeray talks of making some trumpet-blast about it. As the *Vengeur* article is to go into this new *Miscellanies* edition, I must see it myself."[21] Thackeray did make his "trumpet-blast" in defense of Carlyle in a twelve-page article in *Fraser's Magazine* for March 1840, in which he examined all the evidence. The article is entitled

20. See Carlyle's *Works*, IV, 241–42: I. W. Dyer, *A Bibliography of Thomas Carlyle's Writings and Ana* (Portland, Me., 1928), p. 253.
21. MS, Professor Frederick W. Hilles.

"On French Criticism of the English, and Notably in the Affair of the Vengeur" and is printed under the amusing pseudonym "Nelson Tattersall Lee Scupper." It incorporates a second and even more convincing letter from Admiral Griffiths, who quotes from a letter which he had received from Captain Renaudin of the *Vengeur* in confirmation of his testimony. Speaking to one Labédollière, to whom the whole article as one of *Fraser's* "Epistles to the Literati" is addressed, Thackeray insists: "Sir, your country needs no such lies to support its reputation for valour; and if it finds a sham jewel among those ten thousand real stones that ornament its crown of glory, character demands that the paste should be flung away." He quotes and then translates from the French a poem by the "celebrated and sublime Jules Baget" attacking Carlyle as a calumniator but then adds a spoofing last stanza ending in "Aid me, ye Muses nine—'Cockdoodledoodle-doo.'" He also quotes a long letter signed by Captain Renaudin "and seven others" giving a detailed account of how the ship went down. Finally Thackeray concludes in terms of realistic common sense: "That certain men did cry out ['*Vive la République*'] we believe, although Admiral Griffiths did not hear them; that all did their duty most gallantly, none will deny; that they hung their colours *en berne* (in token of distress), implored succour, and all rushed for the boats which were sent to relieve them, we know from Renaudin's own testimony;—but guns firing, colours flying, crew refusing to surrender, and shouting *Vive la République*!—all this is what Mr. Carlyle calls a windbag, which Admiral Griffiths and Captain Renaudin have flapped out. And this made the point of the story, and formed the theme of Barrère's declamation." Carlyle naturally found gratification and satisfaction in Thackeray's article. "Thackeray's article is well enough," he wrote to his brother John on 2 March 1840; "I am glad that I did not write any further on the subject."[22] Possibly the whole episode caused Carlyle to intensify and clarify his thinking on the exact nature of heroism: his lectures for the spring of this year were to be entitled "On Heroes, Hero-Worship and the Heroic in History." Perhaps too it may be a small, shadowy part of the background of a work called *Vanity Fair: A Novel without a Hero*.

In July 1840 Thackeray brought out his first book, *The Paris Sketch Book*. Carlyle took due note of it in a letter to his brother John: "Thackeray has brought out a book; kind of picture-book about Paris."[23] But the year was not a good one for Thackeray. Since his marriage in 1836 his wife had borne him three daughters: Anne Isabella, later Lady Ritchie, born 9 June

22. MS, NLS, 523.77.                    23. MS, NLS, 523.90.

1837; Jane, born 9 July 1838, who died the following year; and Harriet
Marian ("Minny"), later Mrs. Leslie Stephen, born 27 May 1840. In September 1840 on the way from London to Cork Mrs. Thackeray attempted
to drown herself, and the first symptoms of what was to be her lifelong
insanity revealed themselves. After spending a few weeks in Cork, Thackeray took his wife to London and from there to Paris, where for a brief
period he placed her in an institution for the insane. In May 1841 he placed
her in the care of a nurse. Later that year he took her to a sanatorium near
Boppard on the Rhine; and in February 1842 he left her with Dr. Puzin at
Chaillot. Eventually, in 1845, he brought his wife back to England and
placed her in the hands of Mrs. Bakewell in Camberwell. Mrs. Thackeray
lived on until 1894, long after Thackeray's own death. During the early
years of Mrs. Thackeray's illness Carlyle learned of it and wrote about it
with compassion to his mother in a letter of 16 June 1841: "Alas, here is a
poor man, by name Thackeray, just come in from Paris; where his poor
Wife is left, having fallen *insane* on his hands some six or eight months
ago! I believe he is not well off for cash either, poor Thackeray (tho' born
a rich man); he is very clever, with pen and pencil; an honest man, in no
inconsiderable distress! He seems as if he had no better place, of all the
great places he once knew, than our poor house to take shelter in!—Welcome the coming guest, especially him that is in misfortune! I must go down
to poor Thackeray, and bid my Mother farewell." [24]

Another old Cambridge friend of Thackeray's, Edward FitzGerald, had
heard with admiration Carlyle's lectures on *Heroes* in 1840 and later
described the lecturer as "very handsome then, with his black hair, fine
Eyes, *and a sort of crucified expression.*" [25] In September of 1842 the painter
Samuel Laurence brought FitzGerald to meet Carlyle at Chelsea. [26] Fitz-
Gerald proved to be an extremely helpful friend, not only then, when
Carlyle was deeply involved in his book on Cromwell but seven years
later, when he toured Ireland. FitzGerald's father owned the battlefield
of Naseby, which Carlyle had walked over in company with Dr. Arnold of
Rugby. Carlyle wrote to his brother John on 29 September 1842: "A certain
Mr. FitzGerald, an acquaintance of Thackeray's, who had been here before,
called one night about a week ago; told me he had just come from Naseby:

24. MS, NLS, 520.106. There is a letter from Thackeray in Paris to Jane Carlyle, 25
Feb. [1841], in which in considerable distress he writes of his great need of money to
keep his ill wife in a *pension* (MS, NLS, 665.45).
25. David A. Wilson, *Carlyle* (London and New York, 1923–34), III, 88.
26. Ibid., 184.

*he*, or his Father, was now proprietor of Naseby Battle-field.!"[27] Through later meetings with FitzGerald and correspondence with him Carlyle was able to achieve a considerable degree of accuracy and fullness of detail in writing his description of the famous battle. For many years the future translator of *The Rubáiyát of Omar Khayyam* (1859) was known to Carlyle chiefly as the heir to Naseby, the relative of wealthy landowners in Ireland, and the friend of Thackeray. And even some years after the famous translation was published, Carlyle told Charles Eliot Norton: "I've read that little book which you sent to me, and I think my old friend FitzGerald might have spent his time to much better purpose than in busying himself with the verses of that old Mohammedan blackguard."[28]

Thackeray's tour of Ireland which he recorded delightfully in his *The Irish Sketch Book* (1843) took place from 4 July to 1 November 1842. Many of the places which he visited and people whom he saw were the same as those which Carlyle would see and write about after his tour of Ireland in the late summer of 1849. FitzGerald's uncle, Peter FitzGerald, and his family seat Halverstown, near Kildare, figure largely in both narratives. Thackeray wrote in his brilliant conversational style, Carlyle in a somewhat vivid, choppy, emphatic way. Thackeray was more interested in manners, Carlyle in Ireland's horrible economic plight after two years of potato famine. But both were sharp observers and keen critics of Irish institutions, both were very much interested in many individual Irishmen, particularly those who stood out because of either personal oddity or strength of character, and both gave minimum attention to descriptions of places as such.

The Carlyles saw Thackeray soon after his return from Ireland. On 11 November 1842 Carlyle wrote to his brother John: "We had Thackeray here, two nights ago; fresh from Ireland, and full of quizzical rather honest kind of talk: he is now off to Paris; has a Book on Ireland with caricatures nearly ready: I cannot but wish poor Thackeray well. Nobody in this region has as much stuff to make a man out of,—could he but *make* him."[29]

27. MS, NLS, 524.37. See Thomas A. Kirby, "Carlyle, FitzGerald, and the Naseby Project," *Modern Language Quarterly*, 8 (Sept. 1947), 364–66. See also Wilson, *Carlyle*, III, 184.

28. Charles Eliot Norton, *Letters* (Boston and New York, 1913), I, 425–27; see also 471.

29. MS, NLS, 524–39. Among the caricatures made about this time, according to John Sterling, was a "first-rate pen sketch of Carlyle sitting on a tub and smoking—only to be paralleled by the Prophets of Angelo—I never laughed more heartily at anything." See Lionel Stevenson, *The Showman of Vanity Fair* (New York, 1947), p. 105.

During the years immediately following, the Carlyles saw much of
Thackeray, sometimes with feelings that were happy, sometimes with
feelings that were unpleasant if not unhappy, and sometimes with feelings
that were mixed. Thackeray, for his part, maintained his feeling of admiration and affection for the Carlyles consistently. Frequently FitzGerald or
others came to Chelsea with Thackeray. On 23 March 1843 Jane Carlyle
wrote to her cousin Jeannie Welsh:

> Today my head is specially bad and I am not up to a decent letter—in
> compensation I send you a document from Thackeray, which has wit
> enough in it to make up for any sort of scrap. To understand it aright
> I must tell you that he and FitzGerald came here that evening we were
> at the musical lecture, the *only* evening in which they *could* have
> failed to find at least one of us at home— Ever since I have been think-
> ing occasionally that I should write him a note of regrets and fix an
> evening—but my intention like too many others during the last week
> had gone to the paving of *the bad place!* To sharpen my sense of hos-
> pitality there arrived this letter from Fitzboodle two days ago which
> would have made even old Pitrucci [*sic*] in the 'Character of Heracly-
> tus' laugh. Pray return it to be present among my genuine treasures.[30]

A few days later she again wrote to her cousin:

> Thack[era]y and FitzGerald were to dine with us that day (Friday)—
> I baked a mutton pie and a raspberry tart in a state of great suffering
> —got through the dinner—hoped to get through the tea—and then
> promised myself to go to bed—but just before the men came up stairs,
> my affairs reached a consummation—I fainted—and had to be carried
> to bed—and lay for three hours alternating between fainting and retch-
> ing—Helen blubbering over me—and the men, increased by the arrival
> of Spedding and Robertson, raging and laughing in the adjoining
> room—Oh I assure you I have not passed such an evening for a good
> while.[31]

---

Thackeray undoubtedly felt very kindly toward Carlyle in this period. In a letter to
Jane dated 30 March [1842] he expressed his appreciation for the praise which he said
Carlyle had bestowed upon *The Great Hoggarty Diamond*, which had begun to ap-
pear in *Fraser's Magazine* for Sept. 1841 (MS, NLS, 665.46).

30. MS, NLS, 1891.224. Heraclitus of Ephesus (fl. 500 B.C.) was known as "the
weeping philosopher." Scipione Petrucci, whom Jane knew as a member of Mazzini's
circle, had because of his melancholy disposition acquired the nickname of Heraclitus.
See *Jane Welsh Carlyle: Letters to Her Family, 1839–1863*, ed. Leonard Huxley (New
York, 1924), pp. 22, 31.

31. MS, NLS, 1891.247. The letter is undated but was probably written on 8 April.

But there were far more joyous occasions. One of these was the birthday party of Nina Macready, daughter of the actor, who was absent from home at the time. In a letter to Jeannie Welsh of 23 December 1843 Jane Carlyle gave full details. Thackeray, Dickens, John Forster, Daniel Maclise, and others were all there.

> It was the *very* most agreeable party that ever I was at in London—everybody there seemed animated with one purpose to make up to Mrs. Macready and her children for the absence of "the Tragic Actor" and so amiable a purpose produced the most joyous results. . . . Only think of that excellent Dickens playing the *conjuror* for one whole hour—the *best* conjuror I ever saw—(and I have paid money to see several)—and Forster acting as his servant. . . . Then the dancing—old Major Burns with his one eye—old Jerdan of the Literary Gazette, . . . the gigantic Thackeray &c. &c. all capering like *Maenades*!! Dickens did all but go down on his knees to make *me*—waltz with him!

After supper there was champagne and making of speeches.

> A universal country dance was proposed—and Forster *seizing me around the waist*, whirled me into the thick of it, and *made* me dance!! . . . In fact the thing was rising into something not unlike the *rape of the Sabines* . . . when somebody looked [at] her watch and exclaimed "twelve o'clock!" . . . Dickens took home Thack[era]y and Forster with him and his wife "*to finish the night there*" and a *royal* night they would have of it I fancy! . . . After all—the pleasantest company, as Burns thought, *are the blackguards!*— . . . I question if there was as much witty speech uttered in all the aristocratic, conventional drawing rooms th[r]o'out London that night as among us little knot of blackguardist literary people who felt ourselves above all rules, and independent of the universe![32]

In another letter to her cousin (15 February 1844), Jane mentioned an amusing note from Dickens commenting on "an absurd mistake of Thackeray's who put five shillings into Robertson's hand one night in the idea he was reduced to the last 'extremity of fate'!! and then (what was much more inexcusable) told Dickens and myself of the transaction before witnesses in Mrs. Macready's drawing room!"[33]

32. MS, NLS, 1892.95.
33. MS, NLS, 1892.146. Carlyle identifies Robertson as "the blusterous John Robertson, whom Mill had at that time as Sub-editor, or Subaltern generally in the West-

On the more serious side, we find during these years Thackeray proposing to no avail in a letter to Bradbury and Evans of 26 February 1844 that
they put him at the head of a new "slashing brilliant, gentlemanlike, six-
penny, aristocratic, literary paper," a weekly which would carry signed
reviews and articles "by good men, Buller, Carlyle, Forster, Milnes, [Fitz]-
Gerald, and a University man or two."[34] Not until he became editor of the
*Cornhill Magazine* in 1859 was this dream to be in any part fulfilled. His
loyalty to Carlyle continued. "I got angry," he wrote in a letter to Richard
Bedington, 13 May 1844, "on reading 'The Miser's Son' at some reflections
on Thomas Carlyle made by a young author."[35] Yet it was quite possible
even during these years when the friendship was at its best for Thackeray
to catch Carlyle in one of his dour moods. On 30 July 1845 Carlyle wrote to
Jane, who was visiting in Liverpool, that on the day before he had had "a
grand ride" but that "after that, while at tea—Thackeray: no work farther
done. Weary, weary."[36]

The most disagreeable episode in the relationship of Carlyle to Thack-
eray arose, however, in January 1846 from a comment made by Carlyle to
Charles Buller on the trip to the Mediterranean which Thackeray made
from August 1844 to February 1845 as the guest of the Peninsular and
Oriental Steam Navigation Company, a trip which he recorded in his
*Notes of a Journey from Cornhill to Grand Cairo* (1846). Carlyle told
Buller that for Thackeray to accept a free berth for this voyage was like "a
blind fiddler going to and fro on a penny ferry-boat in Scotland, and playing
tunes to the passengers for half-pence." Buller very indiscretely repeated
the remark to Thackeray. Thackeray, hurt and indignant, confronted Carlyle, only to be told by him frankly: "It is undoubtedly my opinion that, out
of respect for yourself and your profession, a man like you ought not to
have gone fiddling for halfpence or otherwise in any steamboat under the
sky."[37] A year or two later, according to Francis Espinasse, Carlyle spoke

---

minster Review; and who took absurdish airs on that dignity." See *New Letters and
Memorials of Jane Welsh Carlyle*, ed. Alexander Carlyle (London and New York,
1903), I, 124.

34. Ray, *Letters*, II, 163.

35. Ibid., II, 167. The author of *The Miser's Son* has not been identified, but William Harrison Ainsworth published a novel called *The Miser's Daughter*, illustrated by
Cruikshank, in 1842. Ainsworth was thirty-eight years old at that time.

36. MS, NLS, 611.191.

37. See Wilson, *Carlyle*, III, 354–57; Ray, *Letters*, I, cvii–cviii; Stevenson, pp. 139,
159. Stevenson says that Carlyle's comment goaded Thackeray to make a sarcastic
retort in *Punch*. Yet Moncure D. Conway says that Carlyle told him that while Thackeray was writing *Cornhill to Cairo* and "with urgent work on hand, [he] escaped from
invitations, callers, and letters, and went off from his house without leaving any ad-

of the sagacity and knowledge of his uneducated father, even though "he could not tell you of the bitter ale consumed in the City of Prophets," a comment interpreted as a thrust at Thackeray's *Cornhill to Cairo*.[38] Thackeray became increasingly critical of Carlyle and showed his resentment in various ways. In a letter to FitzGerald of early 1846 he touched upon the ugly incident and in so doing employed an uglified spelling of Carlyle's name: "Gurlyle has called twice upon me and I've returned the visit once in rather a haughty & patronizing way"; and FitzGerald in a later letter refers to the "Gurlyles."[39] Carlyle, never a great admirer of the novel as a literary genre, in a letter to Browning of 23 June 1847 wrote critically of both Thackeray and Dickens: "Dickens writes a *Dombey and Son*, Thackeray a *Vanity Fair*; not *reapers* they, either of them. In fact, the business of rope-dancing goes to a great height."[40] On his side, Thackeray kept up the fight. In the spring of 1848 he wrote to FitzGerald: "My dear old Yedward It is not true what Gurlyle has written to you about my having become a tremenjuous lion. . . . Gurlyle is immensely grand and savage now. He has a Cromwellian letter against the Irish in this weeks Examiner. I declare it seems like insanity almost his contempt for all mankind, and the way in which he shirks from the argument when called upon to préciser his own remedies for the state of things."[41] And yet the amenities and the sense of fair play were in considerable part preserved. On 4 August 1848 Thackeray wrote to his mother: "Tom Carlyle lives in perfect dignity in a little house at Chelsea, with a snuffy Scotch maid to open the door, and the best company in England ringing at it. It is only the second and third chop great folks who care about Show."[42] On 24 August the Carlyles and John Forster took Jeannie Welsh to hear a concert by Jenny Lind which Thack-

---

dress," a messenger came to him one night from a public house nearby "with a request from Thackeray for the loan of a Bible." *Autobiography* (London, Paris, etc., 1904), II, 4. See also Stevenson, p. 135.

38. Francis Espinasse, *Literary Recollections and Sketches* (New York, 1893), p. 151.

39. Ray, *Letters*, II, 227, 265. Yet there does not seem to have been an open breach, not between Thackeray and Jane Carlyle at least. In an effort to help Thackeray find a proper governess for his daughters, Jane had told her German friend Amely Bölte of the position. Thackeray wrote to Jane on 25 July 1846 (?): "For God's sake stop Mme. Bölte. . . . I don't want a Gerwoman." Ibid., II, 242–43.

40. Wilson, *Carlyle*, III, 384.　　　　41. Ray, *Letters*, II, 365–66.

42. Ibid., II, 418. About this time Jane wrote to Carlyle: "I brought away the last four numbers of *Vanity Fair* and read one of them during the night. Very good indeed, beats Dickens out of the world." Stevenson, p. 166. On 14 July 1848 (her birthday) Thackeray had written to her apologetically, "Our dear little party of pleasure is put off." MS, NLS, 665.65. Very probably they were planning to celebrate the completion of *Vanity Fair*, finished on 29 June.

eray also attended.[43] Perhaps there was some friendly talk with Thackeray there, for just four days later Carlyle wrote to his brother John: "We are next to go and dine with Thackeray, who has been at Spa and back again; not a lovely outlook either."[44] In December of this year Thackeray wrote rather cryptically in a letter to Mrs. Brookfield: "As I was writing to Carlyle last night (I haven't sent the letter as usual and shall not most likely) Saint Stephen was pelted to death by Old Testaments; & Our Lord was killed like a felon by the law which he came to repeal."[45]

The friendship continued to progress on its uneasy, uncertain, irregular course, with a great deal of nip and tuck in the relationship. But it did not die, and neither man quite lost his deep, underlying respect and even affection for the other. On 5 January 1849, Carlyle wrote to James Marshall, secretary of the Duchess of Weimar: "Thackeray, Dickens and the others carry on their affairs; Thackeray has risen quite into fashion since you were here. Nothing can convince me that the like of all that is a noble employment under this Sun; or that it is in fact any employment at all, different from what we see at Astley's Ampitheatre, or what the black Bayaderes perform, in Oriental Countries, for some big surfeited rajah, who pays them surprisingly."[46] But as Gordon Ray points out, "The coolness that had developed between Thackeray and Carlyle did not prevent Mrs. Carlyle from inviting Anny and Minny to her little haven at Chelsea," and he quotes Lady Ritchie's charming account of how Jane served the two little girls hot chocolate on cold winter days.[47] Just the same, Jane wrote to Jeannie Welsh on 27 February 1849: "I must make an end for the present—and try to walk off the headache I got at a dinner at Thackeray's last night where *you* were not."[48] When Jane was away on a visit, Carlyle wrote to her on 5 April 1849: "I have got *Nowvigisch Näturchen* for you; *Pendennis* too (not by myself yet read): hope the tea will be agreeable!"[49] On 12 May following we find the Carlyles, Samuel Rogers, Thackeray, and others at a dinner party given by Dickens.[50] Just five days later Jane wrote to Jeannie Welsh to complain about a rather horrible practical joke perpetrated upon her by Thackeray. "Thackeray is returned from Paris; he was here with Fitz-Gerald the other evening. I was upstairs when they came in, and on coming into the room went to Thackeray first, to shake hands *in enthusiasm—*

43. Wilson, *Carlyle*, IV, 56.  
44. MS, NLS, 512.89.  
45. Ray, *Letters*, II, 472–73.  
46. MS, British Museum, 3032, f.5.  
47. *Thackeray: The Age of Wisdom (1847–63)* (New York, Toronto, London, 1958), pp. 20–21.  
48. MS, NLS, 1893.174.  
49. MS, NLS, 613.292.  
50. Wilson, *Carlyle*, IV, 88–90.

as one does after a journey to Paris—but I gave a loud scream on finding a small, cold, hard hand, as of a dead fairy—laid in mine. It was *your* hand which he had fastened at the end of his sleave! I declared the joke to be a heartless one, which seemed to vex him greatly. He repeated a dozen times during the evening that he wished he had not done it."[51] On 8 June Thackeray wrote to Mrs. Brookfield: "And now concerning Monday. You must please remember that you are engaged to this house at 7—I have written to remind the Scotts—to ask the Pollocks, and the Carlyles are coming."[52]

Early in his tour of Ireland during July and August of 1849 Carlyle visited Edward FitzGerald's relatives Peter FitzGerald and Mrs. Purcell at their home Halverstown near Kildare, as Thackeray had done seven years before. In his letters written at the time and in his *Reminiscences of My Irish Journey in 1849* he gave an account of his experience there. More interesting, however, was a comparison of Thackeray with Dickens which he made in conversation with Charles Gavan Duffy, who acted as his guide during a considerable part of the Irish tour. Duffy's account follows:

> I suggested that the difference between his [Dickens'] men and women and Thackeray's seemed to me like the difference between Sinbad the Sailor and Robinson Crusoe.
>
> Yes, he said, Thackeray had more reality in him and would cut up into a dozen Dickenses. They were altogether different at bottom. Dickens was doing the best in him, and went on smiling in perennial good humour; but Thackeray despised himself for his work, and on that account could not always do it even moderately well. He was essentially a man of grim, silent, stern nature, but lately he had circulated among fashionable people, dining out every day, and he covered this native disposition with a varnish of smooth, smiling complacency, not at all pleasant to contemplate. The course he had got into since he had taken to cultivate dinner-eating in fashionable houses was not salutary discipline for work of any sort, one might surmise.

When Duffy asked Carlyle whether he saw much of Thackeray, Carlyle gave him a detailed account of his comment on Thackeray's Mediterranean tour and the ill-feeling that grew out of it. But he also told Duffy that, as to criticism, Thackeray, John Sterling, and John Mill had written of his work

51. MS, NLS, 1893.187. Just what the "hand" was and in what sense it belonged to Jeannie Welsh has not been determined.
52. Ray, *Letters*, II, 548.

in various quarters with appreciation and more than sufficient applause but that criticism in general on books, men, and things had become the idlest babble.[53] In spite of this comment on Thackeray, Carlyle knew very well that there could never be any agreement between Thackeray and himself on the subject of the hero. George Venables, who knew both men well, wrote: "He [Carlyle] had naturally but little sympathy with Thackeray's instinctive dislike of greatness, as it is exemplified in his antipathy to Marlborough and to Swift. I think it was after a conversation between them on the character of Swift that I heard Carlyle say, 'I wish I could persuade Thackeray that the test of greatness in a man is not whether he (Thackeray) would like to meet him at a tea-party.' He liked Thackeray himself, and I think he never spoke of him with the contempt which, before he became comparatively intimate with Dickens, he expressed for 'the infinitely small Schnüspel, the distinguished novelist.' "[54]

Back at Chelsea, Carlyle wrote to his brother John on 6 October:

> Thackeray has been dangerously ill, still lies close in bed: "slow inflammation," that to be produced by too diligent a course of dinners, —poor Thackeray! He has had formally to suspend his Pendennis nonsense; and everybody says he had better give it up, the total, and even, tiresome inanity of it being palpable to all creatures. Dickens again is said to be flourishing beyond example with his present series of funambulisms [*David Copperfield!*]:—I read one No of it (I am quite fallen behind) last night; innocent waterest of twaddle with a *suspicion* of geniality,—very fit for the purpose in view, which Th's is not.[55]

On 10 November he again wrote to his brother: "Thackeray is still utterly weak, but is reported out of danger."[56] Thackeray's illness was a long one and recovery was slow, but by late November he was pretty well back on his feet again. Henry Reeve reports in his diary that on 19 December he had dinner at Bryan Waller Procter's with Kinglake, Harriet Martineau, the Carlyles, and Thackeray.[57] Thackeray wrote to Mrs. Procter on 3 January 1850: "I will come with much pleasure on Sunday and I should like to have Carlyle and Reeve over again only I know it's wrong and impossi-

53. *Conversations with Carlyle* (London, Paris, Melbourne, 1896), pp. 75–91; Wilson, *Carlyle*, IV, 112; V, 304; C. R. Sanders, "Retracing Carlyle's Irish Journey (1849)," *Studies: An Irish Quarterly Review*, 50 (Spring 1961), 41–42.

54. Ray, *Letters*, I, cix.

55. MS, NLS, 513.23. In a letter to Jane of Oct., probably written some days later, Thackeray reports, "I am getting better." Ray, *Letters*, II, 597.

56. MS, NLS, 513.27.              57. Wilson, *Carlyle*, IV, 235.

ble."[58] Just why it was impossible for Carlyle and Reeve to come is explained in a letter which Thackeray wrote to James Spedding on 5 January: "The fun goes out of a man at 40: where are the jokes that came in such plenty? Ah me as Tom Carlyle says he was here the other day and very kind. I wish you could have heard him though, in a different mood, at Procter's. He fell foul of Reeve who had a stiff white neckcloth, which probably offended the Seer. He tossed Reeve and gored yea as a bull he chased him and horned him: for an hour or more he pitched him about ripping open his bowels and plunging his muzzle into Reeves smoking entrails. Reeves had to appear perfectly goodhumoured all the time of the operation, and indeed bore it with wonderful face and patience."[59] According to an account of the incident which Dickens gave to Yates, Carlyle became furious when Reeve smugly and suavely tried to dismiss a subject, perhaps Ireland, which Carlyle considered important.[60]

Just a few days later at a dinner given by Misses Agnes and Mary Berry, Thackery was much more severe in his judgment upon Carlyle. Miss Kate Perry gives this account of the conversation: "Carlyle was discussed, and Miss Berry asking what his conversation was like, Kinglake said Ezekiel which we all thought a happy illustration of the denouncing style with which he cries out woe and desolation to all existing ordinances, men, and habits of the world. Thackeray said that he was a bully—attack him with persiflage and he was silenced, in fact Carlyle is no longer the Prophet he used to be considered—I remember his palmy days when his words were manna to the Israelites."[61] Thackeray's friend FitzGerald, however, was much more tolerant when Carlyle's *Latter-Day Pamphlets*, written in an extremely angry tone, began to appear in February. He wrote to Tennyson: "Do you see Carlyle's *Latter-Day Pamphlets*? They make the world laugh, and his friends rather sorry for him. But that is because people will still look for practical measures from him. One must be content with him as a great satirist who can make us feel when we are wrong, though he cannot set us right. There is a bottom of truth in Carlyle's wildest rhapsodies."[62]

Whatever their comments on the side and their true feelings toward one another may have been, Carlyle and Thackeray continued to meet and

58. Ray, *Letters*, II, 626.          59. Ibid., II, 628.
60. Wilson, *Carlyle*, IV, 235–36. For an anecdote concerning Thackeray's own use of persiflage to choke off a Unitarian minister's serious theological discussion, see Stevenson, p. 193.
61. Ray, *Letters*, I, cviii.
62. *Tennyson and His Friends*, ed. Hallam Tennyson (London, 1911), p. 132.

maintain the social amenities from time to time. Often they met with other members of the Ashburton circle, which from about 1848 until the death of Lady Ashburton in 1857 was one of the most brilliant groups in the history of British literature and culture. Needless to say, however, things did not always go off well even at Lady Ashburton's parties. In early March 1850 Thackeray wrote to Mrs. Brookfield: "We had a dull dinner at Lady Ashburton's, a party of Barings chiefly. . . . Carlyle glowered in the evening."[63] But on 12 June Carlyle attended a dinner given by Thackeray for Charlotte Brontë.[64] We find both Carlyle and Thackeray at Addiscombe, one of the Ashburton country houses, on 30 June, when word came that Peel had been thrown from his horse the day before, an accident from which he soon died.[65] Thackeray and Mrs. Carlyle were among Lady Ashburton's guests at "The Grange" in early October. Jane wrote to Carlyle on 6 October: "Thackeray is here—arrived yesterday—greatly to the discomfort of Henry Taylor evidently who 'had the gang all to himself' so long. First he (Thackeray) wrote he was coming; then Lady A. put him off on account of some *Punch*-offence to the Taylors. Then Thackeray wrote an apology to Taylor!! Then Lady A. wrote that he was to come after all, and went to Winchester to meet him, and Taylor sulked all yester evening and today is solemn to death. In fact he had been making a sort of superior *agapemone* here in which *he* was the Mr. Price, *The Spirit of Love*—and no wonder he dislikes the turn that has been given to things by the arrival of the *Spirit of Punch*."[66] Soon Carlyle himself came down, as was duly noted by Thackeray in a letter to Mrs. Brookfield.[67] On 10 October Carlyle wrote from the Grange, to his brother John: "We are a shifting party, Thackeray and Rawlinson (Bagdad) went today; a nice little Frenchwoman (Mrs Craven) remains; and here are the *wheels of newcomers* while I write: a shifting party; with whom I have not much to do beyond looking at them."[68]

One of the most delightful records in the story of the relation between the Carlyles and Thackeray is that which Jane Carlyle made concerning her dealings in early 1851 with Theresa Reviss, adopted daughter of Charles

63. Ray, *Letters*, II, 647.                    64. Ibid., II, 674n.

65. Wilson, *Carlyle*, IV, 288–89. Jane wrote to Helen Welsh on Thursday, 4 July: "Mr. C. and Thackeray came to dinner on Sunday but had to return at night every room being taken up." MS, NLS, 1893.231.

66. MS, NLS, 604.344. Two days later Jane wrote to Carlyle: "Henry Taylor and Thackeray have *fraternized* finally, *not* 'like the carriage horses and railway steam engine' as might have been supposed but like *men* and *Brothers!*" MS, NLS, 604.335. An Agapemone is a communistic, free-love institution like that founded about 1849 at Spaxton, England.

67. Ray, *Letters*, II, 699.                    68. MS, NLS, 515.53.

Buller's mother and generally assumed to be one of the most important prototypes of Becky Sharp, although Mrs. Carlyle identifies her with Blanche Amory in *Pendennis*. Thackeray had been in and out of the Buller home many times throughout the years when Theresa was growing up and had always found her to be a detestable brat. Mrs. Carlyle's record is to be found in two letters of early 1851 to John Welsh, her mother's brother in Liverpool. The first is dated 2 January:

> And now I must simply *promise* you a long letter, for today is most unfavorable for *writing* one. There arrived on us yesterday a young Heroine of Romance with a quantity of trunks and a Lady's maid, who is for the moment keeping this poor house and my poor self in a state of utter disquiet. I had invited her to dine one day and, if it suited her better, to stay *over the night*. And she has so arranged her affairs that if she leave here today it must be to live till next week in a Hotel (at nineteen!). What can one do then but let her remain—with protest against the Lady's maid. She is Mrs. Buller's adopted daughter whom you may have heard of, and has just been playing the Sultana in India for a year, and—. Oh dear, here is her *lover* come to see her, and in a quarter of an hour a Prison Inspector is coming to take Mr. C. and me through Pentonville prison. I am bothered to death, my blessed Uncle.[69]

Her second letter to her uncle was written on 7 January:

> Have you been reading Thackeray's *Pendennis*? If so, you have made acquaintance with *Blanche Amory*, and when I tell you that my young lady of last week, is the original of that portrait, you will give me joy that she, Lady's maid, and infinite baggage, is all gone! Not that poor little 'Tizzy' (Theresa Revis[s]) is *quite* such a little devil as Thackeray, who has detested her from a child[,] has here represented, but the looks, the manners, the wiles, the *Larmes*, "and all that sort of thing["] are a perfect likeness—the blame, however, is chiefly on those who placed her in a position so *false*, that it required extraordinary virtue not to become false along with it—She was the only *legitimate* child of a beautiful young 'improper female' who was for a number of years Arthur Buller's mistress. She had *had* a husband, a swindler—his [Buller's] Mother took the freak of patronizing this mistress, saw the child and behold it was very pretty and clever. Poor Mrs Buller had

69. MS, NLS, 604.341.

tired of parties, of Politics, of most things in Heaven and earth; "a sudden thought struck her," she would *adopt* this child; give herself the excitement of *making a scandal* and *braving public opinion*, and of educating a flesh and blood girl into the Heroine of the three volume novel which she had for years been trying to *write*; but wanted perseverance to elaborate!—The child was made the idol of the whole house —even Charles did whatever she pleased—her showy education was fitting her more for her own Mothers profession than for any honest one—and when she was seventeen and the *novel* was just rising into the interest of *love-affairs*—a rich young man having been refused —or rather *jilted* by her—Mrs Buller died—her husband and son [Charles] being already dead and poor Tizzy was left without any earthly stay and with only 250 £ a year to support her in the extravagantly luxurious habits she had been brought up in— She has a splendid voice and wished to get trained for the Opera— Mrs. Buller's fine Lady friends screamed at the idea—but offered her nothing instead— not even their countenance—her two male guardians, to wash their hands of her, resolved to send her to India to Sir Arthur Buller, whose wife hated her—naturally—being the child of her husbands ci-devant mistress— To India she had to go however; vowing that if their object was to marry her off—she would disappoint them, and return "to prosecute the Artist Life"— She produced the most extraordinary *furor* at Calcutta, had offers of Sudar Judges and what not, every week—refused them point blank, terrified Sir Arthur by her extravagance, tormented Lady Buller by her caprices, "fell into consumption," —for the nonce—was ordered by the Doctors back to England! and to the dismay of her two cowardly guardians arrived here sick months ago—*with her health perfectly restored!* But her Indian reputation had preceded her and the fine Ladies who turned their backs on her in her extreme need now invite a girl who has refused Sudar Judges by the dozen— She had been going about from one house to another, while no *home* could be found for her! The guardians had a brilliant idea— "Would *we* take her?"—Not for her weight in gold I said—but I asked her to spend *a day* with me that I might see what she was grown to, and whether I could do anything in placing her with some proper person— The result of this invitation was that alarming arrival, bag and baggage on Newyears day! She has saved me all further speculation about her however by engaging herself to a Capt. Neale (from Ayrshire) who came home in the ship with her and seems a most

devoted Lover—SHE "does not love *him* a bit" she told me—"had been
hesitating some time betwixt accepting him, or going on the stage, or
drowning herself—" I told her, her decision was good, as marrying did
not preclude either 'going on the stage' at a subsequent period, or
'drowning herself'—whereas had she decided on *the drowning*; there
could have been no more of it.— I have my own notion that she will
throw him over yet; meanwhile it was a *blessed calm* after the *Fly*
rolled her away from here on Saturday— "Oh my Dear!" Mr C said
"we cannot be sufficiently thankful!!"— indeed you can have no notion
how the whole routine of this quiet house was tumbled heels over
head—It had been for these three days and three nights *not* Jonah
in the Whale's belly—but the Whale in Jonah's belly!—that little creature seemed to have absorbed this whole establishment into *herself*—[70]

From 22 May to 3 July Thackeray delivered his lectures on "The English
Humourists of the Eighteenth Century." Thackeray's friends, including
the Carlyles, attended them. Thackeray had his misgivings concerning the
merits of lecturing but was grateful for the brilliant circle of friends who
came to hear him. On 23 May he wrote to Abraham Hayward: "But the
truth is that lectures won't do. They were all friends, and a packed house;
though, to be sure, it goes to a man's heart to find amongst his friends such
men as you and Kinglake and Venables, Higgins, Rawlinson, Carlyle, Ashburton and Hallam, Milman, Macaulay, Wilberforce looking on kindly."[71]
The Carlyles were not uncritical. Jane wrote to her cousin Helen Welsh in
early June: "Thursday is Thackeray's Lecture day, and I have a ticket waiting for you. The Lectures between you and me are no great things—as
*Lecture*s—but it is the fashion to find them 'so amusing'! and the *audience*
is the most brilliant I ever saw in one room—unless in Bath House drawing-
rooms."[72] After the last lecture Carlyle wrote to his brother John: "On
Thursday I went to hear Thackeray *end*; Jane and I. The audience inferior
to what I had heard; *item* the performance. Comic *acting* good in it; also
a certain gentility of style notable: but of *insight* (worth calling by the
name) none; nay a good deal of *pretended* insight (morality &c with an

---

70. MS, NLS, 604.343.
71. Ray, *Letters*, II, 777. For a note to the Carlyles which, according to Ray, may
have been written on the day after Thackeray's first lecture and in which he says "you
are both very kind to me: and always have been my kind old friends and I am yours
in return," see ibid., II, 775. The note is accompanied by an amusing sketch of a
tight-rope walker.
72. MS, NLS, 1893.249. Bath House in Piccadilly was the town house of the Ashburtons.

ugly 'do' at the bottom of it) which was worse than none. The air grew
bad; I had only one wish, to be out again, out, out!— Thackeray has not
found his feet yet; but he may perhaps do so in that element, and get (as
Darwin expresses it) into some kind of 'Thackeray at Home,' in which he
might excel all people for delighting an empty fashionable audience."73

Gordon Ray makes clear one reason why Carlyle did not greatly enjoy
Thackeray's lectures: "With regard to doctrine Thackeray intended his
lectures to be pointedly anti-Carlylean. He made 'The Humorist as a Man
of Letters' almost the antithesis of 'The Hero as a Man of Letters' as Carlyle
had described him. . . . He reserved his warmest praise for such completely
unheroic figures as Dick Steele and Noll Goldsmith. This aspect of Thackeray's lectures did not escape Carlyle, who was a faithful member of his
audience."74

Nevertheless, the Carlyles continued to maintain a friendly interest in
Thackeray and his activities, and Thackeray continued to visit them. On
18 October 1851 Carlyle wrote to his brother John: "Thackeray was here
last night; he is going to Edinr to lecture in December, then to America
('to send round the hat'), is meanwhile writing an illustrious Novel [*Henry
Esmond*]:—'poor fellow, after all!' "75 On 24 October he wrote again to the
same brother: "Thackeray was here the other night, 'just waiting for his
dinner hour' somewhere: perhaps I told you?"76 And to Lady Ashburton
Carlyle wrote on 27 October: "Thackeray was here one night; going to
Edinburgh with his Lectures in December; then to Yankeeland with do:
having first published a Novel in 3 volumes; and so smitten heartily on the
big drum."77

Carlyle's *The Life of John Sterling* was published during the second
week in October. Late in the same month Thackeray wrote to Lady Stanley
of Alderley: "Carlyle's Life of Sterling is delightful have you read it?" It
is hard to reconcile this praise with his savage attack on the book and

73. MS, NLS, 513.86. See also Stevenson, p. 238.

74. *Thackeray: The Age of Wisdom*, pp. 144–45. Carlyle wrote to Emerson on 25
Aug.: "Item Thackeray; who is coming over to lecture to you: a mad world, my Masters!" Joseph Slater, ed., *The Correspondence of Emerson and Carlyle* (New York and
London, 1964), p. 474. Slater quotes as follows from a letter of 25 Feb. 1852 by Harriet Martineau to Emerson: 'I saw the Carlyles a few months since;— just saw them, &
O! dear! felt them too. They put me between them, at Thackeray's last lecture; & both
got the fidgets. After the first half hour, C. looked at his watch, & held it across me,
about once in two minutes; & he filled up the intervals with shaking himself, & drum-
ming his elbow into my side." Ibid.

75. MS, NLS, 514.29. "Poor fellow, after all!" is coterie speech, a favorite expression of Carlyle's brother John.

76. MS, NLS, 514.30.                    77. MS, Marquess of Northampton.

Carlyle which appeared in over three long columns in the *Times* for 1 November.[78] Of course there had been rumblings under the surface of Thackeray's mind before in such things as his account of Carlyle's goring of Henry Reeve and his speaking of Carlyle as a bully. It should also be noted that two of Carlyle's chief admirers, John Sterling and Charles Buller, both of whom could have acted as restraining influences on Thackeray, were now dead. Whatever the explanation and however great the inconsistency may be, Thackeray's review was something far removed from the persiflage with which he had said the bully could be silenced; it was veritably the explosion of a volcano. Brief excerpts from it follow:

> Weak minds will be sorely distressed by the last production of the redoubtable Thomas. That angry gentleman is more indignant than ever. His wrath has got to its height . . . . We doubt whether the life would have been written at all but for the matchless opportunity it affords for the pugilistic efforts of the author. . . . We may doubt the prudence of the undertaking, but who shall question the valour of the man who, singlehanded, takes upon himself to thrash the whole world! A memoir of John Sterling has already been written. The reading public, which did not call for that, hardly required another almost upon its heels. . . . The great object of the author of the *Latter Day Pamphlets* in this his last work seems to be—as far as we can gather it—to prove the utter impossibility of an honest man's making way in life, and the absolute rottenness of all existing things. The world, according to Mr. Carlyle, has never been so bad as it is . . . . : There is throughout this book no cessation of abuse; but we have searched throughout it in vain, though most carefully and anxiously, for a single line of wholesome counsel. Mr. Carlyle keeps a school in which scolding goes on from morning till night, but certainly no teaching. . . . Nothing but fighting suits Mr. Carlyle or lies within his scope to recommend. But, if we are to fight, let us at least know against whom and what for. . . . But we altogether deny the wild and incoherent yet very grave accusations which Mr. Carlyle brings against society—accusations which he finds much easier to make than to justify. The age in which we live is *not* the very worst since the fall of man. Would Mr. Carlyle, who asserts that it is, willingly exchange it for any age that has preceded it? . . . It is not always easy, as our readers may have discovered, to have the full benefit of

78. Ray, *Letters*, II, 808. Thackeray's review is included in his *Centenary Works,* (London, 1910–11), XXV, 373–86.

Mr. Carlyle's thoughts, so strangely are they garbed in that gentleman's most peculiar diction. . . . The world, bad as it is, will be grateful to Mr. Carlyle if he will put his shoulder to the wheel and help it to repair a crying evil. But putting a shoulder or even a finger to the wheel is just what this writer will not do. . . . Coleridge is presented to us in glowing colours, sitting "on the brow of Highgate-hill, looking down on London and its smoke tumult, like a sage escaped from the inanity of life's battle." This is a "good man"; the only "good" man of whom especial mention is made in the volume. . . . But Coleridge, coolly leaving Robert Southey to take care of his children, retires to a snug retreat opened for him by his friends at Highgate—a refuge which he had not the chivalry and manly courage to decline; and he, in that very epoch of his life, assumes in Carlyle's eye the form of perfect human grandeur. . . . The moment the philosopher creeps to his chamber, and thereby humbly falls on his knees as a Christian, he is scornfully left to his own devices. . . . Poor Coleridge, in spite of all his metaphysical entanglements, took shelter in his latter days from his many bodily and mental troubles under cover of those simple truths which give peace to the tempest-tossed, hope to the despairing, resignation to the sorely-afflicted; and, for this obvious outrage to philosophy, Carlyle deserts him. . . . It suits the humour of Mr. Carlyle to mock every faith but his own, and to render his own wholly unintelligible even to his disciples.

Finally Thackeray criticizes Carlyle for publishing in the *Sterling* some private correspondence between Edward Sterling, editor of the *Times* and John Sterling's father, and Sir Robert Peel. Thackeray's comment today sounds strangely ironical in view of the controversy later over Froude's revelation of intimate details in his biography of Carlyle. Thackeray wrote: "From the reckless way in which he [Carlyle] had made use of this private communication we cannot refrain from expressing a hope that Mr. Carlyle himself may never be placed in the same position, with regard to any public journal, as that so ably filled by Edward Sterling with regard to *The Times*. Should he be so situated we cannot undertake to say how soon such private communications as that to which we have called attention would become common property." It is even more strikingly ironical that Thackeray's most blistering attack on Carlyle, written just three years after the publication of his own *novel* without a hero, concerned itself with a book in which Carlyle, following the example of Dr. Samuel Johnson's *The Life of Richard Savage,* proved that he could write a truly excellent *biography* without a hero.

One would be hard pressed to draw a nice distinction between Carlyle's pessimism, as Thackeray conceived it, and what Carlyle thought of as Thackeray's "terrible cynicism." Did Carlyle know that Thackeray was the author of the hostile review in the *Times?* Presumably he did. There were other unfavorable reviews of Carlyle's *Sterling,* and he dismissed them all with a disdainful, shrug-shoulder gesture. The book sold extremely well and soon went into a second edition. Carlyle gave some of the credit to the hostile reviews such as that which had appeared in the *Times.*

As formerly, ripples continued to appear in the friendship from time to time, but in the main it proceeded rather pleasantly along its course down to Thackeray's death on 24 December 1863. The Carlyles, Thackeray, and his two little girls spent late December of 1851 and the New Year's season with the Ashburtons at the Grange. On 27 December Jane wrote Helen Welsh from the Grange that Thackeray was coming that day and that she was remaining to help take care of his two little girls.[79] On 29 December Carlyle wrote to his brother John from the same place: "Thackeray is just returned from lecturing and lionizing in Edinburgh; he is not of great profit to talk with, but he is easy and agreeable, and his presence, taking away the burden of talk from others, is so far very welcome."[80] Back at Chelsea on 3 January, Carlyle wrote again to the same brother: "Thackeray and his two girls were with us. . . . I have never seen him so well before. There is a great deal of talent in him, a great deal of sensibility,— irritability, sensuality, vanity without limit; and nothing, or little, but sentimentalism and playactorism to guide it all with: not a good or well-found ship in such water on such a voyage."[81] On 23 February Carlyle wrote to this brother: "We were at dinner on Friday night with one Ellice in Arlington Street (a wide-flowing old Canadian Scotchman, Politician, Negociator &c &c, called 'Bear Ellice' in society here, but rather for his *oiliness* than any trace of ferocity ever seen in him): Thiers, the Ashburtons,

---

79. MS, NLS, 1893.266. In an undated letter written perhaps several days later Jane told Kate Sterling, daughter of John Sterling, "Well! I write to day to tell you that we go home on Friday next—having staid a week longer than bargain on account of the —Misses Thackeray!— 'As they knew *me* and didn't know *her*'; Lady A begged me to stay over their visit in case of their 'being shy'! a needless apprehension on her part!— Besides these little girls and their Father there are no other visitors at present except Miss Farrer [Farrar]—much better humoured and every way more compatible with children than I am." MS, Carlyle House, Chelsea.
80. MS, NLS, 514.42.    81. MS, NLS, 514.47.

Thackeray &c &c were there; and much confused talk, in bad French and otherwise."[82] On 5 April he wrote to him: "Anthony Sterling has finished his Zinc House, and holds *tabagies* (or smoking parties in it, Spedding, Ford, Thackeray &c) in it [*sic*], to none of which do I go."[83]

A very amusing account of two robberies, one of them at the expense of Thackeray, is to be found in a letter which Jane Carlyle wrote to Carlyle in Scotland on 12 August. Carlyle repeated it in a letter to Lady Airlie:

> Jane added a rumour of two robberies: robbery first, the pocket of Thackeray picked of a £100 Note in foreign parts (may it burn the thief's fingers!)—robbery second, Mrs. Ruskin's jewels (pretty Mrs. Ruskin, one of the daintiest Scotch women married to *a Prince* "of Criticism," and I doubt not valuable jewels, for they are rich and she is bright and gay), all stolen, in Italy, by some English-Austrian spy and swindler; and, what makes it worse, the Newspaper narrative of the affair, is headed 'Stones of Venice,' which is the title of her husband's last Book. How mischievous are mankind one to another, with object and without![84]

Thackeray's old dislike of heroes is reflected in a letter to Dr. John Brown of 6 October: "Carlyle is away in Germany looking after *Frederick the Great*. I don't know what Literature is about."[85] Back at the Grange, Carlyle wrote to his mother on 23 October: "Thackeray is coming, for whom I care nothing, though he is a clever and friendly man; he comes today with a nobleman and a Portrait-Painter; comes, but is soon to go:— 'Di tha naither ill na' guid!' "[86] A day or so later he wrote to Joseph Neuberg: "We have agreeable enough people, Thackeray among them."[87]

---

82. MS, NLS, 514.56. "Bear" Ellice is Edward Ellice, who appeared frequently in the Ashburton circle.

83. MS, NLS, 514.61. Anthony Sterling, who was to become a captain and fight in the Crimean War, was John Sterling's brother.

84. MS, NLS, Acc. 2427.                  85. Ray, *Letters*, III, 91.

86. MS, NLS, 514.89. Jane wrote Kate Sterling on the same day: "I hear the carriage come back with Laurence who is to paint Thackeray here in these days—for the world—" MS, Berg Collection, New York Public Library. Laurence is Samuel Laurence (1812–84). Carlyle's dialectal phrase "Di tha etc." is coterie speech, the saying of an Annandale cattle dealer. See the *Letters and Memorials of Jane Welsh Carlyle*, ed. J. A. Froude (London, 1883), I, 278–79. Thackeray wrote to George Bancroft on 18 Nov. 1853: "My friend Mr. S. Lawrence [*sic*] is the bearer of this note: and I recommend him to your good offices during his stay in New York. You have a specimen of his handy-work in the portrait of the undersigned. I think Lawrence is the best drawer of heads since Van Dyke.... Lawrence has done all the philosophers and literary men here Carlyle Dickens F. Maurice Kingsley Ashburton, Monteagle que scais je?" Ray, *Letters*, III, 317.

87. Wilson, *Carlyle*, IV, 445.

*Henry Esmond*, published in October 1852, was soon read by both Carlyles. Carlyle gave their estimate of it in a letter to Lady Ashburton of 10 November:

We have gone thro' Thackeray's Novel; my wife first, with great admiration "for the fine delineations of women"; I next, with aversion and contempt mainly for his feline phantasms of "women," with many reflexions on his singular fineness of sense and singular want of do— and on the whole with fairly more esteem for this Book than seemed likely at the Grange. I find the "style," both of painting and writing, worthy of peculiar recognition, in general quite excellt for clearness, simplicity and grace,—and here and there with a fine *adagio* of affectionate sentimentality, which is almost beautiful, almost pious. Poor Thackeray, God help him, and us, after all![88]

But Thackeray's comment on Carlyle in a letter to Mrs. Procter of 25 November is not so charitable: "I wish you had seen it [the Duke of Wellington's funeral on 18 November]. . . . You can imagine the whole of this large City, but with one idea (except Carlyle who is entirely without sympathy and thinks all enthusiasm wrong, except what is felt for himself), I thought."[89] From Philadelphia in a letter to Lady Stanley of 21 January 1853 he made a lighter and somewhat amusing thrust at Carlyle: "They [his American audiences] are great about pronunciation especially, and take down at my lectures the words which this present Arbiter of English pronounces differently to them. If Carlyle comes I wonder if they'll take *him* as an exemplar."[90]

Thackeray returned to England in early May but after a few weeks went abroad to Paris, Germany, and Switzerland. In a letter of 9 September Carlyle gave Emerson what has become his most quoted pen portrait of Thackeray: "Thackeray has very rarely come athwart me since his return: he is a big fellow, soul and body; of many gifts and qualities (particularly in the Hogarth line, with a dash of Sterne superadded), of enormous *appetite* withal, and very uncertain and chaotic in all points, except his *outer breeding*, which is fixed enough, and *perfect* according to the modern

88. MS, Marquess of Northampton.
89. Ray, *Letters*, III, 126. Carlyle admired the Duke of Wellington, but as he watched the funeral procession from the second-floor windows of Bath House he saw nothing in it "of the least dignity" except the four thousand soldiers and was disgusted with much in it that seemed to him ugly and inappropriate. See Wilson, *Carlyle*, IV, 449–50.
90. Ray, *Letters*, III, 179.

English style. I rather dread explosions in his history. A *big*, fierce, weeping, hungry man; not a strong one."[91]

In 1854 Carlyle saw very little of Thackeray, who was abroad a good part of the time. But on 4 November he wrote to Lady Ashburton: "Thackeray came over to see us one night; was very gentle and friendly-looking; ingenious too here and there; but extremely difficult to talk with, somehow —his talk lying all in flashes, little detached pools, you nowhere got upon a well or vein."[92] On 18 November he again wrote to her: "Thackeray, I hear, has fled the country somewhither, not being well in these weeks: poor soul, busy to[o] and I suppose not in high spirits always—as the like of me. God help us all."[93] Thackeray's one comment on Carlyle for this year comes late and does not amount to much. On 4 December he wrote to Lady Stanley: "Ashburton has grown a beard I hear & Tom Carlyle has a scrubby one."[94]

On 13 October 1855 Thackeray sailed from Liverpool to Boston in order to begin his lecture tour on *The Four Georges*. Two days earlier Carlyle had written to Lady Ashburton: "Thackeray, I suppose, is gone to America? A fortnight ago I saw him once for a moment; poor Thackeray: what a life poor mortals have in this world at present—with all loadstars gone out, locker emptyish, and the sea running high!"[95] Thackeray's American tour lasted all winter and ran into the early spring. A curious bit of confusion involving pronunciation and spelling got him in trouble and at the same time reflected the popularity of Carlyle in the United States, especially in the South, at this time. On 15 March Thackeray wrote to Mrs. Procter from New Orleans: "I am whipped for a malignant attack on Carlyle in my lectures—the fact being that I mentioned in the very most courteous and kindly terms, Lord Carlisle, G. Selwyn's correspondent in the early reign of George III. Only a malignant blundering Paddy-whack could write in this way."[96] It seems inconceivable, as Thackeray suggests, but careless American journalists had misconstrued two points in Thackeray's discussion of Lord Carlisle which offended an American public thinking of Thomas Carlyle: one was a close association with George III, and the other was Thackeray's statement that "Lord Carlisle was one of those English fine gentlemen who was well-nigh ruined by the awful debauchery

---

91. Slater, p. 496.                    92. MS, Marquess of Northampton.
93. Ibid.
94. Ray, *Letters*, III, 404. Carlyle stopped shaving on 9 Oct. when Lord Ashburton, who had already grown a beautiful beard, came to Chelsea and took away his razors to compel him to keep his promise to stop.
95. MS, Marquess of Northampton.          96. Ray, *Letters*, III, 585.

and extravagance which prevailed in the great English society of those days."[97]

On 4 May 1857 Lady Ashburton died at Paris, and an era ended for both Carlyle and Thackeray. Jane Carlyle gave an account of her death to her friend in a letter written several days after the funeral, which took place on 12 May: "I have been long in answering your dear Letter. If you saw Lady Ashburton's death in the Newspapers you would partly guess why; that I was shocked, and dispirited, and feeling *silence* best. . . . I never heard of so easy a death. She was dressing about four o'clock; felt faint, and called for Dr. Rous (her private Doctor); he told her, in answer to her question, 'what is this?' 'you are going to faint, it is nothing; you mustn't mind these faintnesses!' He put his arm round her to support; she clasped her hands over his other arm, leant her forehead on his shoulder, gave a sigh, and was dead!" In the same letter she commented on the funeral, which Carlyle, Thackeray, Henry Taylor, George Venables, and other members of Lady Ashburton's circle attended: "On Tuesday Mr. C. went to the Grange to be present at her funeral. It was conducted with a kind of royal state; and all the men, who used to compose a sort of *Court* for her, were there, *in tears*! I never heard of a gloomier funeral."[98]

In July following Thackeray ran for a seat in Parliament to represent Oxford. His opponent was Edward Cardwell (1813–86), a politician, statesman, and military reformer of considerable note who had held the seat earlier. Carlyle commented in a letter to his wife of 16 July: "Thackeray is candidate for Oxford: Thackeray *versus* Cardwell! It seems to be extremely foolish; but perhaps not *more* so than the rest. Cardwell, at any rate, I suppose, will prevail."[99] Cardwell did prevail, and on 26 July Carlyle again wrote to his wife: "Thackeray has lost his Election, as you see; what a big form of the species Dingle-dousie that is!"[100] According to Gordon Ray, Thackeray did not willingly face so formidable an opponent and afterwards confessed that he was "himself a Cardwellite."[101]

In the middle of May 1858 Thackeray was guest at a dinner in London at which the historian John Lothrop Motley was also present. Motley gave an account of the dinner in a letter to his wife: "Something was said of

97. See the 9th and 10th paragraphs of Thackeray's lecture "George III."
98. *New Lettters and Memorials of Jane Welsh Carlyle*, ed. Alexander Carlyle (London and New York, 1903), II, 135–36.
99. MS, NLS, 614.443.
100. MS, NLS, 614.448. A "dingle-dousie" is Scottish for a stick ignited at one end and swung about for the entertainment of children.
101. *Thackeray: The Age of Wisdom*, pp. 269–70.

Carlyle the author. Thackeray said, 'Carlyle hates everybody who has arrived—if they are on the road, he may perhaps treat them civilly.' Mackintosh praised the description in the 'French Revolution' of the flight of the King and Queen (which is certainly one of the most living pictures ever painted with ink), and Thackeray agreed with him, and spoke of the passages very heartily."[102]

When the Reverend Alexander Scott was planning a trip to America in 1858, Carlyle wrote to him on 30 June: "Have you applied to Thackeray on the matter? . . . He is of course the Cortez and Columbus of that element; —he is a very kind obliging soul too."[103]

Throughout his life Carlyle had grappled with what was to him the formidable problem of finding good pens to write with and good paper to write on. This had been something of a problem to Thackeray too, and between the years 1856 and 1859 they discussed the matter from time to time and even corresponded about it. When in 1856 Thackeray found a steel pen which he liked, he sent one to Carlyle with the following note, dated 3 August: "Perhaps this small present may be useful to you— It is the only steel-pen with w*h* I could ever write comfortably, and if it suits your hand as it does mine, why it will save you much pen-knife work and may make your life easier."[104] In a similar vein of helpfulness we find Carlyle writing to Thackeray on 9 April 1859: "Thanks for your merry little Note and the two Pens. It is like a little pearl of human cheerfulness and friendliness, turning up for one in the dreary wash of commonplace and botheration, wh*h* is one's common lot! — I have been true as Mitchell's own steel to his Pens and him these many years. . . . And observe farther, *here* is a kind of Paper wh*h* I find the best of many for suiting Mitchell. Try that too: It is made partly of *straw*; smooth enough; and bites at the ink with an appetite one likes. 'Parkins & Gotto' Stationers;—and I will send you a ream of it whenever you hold up your finger."[105]

In the late summer of 1859 Thackeray accepted the editorship of the *Cornhill Magazine*, the first issue of which was to appear the following

---

102. Ray, *Letters*, IV, 82n.

103. MS, Berg Collection, New York Public Library.

104. Ray, *Letters*, IV, 147. There is some question about the date of this letter, which Ray dates 1859. I am dating it 1856 because on 7 Aug. of that year Carlyle wrote to Lady Ashburton: "Thackeray sent me a steel Pen which he had found answer; 'just going away somewhither,' he says" (MS, Marquess of Northampton) and Thackeray's note to Carlyle ends: "Yours ever (just on the point of starting somewhither)."

105. MS, NLS, Acc. 2517. For an anecdote of 1858 concerning Thackeray's daughters told by Jane to Mrs. Russell, see Lawrence and Elisabeth Hanson, *Necessary Evil* (London, 1952), p. 471.

January. Carlyle was among those whom he invited to contribute to the periodical. In a letter to Thackeray of 20 October 1859 Carlyle wrote that "crushed to death amid Prussian rubbish," he could not make a contribution then but that if and when he ever got *Frederick the Great* finished he would be glad to write for Thackeray's magazine.[106] On 23 October he wrote to his brother: "Thackeray *is* to do a new Magazine; has applied to me; one of my climbings upstairs was to say handsomely, 'No, can't at all.' "[107] On 30 November he wrote to Edward FitzGerald: "Thackeray *fell* lately in a dark fog and lamed a leg, I am told, which still keeps him prisoner: no doubt he is busy exceedingly with his *Magazine*, with his &c. &c. I cannot get to see him yet."[108] In a letter to Thackeray of 26 May 1860 Carlyle spoke of a French subject on which he had considered writing for the *Cornhill* but which he could not use because he could not get permission to include some of the basic material which he needed. Yet he wished Thackeray and his magazine well: "If I ever in the end of this book have life left, you shall have plenty of things. . . . Fair wind and full sea to you in this hitherto so successful voyage, for which the omens certainly are on all sides good."[109] And although Carlyle never did write anything for the *Cornhill Magazine*, he was delighted when Thackeray published in it four installments of Ruskin's *Unto This Last*, which because of public outcry had to be stopped with the issue of November 1860. He was on the most friendly terms with Thackeray during the first year of the enterprise, as the tone of the following letter, dated 24 May 1860, indicates: "Alas, dear Thackeray, I durst as soon undertake to dance a hornpipe on the top of Bond Steeple, as to eat a white-bait dinner in my present low and lost state! Never in my life was I at such a pass. You are a good brother man; and I am grateful. Pray for me, and still hope for me if you can."[110]

In these last years of Thackeray's life it is clear that the two Carlyles continued to read him. On one occasion, possibly in 1860, Carlyle sent his helper Henry Larkin a note reading: "Wd you now demand *Thackeray's* Chatham at Londn Library, for me," probably a reference to the many passages on the two William Pitts in *The Four Georges*, published as a book that year.[111] Jane wrote to her friend Mrs. Russell on 14 April 1862: "The two numbers of the Story [probably Thackeray's *Philip*, then appear-

---

106. Ray, *Letters*, IV, 157–58.      107. MS, NLS, 516.96.
108. MS, Trinity College, Cambridge.      109. Ray, *Letters*, IV, 188.
110. Ibid., IV, 187. A letter from Thackeray to Carlyle of 16 Oct. [?1860] which I have not seen is in the NLS, 666.82. It may shed further light on Thackeray's relation to both Carlyle and Ruskin at this time. See also Wilson, *Carlyle*, V, 406–7.
111. From an undated fragment of a note in the Huntington Library.

ing in the *Cornhill*] I sent you the other day will be followed up to the end; and I am sure you will like it, and even the Doctor [Mrs. Russell's husband] may read it with satisfaction. The Author is one of the best Novelists of the day."[112] One of the most amusing stories concerning Carlyle and Thackeray in these last years is quoted by D. A. Wilson from Martin Tupper: "Thackeray mentioned to somebody that, were he not himself, he would like to be Martin Tupper. I repeated this to Carlyle. He evidently thought Thackeray presumptuous in hinting at such a thing, for he at once exclaimed,—'Save us frae a guid conceit of ourselves!'" The wits who were listening to Tupper tell the story, Wilson says, "dissolved in inextinguishable laughter," and Tupper laughed along with them, supposing it was Thackeray who was conceited.[113]

On 29 December 1863, five days after Thackeray's death, Carlyle wrote in a letter to Richard Monckton Milnes what may be taken as his obituary, certainly a very moving one:

> Poor Thackeray! I saw him not ten days ago. I was riding in the dusk, heavy at heart, along by the Serpentine and Hyde Park, when some human brother from a chariot, with a young lady in it, threw me a shower of salutations. I looked up—it was Thackeray with his daughter: the last time I was to see him in this world. He had many fine qualities, no guile or malice against any mortal; a big mass of a soul, but not strong in proportion; a beautiful vein of genius lay struggling about in him. Nobody in our day wrote, I should say, with such perfection of style. I predict of his books very much as you do. Poor Thackeray!—adieu! adieu![114]

In the period of about seventeen years in Carlyle's life which remained after Thackeray's death, his experiences and comments relating to Thackeray were of the same mixed nature as those when Thackeray was alive. The Carlyles continued to see and take an interest in Thackeray's daughters. On 24 October 1864 Anne Thackeray wrote in a letter to a friend: "Minny is going out for a drive with Mrs. Carlyle this afternoon,—we met old Thomas the other day on his horse & he suddenly began to cry. I shall always love him in future, for I used to fancy he did not care about Papa."[115] Minny Thackeray wrote to Carlyle on 15 December 1866 to announce her coming marriage to Leslie Stephen, which took place the

112. MS, NLS, 607.587B.                    113. Wilson, *Carlyle*, V, 449.
114. T. Wemyss Reid, *Richard Monckton Milnes* (London, 1890), II, 113.
115. Ray, *Letters*, IV, 304.

following 19 June.[116] In a letter of 1871 to a friend, Anne made a rather curious reference to her father's review of Carlyle's *Sterling*, considering the hostile nature of that review: "The other day I met dear old Mr. Carlyle walking along, and I rushed after him to talk about his *Life of Sterling*. . . . I wonder have you ever come across my father's review of it in the *Times?*"[117] It would indeed be interesting to know just what Carlyle said to Anne on this occasion.

On 2 January 1872 William Allingham wrote in his *Diary*:

> C[arlyle] said Thackeray's *Irish Ballads* were the best things he ever wrote, and quoted (as he often did) with great gusto and a strong brogue—
> 'Twould binifit your sowls
> To see the butther'd rowls,
> laughing heartily afterwards.
> For Thackeray's novels, except *Esmond*, he had little praise. The fact is he had not read most of them.[118]

On 27 December 1872 Carlyle wrote to his brother John: "A knock at the door and word that 'Miss Thackeray,' a very rare individual here, is waiting in the dining room below."[119] The old Carlyle could not always be tolerant and goodnatured in commenting on Thackeray's daughters. To his brother John he wrote again on 9 December 1873; "Alas, alas, here has been a flight of Thackeray ladies and others: beyond expression *un*furthersome to me. I will end I will end."[120] William Black's notes of July 1875 indicate also that he was critical of Thackeray's conception of Goethe: "He regretted he had never seen Goethe face to face, and added: 'Thackeray's recollection of Goethe was vague and inaccurate. Thackeray had a confused memory of Goethe being a dark man.'"[121] Yet on 1 December 1875, just three days after Minny had died, he spoke with deep compassion to Leslie Stephen when he met him on a walk on Cromwell Road. "I am very sorry for you, sir," he said. "My own loss did not come in so grievous a way."[122]

Duffy, who had acted as a guide to Carlyle during his tour of Ireland in 1849, had a very distinguished career afterwards and became Sir Charles Gavan Duffy. In 1856 he emigrated to Australia, where he was very active in reform movements, as he had been in Ireland. At one time he was Prime

116. MS, NLS, 1768.204.
117. Ibid., II, 808n.
118. (London, 1907), p. 208.
119. MS, NLS, 527.78.
120. MS, NLS, 527.103.
121. Wilson, *Carlyle*, VI, 358.
122. Ibid., VI, 379.

Minister of that country and at another Speaker of the House. From time
to time he returned on visits to Great Britain, always making it a point to
see and talk with his old friend Carlyle and to record what Carlyle said.
Some of the talk concerned Thackeray. In his diary Duffy states that about
1866 or 1867 Carlyle told him: "The huge edifice called the New Palace
of Westminster was not insignificant or grotesque, but it wanted the unity
of design which is apt to impress one in a work which is a single birth
from one competent mind. When Thackeray saw the river front he declared he saw no reason why it stopped: it ended nowhere, and might just
as well have gone on to Chelsea."[123] On one of the long walks which
Duffy took with Carlyle some years later, Carlyle reverted to a subject
which they had discussed years before on the Irish tour, the characteristic
qualities and relative merits of Dickens and Thackeray. Duffy reports:

> Speaking of both after they were dead, Carlyle said of Dickens that
> his chief faculty was that of a comic actor. He would have made a
> successful one if he had taken to that sort of life. His public readings,
> which were a pitiful pursuit after all, were in fact acting, and very
> good acting too. He had a remarkable faculty for business; he man-
> aged his periodical skilfully, and made good bargains with his book-
> sellers. Set him to do any work, and if he undertook it, it was altogether
> certain that it would be done effectually. Thackeray had far more
> literary ability, but one could not fail to perceive that he had no con-
> viction, after all, except that a man ought to be a gentleman, and
> ought not to be a snob. This was about the sum of the belief that was
> in him. The chief skill he possessed was making wonderful likenesses
> with pen and ink, struck off without premeditation, and which it was
> found he could not afterwards improve. Jane had some of these in
> letters from him, where the illustrations were produced, apparently
> as spontaneously as the letter.
>   I said I was struck with a criticism which I heard Richard Doyle
> made on Thackeray, that he had a certain contempt for even the best
> of his own creations, and looked down not only on Dobbin, but even
> on Colonel Newcome. He was a good-natured man, however. It was
> notable that he had written over and over again with enthusiasm
> about Dickens, but I could not recall any reference to Thackeray in
> Dickens' writings during his lifetime, and only a lukewarm "In Me-
> moriam" after his death.

123. *Conversations*, pp. 228–29.

I asked him, was it as a practical joke, or to win a bet, that Thackeray named the heroine of "Pendennis" after a famous courtesan then in London? He said he did not know anything of this, but it could scarcely be an accident with a man about town like Thackeray.[124]

From time to time through the years Carlyle had also discussed Thackeray and Dickens with Francis Espinasse, who recorded much of the conversation:

> Of Thackeray's earlier performances Carlyle said that they showed 'something Hogarthian' to be in him, but that his books were 'wretched.' Of course this was before the appearance of *Vanity Fair*, the immense talent displayed in which Carlyle fully recognized, pronouncing Thackeray 'a man of much more judgment than Dickens.' Yet, when *Vanity Fair* in its yellow cover was being issued contemporaneously with *Dombey and Son* in its green ditto, Carlyle spoke of the relief which he found on turning from Thackeray's terrible cynicism to the cheerful geniality of Dickens. The highest praise bestowed by him on Thackeray's lectures was that they were 'ingenious.' Personally Carlyle preferred Dickens, who always treated him with deference, to Thackeray, who often opposed to his inopportune denunciations of men and things at miscellaneous dinner-parties some of that persiflage which was more disconcerting to Carlyle than direct contradition. It was a startling parallel between two surely most dissimilar men which was drawn by Carlyle, when he once said to me, 'Thackeray is like Wilson of Edinburgh (Christopher North), he has no convictions.' Possibly this was said after Carlyle had been more than usually irritated by Thackeray's persiflage.[125]

The same preference is indicated in what Carlyle said to Mrs. James Anstruther in 1874, to whom he spoke of Thackeray as an unsatisfactory and dissatisfied man for whose books he did not care. On the other hand, he did not like the comparisons of Dickens with Shakespeare, such as he had heard recently.[126]

With these comparisons which Carlyle made between his two old friends we may appropriately end this record of his relation to Thackeray. To attempt to arrive at general conclusions or to speak in terms of broad generalizations in dealing with the subject would be unwise and perhaps even

124. Ibid., pp. 77–78.          125. *Literary Recollections and Sketches*, pp. 215–16.
126. Wilson, *Carlyle*, VI, 333.

misleading. Both Carlyle and Thackeray were far too complex in themselves and the relationship between them was too complex for such an
attempt to be very convincing or profitable. We must take human nature
in its individual manifestations and human relationships as they are and
not mold them into the forms of logic unless they flow into them naturally.
Thackeray and Carlyle were two very different human beings, different in
taste and different in temperament, neither of which has much to do with
logic or its processes. Thackeray could never have been or quite understood
the earnest mystic that Carlyle was; Carlyle could never have been or quite
understood the urbane and sophisticated artist and man of the world that
Thackeray was. Yet both were in their own way artists, reformers, and
haters of sham; and they found sufficient common ground to stand on for
their friendship, critical as they were of one another, to be significant and
in some of its most revealing incidents dramatically moving.

# Dickens's Anti-Chauvinism

## Edgar Johnson

*City University of New York*

*For he might have been a Roosian,*
*A French, or Turk, or Proosian,*
   *Or perhaps I-tal-i-an!*
*But in spite of all temptations*
*To belong to other nations,*
   *He remains an Englishman!*

                       W. S. Gilbert

*Some people . . . may be Rooshans,*
*and others may be Proosans; they are born*
*so, and will please themselves. Them which*
*is of other naturs thinks different.*

                       Mrs. Gamp

DICKENS WAS ASSUREDLY VERY ENGLISH, to the core in emotion, in humor, in every significant way. But not least remarkable about him is that in an age of strong national feeling in all countries he reveals hardly a trace of chauvinism, treating national prejudice from the beginning with a burlesque derision that gradually deepens into scornful hostility. And this was not because like Henry James he had any youthful background in other cultures; his early reading was largely in English fiction and drama, his first trip abroad was a mere week in Belgium when he was twenty-five, and his first extended experience of another people was his trip to America in 1842. Nor does Dickens have even a tinge of the other kinds of chauvinism, class-chauvinism, the time-chauvinism that assumes the automatic superiority of the present over the past, or the youth-chauvinism contemptuous of all its elders.

    Though Dickens was and knew himself to be a member of the middle class, he had small respect for that class as such. He disliked its complacency, hated its materialistic greed, and despised the self-abasing snobbery that made it subservient to the aristocracy—in the end, as he put it, "noth-

ing but the poor fringe on the mantle of the upper." As he shows through
the delineation of Mr. Meagles in *Little Dorrit*, even the most useful and
self-respecting members of the middle class were all too often alloyed by a
willingness to bow down to the Tite-Barnacles and Sir Lancaster Stilt-
stalkings. Mr. Gradgrind represents another aspect of the middle class at
its most well-intentioned but most deluded, and Bounderby at its most
sordidly rapacious.

For the conventional notions of gentility Dickens had equally little
reverence. He regarded himself, to be sure, as a gentleman, and yielded to
the vanity of using as his own the crest of the Dickens family of Stafford-
shire; but fundamentally he thought of gentlemanliness as a spiritual at-
tainment and not as an ancestral heritage. From Lord Frederick Verisopht
to Lord Snigsworth "snorting at a Corinthian column" he ridicules "the
tenth transmitter of a foolish face." In *David Copperfield* Dickens has hilarious fun at the exaltation of blood over achievement or intellect; "Other
things are all very well in their way," says Mr. Waterbrook, "but give me
Blood!" and "Hamlet's aunt" agrees: "We see Blood in a nose, and we
know it."

Some of the outer mannerisms of gentility Dickens parodies with riotous
enjoyment—the shabby dandyism and grandiloquence of Mr. Micawber;
Turveydrop's rituals of deportment in *Bleak House*; and, in *Little Dorrit*,
William Dorrit's pathetic tenacity to his status as a "gentleman" and his
horror lest it be compromised by his even knowing that any members of his
family "do anything":—that is, engage in any form of useful work. Throughout the range of Dickens's career he gives no encouragement to the self-
aggrandizements of class pride.

As of class-chauvinism, so of time-chauvinism. Dickens had, to be sure,
no doubt that the nineteenth century had both made material progress and
ameliorated some of the most dreadful evils of the past. He speaks with
enthusiasm of the wires of the telegraph going "like a sunbeam through the
cruel old heart of the Coliseum," and with scorn of "the drivellers" who
regret the railroad crossing the water to Venice "instead of going down on
their knees . . . and thanking Heaven that they live in a time when iron
makes roads, instead of . . . engines for driving screws into the skulls of
innocent men." He could hardly control the almost hysterical loathing he
felt for the dark medieval record of persecution and cruelty; everywhere
he went in Europe he visited the dungeons of the Papacy and the Inquisition, sickening at the hammers that smashed men's limbs, the irons once
heated red hot, the stone trough of the water torture; and his voice vibrates

with hatred when he gazes on those instruments of inhumanity: "Gurgle, swill, bloat, burst for the Redeemer's honour! Suck the bloody rag, deep down into your unbelieving body, Heretic, at every breath you draw!"

But these relics of the past never made Dickens forget that in the present men's hands were still bitterly stained with evil. He never ceased girding at the greed of industrial exploitation, the horrors of mine and mill, the dirt and disease of the slums. From his first horrified glimpse of the Black Country in 1838 he had determined that he should some day "strike the heaviest blow in my power" against these enormities.

His career was a lifelong fulfillment of that resolution. The stews of Whitechapel and Saffron Hill in *Oliver Twist*; the pestilence seeping through the foul rookeries of Tom-all-Alone's in *Bleak House*; the black canal, the river purple with ill-smelling dye, the stifling odor of hot oil, the soot and smoke of Coketown in *Hard Times*; the rackrented tenements of Bleeding Heart Yard in *Little Dorrit*;—the campaign runs through all of Dickens's work. And not only in his fiction; the pages of *Household Words* and *All the Year Round* endlessly point out how typhus, cholera, disease and death in every form, are engendered by polluted sewers, bad and insufficient water, lack of light and air, crowded and dirty houses, and how in mines and factories bodies are rotted, limbs maimed, lives destroyed. One article alone, "Ground in the Mill," details dozens of hideous deaths and mutilations: boys caught in the belting and smashed a hundred and twenty times a minute against the ceiling, men wedged in a shaft and battered to pulp, their lungs broken, their heads scalped, their skulls smashed. Dickens leaves his contemporaries no excuse for feeling vainglorious about progress or preening themselves on their moral superiority to their ancestors.

But neither does he provide any ammunition for the youth-chauvinism that scorns all the older generations as fools and scoundrels and rejects their entire world as a monstrous failure. Though he had himself small reverence for the wisdom of eld, he did not believe that virtue was the monopoly of those under thirty. The hero of his very first novel was not a brilliant young messiah but the elderly Mr. Pickwick, who begins, to be sure, as a foolish gull. But Pickwick develops into a man of sense and a savior of injured innocence, whom his sharp Cockney servant Sam Weller describes as an "angel in tights and gaiters." The surrounding figures of Mr. Nupkins, Dodson and Fogg, Serjeant Buzfuz, Justice Stareleigh, Pott and Slurk, Fizkin and Slumkey, Mrs. Leo Hunter, and hosts of others show clearly enough what Dickens thinks of the "Establishment"; but Mr. Winkle and

Mr. Snodgrass and those two precious rascals Mr. Jingle and Job Trotter reveal no less clearly that he does not regard youth as necessarily endowed with either brains or stainless probity. And, throughout all his novels, a range of characters from the Artful Dodger and Mr. Justice Fang to Charley Hexam and Mr. Podsnap holds the balance fairly evenly distributed between youth and age, giving no support to any complacent age-chauvinism among the members of either generation.

Of chauvinism in its more usual meaning Dickens had from the start hardly a trace. On his first trip to Belgium, in 1837, it must be admitted, he commented on an elegantly patronizing chance acquaintance who turned out to be the Boots at his hotel, "Isn't this French?" But not long afterward, in *Nicholas Nickleby*, he has fun at the expense of British insular superiority; when Mr. Lillyvick learns that *"l'eau"* is the French for "water," that worthy remarks with gloomy dissatisfaction, "Lo, eh? I don't think anything of that language—nothing at all." And in later years, as Dickens became acquainted with the French, the Italians, and the Swiss, he never looked on them with patronage, and came to feel an increasing regard for all three.

His central criticism of the United States during his visit there in 1842 was the widespread chauvinism he found in the American people. During a pelting downpour near Harrisburg, Pennsylvania, he reported, a small boy with "a mingled expression of complacency, patronage, national independence, and sympathy for all outer barbarians and foreigners, said, in shrill piping accents, 'Well, now, stranger, I guess you find this almost like an English a'ternoon, hey?'" A flamingly patriotic Cleveland newspaper boasted that America had "whipped" England in her infancy, whipped her again in her youth, and must whip her once more in her maturity, and proclaimed that within another two years "True Americans" would "sing Yankee Doodle in Hyde Park, and Hail Columbia in the scarlet courts of Westminster." Many Americans were convinced, Dickens learned, that they were the only progressive nation on the face of the globe; one of them asks Martin Chuzzlewit, "How's the unnat'ral old parent?"—England; and adds, "Progressing back'ards, I expect, as usual?" And everywhere among this violent people, still addicted to lynch law and tar-and-featherings, Martin finds the conviction that European courts of justice employ the stake, the block, the thumb-screw, and the rack.

And everywhere, too, Martin, like his creator, discovers a national belief that the country consists mainly of outstanding characters. Colonel Diver, his war-correspondent Jefferson Brick, General Choke, the Honorable Elijah Pogram, Mr. Lafayette Kettle, each is "one of the most re-markable men in our country, sir." That backwoods bully and assassin Hannibal Chollop is "a splendid example of our na-tive raw material, sir." "He is a true-born child of this free hemisphere . . . unspoiled by conven-tionalities as are our broad and boundless Perearers! . . . He is a child of nature and a child of freedom, and his boastful answer to the Despot and the Tyrant is, that his bright home is in the Settin' Sun."

Combined with these grotesque delusions about other countries and this fantastically inflated national egoism, Dickens discovered the most furious intolerance of even the mildest adverse criticism. What had Miss Martineau done, he asked some Americans, to arouse their resentment? "Surely she praised America enough?" "Yes, but she told us some of our faults, and Americans can't bear to be told of their faults. Don't split on that rock, Mr. Dickens." "We must be cracked-up, sir," the egregious Hannibal Chollop tells Mark Tapley menacingly. "You are not now in A despotic land." And he goes on ,"I have know'd men lynched for less, and beaten into punkin-sarse for less, by an enlightened people. We are the intellect and virtue of the airth, the cream Of human natur', and the flower Of moral force. Our backs is easy ris. We must be cracked-up, or they rises, and we snarls."

There were, on the other hand, Dickens warmly admitted, indeed "a great many very remarkable men" in America to whom none of these stric-tures applied. "The professors of the Cambridge university, Longfellow, Felton, Jared Sparks, are noble fellows," and to them he added Ticknor and Bancroft. In Congress there were John Quincy Adams, Clay, Calhoun. "Clay is perfectly enchanting, an irresistible man. There are some very noble specimens, too, out of the West. Splendid men to look at, hard to deceive, prompt to act, lions in energy, Crichtons in varied accomplish-ments, Indians in quickness of eye and gesture, Americans in affectionate and generous impulse."

But for Congress in the mass Dickens had much less admiration, though, as he was to remind the readers of *American Notes*, he had no higher an opinion of the British Parliament. He had never, he said drily, "fainted away" or "even been moved to tears of joyful pride, at the sight of any legislative body." He had borne the House of Commons "like a man" and "yielded to no weakness but slumber" in the House of Lords; had seen elec-tions without ever having been "impelled (no matter which party won) to damage my hat by throwing it up into the air in triumph."

Thus little was Dickens's view of America tainted by any notions of the superiority of British institutions. Further, he found much to praise in the United States—more, perhaps, than he would easily discern today. "The American poor, the American factories, the institutions of all kinds—I have a book already. There is no man in this town, or this State of New England, who has not a blazing fire and a meat dinner every day of his life. A flaming sword in the air would not attract as much attention as a beggar in the streets." The American people were "by nature, frank, brave, cordial, hospitable, and affectionate. Cultivation and refinement seem but to enhance their warmth of heart and ardent enthusiasm."

When Americans compared themselves with other peoples, however, all these virtues were almost overwhelmed by their national complacency. Though there were, of course, some like Cornelius Felton, Professor of Greek at Harvard, who were not, as Dickens said, "at all starry, *or* stripy," such exceptions were rare. "The national vanity swallows up all other countries on the face of the earth, and leaves but this above the ocean." Twenty-five years later, when he returned to the United States in 1867, though he observed vast improvements and "amazing changes," he thought this towering self-conceit as rampant as ever. Newspapers could not get over the "extraordinary composure" he displayed in public. "They seem to take it ill," he commented, "that I don't stagger on the platform overpowered by the spectacle before me, and the national greatness."

But Dickens was well aware of the fact that his own compatriots were by no means devoid of the same national vanity. If they did not always display it as blatantly, that was because deep down they were even more convinced of Britain's innate superiority. During the years following his first American visit, he devoted himself to attacking England's failings with an ever-growing violence. He would have none of the insular ostentation that lauded English ways as transcending those of all other nations, none even of the European vanity that saw occidental civilization as free from the shortcomings and superstitions that afflicted other more benighted parts of the globe. Day in day out, year after year, he never ceased girding at his countrymen, using every conceivable weapon: argument, cajolery, humor, facts and figures, irony, sarcasm, repetition, angry diatribe.

These aims animate many of even his most casual magazine articles. In 1848, for example, describing in the *Examiner* a visit to a Chinese junk moored in the Thames, he pictures the mimic eye in the vessel's prow by which she was supposed to see her way, the red rags fastened to her mast to ensure her safety at sea, and the joss-stick burning before the idol Chin-Tee. But then, instead of bursting into a noisy fanfare about western enlightenment, as the singers of Rule Britannia—or Hail Columbia—would have done, he adds sardonically, "It is pleasant to think that WE trust no red rags in storms, and burn no joss-sticks before idols; that WE never grope our way by the aid of conventional eyes that have no sight in them . . . Our seamen—far less our bishops, priests, and deacons—never stand out upon points of silvered paper and tinfoil, or the lighting-up of joss-sticks upon altars!"

Nor did Dickens confine himself to generalities. The inefficiency, red tape, jobbery, and corruption of British politics; the heartless cruelty with which her industrialists exploited the working class; the ugliness, dirt, and disease of the slums; the failure to create any system of public education and the almost deliberate way in which the poor were thus left ignorant and helpless; the inhumanity of an economic theory that made starvation a matter of supply and demand, and told unfed infants to die and decrease the surplus population—all these evils Dickens deluged in floods of burning denunciation.

Nothing could be plainer, he insisted, than that Parliament, "with its feeble jokes, logic-chopping, straw-splitting, tape-tying, tape-untying, to tie again; double-shuffling, word-eating," was "the house of Parler and Mentir," the place of wordiness and lies. Was it not obvious "that any half-dozen shopkeepers taken at random from the London Directory and shot into Downing Street out of sacks" could do a better job than these Red-Taper and Sealing-Wax-Chafers? How fantastic was a system in which there were "Chancery suits sixty years old, and admirals and generals on active service eighty"! What of the addled theorists who would "comfort a labourer travelling twelve miles a day to and from his work by telling him that the average distance of one inhabited place from another in the whole area of England is not more than four miles? Bah!" And meanwhile there were bread riots in the East End of London, with out-of-work dock laborers looting bakers' shops, and "an enormous black cloud of poverty . . . spreading and deepening every hour."

More and more often through the years, too, Dickens emphasized England's failures by contrasting what he scarified as her bitter record of drift, incompetence, and wrong-headedness with the more rational behavior of other nations. Throughout the rest of northern Europe, he recorded, one child out of every two-and-a-quarter of the population received at least the rudiments of an education; in England there was only one such pupil to every *fourteen* inhabitants. How was it that foreign governments could encourage invention and technological improvement, whereas English

patent procedures subjected inventors to a labyrinthine and expensive run-
around seemingly designed to strangle innovation? Even the *abattoirs* of
Paris were models of humane cleanliness; London's Smithfield was a sham-
bles of filth, blood, and cruelty.

For those so purblind as not to see these facts Dickens painted England's
defects in the most lurid colors. The arrogant national self-esteem that
looked down pityingly on all other nations and regarded English ways as
the only standards of right he caricatured with savage ferocity. Mr. Podsnap, in *Our Mutual Friend*, is the supreme embodiment of England's infatuated smugness. "Mr. Podsnap's world was not a very large world,
morally; . . . he considered other countries . . . a mistake, and of their
manners and customs would conclusively observe, 'Not English!' when,
PRESTO, with a flourish of the arm, and a flush of the face, they were swept
away." He consistently regrets "that foreign nations do as they do." Podsnap is the incarnation of British chauvinism.

Even in Dickens's last novel, the unfinished *Mystery of Edwin Drood*,
he cannot resist the temptation to another fling of derision. Young Drood
is both a race-chauvinist and an imperialist who voices the catchwords of
those attitudes in their most infuriating forms. Headed for the Near East
to take charge of his family's engineering business there, he is "Going to
wake Egypt up a little," he says patronizingly. He talks with insolent and
insular contempt of other races. "Pooh, pooh," he sneers to the dark-skinned
Neville Landless. "You may know a black common fellow . . . but you are
no judge of white men." His words epitomize the whole vainglorious gospel
of backward races and the white man's mission.

The judgments that Dickens expressed in his published writings he consistently voiced to his friends. "Don't think it a part of my despondency
about public affairs," he wrote John Forster, ". . . when I say that mere form
and conventionalities usurp, in English art, as in English government and
social relations, the place of living force and truth." How much better than
the work of almost all English painters was that of the Belgian and the
French artists in the international exposition at Paris in 1855: "the fearless-
ness of them; the bold drawing, the dashing conception, the passion and
action in them!" Even in the work of his own friends, Leslie, Frith, Ward,
Egg, and "dear old Stanny,"—Clarkson Stanfield—he was obliged to admit
the deficiency. "It is of no use disguising the fact that what we know is
wanting in the men is wanting in their works . . . . There is a horrid respectability about the best of them—a little, finite, systematic routine in
them, strangely expressive to me of the state of England."

These same respectabilities were responsible for the deficiencies of English literature. The novelists were all terrified by Mrs. Grundy; they dared not write unpalatable truth. (Thackeray was to make the same complaint; the eighteenth-century freedom of *Tom Jones* was impossible in the England of Victoria.) And once again Dickens looked abroad for contrast. What intellectual dishonesty there was in some smooth gentleman complaining that the hero of an English novel was always "uninteresting—too good-not natural, &c," and extolling the heroes of George Sand and Balzac. "But O my smooth friend, what a shining impostor you must think yourself and what an ass you must think me," when both the critic and the author knew "that this same unnatural young gentleman . . . *must* be presented to you in that unnatural aspect by reason of your morality, and is not to have, I will not say any of the indecencies you like, but even of the experiences, trials, perplexities, and confusions inseparable from the making or unmaking of all men!"

Dickens had reached the point, in fact, where he could not bear the smugness with which the English assumed their own rightness and the wrongness of all others. Dropping in to see his friend Miss Burdett Coutts at Stratton Street, he argued hotly with her companion, Mrs. Brown, when she talked "nonsense about the French people and their immorality." In England, Dickens said, people hypocritically pretended that social evils and vices did not exist; in France they were honest about them. "Don't say that!" she cried. "Don't say that! It gives me such pain to hear you say anything I can't agree with!" But he must say it, Dickens insisted, "when, according to our national vanity and prejudice, you disparage an unquestionably great nation." Mrs. Brown burst into tears; Dickens remained rigidly unyielding.

He had become what he had always been in essence, a citizen of the world. The smart young Londoner amused at Mr. Lillyvick's ignorant provincialism had matured into a man at home in international circles and sharply aware of the narrowness of parochial judgments.

This was only one aspect, of course, of Dickens's many-faceted genius. His sympathy with the richness and variety of human life, with all that was fruitful in experience, made him at the same time a fierce critic of whatever impoverished and destroyed. In comparison with the cruelty, ignorance, and lust for power that he assailed again and again in his works, chauvinism was, no doubt, only a contributory evil. But the group vanities and group intolerances it represented were allied with all these other forces.

Dickens consequently opposed chauvinism in all its manifestations. He was unwaveringly hostile to the chauvinism of class. Though he knew that there were many old fools and rascals, and that they often wielded harmful power, he also knew that there were many young fools and rogues, and he gave no support to the chauvinism of either youth or age. He felt no doubt that the world had progressed, but instead of making that an excuse for satisfaction he redoubled his demands for further advance; he detested those who lauded the good old times, but he also disliked the time-chauvinism complacent about the present. And, last, he developed a deepening scorn and hatred for all the national and racial chauvinisms that buttressed national self-righteousness with contempt for other nations and peoples. No leading man of his age was freer from such prejudices.

# Change in CHUZZLEWIT

## Carl Woodring

### Columbia University

" 'IF YOU HAVE CHANGED at all, my love, since we parted,' said Martin at length, as he looked upon her with a proud delight, 'it is only to be more beautiful than ever!' . . . .

" 'What change is there in *you*, Martin,' she replied; 'for that concerns me nearest? You look more anxious and more thoughtful than you used.' "[1]

He ought to, he answers; he has undergone a great deal of vexation and privation. Young Martin Chuzzlewit has brought Mary Graham out into the dankest dawn of the year to tell her of his impending journey to America for the purpose of turning vexation and privation into fortune. The conversation is given to us ironically. On this "raw, damp, dark, and dismal" morning, Martin thinks only of his own discomfort, not of Mary's endangered health. Is the irony at a single level only? Unconscious of all but his own interest, is there a truth in Martin's expression of self-interest of which he is just as unaware as he is of his selfishness? Has Dickens not begun to alert us here to the effects of privation?

In *Martin Chuzzlewit* Dickens undertook the most complex and demanding work of his career to that point. Among other developments and challenges, he was more concerned with the internal life of his characters than he had been in the books from *Pickwick* through *Barnaby Rudge*. As the new novel progressed, he could communicate to John Forster his certainty of comic genius and moral power, but the twenty parts of *Martin Chuzzlewit* reveal an authorial struggle with experiments to show modification within an individual. Of all the varieties of change that intrigued Dickens, unseen spiritual growth within a character was the most difficult to communicate. He was never to solve the problem perfectly, not even in *Great Expectations*, itself to be written partly out of dissatisfaction with the depiction of spiritual growth in *David Copperfield*. Had Fielding adequately

---

1. Chapter 14. All quotations in this paper, except where otherwise indicated, are from Charles Dickens, *The Life and Adventures of Martin Chuzzlewit*, The New Oxford Illustrated Dickens (Oxford, 1951). Except for a few accidentals of spelling and punctuation, the passages quoted are unchanged from the first edition in book form, Chapman and Hall, 1844.

traced the spiritual development of Tom Jones? If so, Fielding's method could not be Dickens's, except in so far as he had subordinated gradual revelation to the splashier devices of concealment and surprise. Coleridge declared the plot of *Tom Jones* to be one of the finest in literature, but the intricacies of the plot are evident only when the reader has reached the end; Fielding's anticipatory hints are more deliberately hidden, less available on a first reading, than those in *Martin Chuzzlewit*.

Dickens makes the working of change by time a prominent theme. The opening of chapter 18 is often quoted:

> Change begets change. Nothing propagates so fast. . . . Things cemented and held together by the usages of years, burst asunder in as many weeks. The mine which Time has slowly dug beneath familiar objects, is sprung in an instant; and what was rock before, becomes but sand and dust.

The metaphor of time as a burrowing mine has important implications for the portrayal of change in Chuzzlewits and other erring creatures. Among other effects, it encourages a structural emphasis on dramatic surprise.

An overvaluation of surprise can be counted among the reasons that Martin is shown blandly selfish in episode after episode until the fevers of Eden teach him suddenly to have regard for those about him. A more general explanation, one that helps account for the melodramatic reversals throughout English fiction of the nineteenth century, is the pervasive inevitability of religious conversion. Evangelical conviction of sin required a specific moment of rebirth in every Christian life. In an epochal book, *The Victorian Temper* of 1951, J. H. Buckley called attention to the pattern of conversion in diverse works of nearly every genre of Victorian literature, biography and autobiography as well as fiction. Dickens also called attention to the pattern, as when he had the evangelical Mr. Chadband attempt to convert Jo the sweeping boy in *Bleak House*: "When this young Heathen now among us—who is now, my friends, asleep, the seal of indifference and perdition being set upon his eyelids; but do not wake him, for it is right that I should have to wrestle, and to combat and to struggle, and to conquer, for his sake . . ." ( ch. 25 ). Finding the seal of indifference set upon the eyelids of young Martin, Dickens himself struggled to redeem him.

William James devoted to the phenomena of conversion two of the Gifford Lectures published as *The Varieties of Religious Experience*. He accepted a distinction between the volitional type of convert who is changed by act of will through gradual stages and the type that surrenders suddenly to regenerative change; but in summary he explained the phe-nomena of conversion "as partly due to explicitly conscious processes of thought and will, but as due largely also to the subconscious incubation and maturing of motives deposited by the experiences of life."[2] Arthur Darby Nock illustrated the point by reference to the *Confessions* of St. Augustine, wherein "Christianity is throughout presupposed and present in the subject's subconsciousness."[3] St. Augustine differed from the fa-miliar nineteenth-century type in that his "progress in a continuous line" was not a conversion from indifference.

The methods of drama and the evangelical insistence upon a perceptible moment of redemption, however long the maturation, coincide in Dickens's fictional technique. I am not trying to suggest that Dickens is an uncon-scious friend to Stiggins and Chadband, but merely that he, along with most of his contemporaries, had absorbed the evangelical sense of dramatic revelation as the expected outcome of the cumulative force of change within each fallen creature. The coming of grace should be an occasion evident to one's associates.

One of our best critics, quoting the passage in *Martin Chuzzlewit* be-ginning "Change begets change," has observed: "In this metaphor time is a mine, long in the laying but sudden to explode."[4] Circumstances work upon the individual as an unseen oxydizing atmosphere. Dickens subtly follows the disquisition on change by noting the alterations among those left behind in London while the narrator followed Martin and Mark Tap-ley to the New World of slogans and slavery. Whether the narrator is away or at hand, time burrows like a mole.

The colloquy between Martin and Mary Graham, with which we began, illustrates a paradox of Dickens's method. In due time sufferings in the deleterious Eden are destined to change Martin. The scene before his de-parture, with its comic irony, is set up as preparation within the plot. Mary is made to remark on the apparent change in Martin chiefly because no significant change has then occurred. The ironic preparation for the trans-formation in Eden is a device of plot to assure an adequate jolt to the reader when Martin begins to show consideration for others. At the same time, observed but not directly declared by the novelist, Martin *is* under-going change. Psychologically, the vexation under Pecksniff and embar-rassments of poverty after dismissal have had an effect. Dickens has seen

2. Lecture X; Modern Library Edition, p. 226.
3. *Conversion* (Oxford, 1933), p. 266.
4. John Henry Raleigh, *Time, Place, and Idea: Essays on the Novel* (Carbondale, Ill., 1968), p. 132.

to it that the reader who did not detect the beginnings of change in Martin nonetheless felt the necessity of change. And now the perceptive Mary has noticed the beginnings of a change that the reader must eventually come to accept as genuine.

In addition, as something more than protective plotting of Fielding's kind, Dickens has already laid one stone for the path that the reader needs. In chapter 13, after Martin was discovered by Tigg at the pawnbroker's, the novelist has afforded evidence of both change and awareness of change in Martin: "And it was strange, very strange, even to himself, to find how, by quick though almost imperceptible degrees, he lost his delicacy and self-respect, and gradually came to do that as a matter of course, without the least compunction, which but a few short days before had galled him to the quick." The positioning of this passage, in a chapter labeled by the Oxford editors "A Rapid Descent," masks it as a step, not in the hardening of Martin that it might appear to be, but as a step in his regeneration. He remains centered in self, but he has learned that his identity is not a rock, and he has made the discovery while in full view of the reader. Dickens paradoxically shows Martin to be changing and not changing simultaneously.

With Martin's regeneration as a central exhibit, Steven Marcus has described the essence of this novel as "the comedy of soul-making, of creating an identity in a world of circumstance."[5] This is excellently said. The conception of Keats's referred to, however, the gradual working of circumstance in the process of making a human soul, refers only to what is generally unconscious and mostly unseen in *Martin Chuzzlewit*. In the work of Keats, one would need to turn rather to the sudden metamorphoses, the painful moments of "dying into life," for a parallel to the episodes of overt conversion in *Chuzzlewit*.

Dickens's mastery of description, variously symbolic, atmospheric, and hypnotic, did not deflect him from the methods of drama in conveying to the reader the processes of soul-making. Seldom describing the processes of change within a consciousness, he marks instead—usually with the mirror-reversal of irony—the dramatic stages of redemption or transformation. Some of these dramatic changes add the strength of pattern to others that follow. The redemption of Mercy Pecksniff begins with the unexpected proposal of marriage from Jonas Chuzzlewit in chapter 20. She thought she would accept only "that I might hate and tease you all my life," but the opportunities for teasing do not in the outcome equal those

---

5. *Dickens: From Pickwick to Dombey* (London, 1965), p. 259.

for hating. Her nickname Merry, like the sisters' given names Mercy and Charity, has seemed earlier to refer in irony to the effect on others of her tartness; it now begins to refer to her misery under the meanness and cruelty of Jonas. She becomes Mercy meek and mild, under Satanic, Blake-ian, painful redemption as Merry, wretched and numb. By a similarly slow maturation, apparent to the reader only as a slight uneasiness under re-peated provocation, honest Tom Pinch leaps within a few pages, in chapter 31, from declaring Pecksniff "the best of men" to accepting Mary's view of one who had done as Pecksniff had done as the "falsest, craftiest, meanest, cruellest, most sordid, most shameless" of men. Since Tom can think such of no living Dick or Harry, much less of Seth Pecksniff, it suddenly "was not that Pecksniff, Tom's Pecksniff, had ceased to exist, but that he never had existed." In the structure of the novel, such reversals as Mercy's and Tom's help prepare for the regeneration of Martin in chapter 33: "being newly risen from a bed of dangerous sickness, to watch by such another couch, he felt how nearly Self had dropped into the grave, and what a poor, de-pendent, miserable thing it was." [6] Not in contradiction to this evangelical language of rebirth, but supplementary to it, Martin resolved that he would fight hereafter against his rooted selfishness. Looking to the past as well as to the future, he recognized the generosity and sacrifice of others in episodes that he was now able to reinterpret. Here Dickens was accentu-ating the positive where an evangelical preacher would have called upon the sinner to concentrate upon the past of his own now-dying miserable self.

The Merry, Tom, and Martin now evident have been implicit in those characters from the beginning. The final chapters of the novel provide a complex pattern of experiments in the presentation of changing and emerg-ing personalities. This pattern of emergence has been described, and cor-rectly so, as like the transformation scene at the end of a Christmas panto-mime.[7] Nonetheless, just as melodrama has obligations to a Christianity of emotion, so the closing chapters of *Martin Chuzzlewit* contain emblems of the transformed soul. Persons are transformed at the end of this novel as *things* are in "The Rape of the Lock." Jonas, who has been a murderer in intent and in his own estimation, becomes one in fact (ch. 47) just before the ghostly Mr. Lewsome emerges to assure everybody concerned that

6. The comma after *poor* is supplied from 1844.
7. See, e.g., Edgar Johnson, *Charles Dickens: His Tragedy and Triumph* (New York, 1952), II, 807; K. J. Fielding, *Charles Dickens: A Critical Introduction* (London, 1958), p. 75. Versions of Mrs. Gamp's teaparty were among the adaptations of *Martin Chuzzlewit* to hold the stage for the rest of the century; see S. J. Adair Fitz-Gerald, *Dickens and the Drama* (London, 1910), pp. 173–84.

Jonas was guiltless of the death that had soured his dreams. Chevy Slyme, who has been coming around the corner throughout the novel, finally negotiates the turn—except that aspiration remains a part of his character. Nadgett, who is Secrecy itself, comes into the open.

The guilty confront their worst dreams. The nightmares that ride through the cluster of villains reveal the submerged consciousness and conscience that we knew each must have. Suddenly it is apparent that everybody, and especially each of the wicked, has an alter ego, and most have an external agent. "It is your wishes," Mrs. Gamp asks in a quavering croak, "to see the t'other person. Is it?" (ch. 51). Each of the guilty confronts the "other person." In the sustained melodrama, the other person is not quite Old Martin, nor Chuffey, nor Westlock, who each enter as candidates, but the previously concealed Lewsome. More to our point, another person has been concealed inside Old Martin, Mrs. Gamp, Pecksniff, even Nadgett, and each such other person emerges. In each emergence, essential being stands revealed. The transformations are circumferential to, emblems of, and dramatic substitutions for, the kind of conversion that Martin experienced in America. The reborn soul of Evangelical self-discovery blends into discovery by the reader. For his congregation of readers, the novelist is the shepherd who has led each sinful, selfish character to the mourner's bench for apocalyptic disclosure, what William Blake calls a last judgment, where each divided soul can be reintegrated.

Dickens, knowing that some E. M. Forster would declare his finest creations not only incredible but flat, gave Mrs. Gamp one of the richest internal lives since Don Quixote, open to any who will perceive it when Mrs. Harris emerges in all her richly imagined, accumulated detail from a teapot filled with gin. Mrs. Gamp's extraordinary difficulty in giving the name of her other person as the nonexistent Mrs. Harris comes partly from fear of exposure as the criminally negligent nurse she is, but it comes also from sudden awareness that the companionship and flattery of her alter ego is about to be forever banished from her dreams. Professionally Mrs. Gamp is both despicable and terrifying—the latter for those especially who find her reincarnated in urban hospitals today—but the traumatic jolt to her creative inner life, which has been freely and continuously shared with others, has an inexpressible poignance for the rapt reader. Poetic justice does not normally involve the squashing of a true artist, and it is only the Wagnerian completion of the cycle of Mrs. Harris that reconciles the reader to the dissolution of Mrs. Gamp the creator along with the downfall of the bestial nurse.

The final exposures multiply in a sequence determined by a pecking order: Mrs. Gamp over Poll Sweedlepipe the hairdresser, Jonas over Mrs. Gamp, Nadgett over Jonas, Pecksniff superior to the assemblage until struck down by Old Martin. Fate, for the ultimate comeuppance, strides over all as the grim reaper, in a transformation foreshadowed as early as chapter 9, where the description of swarming life at Todgers's turns to a description of death, of graveyards where those who were once watchmen are now "in another kind of box" and themselves watched. Throughout this novel, the ultimate transformation by death subdues the comedy and lessens the secular significance of change in life.

Steven Marcus aptly quotes chapter 27 on Montague Tigg, now become Tigg Montague of the Anglo-Bengalee Assurance Company: "Though turned and twisted upside down, and inside out, . . . still it was Tigg; the same Satanic, gallant, military Tigg."[8] Conflicting characters were latent in Tigg from the outset. He does not change essentially, *and* he is murdered. In Christian melodrama, the alternative to conversion is either death or a miserably prolonged life. The predictable exception is Tom Pinch, the saint for whom all questions of character have been resolved before the curtain rises. Tom, however, grows with experience, from illusioned innocence to unillusioned goodness. Without losing his humility, he becomes a militant Christian soldier striking blows for any oppressed maiden needing his protection. Doddering old Chuffey, although a memorable figure, is a more easily predictable norm, the more grotesque because the normality of his generous spirit (he is unselfish almost to the point of nonentity) survives among moral grotesques of utter selfishness. Tom Pinch's essential nature, like Mark Tapley's, is unchanging and predictable; his growth from experience surprises. Old Chuffey was almost totally predictable, perhaps even to his role in the final unraveling.

In contrast, what Dickens does with Pecksniff was totally unpredictable. The hypocrisies of Pecksniff are successively exposed and peeled away like an onion. He ought by all the rules of fiction to submit finally to eternal truth. Instead, as in an onion, what is left is the essential Pecksniff, a hypocrite still, as unconverted in his stubborn pride as Milton's Satan. The world of Pecksniff's rhetoric, the world in which he named his daughters, is that world of allegory associated by Dickens with the plaster ceilings of manor houses, with everything aristocratic, heraldic, and unprogressively medieval. The parody of genealogy with which the novel begins is followed up in Pecksniff more than in the Chuzzlewits.

8. P. 429. See Marcus, p. 227.

Abstraction-filled rhetoric, shared by Tigg as well as by Pecksniff, also pervades the United States, and helps explain why the populace there inhabits a satiric world of fixed personalities. In the scenes observed by Martin and Mark in America, Dickens confronts us with an emptied Utopia. If old families like the Chuzzlewits act as if others could not rise, the population across the Atlantic acts as if expectancy of perfection could be satisfied with the rhetoric of what is not. Conversion and perfection can be had to the satisfaction of Americans by a series of declarations that the false is its opposite. Bill Simmons's irony in chapter 13 anticipates and equals the self-deception of Americans: "It makes no odds whether a man has a thousand pound, or nothing, there." So New Yorkers *say*.

The transformations in the final chapters contrast a life of regeneration and change with the deadening hand of unredeemed rhetoric. We have heard that rhetoric from Pecksniff, Tigg, and all the spokesmen of the retarded spirit of the United States. A few critics feel that they have heard quite enough of it from the novelist Dickens. "But"—most of us can apply to Dickens, except for the irony, his words in chapter 6 concerning the architect Pecksniff—"such is the magic of genius, which changes all it handles into gold!" We can accept the cosmic irony in his words on the power of fancy in a lover of home, "stronger than magician ever spoke, or spirit answered to, in strongest conjuration." The magician has given paradoxical evidences of change in the apparently unchanging who are in time to be dramatically transformed.9

9. On the general question of Evangelical influence, see the excellent work by Harland S. Nelson, "Evangelicalism in the Novels of Charles Dickens," Ph.D. dissertation, University of Minnesota, 1959.

# The "Soothing Songs" of LITTLE DORRIT:
## New Light on Dickens's Darkness

Jerome Beaty

*Emory University*

LITTLE DORRIT IS AMONG the very darkest of Dickens's novels. It sees, we have often been told, society as a prison: all of its characters are in one way or another prisoners, and man's life on earth may be epitomized by its sweeping description of the "bars of the prison of this lower world."[1] It is thus in theme and form one of "our novels."

That *Little Dorrit* is dark and that prisons and imprisonment, real and metaphorical, are important in the novel would be foolhardy to deny. What I wish to argue, however, is that prison is not the *central*, unifying image or "spine" of the novel[2] but is subsumed by a larger, and quite different cosmological view. By denying the centrality of the prison image and placing it in its larger context, we find the novel not less but more unified, since the character of Amy Dorrit, the happy ending and other "bright" elements become integral to the work and we can view the residual optimism of the novel not as pablum for the public but as essential to Dickens's total vision.[3]

1. Charles Dickens, *Little Dorrit* (Baltimore: Penguin Books, 1967), Book II, ch. xxx, p. 831. Hereafter book, chapter and page numbers to this edition will be inserted in the text parenthetically thus: (II, xxx, 831).

2. Most of the discussions of "organic unity" in the novel, at one time so popular, seem to assume a center or "spine" running through an entire work, something to which all other elements, especially images, are more or less directly related. This has led, I believe, to a good deal of critical acrobatics and distortion, the search for "the" theme and "the" image cluster or other structure which bears the single, central theme. Many organisms fitly survive without such a centralized nervous system, though novels so structured look to critical anatomists like "loose baggy monsters." Whether they are higher or lower forms of fictional life, *War and Peace* and *Middlemarch* and many other nineteenth-century novels—and much of Dickens—have organic forms without wholly unitary "spines." I hope to demonstrate this tangentially here and in more detail elsewhere.

3. In recent criticism the most evenly balanced view of *Little Dorrit* is that of John Butt and Kathleen Tillotson in *Dickens at Work* (London, 1957), where the change from the original intention of a novel to be called "Nobody's Fault" to *Little Dorrit* is viewed largely as a change of emphasis from negation to affirmation, "the optimism about humanity which sets the rest in perspective." Amy's virtue, however, "must be seen as expressing what still survived of Dickens's own indestructible faith—expressing

I

A good deal of the action of the novel takes place in prison, especially in the Marshalsea, and most of the major characters and many of the minor ones are in prison, have been in prison or visit a prison. There are, in addition, several prison-like places of confinement: quarantine and the workhouse, for example.

There are, further, several prison metaphors or analogues *verbally indicated* in the novel. Arthur has somehow got the fixed but superficially erroneous idea that his mother is responsible for Dorrit's imprisonment and that her paralysis imprisons her for that crime (I, viii, 129). Much later in the novel, she herself sees the paralysis as prison (II, xxx, 843). When Dorrit is at long last released from prison and with his new-found wealth is making the Grand Tour of the Continent, his daughter finds the English tourists very much like Marshalsea prisoners (II, vii, 565). There is, as well, the all-encompassing metaphor mentioned earlier, "the prison of this lower world."

It is no wonder, then, that critics have extrapolated this image beyond what is verbally justified in the text. Thus, at least since Edmund Wilson's important essay,[4] Miss Wade has been said to be a prisoner of her temperament, though Dickens, who usually insists upon such analogues, never, to my knowledge, makes the connection, and Flora may be said to be a prisoner of the past—but *Dickens* does not say so.

The question I wish to raise is not whether prisons function as major scenes or setting for much of the novel, or whether Dickens extends imprisonment metaphorically in the novel, or even whether specific critical extrapolations of a metaphor not verbally indicated in the text are justified, but whether the prison image is the major structural or unifying factor of the novel; whether it is the formal and thematic "spine" to which all else is related; whether the form of *Little Dorrit* is, as it were, centripetal—

---

it almost allegorically, with the validity of fairy tale" (pp. 230–31). The identification of the "dark" as the "realistic" and the "bright" as "fairy tale" is common among twentieth-century critics and is not, I shall argue, just to Dickens's integral vision. More generally, George Ford, in his excellent *Dickens and His Readers* (1953; rpt. New York, 1965), p. 258, sees the possibility of a critical presentation of "a benevolent and cheerful Dickens" though he fears the critic would encounter "certain obvious difficulties," and he finds the issue of whether Dickens is optimistic or pessimistic "a question dear to the hearts of the luncheon clubs" (p. 250). I hope here to be able to digest the question a little more fully than that and to show its relevance to matters of theme, imagery and structure in the novels.

4. "Dickens: The Two Scrooges," *The Wound and the Bow* (Cambridge, Mass., 1941). See especially pp. 56ff.

pulling everything in the novel together—or centrifugal—opening out into larger and larger contexts; whether, finally, it emblemizes Dickens's deeply dark world-view.

Let us first examine three passages, two of them major prison images referred to earlier, the third the opening of the novel. The first of these is the tourists-as-prisoners passage:

> It appeared on the whole, to Little Dorrit herself, that this same society in which they lived, greatly resembled a superior sort of Marshalsea. Numbers of people seemed to come abroad, pretty much as people had come into the prison; through debt, through idleness, relationship, curiosity, and general unfitness for getting on at home. They were brought into these foreign towns in the custody of couriers and local followers, just as the debtors had been brought into the prison. They prowled about the churches and picture-galleries, much in the old, dreary, prison-yard manner. They were usually going away again to-morrow or next week, and rarely knew their own minds, and seldom did what they said they would do, or went where they said they would go: in all this again, very like the prison debtors. They paid high for poor accommodation, and disparaged a place while they pretended to like it: which was exactly the Marshalsea custom. They were envied when they went away by people left behind, feigning not to want to go: and that again was the Marshalsea habit invariably. A certain set of words and phrases, as much belonging to tourists as the College and the Snuggery belonged to the jail, was always in their mouths. They had precisely the same incapacity for settling down to anything, as the prisoners used to have; they rather deteriorated one another, as the prisoners used to do; and they wore untidy dresses, and fell into a slouching way of life: still, always like the people in the Marshalsea. (II, vii, 565)

This oft-quoted passage is the very marrow of the spinal interpretation of the novel, and I have quoted it at length in order to make two points: first, that it does not make prison analogous to English or Victorian society as a whole but only to English tourists on the Continent; second, that it is not Marshalsea or the Grand Tour as institutions but the prisoners-tourists as individuals or as a group that Little Dorrit here views so critically. If this were, in fact, a paradigm of Dickens's vision, that vision would be very dark indeed, for it is humanity rather than society that would be indicted by extrapolating the reference of this passage.

It is only those who see the central prison image as social, a symbol of Victorian or capitalist society, who would object to the wider reading, however. Those who see the prison image as central and cosmic—a symbol of modern man's condition in the wasteland without God—might well agree with such a sweeping interpretation, and it is they, too, who would cite the "prison of this lower world" image:

> Black, all night, since the gate had clashed upon Little Dorrit, its iron stripes [the bars of the Marshalsea gate] were turned by the early-glowing sun into stripes of gold. Far aslant across the city, over its jumbled roofs, and through the open tracery of its church towers, struck the long bright rays, bars of the prison of this lower world. (II, xxx, 831)

That "this lower world," our world, is a prison is not, admittedly, a very happy thought, and the last phrase out of context offers a dark view indeed. In context, however, the "bars" of the prison are not black but golden, "long bright rays" of the sun, the sun that is the traditional image for God and life. This force disperses the blackness of night and turns even the bars of the Marshalsea into gold. If we are in a prison here in this lower world, it is one whose bars are golden, insubstantial, life-giving, part of a superterrestrial if not supernatural force that can redeem even prisons.

Dickens uses the traditional or natural images of light-dark, sun-shadow, day-night frequently, even insistently throughout his career, and *Little Dorrit* is not exceptional in this regard. It would be tedious to list a great many here and in any case several will appear later in this essay. There is one puzzling but emphatic exception to the traditional association of sun with life or the good and shadows with death or evil, and it appears in the third of the passages I wish to cite, the very opening of the novel.

*Bleak House* opens immediately with the fog and mud and moves immediately to the heart of the fog where sits Chancery. The first scene of *Little Dorrit* takes place in the Marseilles prison which is in the shadows, physically and morally. But the title of the first chapter is "Sun and Shadow," and the novel begins in the bright sunlight, a sunlight that is not, however, beneficent or life-giving or good, but "burning," "blazing," staring and oppressive:

> Thirty years ago, Marseilles lay burning in the sun, one day. A blazing sun upon a fierce August day was no . . . rarity in southern France . . . . Everything in Marseilles, and about Marseilles, had stared

at the fervid sky, and been stared at in return, until a staring habit had become universal there. . . .

There was no wind to make a ripple on the foul water within the harbour, or on the beautiful sea without. . . . [Everyone who had] come to trade at Marseilles, sought the shade alike—taking refuge in any hiding-place from a sea too intensely blue to be looked at, and a sky of purple, set with one great flaming jewel of fire.

The universal stare made the eyes ache. . . . Everything that lived or grew, was oppressed by the glare; except the lizard, passing swiftly over rough stone walls, and the cicala, chirping his dry hot chirp, like a rattle. The very dust was scorched brown, and something quivered in the atmosphere as if the air itself were panting.

Blinds, shutters, curtains, awnings, were all closed and drawn to keep out the stare. . . . The churches were the freest from it. To come out of the twilight of pillars and arches . . . was to plunge into a fiery river, and swim for life to the nearest strip of shade. So . . . Marseilles . . . lay broiling in the sun one day.

It is only then that we are introduced to the prison. What a strange way to begin a novel whose dominant image is alleged to be prison and whose vision is both physically and morally "dark." And what a strange use of the sun, traditionally and elsewhere in Dickens the life-giver, the eye of God. In seeking the significance of this puzzling but emphatically-placed initial passage, we are led to explore Dickens's use of conventional imagery, his cosmology in this novel and elsewhere and to "place" the prison and other images in relation to his total vision.

II

The traditional day-night imagery and images of light associated with it readily extends to times of day, seasons, times of life and ultimately the entire temporal condition of man. Morning, spring and youth; midday, summer and maturity; evening, autumn, middle-age; night, winter, old age and death—these are conventional parallels which not only require no explication but frequently escape notice. Man in his life on earth inhabits a temporal and cyclical universe created, the convention holds, by a benevolent God outside time. Virtue in such a universe consists in believing not only in God but in His creation and in His benevolence: His creations, including man and time, are essentially good; if the wicked temporarily prosper, the good will ultimately prevail and those with faith will be able to endure the dark, confident that light and good will come again.

To lack faith in life, in the ultimate triumph of good, is to lose purpose, hope and will, but to believe that the world, life and man are evil is itself evil, a perversion. It is this that is the sin[5] of all those Calvinistic evangelical characters who appear in Dickens's novels, including, in *Little Dorrit*, first and foremost, Mrs. Clennam: she believes "Earth is expressly meant to be a scene of gloom" (I, xxx, 407). She was brought up to believe man cursed and his heart corrupt and therefore in need of "wholesome repression": "Mine were days of wholesome repression, punishment, and fear. The corruption of our hearts, the evil of our ways, the curse that is upon us, the terrors that surround us—these were the themes of my childhood" (II, xxx, 843). Arthur, a "love child," needs even more such "wholesome repression" to save his soul, and so she raises him: "I devoted myself to reclaim the otherwise predestined and lost boy . . . to bring him up in fear and trembling, and in a life of practical contrition for the sins that were heavy on his head before his entrance into this condemned world" (II, xxx, 846). It is Mrs. Clennam, not Dickens, who views human life as a "condemned world."

Though she herself was victim of such an upbringing and this may extenuate her guilt, it does not, for Dickens, exonerate her, for the Reality of God's good creation is there to be seen by those who will look outside themselves, those who are not guilty of a second perversion, the cardinal sin of pride, putting self in the place of God:

> More than forty years had passed over the grey head of this determined woman, since the time she recalled. More than forty years of strife and struggle with the whisper that, by whatever name she called her vindictive pride and rage, nothing through all eternity could change their nature. Yet, gone those more than forty years, and come this Nemesis now looking her in the face, she still abided by her old impiety—still reversed the order of Creation, and breathed her own breath into a clay image of her Creator. . . . [N]o human eyes have

5. Humphry House, *The Dickens World* (London, 1941), p. 112, rightly argues that Dickens "rejected Original Sin," a concept which clearly would be antithetical to the world-view I am here describing; he points out, too, that " 'sin' is scarcely mentioned at all," and cites E. L. Woodward, *The Age of Reform*, p. 535: " 'Acton once said that Dickens knew nothing of sin when it was not crime.' " Acton, I believe, is wrong. What I here describe as "perversions" of Dickens's religion are at least closer to sin than to crime and indeed are, I feel, the moral conditions of crime in much of Dickens's fiction.

ever seen more daring, gross, and shocking images of the Divine nature than we creatures of the dust make in our own likenesses, of our
own bad passions. (II, xxx, 844)[6]

A third "sin," closely allied to these two, and one of which Mrs. Clennam
and many others in *Little Dorrit* are guilty, is to ignore or defy the temporality of life on earth, to try to stop time and cyclicality. For this, too, is
to usurp God's role. Cycles, of course, may be seen pessimistically as well
as optimistically: though it may be true that if winter comes spring is not
far behind, it is also true that if summer comes, fall and winter are not far
behind. Indeed, life on earth ends the cycle with winter, midnight, death,
and it is only belief in God and the immortality of the soul which sees in
death a rebirth into eternity. And eternity, in the convention within which
Dickens is working, is rebirth into the morning which has no night; the
end of the cycle is, to the believer, a happy one.[7] There Reality will be
known, true faith will be justified, answers to this perplexing life will be
found. Death will bring Truth even to those who, like Dorrit, have a "poor
weak breast, so full of contradictions, vacillations, inconsistencies, the little
peevish perplexities of this ignorant life, mists which the morning without
a night only can clear away" (II, xix, 699–700). Even the bright sunlight
of this world is as mist or twilight to the bright light of eternity: when the
Dorrit brothers die, "removed by an untraversable distance from the teem-
ing earth and all that it contains," they are "far beyond the twilight judgment of this world; high above its mists and obscurities" (II, xix, 715).

This conventional cosmology with its natural and traditional images per-
tains to all of Dickens's novels, I believe. This third "sin," however, the attempt to stop time and time's cyclicality, is more emphatically presented in
those novels which coincide with Dickens's consciousness of middle-age.
Sir Leicester Dedlock, the worn-out aristocrat, is connected with Chancery
in more ways than merely through the Jarndyce suit in which his wife has
a secret part: he and his class are agents and victims of precedent and
usage, the impeding of progress through the burden of the past, the clog-
ging of time and change and cyclicality, so that Chesney Wold is as fog-
bound and misty and dark as the Court of Chancery. Miss Havisham tries
to stop the clock on the day of her wedding that never came to pass, sitting
paralyzed among the ruins of the wedding banquet and trying to pervert
Estella so that time can run again. But in neither *Bleak House* nor *Great*

---

6. Compare Murdstone, who "sets up an image of himself, and calls it the Divine
nature," in *David Copperfield* (Baltimore: Penguin Books, 1966), p. 906.
7. If, unlike Acton, I find sin in Dickens, I find no evidence for Hell.

*Expectations* is the theme of stagnation, stasis, the attempt to stop time's onward movement through its cycles so pervasive or so fully explored as in *Little Dorrit*.

III

The worst of Hell is not the fires or the torture devices, but the deprivation of the sight of God's countenance. So it is in prison. It is not so much the internal conditions—William Dorrit can make of his existence there something approaching comfort—but the deprivation of time's cyclicality —days and seasons—of the face of Nature, of life. The sun rarely penetrates and never dispels the shadow of the Marshalsea, sometimes merely touching the spikes of the prison with golden light. The bars, though lifeless parodies of trees—as Dorrit's prison life is a parody of life in society—know no seasonal change, never bloom or bear fruit: "Changeless and barren, looking ignorantly at all the seasons with its fixed, pinched face of poverty and care, the prison had not a touch of any of these [autumn] beauties. . . . Blossom what would, its bricks and bars bore uniformly the same dead crop" (II, xxxiv, 883).

This, too, is the nature of Mrs. Clennam's gloomy world. On the first gloomy Sunday of his return home, Arthur finds her out of the reach of nature's seasonal cycle:

"All seasons are alike to me," she returned, with a grim kind of luxuriousness. "I know nothing of summer and winter, shut up here. The Lord has been pleased to put me beyond all that." . . . her being beyond the reach of the seasons seemed but a fit sequence to her being beyond the reach of all changing emotions. (I, iii, 74)

Indeed, it is the avoidance of emotions and change, of human involvement, that compensates her for her psychosomatic paralysis; as she says to Flintwinch: "If it is any compensation for my long confinement within these narrow limits . . . , that while I am shut up from all pleasant change I am also shut up from the knowledge of some things that I may prefer to avoid knowing, why should you . . . grudge me that belief?" (I, xv, 226). Her confinement and the changeless passage of her days in the gloomy house permit her to maintain the illusion that she is the center or measure of the world, that just as she is unchanging, so the rest of the world is motionless:

The house in the city preserved its heavy dulness through all these transactions, and the invalid within it turned the same unvarying round of life. Morning, noon, and night, morning, noon, and night, each recurring with its accompanying monotony, always the same reluctant return of the same sequences of machinery, like a dragging piece of clockwork.

. . . To stop the clock of busy existence at the hour when we were personally sequestered from it, to suppose mankind stricken motionless when we were brought to a stand-still, to be unable to measure the changes beyond our view by any larger standard than the shrunken one of our own uniform and contracted existence, is the infirmity of many invalids, and the mental unhealthiness of almost all recluses. (I, xxix, 387–88)

As William Dorrit has been in the barren and changeless Marshalsea for twenty-five years, Arthur Clennam has been in China for more than twenty. Returning home, middle-aged, without a wife or a profession, he finds not so much bewildering change as stultifying stasis. Just as the woman he thinks his mother remains unchanged in her wheelchair and her home the same gloomy, monotonous place of confinement, so the home of his adolescent sweetheart, Flora Casby Finching, has remained unchanged: " 'The house,' thought Clennam, . . . 'is as little changed as my mother's, and looks almost as gloomy. But the likeness ends outside. I know its staid repose within' " (I, xiii, 186). The "staid repose" is incarnate in Flora's father, "The Last of the Patriarchs," whose kindly exterior not only masks the avaricious slum landlord but also freezes time unnaturally:

This was old Christopher Casby—recognisable at a glance—as unchanged in twenty years and upward as his own solid furniture—as little touched by the influence of the varying seasons as the old roseleaves and old lavender in his porcelain jars.

Perhaps there never was a man, in this troublesome world, so troublesome for the imagination to picture as a boy. And yet he had changed very little in his progress through life. Confronting him, in the room in which he sat, was a boy's portrait, which anybody seeing him would have identified as Master Christopher Casby, aged ten . . . . (I, xiii, 186)

Flora, fat and fortyish, protests against her father's changelessness while calling attention to her own change, claiming she will soon be considered "Papa's Mama." Having been married and widowed in the intervening years, Flora ludicrously and pathetically sets Arthur "free" from their one-

time engagement. As "the relict of the late Mr. F." she admits the passage
of time and her own physical change, but acts out an unconscious parody
of coyness and girlishness, trying at once to admit and deny change, "thus
making a moral mermaid of herself" (I, xiii, 196–97).

To avoid pain by avoiding pleasure and all human emotions; to attempt
to forestall life's ups and downs;[8] to be outside the organic cyclicality of
time and nature—whether through imprisonment imposed by society, self-
imposed paralysis or reclusion, or the imposition of an unchanging mask
of hypocrisy—is to exist without life. Existence, life without cyclical change,
nonetheless takes place in time. The river, here as elsewhere in Dickens
the traditional image of time flowing into the sea of eternity, is nowhere
in *Little Dorrit* an agent for resurrection or baptism, as it may be in *Our
Mutual Friend*. Instead, it is for Arthur, as for John Chivery,[9] a pastoral
retreat from life, associated with idyllic love, in which life and death
merge:

> A tranquil summer sunset shone upon him as he . . . passed through
> the meadows by the river side. He had that sense of peace . . . which
> country quiet awakens in the breasts of dwellers in towns. . . . Be-
> tween the real landscape and its shadow in the water, there was no
> division; both were so untroubled and clear, and, while so fraught
> with solemn mystery of life and death, so hopefully reassuring to the
> gazer's soothed heart, because so tenderly and mercifully beautiful.
> (I, xxviii, 381–82.)

He is at this point infatuated with Pet Meagles, who comes to meet him
in this very scene, gives him roses and then stuns him with the news that
she and Gowan are to be married. When she goes in, he gently launches
the rose petals on the river where "the flowers, pale and unreal in the
moonlight, floated away upon the river; and thus do greater things that
once were in our breasts, and near our hearts, flow from us to the eternal
seas" (387).[10] When he first tried to keep from his troubled consciousness

8. Mr. Plornish, visiting Arthur in prison, "amiably growled, in his philosophical
but not lucid manner, that there was ups you see, and there was downs. It was in vain
to ask why ups, why downs; there they was, you know. He had heerd it given for a
truth that accordin' as the world went round, which round it did rewolve undoubted,
even the best of gentlemen must take his turn of standing with his ed upside down
. . ." (II, xxvii, 799).

9. In his love reverie, he and Little Dorrit, "[w]ith the world shut out . . . would
glide down the stream of time, in pastoral domestic happiness"; he ends the daydream
"with a tombstone in the adjoining churchyard" (I, xviii, 256) marking his and Amy's
grave. Gliding down the stream of time and death are near-allied.

10. It is this association of the river and love which makes him later, on the Iron

the knowledge of his infatuation for Pet, he saw in the tranquility of the river escape from pain and love and life: "And he thought . . . that it might be better to flow away monotonously, like the river, and to compound for its insensibility to happiness with its insensibility to pain" (I, xvi, 244). Thus the river, though it may emblemize time, is escape from change, sun and shadow, seasons, ups and downs, from human emotions and human life, human time. Though it flows on, it is impervious to pain and change and uncertainty, more like the escape from life in the prison, the wheel-chair or the mask than it is like true life itself. Human life in time is not like the river but the road:

> Within view was the peaceful river and the ferry-boat, to moralise to all the inmates saying: Young or old, passionate or tranquil, chafing or content, you, thus runs the current always. Let the heat swell into what discord it will, thus plays the rippling water on the prow of the ferry-boat ever the same tune. Year after year, so much allowance for the drifting of the boat, so many miles an hour the flowing of the stream, here the rushes, there the lilies, nothing uncertain or unquiet upon this road that steadily runs away; while you, upon your flowing road of time, are so capricious and distracted. (I, xvi, 235)[11]

Neither the tranquil river with its changeless flow nor the fixedly staring sun of Marseilles, much less the shadow of its prison or that of the Marshalsea, the gloom of Mrs. Clennam's religion or of her house or the unaging mask of Casby, are adequate guides for or modes of human life. Life is a strait and narrow roadway on solid earth (I, xxvii, 368).

As Doyce tells Arthur, life is struggle: "You hold your life on the condition that to the last you shall struggle hard for it. Every man holds a discovery on the same terms" (I, xvi, 233).[12] Arthur and Amy, "married with the sun

---

Bridge, think that Little Dorrit too may be hopelessly in love (as indeed she is, though it is Arthur himself she loves): "Something had made her keenly and additionally sensitive just now. Now, was there some one in the hopeless unattainable distance? Or had the suspicion been brought into his mind, by his own associations of the troubled river running beneath the bridge with the same river higher up, its changeless tune upon the prow of the ferry-boat, so many miles an hour the peaceful flowing of the stream, here the rushes, there the lilies, nothing uncertain or unquiet?" (I, xxii, 309; compare I, xvi, 235 quoted below).

11. There are numerous references to the "road of life"—see, e.g., I, xii, 179 and I, xxvi, 367—and these are connected to the theme of traveling so prominent in the novel and to the Bunyan-like image of life as pilgrimage.

12. It is this moral imperative, the necessity for struggle, that lies, I think, at the heart of Dickens's politics—his social satire, indignation, didacticism; his attack on contemporary institutions and abuses; his warnings that failure to improve society will bring violent revolution—despite both his scepticism about elections and Parliament as

shining on them through the painted figure of Our Saviour on the window," cannot mount to Heaven even yet. They cannot, like Pickwick, retreat to Dulwich and a garden, nor does Arthur, like David, look forward to the moment of death when his wife will angelically be pointing ever upward. They must bear both sun and shadow. They can only pause on the porch of the church[13] before descending, not to an idyllic retreat but to the Earth, to the hard and narrow road, to worse than a road, perhaps, to the untranquil and crowded streets of London.

IV

Before they can descend into the roaring streets inseparable and blessed to engage in the necessary struggle that is life, Arthur and Amy must be restored to the natural, organic growth that, in the Dickens cosmology, is moral health.

Amy's restoration is the easier, and it is presented less dramatically and less explicitly in the novel than is Arthur's. Though a young woman in her twenties, physically—and emblematically—she is little more than a child, the Child of the Marshalsea, and it is no wonder Arthur considers her so for much of the novel. Despite the harsh conditions into which she is born and in which she is reared, and the adult, workaday role into which she is prematurely forced, she has somehow maintained an innocence that is akin to ignorance: "born and bred in a social condition, false even with a reference to the falsest condition outside the walls" (I, vii, 111), "[w]orldly wise in hard and poor necessities," Amy is "innocent in all things else," her moral vision blurred by her narrow environment, by "the mist through which she saw her father, and the prison, and the turbid living river that flowed through it and flowed on" (I, vii, 118). Even the otherwise omniscient narrator does not know "how much, or how little of the wretched truth it pleased God to make visible to her" (I, vii, 111). Out of the prison and away from the river, however, the mist rises, and the narrator can penetrate the mystery of her mind and see that she sees the wretched

---

instruments of reform and his ultimate faith that in God's world all will be well (a position that can lead to moral as well as political complacency and inaction). This pronouncement of Doyce's in context is a response to Arthur's suggestion that he might be better off not to struggle against that institution which in *Little Dorrit* is the chief representative of English government practices, the Circumlocution Office.

13. In the first paragraphs of the novel the churches are "freest" from the staring Marseilles sun; like the prison, they are in shadow. Not to "go down" from the portico of the church here in the last paragraph into the sunshine and shade of the street would seem to be a shirking of social, secular responsibility.

truth of the expatriate and tourist English society on the Continent; it is she who sees through prunes and prisms, through the debacle of Pet's marriage to Gowan, and she who describes the Dorrits' life on the Continent as another Marshalsea. While her father, in his new-found wealth, tries to deny the past and in the madness brought on by its suppression is sentenced to relive it, she keeps the past alive in her present memory, sees the connection between poverty and riches, and maintains the integrity of her mind and soul. In Venice, looking down at the Grand Canal, she sees the past through the flow of time:

> She would think of that old gate . . . ; and of other places and of other scenes associated with those different times. And then she would lean upon her balcony, and look over at the water, as though they all lay underneath it. When she got to that, she would musingly watch its running, as if, in the general vision, it might run dry, and show her the prison again, and herself, and the old room, and the old inmates, and the old visitors: all lasting realities that had never changed. (II, iii, 520)

Riches, so corrupting to the rest of her family, not only fail to corrupt Little Dorrit, but in widening her experience and opening her eyes, they mature her; her ignorant, "cloistered" virtue becomes true innocence.

Amy's growth has not only been stunted, however; it has been perverted: she has had to become a mother before she has had a chance to become a woman. She has been mother to her older brother and sister and even to her own father; she has extended her maternal protectiveness outside her own family to the dim-witted Maggie, who calls her "Little Mother." The term is not, I believe, merely Victorian sentimentality but suggests the grotesque (just as "Little Dorrit" suggests limitation, immaturity, as well as sweet innocence): Amy's acceptance of the role is an act of virtue, its imposition is cruel and unnatural.

The scene in the Marshalsea in which Arthur and Amy confess their love (II, xxxiv) can be readily reduced, on the one hand, to embarrassingly obvious Freudian terms, and, on the other, to almost equally embarrassing Victorian melodrama. In the organic psychological terms of Dickens's moral vision, however, though it may not be wholly redeemed as an artistically effective scene, it can be understood as thematically consistent and even necessary. Little Dorrit has twice lost her father. Once his wealth removes him from under her protective devotion, but his madness restores him to her care; the second time, death removes him finally from her.

Arthur replaces her father: though he is virtually old enough to be her father, and though he has always acted avuncular if not paternal towards her, she has fallen in love with him, and now she finds him in her father's place, a debtor in Marshalsea, ill and in need of her. With him, she can resume her dual role of Child of the Marshalsea and Little Mother. Arthur, as we shall see, needs a mother before he can take a bride, must know childhood before he can recover youth and reach anything like a maturity that befits his age. Ill and impoverished, robbed of physical and worldly manhood, he thinks Little Dorrit comes to him swathed in her wealth offering him physical freedom but emotional dependence, a love that affords not renewal, growth, or maturity but only Oedipal regression. He "nobly" refuses to say he loves her; she somewhat coyly teases him into admitting that it is only her wealth that is an impediment and then announces that all her money has been lost. Though she can offer him something of the maternal affection he has never known and the innocent young love he had thought he had known but had found to be mere folly, these can be subsumed in mature love, with Amy as bride and helpmate, the two of them inseparable and blessed. And, for her part, Amy can now grow into womanhood. She had to return to the Marshalsea, the point at which her growth stopped, and she must undertake consciously the burden she once accepted ignorantly, with shrouded vision.

It is on Arthur's growth to psychological and moral maturity that the novel dramatically centers, however, and where the organic images that define such growth are most explicit. Raised within the shadows of Mrs. Clennam's gloomy, oppressive and guilt-ridden religion, he has never known the innocence, the hopefulness, the protecting and nurturing love and cultivation of the emotions and imagination that is, for Dickens, the proper and healthy environment for childhood. His adolescent illusion of love thwarted, he is packed off in virtual exile to China for more than twenty years. He returns to England at forty never having lived, having had neither childhood nor youth, having neither vocation nor love. He feels, somehow, that the family business he is meant to resume is, if not criminal, at least immoral. He thinks his family is in some way responsible for William Dorrit's imprisonment and Little Dorrit's plight; though literally wrong, he is symbolically right, for what Mrs. Clennam has sinned against is childhood and maternity, both emblemized in the "Little Mother" that Amy Dorrit has been forced to become. Quitting the family business immediately upon his return, Arthur must begin all over again, more like a youth of twenty than a man of forty. He tries to pick up the lost thread of his youth by visiting his boyhood sweetheart. He finds that Flora, "the relict of Mr. F.," is not only fat, forty and foolish, but realizes that his infatuation years ago must have been mere illusion. At forty, when his life should be in the full flower of maturity, it is instead a blighted tree:

> To review his life was like descending a green tree in fruit and flower, and seeing all the branches wither and drop off, one by one, as he came down towards them.
>
> "From the unhappy suppression of my youngest days, through the rigid and unloving home that followed them, through my departure, my long exile, my return, my mother's welcome, my intercourse with her since, down to the afternoon of this day with poor Flora," said Arthur Clennam, "what have I found!" (I, xiii, 207)

The answer to the question he asks himself rhetorically is, in fact, immediately answered—"His door was softly opened, and these spoken words startled him, and came as if they were an answer: 'Little Dorrit.'" But it will be a long time before he can recognize her for what she is, or, indeed, before she can become what she must be, his Amy (or *aimée*).

Deprived even of the memory of childhood and youth, Arthur's crippled psyche first weaves a May-time fantasy around another woman-child, Pet Meagles. Spoiled and petted, she has been kept a child, protected from experience, reality and growth by doting parents since the death of her twin sister in infancy. Arthur knows his romantic fantasy is mere weakness and he denies responsibility for his foolish dreams by attributing them to "Nobody." The Arthur who has such dreams is, indeed, a "nobody," a dreamer without a childhood, without a youth, without maturity. When Pet confides in him that she is to marry the worthless Henry Gowan, he drowns "Nobody" and his ghostly love for Pet along with the roses she had given him, themselves ghostly in the moonlight (I, xxviii, 387). Mr. Meagles, who had always fancied that his dead child was accompanying her twin sister in growth and change, recognizes Arthur's pain, and apparently also the unreal nature of Arthur's love for Pet, "Nobody's" beloved having been not Pet herself but her ghostly sister: "I feel to-night, my dear fellow, as if you had loved my dead child very tenderly, and had lost her when she was like what Pet is now" (I, xxviii, 387).

Arthur must not only be purged of his false guilt and false love, but must also learn the truth of his own past before his life can resume healthy growth. His father's watch and admonition—"Do Not Forget"—must be given meaning, not just in measuring time or reviving memory, but in re-

storing to Arthur the right to live and grow, removing the suppression that
has robbed him of healthy life. As Flintwinch tells Mrs. Clennam: "You
know very well that the Do Not Forget . . . could only mean . . . Do Not
Forget the suppression. Make restitution!" (II, xxx, 851). In her unloving
severity Mrs. Clennam had not been a natural mother to Arthur; now he
learns that she is not, in fact, his natural mother: he is his father's "love
child." Discovering the facts of his parentage, Arthur can be connected with
his true past, and his potentiality for growth restored. The mysterious feelings he had had throughout his life in the presence of the only "mother" he
has known, Nature; intuitions that there are mercy, love, justice, in the
world, he finds aroused again by Little Dorrit's voice reading to him in the
Marshalsea cell. In the autumn of his life, and on an autumn day in which
vestiges of summer's fruitfulness are still present and the coming winter is
a promise rather than a threat; when the ocean into which we must all
descend is not, as it was at Marseilles "asleep in the heat," an image of
finality, but sparkling, open-eyed with promise of resurrection and continuing life, Arthur can be restored to health. Nature's "soothing songs" of
the goodness of life that he had heard since childhood, he hears echoed in
Amy's voice as she reads to him. The past, present and future are now
organically related and prove that God's creation and human life are good
(II, xxxiv, 883–84).

Little Dorrit's moral nature, stunted and perverted in the barren Marshalsea, is capable of growth because she has been inspired to a life of
active if child-like virtue: "Inspired? Yes. Shall we speak of the inspiration
of a poet or a priest, and not of the heart impelled by love and self-devotion
to the lowliest work in the lowliest way of life!" (I, vii, 111). Arthur's blighted life is capable of renewal even in middle-age because, as we have seen,
he has heeded Nature's soothing songs, and has believed that this world,
this "great scheme," God and God's creation are good, a faith accessible to
us all. Despite the false religion he was taught but never accepted and the
deprivation of love in his own life, he has never been guilty of the fundamental sin of creating God in his own image and making of his own lot an
image of the universe (I, xiii, 206–7).

If Amy and Arthur can bear with hardship without making themselves
and their lot a microcosm of God's world, Mrs. Clennam, Gowan, Miss
Wade cannot. Gowan, unsure of his own character and ability, "has no
belief in anybody else, because he has no belief in himself" (II, xi, 606),
and levels all accomplishment and virtue to his own measure. Miss Wade,
admittedly a victim of social injustice, in her resentment refuses to see

kindness anywhere,[14] and tries to pervert all reality to her vision. She tries to corrupt Tattycoram because she takes "a perverted delight in making a sister-woman as wretched as she is" (I, xxvii, 379), and "twisting all good into evil" (II, xxxiii, 880). In a world of sun and shadow it makes all the difference whether one sees the shadow and dismisses the sunshine, or vice versa. One can maintain trust by innocence, failing perhaps to see reality clearly through the mist, like Little Dorrit in the first half of the novel, but one can in maturity and experience also see both the good and evil and, like Arthur, emphasize the good, believing it to be the Truth of the universe. This distinction descends even to the most minor of characters. Even the mere types, Bar and Physician, are distinguished by their moral view of reality, and it is, significantly, Bar, the cynical man of the world, who admires Physician, no less worldly but witness to man's essential goodness (II, xxv, 769). To acknowledge man's tenderness and affections is not to praise ourselves but to witness to the ultimate benevolence of the universe and all-powerful good of its Creator. To deny that good, whatever our personal lot, is to deny the Creator and to replace him with a projected image of ourselves, spiritual pride; it is pride, too, to claim credit for ourselves for our virtues or accomplishments, for they are, ultimately, His; and if successful, we ought to have the humility of the inventor Doyce, who never said: "I discovered this adaptation or invented that combination; but showed the whole thing as if the Divine artificer had made it, and he had happened to find it . . . , so calmly convinced he was that it was established on irrefragable laws" (II, viii, 570). This may, in fact, be a paradigm of Dickens's attitude towards his own fiction, his own vision: the "great scheme" is not his invention but is the creation of "the Divine artificer" and "established on irrefragable laws."

Dickens did not, in fact, "invent" a "great scheme" but found a rather conventional one which he held to rather systematically and consistently throughout his career. The scheme itself, however, is not the spine or center of any one of the novels or of all of them taken together. It is, rather, the circumference, the horizon of his vision within which the world of his fiction operates. *Little Dorrit* explores more insistently than the others one arc of the circle of his cosmology: the moral necessity of seeing the temporality of this world as organically cyclical and benevolent. All of the elements of the novel are related, however, not because they are subsumed

14. See II, xxi, "The History of a Self-Tormentor," especially p. 728, where she describes the nurse, "a rosy-faced woman always making an obtrusive pretence of being gay and good-humoured," whose "most crafty" subtlety "was her feint of seeking to make the children fonder of me."

by this arc or theme but because they are consistent with the horizons of Dickens's vision of which this arc is one portion. This theme and many of its elements—prison, paralysis, precedent—appear elsewhere, of course, in the novels, and many of the elements here—children-as-parents, centering the universe on the self, the role of the imagination in childhood and later, etc.—are explored more fully in other novels. Some of the recurrent images and issues may well be the result of psychic wounds, obsessions of Dickens the man, but in the fiction they are transmuted into art, they have become integrated into a cosmological vision. And the vision of *Little Dorrit*, perhaps the "darkest" of Dickens's novels, is still that of a world in which Nature sings to man "soothing songs" of the ultimate goodness of God's world audible even amidst the turbulent uproar of the contemporary urban world. Amy and Arthur are inseparable and blessed as they pass along in sunshine and shade. It is not Dickens but the Mrs. Clennams who, with the vision of owls or bats, see the world as gloomy and condemned, from their darkened rooms seeing only the shadows. The affirmation of the final paragraph of *Little Dorrit* is at least as strong and at least as integral to the vision of the novel as is that of the final paragraph of *Pickwick*:

> Let us leave our old friend in one of those moments of unmixed happiness, of which, if we seek them, there are ever some to cheer our transitory existence here. There are dark shadows on the earth, but its lights are stronger in the contrast. Some men, like bats or owls, have better eyes for the darkness than for the light. We, who have no such optical powers, are better pleased to take our parting look at the visionary companions of many solitary hours when the brief sunshine of the world is blazing full upon them.

# Education, Print, and Paper
## in Our Mutual Friend

Richard D. Altick

*Ohio State University*

"IN THESE TIMES of ours . . .": so begins *Our Mutual Friend,* in Dickens's most explicit statement of the contemporaneity of a novel's setting. "Concerning the exact year," he continues, "there is no need to be precise." Nor is there, because the setting is certainly the period just before and during that of the novel's composition, January 1864–September 1865. In each of Dickens's novels, whatever the ostensible setting, there hovers the author's sense of the *Zeitgefühl,* the elusive, intangible, often largely undefined quality of the moment. Such a sense usually is dominated by some easily apprehensible symbol, a "characteristic" of the time such as the railway in *Dombey and Son,* Chancery in *Bleak House,* the Circumlocution Office in *Little Dorrit,* and, in *Our Mutual Friend,* the dust mounds and the filth-laden Thames. These last, however, are not as precise indications of the moment as is the cluster of time-evidences—themes and incidental references—that I propose to examine here, in quest of those "finer threads" which, in Dickens's words at the end of this very novel, are related "to the whole pattern which is always before the eyes of the story-weaver at his loom" (p. 821).[1]

In a metropolis symbolically and geographically defined by the dust heaps to the north (between Battle Bridge, near King's Cross, and Holloway) and by the dirty river to the south, the spirit of the moment as Dickens felt it—or at least that element which he chose to emblematize it—was marked by a particular concern over popular education and over literacy as the leading product of that education; and the physical reflection of that concern was printed paper. Put another way, a link, additional to those already perceived by Dickens critics, which connects the dust mounds (and the illiterate Boffin) with the river (and the illiterate Gaffer Hexam) is Dickens's interpretation, in 1864–65, of the present state and consequences of the Victorian desire for education and self-improvement. The

---

1. Page references are to the New Oxford Illustrated Dickens edition (1952).

expectations are epitomized in Noddy Boffin's sanguine "Print is now opening ahead of me" as he looks forward to the advent of "a literary man—
*with* a wooden leg" who "will begin to lead me a new life!" (p. 53). The
realities are a leading topical subject of the novel.

Education in a wider sense is, of course, a theme of *Our Mutual Friend*,
though it is not as conspicuous or as central as in, say, *David Copperfield* or
*Great Expectations*. "The school of life"—moral education through experience, finding out the path to happiness the hard way—is an implicit motif.
Bella Wilfer is the chief pupil, and her father sums up her gain from Boffin's benevolent tutelage in his not very original observation, "There's no
royal road to learning; and what is life but learning?" (p. 684). Eugene
Wrayburn is redeemed from a life of aimless vacuity and made a fit husband for Lizzie almost at the cost of his life; before his redemption, he
describes his indolent habits to Mortimer Lightwood in a school analogy:
"When we were at school together, I got up my lessons at the last moment,
day by day and bit by bit; now we are out in life together, I get up my
lessons in the same way" (p. 537).

But education enters *Our Mutual Friend* not only as a moral theme but
also as a social topic. In the early sixties discussion of the perennial Victorian issue of popular education—the "democratizing" of learning to the
extent of giving working-class children a minimal ability to read—acquired
current relevance from the agitation for an enlarged franchise which
would eventually result in the Second Reform Bill of 1867. The sardonic
"We must educate our masters" had not yet been attributed to Robert
Lowe, vice-president of the Committee of Council on Education, but the
necessity, difficulties, and perils of universal education were already being
debated in connection with the movement to double the electorate.

From the early 1840's, when he became Miss Burdett-Coutts's almoner,
Dickens had taken a deep interest in the voluntary "ragged schools" which
constituted the lowest rung on the educational ladder in the London slums,
and in an indignant passage in *Our Mutual Friend* he returned to a favorite theme of his, the ludicrous unsuitability of the reading books used in
these well-meaning but misguided institutions, one of which Charley
Hexam had attended:

Young women old in the vices of the commonest and worst life, were
expected to profess themselves enthralled by the good child's book,
the Adventures of Little Margery, who resided in the village cottage
by the mill; severely reproved and morally squashed the miller when

she was five and he was fifty; divided her porridge with singing birds; denied herself a new nankeen bonnet, on the ground that the turnips did not wear nankeen bonnets, neither did the sheep who ate them; who plaited straw and delivered the dreariest orations to all comers, at all sorts of unseasonable times. So unwieldy young dredgers and hulking mudlarks were referred to the experiences of Thomas Two-pence, who, having resolved not to rob (under circumstances of uncommon atrocity) his particular friend and benefactor, of eighteen-pence, presently came into supernatural possession of three and six-pence, and lived a shining light ever afterwards. (Note that the bene-factor came to no good.) Several swaggering sinners had written their own biographies in the same strain; it always appearing from the les-sons of those very boastful persons, that you were to do good, not be-cause it *was* good, but because you were to make a good thing of it. Contrariwise, the adult pupils were taught to read (if they could learn) out of the New Testament; and by dint of stumbling over the syllables and keeping their bewildered eyes on the particular syllables coming round to their turn, were as absolutely ignorant of the sublime history, as if they had never seen or heard of it. (pp. 214–15)[2]

A degree more advanced than the ragged schools were those taught by Bradley Headstone and Miss Peecher: working-class schools, conducted by Anglican and Nonconformist educational agencies but partially subsi-dized by the state, and taught by men and women who had themselves come from "the million" and been prepared for their occupation in teacher training colleges. These schools were not a novelty in the period of *Our Mutual Friend* (the government subsidies, for example, had begun in a small way in 1833, and inspection in 1839) but they had become more numerous with every passing year, and their proliferation was a visible social phenomenon of the sixties. Dickens specifically associated Head-stone's and Miss Peecher's schools with the building boom he and his London readers were witnessing at the moment:

The schools—for they were twofold, as the sexes—were down in that district of the flat country tending to the Thames, where Kent and Surrey meet, and where the railways still bestride the market-gardens that will soon die under them. The schools were newly built, and there

2. Matthew Arnold commented trenchantly on school reading books, as well as on other aspects of contemporary education touched upon in *Our Mutual Friend*, in his inspector's reports for 1860–69. See *Reports on Elementary Schools 1852–1882*, ed. Sir Francis Sandford (London, 1889), pp. 82–152.

were so many like them all over the country, that one might have
thought the whole were but one restless edifice with the locomotive
gift of Aladdin's palace. (p. 218)

But it was with the teachers, not the buildings as features of the changing urban landscapes, that Dickens was concerned. As Philip Collins has
pointed out, his "main educational interest in this novel is the sociology of
the new race of trained teachers. . . . The college-trained teacher of Dickens's later years [unlike his ill-paid, overworked predecessors] could not be
regarded as a subject for pathos; . . . he was relatively well paid. Usually
he had risen, like Headstone and Hexam, from a humble origin; his success
in doing so might be regarded as admirable, and his decent salary a well-
earned reward for hard work. At least as often, however, it touched off
lower-class prejudices against the man who deserts his kind, and middle-
class prejudices against the *parvenu.*"[3] Headstone and Hexam are, in fact,
poor relations of the Veneerings. The attempted upward thrust of the new
breed of teachers is part of the problem of social mobility and pretension
which is among the novel's chief themes. "A higher social position, . . . they
felt, was their right, as men of superior education engaged in an important
and respectable job, and they were the more bitterly insistent on this because generally they had risen from poor families, and wanted reassurance
that they were accepted into middle-class society . . . ."[4]

The schoolmasters had brought their grievances into the public eye
which had so far been indifferent to their very existence, as a consequence
of a crisis within the profession. In 1861 the Newcastle Commission, set up
three years earlier to make a comprehensive study of popular education,
recommended instituting regular formal examinations as a means of testing

3. Philip Collins, *Dickens and Education* (London, 1963), p. 159. Pages 159–71 of
this book contain the fullest discussion of the subject. See also Asher Tropp, *The
School Teachers: The Growth of the Teaching Profession in England and Wales from
1800 to the Present Day* (New York, [1957]), ch. 3 ("The 'Social Condition' of the
New Schoolmasters").

4. Collins, p. 160. Mary Sturt, *The Education of the People* (London, 1967), p. 198,
quotes a professional paper of the time, *The School and the Teacher*: "It is no strange
thing that men who in education, tastes and habits have all the qualifications of 'gentlemen' should regard themselves as worthy of something very much higher than the
treatment of a servant and the wages of a mechanic. What in short the teacher desires
is that his 'calling' shall rank as a 'profession'; that the name of 'schoolmaster' shall ring
as grandly on the ear as that of 'clergyman' or 'solicitor'; that he shall feel no more
that awful chill and 'stony British stare' which follows the explanation that 'that interesting young man is only the schoolmaster.'" Such a passage enables us to understand
the precise intonation and intention of Eugene's repeated contemptuous use of "Schoolmaster" ("a most respectable title") as he addresses Headstone in the scene in the
Temple (pp. 288–93).

what would today be called the cost effectiveness of the schools. Lowe readily agreed. "If education is not cheap," he declared in the accents of true Benthamism, "it should be efficient; if it is not efficient it should be cheap." In response, the Committee of Council on Education promulgated the so-called "Revised Code" of 1863 which made government grants to each school contingent upon the results of examinations conducted by the visiting government inspector. Each satisfactory performance won the management 6s 6d (in the case of an infant-school pupil) or 12s (in that of an older one) for the coming year. Penalties were assessed for faulty performance and irregular attendance. Among the major effects of the "payment by results" system were a large increase in the membership of the two professional organizations, as angry teachers, who got all the blame if their pupils failed and none of the money if they passed, rose to arms; more stress on rote memorizing (to which we will return in a moment); and continual publicity for the state-assisted school system as the merits and iniquities of the Revised Code and the claims of the teachers were debated in Parliament. Lowe, who as deviser of the code and its most voluble and prominent apologist was one of the best-hated men of the day, was driven from office in April 1864, just before the first monthly part of *Our Mutual Friend* was published.[5]

Schools and schoolmasters, then, were very much in the news. Here as elsewhere in his fiction, Dickens deftly exploited a topicality for artistic purposes. As he developed the novel, education, and specifically literacy, a cultural value which was enjoying fresh attention as a result of the controversy over the Revised Code, directed the plot and helped delineate character; as much as the dust mounds and the river, it supplied not only scene but framework and motivation. Lizzie Hexam, whose books at the outset of the novel are the fire into which she gazes in her waterside mill-turned-hovel (pp. 28–30), at first sacrifices her own education for the sake of her brother Charley's. (The value of the boon she confers upon the ingrate Charley is quietly suggested by Dickens's comment when Charley awaits Mortimer in the Veneerings' "library of bran-new books, in bran-new bindings liberally gilded": "he glanced at the backs of the books, with an awakened curiosity that went below the binding. No one who can read, ever looks at a book, even unopened on a shelf, like one who cannot" [p. 18].)

5. Although the immediate cause of Lowe's resignation was the charge that he had doctored the inspectors' annual reports to suppress criticism of the Committee of Council's doctrines, it is clear that his sponsorship of "payment by results" had much to do with it. Chs. 6 and 7 of Tropp's book, cited above, supply a detailed narrative of the whole Revised Code controversy.

Gaffer, their illiterate father, strenuously opposes schooling for either one because it would make him their inferior. "Let him never come within sight of my eyes," he says of Charley, "nor yet within reach of my arm. His own father ain't good enough for him. He's disowned his own father. His own father, therefore, disowns him for ever and ever, as an unnat'ral young beggar" (p. 75). Thus the issue defines each character and the relationship of the three. Gaffer's brute nature is exemplified by his attitude, which places him in grotesque juxtaposition with those on a higher level of society who suffer the same gnawing social anxiety. Lizzie's initial self-abnegation in respect to learning is the particular mark, in this novel, of the heroine; and Charley's selfishness and social ambition are expressed by the humiliation he feels because of Lizzie's illiteracy. "It's a painful thing," he tells Headstone, "to think that if I get on as well as you hope, I shall be— I won't say disgraced, because I don't mean disgraced—but—rather put to the blush if it was known—by a sister who has been very good to me" (p. 231).

Lizzie's illiteracy, moreover, provides Dickens with a new twist for a familiar theme.[6] The social differences that form so frequent and imposing an obstacle to lovers' happiness in Victorian fiction are expressed here in the unusual terms of disparate education. Eugene Wrayburn proposes, from motives purer than those exhibited by other of Dickens's idle young men, to pay "some qualified person of your [Lizzie's] own sex and age, so many (or rather so few) contemptible shillings, to come here, certain nights in the week, and give you certain instruction which you wouldn't want if you hadn't been a self-denying daughter and sister" (p. 235). Similar education for Jenny Wren is included in the arrangement. Lizzie's acceptance, after an interval of prudent hesitation, precipitates Headstone's insane jealousy, for Headstone has already decided to make the necessity of Lizzie's being educated the pretext for paying suit to her. "Some man who had worked his way," he disingenuously explains to Charley, "might come to admire—your sister—and might even in time bring himself to think of marrying—your sister—and it would be a sad drawback and a heavy penalty upon him if, overcoming in his mind other inequalities of condition and other considerations against it, this inequality and this consideration remained in full force" (p. 231). Headstone's fury when he

6. Lizzie's education exemplifies a notable trend in the years just before the novel was written. The literacy rate among girls of her generation (i.e., those who were able to sign the marriage register) rose from 54.8 percent in 1851 to 65.3 percent in 1861. This increase of 10.5 percentage points was the largest recorded for either sex in any single Victorian decade.

learns that Eugene has anticipated him is shared by Charley, his *protégé*, who thereupon becomes allied with his schoolmaster against his sister. "What right," he demands, "has he [Eugene] to do it, and what does he mean by it, and how comes he to be taking such a liberty without my consent, when I am raising myself in the scale of society by my own exertions and Mr. Headstone's aid, and have no right to have any darkness cast upon my prospects, or any imputation upon my respectability, through my sister?" (p. 290).

The conflict between Headstone and Wrayburn thus originates in the disputed claim to supply her education. She is an eager pupil. Soon after her teacher (who, she assures Charley, "comes from an institution where teachers are regularly brought up" [p. 345] and therefore enjoys formal certification) has begun operations, she and Jenny are spending their holidays with pleasure and profit in "book learning." This result is agreeable enough, but one should note that it is accomplished not in the classroom but through private instruction; and, indelibly associated as they are with the popular educational system, the conduct of Charley and Headstone throughout the novel casts a deep shadow upon that system. Dickens indeed goes so far as to ascribe Headstone's villainy to his profession:

> Tied up all day with his disciplined show upon him, subdued to the performance of his routine of educational tricks, encircled by a gabbling crowd, he broke loose at night like an ill-tamed wild animal. Under his daily restraint, it was his compensation, not his trouble, to give a glance towards his state at night, and to the freedom of its being indulged. (p. 546)

And as Gissing later remarked of Charley, "This youth has every fault that can attach to a half-taught cub of his particular world. He is a monstrous egotist, to begin with, and 'school' has merely put an edge on to the native vice."[7] In *Our Mutual Friend*, the contemporary school system suffers guilt by association.

Dickens was unenthusiastic, to say the least, about the methods employed in its classrooms. Mr. Podsnap's condescending didacticism as he instructs the Frenchman in the subtleties of English grammar and pronunciation and the glories of the British Constitution would qualify him, Dickens remarks, to teach him in an infant school (p. 132). There was, too, the sterile Gradgrindery of the teaching routine, a favorite target in Dickens's criticism of educational method. Headstone, he says,

7. George Gissing, *Charles Dickens* (New York, 1924), p. 257.

had acquired mechanically a great store of teacher's knowledge. He could do mental arithmetic mechanically, sing at sight mechanically, blow various wind instruments mechanically, even play the great church organ mechanically. From his early childhood up, his mind had been a place of mechanical stowage. The arrangement of his whole-sale warehouse, so that it might be always ready to meet the demands of retail dealers—history here, geography there, astronomy to the right, political economy to the left—natural history, the physical sciences, figures, music, the lower mathematics, and what not, all in their several places—this care had imparted to his countenance a look of care; while the habit of questioning and being questioned had given him a suspicious manner, or a manner that would be better described as one of lying in wait. (p. 217)

"The habit of questioning and being questioned": every reader of the novel who had seen accounts of the squabble over the Revised Code, whether or not he had ever set foot inside a M'Choakumchild classroom, knew what Dickens meant. It was notorious that "payment by results" placed a premium on sheer memory work; every pupil who glibly parroted the right answers to the questions the inspector set was worth as much as 12s per subject to the next year's grant. No wonder the question-and-answer method was so popular with efficiency- and economy-minded bureaucrats and so bitterly execrated, if sometimes for the wrong reasons, by the teachers.

In *Our Mutual Friend*, a succession of widely separated scenes is given a common point by Eugene's remark, after Headstone's and Charley's visit to the Temple and Mortimer's subsequent questioning of Eugene about his intentions toward Lizzie, that "the schoolmaster had left behind him a catechizing infection" (p. 295). The origin and seat of the infection had already been indicated in the brief scene between Miss Peecher and her pupil-assistant Mary Anne:

... "When you say *they* say, what do you mean? Part of speech They?"

Mary Anne hooked her right arm behind her in her left hand, as being under examination, and replied:

"Personal pronoun."

"Person, They?"

"Third person."

"Number, They?"

"Plural number."

"Then how many do you mean, Mary Anne? Two? Or more?" (p. 220)

Later, in the same setting of the schoolmistress' off-duty hours, the catechetical method is resumed when she questions Mary Anne about Charley's sister:

"She is named Lizzie, ma'am."
"She can hardly be named Lizzie, I think, Mary Anne," returned Miss Peecher, in a tunefully instructive voice. "Is Lizzie a Christian name, Mary Anne?"
Mary Anne laid down her work, rose, hooked herself behind as being under catechization, and replied: "No, it is a corruption, Miss Peecher."
"Who gave her that name?" Miss Peecher was going on, from the mere force of habit, when she checked herself, on Mary Anne's evincing theological impatience to strike in with her godfathers and her godmothers, and said: "I mean of what name is it a corruption?"
"Elizabeth or Eliza, Miss Peecher."
"Right, Mary Anne. Whether there were any Lizzies in the early Christian Church must be considered very doubtful, very doubtful." Miss Peecher was exceedingly sage here. (p. 339)

This out-of-school interrogation recurs in another context later on, in a domestic scene between Bella and John Rokesmith, which begins with a catechism on the same subject of naming:

"Now, sir! To begin at the beginning. What is your name?"
A question more decidedly rushing at the secret he was keeping from her could not have astounded him. But he kept his countenance and his secret, and answered, "John Rokesmith, my dear."
"Good boy! Who gave you that name?"
With a returning suspicion that something might have betrayed him to her, he answered, interrogatively, "My godfathers and my godmothers, dear love?"
"Pretty good!" said Bella. "Not earnest good, because you hesitate about it. However, as you know your Catechism fairly, so far, I'll let you off the rest. . . . " (p. 686)

In a climactic variation, in which Dickens adapts a familiar classroom technique to dramatic purpose, Rogue Riderhood, assuming for the moment the role of an illiterate Matthew Arnold, becomes H.M. Inspector of Schools in Headstone's classroom, while the appointed teacher, for a reason admittedly unconnected with the annual grant, agonizes:

"Wot's the diwisions of water, my lambs? Wot sorts of water is there on the land?"

Shrill chorus: "Seas, rivers, lakes, and ponds."

"Seas, rivers, lakes, and ponds," said Riderhood. "They've got all the lot, Master! Blowed if I shouldn't have left out lakes, never having clapped eyes upon one, to my knowledge. Seas, rivers, lakes, and ponds. Wot is it, lambs, as they ketches in seas, rivers, lakes, and ponds?"

Shrill chorus (with some contempt for the ease of the question): "Fish!"

"Good agin!" said Riderhood. "But what else is it, my lambs, as they sometimes catches in rivers?"

Chorus at a loss. One shrill voice: "Weed!"

"Good agin!" cried Riderhood. "But it ain't weed neither. You'll never guess, my dears. Wot is it, besides fish, as they sometimes ketches in rivers? Well! I'll tell you. It's suits o' clothes."

Bradley's face changed.

"Leastways, lambs," said Riderhood, observing him out of the corners of his eyes, "that's wot I my own self sometimes ketches in rivers. For strike me blind, my lambs, if I didn't ketch in a river the wery bundle under my arm!"

The class looked at the master, as if appealing from the irregular entrapment of this mode of examination. The master looked at the examiner, as if he would have torn him to pieces. (pp. 794–95)

In such a fashion, Dickens achieved three results: he reiterated the criticism of the mechanical method of education he had made, in terms too uncomfortably close to reality to be called satire, in the famous second chapter of *Hard Times*; he enhanced the temporal immediacy of the novel; and, perhaps most important, by transferring the catechetical device to informal settings outside the schoolroom he managed a variety of comic effects in addition to the most brilliant one in the passage just quoted. Topicality, in a word, inspired technique.

The schoolmaster is assuredly abroad in this novel, as Eugene says (p. 541). In her dedication to running a respectable waterfront public house, Miss Abbey Potterson has "more of the air of a schoolmistress of the Six

Jolly Fellowship-Porters" and her rough patrons are "pupils . . . who exhibited, when occasion required, the greatest docility" as she sends them
home, with wholesome admonitions, at closing time (pp. 63, 65). One of
them, "Captain Joey, the bottle-nosed regular customer in the glazed hat,
is a pupil of the much-respected old school" (p. 443). R. Wilfer remarks
to Bella that he attends "two schools. There's the Mincing Lane establishment [where he works] and there's your mother's Academy [an abortive
venture, like that of Dickens's mother, where he is the only pupil]" (p.
684). By inference, therefore, the "tragic Muse with a face-ache" and the
strict but well-meaning proprietress of the Six Jolly Fellowship-Porters are
Miss Peecher's colleagues. Betty Higden keeps a "minding school" or day
nursery (p. 199), and Jenny Wren belongs to the profession by virtue of her
own analogy. Old Riah is her prize pupil. "If we gave prizes at this establishment," she tells him, "(but we only keep blanks), you should have the
first silver medal . . ." (p. 433). Jenny's problem pupil, by contrast, is her
alcoholic father, toward whom she behaves with schoolmistressly exaspera-
tion. The inverted parent/teacher-child relationship, grotesque in their
case, makes a playful reappearance in the affectionately assumed relationship between Bella and her own father (p. 684). Bella, in turn, is Noddy
Boffin's pupil, as Noddy, in a certain sense, is Silas Wegg's.

Even the Limehouse police station, like Miss Abbey's nearby house of
refreshment, has the air of a schoolroom. The Inspector is seen busy "with
a pen and ink, and ruler, posting up his books in a whitewashed office, as
studiously as if he were in a monastery on the top of a mountain" (p. 24),
and his fellow-officer, similarly occupied, "might have been a writing-
master setting copies" (p. 763). The ruled books of the police station—
schoolroom equipment transferred to another, not wholly incongruous,
setting—have their counterpart in the "ruled pages and printed forms" of
the Registrar of Deaths (p. 14), and the Inspector in his scriptorium has
his in Riah, who at one point (p. 440), standing at the desk in a corner of
the Six Jolly Fellowship-Porters, is also momentarily cast in the role of
copyist, an "ancient scribe-like figure."

In a social atmosphere increasingly affected by the presence of schools
for "the people," literacy and its converse acquire special significance. Illiteracy on the part of several characters figures among the many instances
of "doubleness" for which *Our Mutual Friend* is noted. Lizzie Hexam,
herself illiterate, makes it possible for Charley to learn to read, and in turn
is enabled to read by Eugene; meanwhile the illiterate Boffin hires the

barely literate Wegg to read to him. Boffin inherits a fortune made from salvage on land, and the equally illiterate Gaffer Hexam squeezes a tiny living from salvage, of quite another kind, on water.

Illiteracy is total in some characters and partial, or intermittent, in others. Rogue Riderhood can neither read nor write, and like many such persons, he is intensely superstitious about the art: he has a "sense of the binding powers of pen and ink and paper" (p. 149), particularly in the form of an Alfred David. The eighty-year-old Betty Higden says she "ain't . . . much of a hand at reading writing-hand, though I can read my Bible and most print" (p. 198). She is meant to be identified as a product of another age, when literacy was far less common than in the 1860's. "Letter-writing —indeed, writing of most sorts—hadn't much come up for such as me when I was young" (p. 385). Boffin's illiteracy, also an instrument of plot in that it brings Wegg into his service, is somewhat spasmodic. Normally, as when Wegg reads from *The Decline and Fall of the Rooshan Empire* and the lives of celebrated misers, it prevails. But he copes, apparently with some expectation of success, with business papers (Rokesmith's function is merely to organize and interpret these disorderly and thumb-smeared notes [p. 178]), and before Rokesmith's advent he seems to have had no trouble writing proposals to parishes desiring to have their waste removed on the most favorable terms (p. 180). He is also able to read a note from Venus (p. 576) and later to slowly spell out the will which the triumphant taxidermist shows him (p. 658).

A curiously gratuitous digression by Eugene Wrayburn suggests that when Dickens wrote *Our Mutual Friend* he was for some reason—perhaps his current involvement with the platform recitals he called "readings"?— extraordinarily conscious of the word in a special sense:

> "You charm me, Mortimer, with your reading of my weaknesses. (By-
> the-bye, that very word, Reading, in its critical use, always charms me.
> An actress's Reading of a chambermaid, a dancer's Reading of a horn-
> pipe, a singer's Reading of a song, a marine painter's Reading of the
> sea, the kettledrum's Reading of an instrumental passage, are phrases
> ever youthful and delightful.)" (p. 542)

Whatever its origin in Dickens's free-associational storehouse, the paren-
thetical embroidery on the theme of the word "reading," so unusual in a writer who ordinarily relates the contents of his asides in some more immediate way to the business in hand, contributes to our sense of the im-

portance of reading—the ability, the act—in this novel. Writing and reading dominate the Boffins' memory of the child John Harmon and his sister:

"... I've seen him sit on these stairs, in his shy way, poor child, many a time [says Boffin]. Me and Mrs. Boffin have comforted him, sitting with his little book on these stairs often."

"Ah! And his poor sister too," said Mrs. Boffin. "And here's the sunny place on the white wall where they one day measured one another. Their own little hands wrote up their names here, only with a pencil; but the names are here still, and the poor dears gone for ever." (p. 184)

Bella, like some of Dickens's other young ladies, carries a book to read while she walks—a book, however, which is not the love story Rokesmith reasonably assumes it to be, but "more about money than anything else" (p. 205). Her home study course after she becomes Mrs. Rokesmith supplies a further nexus between the novel's themes of education and print. She was "under the constant necessity of referring for advice and support to a sage volume entitled The Complete British Family Housewife . . ." (p. 682).[8] While communion with a cookbook is nothing new in the annals of the Victorian heroine, it may be taken as a sign of the times that Bella, in 1865, applies herself to the daily newspaper as a means of delighting her husband. "Wonderful was the way in which she would store up the City Intelligence, and beamingly shed it upon John in the course of the evening, incidentally mentioning the commodities that were looking up in the markets, and how much gold had been taken to the Bank . . ." (p. 682).

In Our Mutual Friend, allusions to newspaper reading as an ordinary habit of everyday life and to newspapers as a means of communication have a frequency unapproached in the social milieux of the earlier novels. Betty Higden's chief contact with print is through the newspaper, a source of information and popular entertainment which scarcely existed, as far as the masses of people were concerned, in her own girlhood before the turn of the century. "I do love a newspaper," she asserts (p. 198). "Sometimes she would hear a newspaper read out, and would learn how the Registrar General cast up the units that had within the last week died of want and of exposure to the weather" (p. 506). But her special delight, as it was of millions, was the police news. "You mightn't think it, but Sloppy

8. Dickens may be casting a side glance at the popularity of Mrs. Beeton's *Book of Household Management*, which in its first year of publication, 1861, had sold 60,000 copies.

is a beautiful reader of a newspaper. He do the Police in different voices" (p. 198). The newspaper is Miss Abbey's favorite study as she sits enthroned at the bar of her temperate public house (pp. 63, 437); Twemlow reads it over his dry toast and weak tea in his stable-flat in Duke Street, St. James's, and in his Pall Mall club (pp. 115, 247); Podsnap reads it at his place of business (p. 247).

Newspapers, enjoying greatly increased circulations as a result of the repeal of the paper tax in 1861 and the consequent reduction of price, afforded Dickens a convenient device of realism at a time when readers expected to be assured that the events they read about in a novel actually happened, or at least could very well have happened. If one were skeptical, Dickens's implication went, one need only look up the files of the papers. For not only were the sensational incidents themselves reported: the newspapers were a constant vehicle of communication among the characters, and a file-searcher could turn up their messages in the agony columns. John Harmon, after he has become John Rokesmith, "examined the newspapers every day for tidings that I was missing" (p. 371); after some days, the inquest over his supposed body is "duly recorded in the newspapers" (p. 30), and the publicity given to Gaffer Hexam's grisly trade impels a "rapturous admirer subscribing himself 'A Friend to Burial' (perhaps an undertaker)" to send "eighteen postage stamps, and five 'Now Sir's' to the editor of the *Times*" (p. 31). The mysterious stranger, Julius Handford, is advertised for, without result, "every day for six weeks . . . at the head of all the newspapers" (p. 195). The eventual disclosure of the real and living John Harmon is announced to Wegg through the papers (p. 787). Meanwhile, Mrs. Boffin has proposed advertising in the newspapers for suitable orphans (p. 102). At a later stage of the plot, Lizzie, in the country, is "afraid to see a newspaper, or to hear a word spoken of what is done in London, lest he [Headstone] should have done some violence" (p. 525), and still later Rogue Riderhood tells Headstone, no doubt facetiously, that he had contemplated the same means of locating *him*: "I had as good as half a mind for to advertise you in the newspapers to come for'ard" (p. 703). Remembering the remark, after his return to London from his brutal assault on Eugene, Headstone "examined the advertisements in the newspapers for any sign that Riderhood acted on his hinted threat of . . . summoning him to renew their acquaintance, but found none" (p. 792).

Side by side with the newspapers, however, remained handbills and placards, much older forms of printed announcement. The freshly printed police notice concerning John Harmon, headed BODY FOUND, another copy of which Rokesmith will carefully preserve (p. 451), takes its place among the other mementoes of similar discoveries that serve Gaffer Hexam's room as wallpaper: descriptions of bodies with money still in pocket, bodies without money, "a sailor, with two anchors and a flag and G. F. T. on his arm," a young woman in grey boots and linen marked with a cross, a body with a nasty cut over the eye, "two young sisters what tied themselves together with a handkecher,"9 and "the drunken old chap, in a pair of list slippers and a nightcap, wot had offered—it afterwards come out—to make a hole in the water for a quartern of rum stood aforehand, and kept to his word for the first and last time in his life" (p. 22).10 These same placards are Charley's shame. His reaction to Lizzie's mention of them is an early clue to his character: "Confound the bills upon the walls at home! I want to forget the bills upon the walls at home, and it would be better for you to do the same" (p. 227).

And just as handbills advertising violent deaths and inquiring for missing men—sometimes proclaiming a reward of £100 for information leading to a murderer (p. 31)—dominate the opening of the novel, so they recur at its close, when the guilty Headstone haunts the railway station to read the printed notices on the walls (pp. 749, 791). Handbills were an old accessory of English daily life, and they may well have decorated an occasional riverman's dwelling centuries earlier; but the locale in which they are now found, a railway station, is a novel one. This suggestion of the ancient lineage and continuity of print is also conveyed by Wegg's ballads. Hexam's walls have their outdoor counterpart in the clotheshorse-turned-screen upon which Wegg displays his stock. The ballads, which Wegg liberally (in a double sense) quotes in the course of the novel, link the new world of sensational daily newspapers with the old one of Autolycus.

In view of the ubiquity of print in *Our Mutual Friend*, it is fitting that Dickens should use dicta on reading to illustrate the philistinism, assumed

9. Unless the event was duplicated nearer the time of the novel, the bill Dickens mentions alludes to an incident of 1840, when two sisters were prevented from jumping off Southwark Bridge, "both firmly tied together round the waists with two strong scarfs knotted, and which went round their bodies two or three times" (*Annual Register* for 1840, Chronicle, pp. 122–23). Although the attempt, having been frustrated, would actually have resulted in no such bill, it may well have stuck in Dickens's mind over the years in connection with the notorious determination of Sir Peter Laurie, a Middlesex Magistrate of the early forties and the model for Alderman Cute in *The Chimes*, to "put down suicide," especially suicide from the Thames bridges, by imposing severe punishment on the unsuccessful.

10. In ironic contrast, the walls of the murderous Bradley Headstone's schoolroom were decorated with "peaceful texts from Scripture" (p. 555).

or real, of two characters. The beginning of Boffin's playacting as a tyrannical employer is signalized when he tells Rokesmith with self-canceling
magnanimity, "it ain't that I want to occupy your whole time; you can take
up a book for a minute or two when you've nothing better to do, though
I think you'll a'most always find something useful to do" (p. 463). And the
essence of Podsnappery is that estimable moralist's view of Literature,
among the other arts, as "large print, respectively descriptive of getting up
at eight, shaving close at a quarter-past, breakfasting at nine, going to the
City at ten, coming home at half-past five, and dining at seven" (p. 128),
as well as being devoid of anything that would bring a blush to the cheek
of the young person.

It is appropriate, too, that when Dickens sends Lizzie to work in the
country, he rejects the more obvious choices of occupation and places her
instead in a paper mill, representative of an industry that seldom appears
in fiction despite the affinity of the two commodities.[11] As part of his
amends to Mrs. Eliza Davis, who had protested his treatment of Jews,
Dickens designated Jews as the proprietors of this mill, which he depicts
as an ideal establishment, benevolently managed, with good labor relations
and a pleasant workers' village to which was attached a "'Christian school"
—a tribute to the millowners' broadmindedness but also an implicit contrast,
in its wholesome traditionalism and piety, with the dismal urban schools
that produced and harbored Charley Hexams and Bradley Headstones.

The prevalence of paper in many contexts is one physical detail that sets
*Our Mutual Friend* apart from its predecessors. It is true that in *Bleak
House* paper is equally prominent; but its quite different nature and the
uses to which it is put there help define the particularity of the later novel.
In *Bleak House* the paper which has the most significant function, as both
symbol and accessory detail, is what might be called "institutional" or
"private" paper, the mass of dusty detritus—parchment as well as paper
properly speaking—generated by Chancery and ending up either in the
despondent archives of the litigants or in Krook's junk shop. It is upon the
existence and interpretation of certain written legal documents that the
plot hinges.[12] In *Our Mutual Friend*, by contrast, the paper that is themat-

11. The paper industry was much in the news in the years just before Dickens wrote
*Our Mutual Friend*. In 1861, as was noted above, the excise duty on paper was re-
pealed. The growing insufficiency of standard raw materials, mainly rags, to meet the
increased demand for paper stimulated a search for other materials which resulted in
the adoption of esparto grass and, later, of wood pulp. For one example of the popular
interest in the topic, see "Paper," *Cornhill Magazine*, 4 (1861), 609-23.

12. One interpretation of the place of paper in *Bleak House* is Trevor Blount's: "the
paper symbolism of Chancery documents, begging letters, and philanthropic corre-

ically and dramatically important is both printed and public: newspapers, police notices, election bills (pp. 251–52) rather than pleas and judgments. It circulates not in the limited sphere of Chancery, its victims and parasites, but in the wide ambience of a metropolis, open to everyone's gaze. Its thematic reference, finally, is not to Law but to Literacy.[13]

Just as the railway defines the contemporaneity of *Dombey and Son*, therefore, so the more diffuse and variegated references to education, print, and paper are Dickens's expression of the special tone of urban England twenty years later. This was the condition of the country five years before the passage of Forster's Education Act, whose consequences Dickens did not live to see, but of whose basic principle he presumably would have approved.[14] His allusions to printed matter and the ability to read are, on the whole, period color rather than commentary; their function is sociological, not symbolic except insofar as they are connected with the theme of education. Yet (though the association is not expressed in the novel) it is impossible not to think of the dust heaps in this connection, for waste paper was one of their many components; and it is waste paper, swirling through the streets on the wind that is blowing throughout the novel, which seems to define the physical and social milieu:

> That mysterious paper currency which circulates in London when the wind blows, gyrated here and there and everywhere. Whence can it come, whither can it go? It hangs on every bush, flutters in every

---

spondence ... [is] meant to show the substitution (as Dickens saw it) of paper resolutions, vapid theorizings, and wordy protestations for actual help when and how it was needed." ("Poor Jo, Education, and the Problem of Juvenile Delinquency in Dickens' *Bleak House*," *Modern Philology*, 62 [1965], 331.) For another, more comprehensive statement, see Alan R. Burke, "The Strategy and Theme of Urban Observation in *Bleak House*," *Studies in English Literature*, 9 (1969), 666–67, 672–73.

13. But at least two commentators have linked paper with Shares—that is, as physical symbols of the worship of stock-exchange values which is a dominant motif of the novel. Arnold Kettle quotes the second paragraph of ch. X, "As is well known to the wise in their generation, traffic in Shares is the one thing to have to do with in this world" (p. 114), and observes: "The dust-heaps are the dominant visual image of the accumulation of wealth and power; but it is a feature of that power that it operates mysteriously, through bits of paper: wills, promissory notes, the offer of reward which Rogue Riderhood clutches, above all, through shares." (*"Our Mutual Friend,"* *Dickens and the Twentieth Century*, ed. John Gross and Gabriel Pearson [London, 1962], p. 219.) J. Hillis Miller, in his Afterword to the Signet edition of the novel, quotes both the former passage and the one with which the present paper ends as the basis for his remark, " 'Shares,' which, in their inexhaustible power to duplicate themselves and make everything of nothing, Dickens describes as the virtual god of a moneyed society." In Dickens's text, however, shares are not explicitly spoken of as pieces of paper.

14. See his letter of 7 June 1850, quoted on p. 252 of the Papermac edition of Collins's *Dickens and Education*.

tree, is caught flying by the electric wire, haunts every enclosure, drinks at every pump, cowers at every grating, shudders upon every plot of grass, seeks rest in vain behind the legions of iron rails. (p. 144)[15]

15. This brief passage contains one further topicality. The "electric" wires are, of course, those of the telegraph (pp. 252, 253), which had come into general use for the transmission of private messages only a few years earlier. By 1865 the several independent companies had offices throughout commercial London. When Society, assembled at the Veneerings', reviews and passes authoritative judgment on the late melodramatic events up the Thames, the Wandering Chairman gives it as his opinion that the proper reward for Lizzie's heroism would be to "have got her a berth in an Electric Telegraph Office, where young women answer very well" (p. 818). This bran-new occupation was one of the very first which enabled women to enter the Victorian business world.

# Poor Mr. Casaubon

## Gordon S. Haight

*Yale University*

EVERY TEACHER of *Middlemarch* has encountered the disgust that under-graduates feel at the marriage of nineteen-year-old Dorothea Brooke to "loathsome old Edward Casaubon." Though he was only forty-eight, they never hesitate—despite a generation of sex-education—to describe him as "impotent." Victorian novels supply many other examples of such marriages. Dr. Strong in *David Copperfield* was sixty-two when he married his nineteen-year-old Annie. Charlotte Brontë created Mr. Rochester twice the age of Jane Eyre, and in *Villette* married Augusta Fanshawe to a man "much older than papa." Even in real life these disparate matches were not at all uncommon. Sir James Hope was fifty when in 1858 he married Victoria, the nineteen-year-old daughter of the Duke of Norfolk. Sir Charles Murray at the age of fifty-six married a daughter of George Eliot's friend Lord Castletown, who was three years younger than his son-in-law. In 1863 the second Earl of Wilton at the age of sixty-four took as his second wife a girl who was younger than her step-children. According to Greville's Diary the third Viscount Melbourne had the good fortune "at sixty years old, and with a broken and enfeebled constitution, to marry a charming girl of twenty." Most of these matches were made to provide heirs, and (as the records show) often with success. Faced with a class of under-graduates particularly vociferous on the subject of Casaubon's impotence, I once pointed out the window to a statue of President Woolsey of Yale, the youngest of whose dozen children was born when he was seventy-one years old; and I might have cited the contemporary example of Charlie Chaplin, who at the age of fifty-four married Oona O'Neill and had eight children by her. Viewed in the light of these examples there was nothing unusual in the Casaubon marriage.

George Eliot had always been fascinated by the theme. In her Journal, 2 December 1870, noting the beginning of "Miss Brooke," she wrote that the subject "has been recorded among my possible themes ever since I began to write fiction." In a notebook kept when she was a pupil at Miss

Franklin's school in Coventry, the earliest work we have in her hand, she copied a poem by Thomas Haynes Bayly entitled "The Unwilling Bride":

> The joybells are ringing—oh! come to the church
> We shall see the bride pass if we stand in the porch;
> The bridegroom is wealthy; how brightly arrayed
> Are the menials who wait on the gay cavalcade. . . .
>
> Yon feeble old knight the bride's father must be
> And now walking proudly, her mother we see;
> A pale girl in tears, slowly moves by her side;
> But where is the bridegroom, and where is the bride?

The answer comes in the next stanza:

> A Bridal like *this* is a sorrowful sight
> For *that* pale girl is bride to the feeble old knight.

In "Silly Novels by Lady Novelists," which she wrote for the *Westminster Review* in 1856, George Eliot comments on some of these ill-assorted matches. The brides are sometimes learned young ladies, who

> read the Scriptures in their original *tongues*. Greek and Hebrew are mere play to a heroine; Sanscrit is no more than *a b c* to her; and she can talk with perfect correctness in any language except English. She is a talking polyglott, a Creuzer in crinoline.

More often than not she will marry the wrong person to begin with. But, though she suffers terribly from the mistake, in the end "the tedious husband dies in his bed, requesting his wife, as a particular favour to him, to marry the man she loves best, and having already dispatched a note to the lover informing him of the comfortable arrangement."

George Eliot is a little kinder to her own heroines. Romola, for example, longed to become as learned as Cassandra Fedele, the famous young philosopher of the fifteenth century, "and then perhaps some great scholar will want to marry me" (ch. 5). The recurrence of this trait in Dorothea was noted by Harriet Martineau; in commenting on the "prodigious" advance George Eliot had made between *Romola* and *Middlemarch* she wrote: "Nobody seems to realise the likeness—almost identity—of the leading conceptions in the two books: e.g. old Bardo and Casaubon—and Romola and Dorothea." [1]

In a passage near the end of the Finale George Eliot wrote:

1. To an unidentified correspondent, 29 Aug. 1873. MS: Huntington Library.

Among the many remarks passed on her mistakes, it was never said in the neighbourhood of Middlemarch that such mistakes could not have happened if the society into which she was born had not smiled on propositions of marriage from a sickly man to a girl less than half his own age.[2]

In revising for the one-volume edition this passage was deleted, possibly to eliminate the repetition of "a fine girl who married a sickly clergyman, old enough to be her father" in the previous paragraph. Both passages emphasize Mr. Casaubon's sickliness. Chapter 5, containing his letter of proposal, takes for its epigraph a sentence from the famous digression on the misery of scholars in Burton's *Anatomy of Melancholy*:

> Hard students are commonly troubled with gowts, catarrhs, rheums, cachexia, bradypepsia, bad eyes, stone, and collick, crudities, oppilations, vertigo, winds, consumptions, and all such diseases as come by over-much sitting: they are most part lean, dry, ill-coloured . . . and all through immoderate pains and extraordinary studies.

Besides his sallow complexion and leanness the only defect on this repulsive list found in Mr. Casaubon is bad eyes. He shows no obvious signs of sickliness. And the difficulty with his eyes is a definite attraction for Dorothea, since it provides her with opportunities to read to him. The deep eye-sockets in which they are set are perhaps the only resemblance he bears to the familiar portrait of John Locke. Dorothea herself suffers from short-sightedness and had never noticed the two white moles with hairs in them which so troubled Celia. Though Mr. Casaubon was "fastidious in voices" of those serving him as readers, his own voice was an unpleasant sing-song, in which he delivered his balanced periods with occasional nodding movements of the head. He disliked music. "I never could look on it in the light of a recreation to have my ears teased with measured noises," he said (p. 48). Yet he never seemed to hear the noise of his spoon scraping the bottom of the dish, which also annoyed Celia when he was eating his soup.

The harshest opinion of his physical deficiencies comes, naturally, from Sir James Chettam, the suitor Mr. Casaubon has displaced: "He is no better than a mummy" (p. 43), "a dried bookworm" (p. 17), with "no good red blood in his body" (p. 52). At each stage of Sir James's indignation, Mrs. Cadwallader, whose plans for Dorothea have been shattered by

---

2. *Middlemarch*, edited by Gordon S. Haight, Riverside edition (Boston, 1956), p. 612. Quotations from the novel are all from this text.

the preposterous engagement, caps his gibes: "A great soul.—A great blad-
der for dried peas to rattle in!" she exclaims (p. 43); under a microscope
his blood would be all semicolons and parentheses; he dreams footnotes,
and they run away with all his brains (p. 52). She wishes Dorothea joy
of her hairshirt, and comforts Sir James, by declaring that he is well rid of
"a girl who would have been requiring you to see the stars by daylight.
Between ourselves, little Celia is worth two of her, and likely after all to
be the better match. For this marriage to Casaubon is as good as going to
a nunnery" (p. 43).

Mrs. Cadwallader's shrewd eye and sharp tongue distinguish the sexual
inadequacy in Casaubon, at which Sir James can hardly hint. Yet it is not
due entirely to his age. Lydgate, conscious of his own large and energetic
frame, watches Casaubon walking slowly with bent shoulders and thin
legs and thinks: "Poor fellow, some men with his years are like lions; one
can tell nothing of their age except that they are full grown" (p. 309). Sir
James believed that at any age Casaubon would never have been "much
more than the shadow of a man. Look at his legs!" (p. 50). Weakness of
body does not always correspond with weakness of sexual passion. In
Casaubon's case, however, we infer that he never felt a strong sexual
interest in women. He assures Dorothea in his letter that he can offer her
"an affection hitherto unwasted" and (in a most characteristic metaphor)
a life with no "backward pages whereon, if you choose to turn them, you
will find records such as might justly cause you either bitterness or shame"
(p. 32). Despite his conventional allusions to "bloom of youth" and "femi-
nine graces," he is clearly attracted most to Dorothea's mental qualities,
which are "adapted to supply aid in graver labours and to cast a charm
over vacant hours." What he wants is a secretary for the graver labors in
that row of notebooks for his Key to All Mythologies. Courtship proves a
sad hindrance to its progress.

But he had deliberately incurred the hindrance, having made up his
mind that it was now time for him to adorn his life with the graces of
female companionship, to irradiate the gloom which fatigue was apt
to hang over the intervals of studious labour with the play of female
fancy, and to secure in this, his culminating age, the solace of female
tendance for his declining years. Hence he determined to abandon
himself to the stream of feeling, and perhaps was surprised to find
what an exceedingly shallow rill it was. As in droughty regions baptism
by immersion could only be performed symbolically, so Mr Casaubon

found that sprinkling was the utmost approach to a plunge which his stream would afford him; and he concluded that the poets had much exaggerated the force of masculine passion. (p. 46)

As the wedding day came nearer, he did not find his spirits rising, nor did the contemplation of that flower-bordered matrimonial garden scene "prove persistently more enchanting to him than the accustomed vaults where he walked taper in hand" (p. 63). In discussing plans for their wedding journey to Rome he more than once urged Dorothea to take Celia with her. "I should feel more at liberty," he said, "if you had a companion" (p. 64).

The conventions of family reading and the circulating library, which determined what Victorian novelists could write about the marriage bed, necessarily relegated details of the Casaubons' honeymoon to the reader's imagination. For Dorothea with her "enthusiastic acceptance of untried duty" it was an experience of "dream-like strangeness":

> the dimmer but yet eager Titanic life gazing and struggling on walls and ceilings; the long vistas of white forms whose marble eyes seemed to hold the monotonous light of an alien world: all this vast wreck of ambitious ideals, sensuous and spiritual, mixed confusedly with the signs of breathing forgetfulness and degradation, at first jarred her as with an electric shock, and then urged themselves on her with that ache belonging to a glut of confused ideas which check the flow of emotion. Forms both pale and glowing took possession of her young sense, and fixed themselves in her memory even when she was not thinking of them, preparing strange associations which remained through her after-years. . . . In certain states of dull forlornness Dorothea all her life continued to see the vastness of St Peter's, the huge bronze canopy, the excited intention in the attitudes and garments of the prophets and evangelists in the mosaics above, and the red drapery which was being hung for Christmas spreading itself everywhere like a disease of the retina. (p. 144)

This red drapery "spreading itself everywhere" is particularly interesting as a clue to Dorothea's experience.[3] The liturgical color for Christmas, of course, is white. George Eliot had been in Rome in 1860 during Holy Week, and may have assumed that the red draperies symbolizing the

3. A perceptive analysis of this passage by A. L. French is found in "A Note on *Middlemarch*," *Nineteenth-Century Fiction*, 26 (Dec., 1971), 339–47. But Mr. Little regards the "disease of the retina" as an allusion to Casaubon's bad eyes.

Passion would also be used at Christmas. But such a mistake is unusual in her books. Through the turbulent imagery in which Dorothea clothes her thoughts a sympathetic reader perceives that her initiation into matrimony had been violent and painful. To have done it differently called for more tact and tenderness than the novice Casaubon possessed. "No one would ever know what she thought of a wedding journey to Rome" (p. 204).

"Dorothea—but why always Dorothea?" George Eliot asks at the beginning of chapter 29. What were poor Mr. Casaubon's feelings on this disastrous honeymoon?

> In spite of his blinking eyes and white moles objectionable to Celia, and the want of muscular curve which was morally painful to Sir James, Mr Casaubon had an intense consciousness within him, and was spiritually a-hungered like the rest of us. He had done nothing exceptional in marrying—nothing but what society sanctions, and considers an occasion for wreaths and bouquets. In had occurred to him that he must not any longer defer his intention of matrimony, and he had reflected that in taking a wife, a man of good position should expect and carefully choose a blooming young lady—the younger the better, because more educable and submissive—of a rank equal to his own, of religious principles, virtuous disposition, and good understanding. On such a young lady he would make handsome settlements, and he would neglect no arrangement for her happiness: in return, he should receive family pleasures and leave behind him that copy of himself which seemed so urgently required of a man—to the sonneteers of the sixteenth century. (p. 205)

Whether Dorothea would find his "family pleasures" equally agreeable it was not in him to inquire. He is one of George Eliot's prime egoists.

As with Dorothea we must guess at Casaubon's experience from the imagery. Sigmund Freud, to whom *Middlemarch* appealed very much because "it illuminated important aspects of his relations with [his wife] Martha,"[4] taught the world that the mind masks painful sexual experiences in symbolic terms. How else can we read this sentence?

> Mr Casaubon had never had a strong bodily frame, and his soul was sensitive without being enthusiastic: it was too languid to thrill out of self-consciousness into passionate delight; it went on fluttering in the

4. Ernest Jones, *Life and Work of Sigmund Freud* (New York, 1953), I, 174.

swampy ground where it was hatched, thinking of its wings and never flying. (p. 206)

He lived at Lowick—and names are never negligible in George Eliot's novels—spending most of his time in the gloomy library and taking his exercise only in the walk to the shady summerhouse, lined with dusky yews. Though he had a trout stream on the Lowick estate, he never fished in it. Strong light always bothered him; almost the first remark he made to Dorothea is, "We must keep the germinating grain away from the light" (p. 16). His life was full of pigeon-holes, locked drawers, small closets, winding stairs, labyrinths, mines, catacombs, museums. In the dark regions of mythology he was "carrying his little taper among the tombs of the past," at work on "a ghastly labour producing what would never see the light" (p. 348). Here George Eliot tosses in without comment the remark that Celia "had lately had a baby."

On the last night of his life Casaubon allows Dorothea to read to him from the table of contents of his Key to All Mythologies and at each point where he said "mark" to make a cross with her pencil. "After she had read and marked for two hours, he said, 'We will take the volume upstairs—and the pencil, if you please—and in case of reading in the night, we can pursue this task. It is not wearisome to you, I trust, Dorothea?'" (p. 349). The reading in the night did come. There is something grimly comic in the spectacle of the bridegroom of fifteen months awakening his bride to take down notes on the fertility rites of Crete for his Key to All Mythologies, which Dorothea now saw as

> shattered mummies, and fragments of a tradition which was itself a mosaic wrought from crushed ruins—sorting them as food for a theory which was already withered in the birth like an elfin child. Doubtless a vigorous error vigorously pursued has kept the embryos of truth a-breathing: the quest of gold being at the same time a questioning of substances, the body of chemistry is prepared for its soul, and Lavoisier is born. But Mr Casaubon's theory of the elements which made the seed of all tradition was not likely to bruise itself unawares against discoveries.... (p. 351)

Before their marriage—in one of his lighter moments—he had pronounced the aphorism "See Rome and die" an extreme hyperbole, proposing to emend it to "See Rome as a bride, and live thenceforth as a happy wife"

(p. 148). Like most of Mr. Casaubon's emendations this proved less true than the original.

His scholarly reputation was limited. At the first mention of his name we are told that he was "noted in the *county* as a man of profound learning" (p. 8). Oxford, however, questioned the value of his studies. The

> pamphlets—or "Parerga" as he called them—by which he tested his public and deposited small monumental records of his march, were far from having been seen in all their significance. He suspected the Archdeacon of not having read them; he was in painful doubt as to what was really thought of them by the leading minds of Brasenose, and bitterly convinced that his old acquaintance Carp had been the writer of that depreciatory recension which was kept locked in a small drawer of Mr Casaubon's desk, and also in a dark closet of his verbal memory. (p. 206)

In one of his pamphlets he had published

> a dedication to Carp in which he had numbered that member of the animal kingdom among the *viros nullo aevo perituros*, a mistake which would infallibly lay the dedicator open to ridicule in the next age, and might even be chuckled over by Pike and Tench in the present. (p. 207)

His chief purpose in the pamphlet he was writing at the time of his death was vengeance against the sneers of Carp & Company, "for even when Mr Casaubon was carrying his taper among the tombs of the past, those modern figures came athwart the dim light, and interrupted his diligent exploration" (p. 308).

During his brief employment as Casaubon's secretary Will Ladislaw, whose schooling had gone no farther than Rugby, saw the futility of spending a lifetime correcting the mistakes of Jacob Bryant and Warburton a century before. His glib remark to Dorothea that "If Mr Casaubon read German he would save himself a great deal of trouble" was superficial. The two most important studies by Germans were already available to him: Creuzer's *Mythologie* (1810–12) had appeared in a French translation and Lobeck's *Aglaophamus* (1829) was written in Latin. George Eliot comments, "Young Mr Ladislaw was not at all deep himself in German writers; but very little achievement is required in order to pity another man's shortcomings" (p. 154). Yet the shortcomings were there, and Mr. Casaubon was morbidly afraid of their being exposed. He had sent Will away, not because of any lack of thoroughness, but from conviction of his scorn for the futility of the Key to All Mythology. Now he "foresaw with sudden terror" that Dorothea's blind worship of his learning might be replaced with the same sort of critical judgment. Jealousy for his reputation mingled with jealous foreboding that, if he should die, Will and Dorothea might marry and be the happier that he was gone. He prepared the codicil to his will withdrawing his estate from Dorothea if she should marry Will Ladislaw.

Casaubon's antecedents are rather shadowy in *Middlemarch*. His mother was the younger of the two ladies of Lowick Manor. When his Aunt Julia, the elder and prettier of them, was disinherited for marrying the Polish refugee Count Ladislaw, the estate passed to the younger sister, who married a Mr. Casaubon and had two sons. The elder inherited the estate; Edward, the younger, became a clergyman and on the death of his brother in 1819 came to live at Lowick. No one in the novel speaks of the earlier members of the family. Casaubon told Dorothea that he had "none but comparatively distant connections" (p. 274); we hear from Mr. Cadwallader that he "is very good to his poor relations: pensions several of the women" (p. 51), but we learn nothing further about them. Will Ladislaw's father was one of these poor relations, a first cousin, towards whom he recognized a duty. Having learned of his desperate plight, ill and starving at Boulogne, Casaubon sent Ladislaw money and, after his death, continued an allowance to his widow and son Will, whose education he paid for. As the only male in the family, of course, Ladislaw should have been the heir of the Lowick estate.

Though George Eliot was always obsessively anxious about the legal details of her novels, there is nothing in her notebooks or papers concerning the codicil to Casaubon's will. My friend Romilly Ouvry, an English solicitor and great-grandson of George Henry Lewes, who has studied the question, suggests that on her marriage Dorothea brought a dowry of about £20,000, which was comprised in the settlement. Apparently Casaubon contributed nothing to it, but, with the knowledge of Mr. Brooke, made a will leaving the Lowick property to Dorothea, whether for life or absolutely is not stated. Though George Eliot was "quite right in her law," Mr. Ouvry tells me, she was "wrong in her practice," for it was most unlikely that Mr. Brooke's solicitor would have agreed to such an arrangement; he would have insisted on at least an equivalent to the £20,000 being brought into the settlement by Casaubon, and would never have been content with a will which could be torn up next day. Provision might have been made in the settlement for Dorothea's life interest in the Lowick property to cease on remarriage, but it would have been unusual to provide for such termination by will or codicil. Had Dorothea deigned to challenge it, the Court of Chancery might have set it aside, particularly since Will Ladislaw was the nearest blood relation. Until 1936, however, such a codicil could not have been challenged by a widow.

I suspect that George Eliot's treatment of the codicil was determined by the case of Branwell Brontë, who, according to Mrs. Gaskell's account, was dismissed as tutor in the family of the Reverend Edmund Robinson because of the "criminal advances" made to him in a love affair with Mrs. Robinson. In her *Life of Charlotte Brontë* Mrs. Gaskell declared that the Reverend Mr. Robinson altered his will to bequeath his property to his wife "solely on the condition that she should never see Branwell Brontë again."[5] Threatened with a libel suit, Mrs. Gaskell made a public apology in a letter to *The Times*,[6] retracting every statement imputing any breach of conjugal duties or "guilty intercourse with the late Branwell Brontë," and removed the offensive passages from the revised edition. George Eliot read Mrs. Gaskell's book as soon as it appeared and was deeply moved by it, but regretted her setting down Branwell's alcoholism and opium addiction as due entirely to remorse over the alleged affair with Mrs. Robinson, which "would not make such a life as Branwell's was in the last three or four years unless the germs of vice had sprouted and shot up long before."[7] Mr. Robinson's will contains no reference to Branwell, who was probably dismissed for some indiscretion with his pupil, thirteen-year-old Edmund Robinson, Jr.

The ironic echoes in the name *Casaubon* made it a happy choice for George Eliot. She had long known about the great Renaissance scholar Isaac Casaubon, who died in England in 1614 and was buried in Westminster Abbey. She had used his edition of Theophrastus, and was familiar with the part he had played in the Catholic-Protestant disputes that brought him from France as a refugee after the assassination of Henry IV. In the notebook containing extracts from her reading in the 1860s and 1870s—Sophocles, Euripides, Theocritus, Drayton, Sidney, Shakespeare, Marlowe, Donne, Browne, Milton, and most of the nineteenth-century poets—between two long passages from Spenser's *Shepherd's Calendar* she wrote: "Spenser, born 1552, twelve years older than Shakspeare, died 1598–9.

5. (London, 1857), I, 226.  6. 30 May 1857, p. 5b.
7. *The George Eliot Letters* (New Haven, 1954–55), II, 319–20.

Curious to turn from Shakspeare to Isaac Casaubon, his contemporary."[8]
To use the name for the pseudo-scholar of *Middlemarch* was a touch that
delighted her.

In 1875, four years after the novel was written, Mark Pattison, the Rector
of Lincoln College, Oxford, published his *Isaac Casaubon 1559–1614*. He
and his wife had been acquainted with George Eliot since 1869, and until
her death they remained warm friends. Mrs. Pattison, the daughter of an
Oxford bank manager, had raised her position socially by the match, marrying him in 1861 (according to A. H. Sayce) "from ambition rather than from
love."[9] He was forty-eight and she was twenty-one. It was not a happy
marriage. Fifteen years later in a letter to Pattison she spoke of her
"physical aversion" to their sexual relation and her "fear of its renewal."[10]
But her intimacy with Sir Charles Dilke had already begun. There could
hardly be greater contrast in moral character between the sophisticated
worldly-minded Mrs. Pattison and the serious, naive Dorothea Casaubon
—unless it was that between the foolish pedant of Lowick and the energetic
and learned Rector of Lincoln. In an obituary article on him Henry Nettle-
ship wrote:

> There have been those who judging from a very imperfect knowledge
> of a few facts, and from the name of the book by which he is best
> known, have fancied that George Eliot had the Rector's studious
> habits in mind to a certain extent when she drew the character of Mr.
> Casaubon in *Middlemarch*. There was, however, nothing in common
> between the serious scholar at Lincoln and the mere pedant frittering
> away his life in useless trivialities; nor was George Eliot, Mark Pat-
> tison's friend, at all likely to draw a caricature of one she loved and
> valued.[11]

In a manuscript "Memoir of E. F. S. Dilke," later prefixed to her *The Book
of the Spiritual Life* (1905), Dilke, who became her second husband,
declared:

> To those who know, Emilia Strong was no more Dorothea Brooke than
> Pattison was Causaubon; but it is the case that the religious side of
> Dorothea Brooke was taken by George Eliot from the letters of Mrs.

8. MS: Folger Library, M.a. 13, p. 159.
9. *Reminiscences* (London, 1923), p. 86.
10. MS: Bodleian, 21 Jan. 1876. Published in Betty Askwith, *Lady Dilke* (London,
1969), p. 60.
11. *Academy*, 9 Aug. 1884, p. 94.

Pattison. . . . It was of Emilia Strong that George Eliot was thinking when she wrote "Dorothea knew many passages of Pascal's *Pensées* and of Jeremy Taylor by heart."[12]

But just what was "the religious side of Dorothea"? A single sentence in the first chapter of *Middlemarch* alludes to her girlish notion of praying at the bedside of sick laborers and her "strange whims of fasting like a Papist, and of sitting up at night to read old theological books." Casaubon's fancied learning, not his clerical function, attracted her. Her asceticism was not Puseyite, like Mrs. Pattison's, but sprang from Evangelical seriousness before the Oxford Tracts began. The only time Dorothea lay all night on the floor, she was impelled, not by penance, but by a paroxysm of sexual jealousy, which George Eliot had no need to study in any one's letters. She was quoting Jeremy Taylor to her governess when Mrs. Pattison was only a year old. As for Pascal, the *Pensées* were the first prize George Eliot won at school, and she had learned many of them by heart before Mrs. Pattison was born.

No manuscript has ever been found to support Dilke's categorical assertion that "Casaubon's letter to Dorothea at the beginning of the 5th chapter of Middlemarch, from what G. E. herself told me in 1875, must have been very near to the letter that Pattison actually wrote, and the reply very much the same." Betty Askwith in her *Lady Dilke* is commendably skeptical of this story; she finds it hard to believe that any real man ever wrote that letter. Besides, she adds, the style "is totally unlike Pattison's lucid, sinewy writing."[13] George Eliot was always reluctant to discuss her works, even with her most intimate friends, among whom Sir Charles Dilke never figured. Indeed, in 1875 she had never met him; it was not till 1878 that Lewes first made his acquaintance at Lord Houghton's.

The most absurd hypothesis was advanced by Mr. John Sparrow: that Mrs. Pattison "sanctioned and actually encouraged George Eliot to caricature her husband as Casaubon."

> As for the Rector, George Eliot—the confidant of the suffering wife —must have meant to make him suffer in his turn, and she was shrewd enough to know that she could do so safely: Pattison was not so vain as to be blind to the odious resemblance, but he was too proud to admit by any public gesture that a resemblance existed. He had to endure seeing his own stilted proposal of marriage reproduced almost

12. *The Book of the Spiritual Life*, (London, 1905), pp. 16–17.
13. *Lady Dilke*, p. 16.

word for word and held up to ridicule, in the knowledge that his wife had repeated it *verbatim* to her friend the novelist. George Eliot could be sure both that he would suffer and that he would suffer in silence. The story, in fact, is of strong action by one high-minded woman on behalf of another.[14]

If any evidence ever existed in Mrs. Pattison's or George Eliot's correspondence to support this melodramatic plot, it has vanished under the mutilation of Sir Charles Dilke's notorious scissors; both Mrs. Pattison and Sir Charles, were (according to Betty Askwith) "uncommonly handy with the eraser and with the scissors."[15] But to Mr. Sparrow that makes the evidence, not more dubious, but less, suggesting only that "Dilke took great care about the accuracy of his text"![16] Mr. Sparrow is so enthralled by his hypothesis that he discovers "parallels that George Eliot could not have been aware of, except prophetically, when she wrote her novel."

Dorothea Casaubon found consolation for her husband's lack of sympathy in a romantic attachment formed before his death, to a man whom she married when she became a widow. Three years after *Middlemarch* was published, Sir Charles Dilke, who had known Mrs. Pattison slightly as a girl, resumed his friendship with her; he then played in her life a *rôle* exactly corresponding with the part played in *Middlemarch* by Will Ladislaw—a romantic friendship was followed, after the death of the detested husband, by marriage to the widow.[17]

The exactness of the parallel is somewhat blurred by the fact that Mrs. Pattison's intimacy began some years before her husband died—an example, Mr. Sparrow says, of "life imitating art." Even the jealous Mr. Casaubon entered into no such "coarse misinterpretation" of Dorothea (p. 307). The closest approach Will ever made to the romantic in Casaubon's lifetime was going to church one Sunday to look at her and getting nothing but a grave bow as she walked out on her husband's arm. She was a widow more than a year before they became engaged.

Pattison himself never betrayed the least sign that he recognized the "odious resemblance"—quite understandably, since there was none, either physical or intellectual. He continued to call on George Eliot when in Lon-

14. John Sparrow, *Mark Pattison and the Idea of a University* (Cambridge, 1967), pp. 16–17.
15. *Lady Dilke*, p. 10.
16. *Notes and Queries*, 213 (Dec. 1968), 469.
17. *Mark Pattison and the Idea of a University*, p. 17.

don, often accompanied by that "high-minded" conspirator his wife. When Lewes and George Eliot were in Oxford they usually spent an hour or two with the Pattisons. Their contemporaries were equally unaware of the alleged caricature. John Morley, who (though not an enthusiastic admirer of George Eliot) knew them all well, dismissed the identification as an "impertinent blunder."[18] Mrs. Humphry Ward, also a friend of them all, said explicitly: "I do not believe that she ever meant to describe, the Rector . . . in the dreary and foolish pedant who overshadows *Middlemarch*."[19]

A number of other candidates have been proposed, most of them—like Pattison—for no stronger reason than that they had married younger wives. Thus Frances Power Cobbe suggested the shy, kindly Robert William Mackay, a scholar of real distinction, who bore no other resemblance to Casaubon.[20] Eliza Lynn Linton was convinced that he was modelled on Dr. R. H. Brabant, and her evidence is important, because, like George Eliot, she had visited Dr. Brabant during her girlhood. She describes him as

> a learned man who used up his literary energies in thought and desire to do rather than in actual doing, and whose fastidiousness made his work something like Penelope's web. Ever writing and rewriting, correcting and destroying, he never got farther than the introductory chapter of a book which he intended to be epoch-making, and the final destroyer of superstition and theological dogma.[21]

After the marriage of his daughter Rufa to Charles Hennell in 1843, Dr. Brabant invited Marian Evans, who had been a bridesmaid, to visit him at Devizes "to fill the place of his daughter." The best one can say of Dr. Brabant is that he was a pompous and foolish man who at the age of sixty-two, thanks to an ample fortune, found leisure to impress young ladies with his supposed learning. Naturally Marian was gratified to have her intellectual achievements recognized, and was eager to serve him in any capacity. According to Mrs. Linton "she knelt at his feet and offered to devote her life to his service."[22] He showed her his library, which he said she was to consider *her* room. To her friends back in Coventry Marian wrote: "I am in a little heaven here, Dr. Brabant being its archangel. . . . We read, walk,

---

18. "On Pattison's Memoirs" in Morley's *Critical Miscellanies, Works*, VI (London, 1921), 240.
19. *A Writer's Recollections* (New York, 1918), p. 110.
20. *Life of Frances Power Cobbe* (London, 1894), II, 430–31.
21. Eliza Lynn Linton, *My Literary Life* (London, 1899), p. 43.
22. Ibid., p. 44.

and talk together, and I am never weary of his company." He taught her some Greek, and after reading German aloud to him for two hours, she was sometimes so faint as to be obliged to lie down on the sofa till walking time.

But there was a *Mrs.* Brabant, too, in this little heaven, a blind lady, the affable archangel's wife, and her rather formidable sister, Miss Susan Hughes, who became alarmed at the young lady's failure to practise the required conventionalisms, made a great stir, and excited the jealousy of the blind Mrs. Brabant. Miss Evans was forced to leave—some time before she had expected to go. Rufa Hennell, who supplied this account years later in a conversation with John Chapman, blamed her father for acting ungenerously and worse towards George Eliot.[23]

Lewes used to joke occasionally about his being George Eliot's Casaubon.[24] From the compelling realism of the character those who did not know them sometimes imagined that she had studied Dorothea's marriage from her own. Harriet Beecher Stowe was one of these. In replying to her letter George Eliot wrote:

> But do not for a moment imagine that Dorothea's marriage experience is drawn from my own. Impossible to conceive any creature less like Mr. Casaubon than my warm, enthusiastic husband, who cares more for my doing than for his own, and is a miracle of freedom from all author's jealousy and all suspicion. I fear that the Casaubon-tints are not quite foreign to my own mental complexion. At any rate I am very sorry for him.[25]

Frederic W. H. Myers tells in his obituary article on George Eliot how

> Mr. Lewes and she were one day good-humoredly recounting the mistaken effusiveness of a too-sympathizing friend, who insisted on assuming that Mr. Casaubon was a portrait of Mr. Lewes, and on condoling with the sad experience which had taught the gifted authoress of *Middlemarch* to depict that gloomy man. And there was indeed something ludicrous in the contrast between the dreary pedant of the novel and the gay self-content of the living *savant* who stood acting his vivid anecdotes before our eyes. "But from whom, then," said a friend,

23. G. S. Haight, *George Eliot and John Chapman*, 2nd. ed. (New Haven, 1969), p. 24.
24. See, for example, *The George Eliot Letters*, V, 291, 332.
25. Ibid., V, 322.

turning to Mrs. Lewes, "did you draw Casaubon?" With a humorous solemnity, which was quite in earnest, nevertheless, she pointed to her own heart.[26]

There in the pain and humiliation of the episode with Dr. Brabant, I believe, lay the venom that was to give poor Mr. Casaubon his horrible vividness.

26. "George Eliot," *Century Magazine*, 23 (Nov. 1881), 60.

# Qualifications of the Medical
# Practitioners of MIDDLEMARCH

## C. L. Cline

*The University of Texas at Austin*

"MEDICAL DEGREES," *The Times Literary Supplement* remarked recently (1 January 1971), "have always been a mystery to the layman, who discovers with surprise that his alleged doctor merely holds the bag of letters known as Conjoint, or the diploma of the Society of Apothecaries." Except for "the bag of letters known as Conjoint"—that is the diploma earned by passing the conjoint examinations of the Royal College of Physicians and the Royal College of Surgeons, instituted in 1885—there is little difference in the mystery today and in 1829, the year that Tertius Lydgate came to Middlemarch.

It is my intention in this paper to consider the physicians and surgeons who practiced in Middlemarch, the kind of training which they must have undergone, and their general status and that of their profession at the time.[1] We may be sure that George Eliot was clear in her own mind about these matters—the *Quarry for Middlemarch* is ample testimony—but the art of the novel she was writing did not require her to tell all she knew. Moreover she may have assumed more familiarity with such matters than general readers possessed at the time and certainly more than readers—especially Americans—possess today.

On the state of medicine in 1829 she tells us ironically that it was "a dark period . . . in spite of venerable colleges which used great efforts to secure

---

1. Asa Briggs, in "*Middlemarch* and the Doctors" (*The Cambridge Journal*, Sept., 1948, pp. 749–62), adds little specific information to that contained in Anna Theresa Kitchel's *Quarry for Middlemarch* (Berkeley and Los Angeles, 1950). Even so, in the discussion of Lydgate I shall be covering ground shared in common with him. In the Leavises' *Dickens the Novelist* (New York, 1970) Mrs. Leavis has an interesting Appendix to the chapter on *Bleak House* entitled "The Symbolic Function of the Doctor in Victorian Novels" (pp. 179–83). As she points out, the necessity for sanitary reforms and public health services produced in fiction a new type of doctor, "a modern figure concerned not for private practice among the well-to-do but for public health and the scientific advancement of medicine. . ." (p. 180). Lydgate she quite correctly assigns to this category before his defeat. In regarding him as the general practitioner that he was, however, she surprisingly confers upon him the title of "Dr."

purity of knowledge by making it scarce. . . ."[2] It was an Age of Darkness indeed. By 1800 the zest for experiment that had marked the period from Harvey to Newton had been followed by a complete collapse of the spirit of inquiry.[3] The single exception of consequence, before the introduction of anaesthesia in 1846 and of antisepsis in 1865, was the first successful vaccination with cowpox vaccine by Edward Jenner in 1796. Even so, vaccination was not made compulsory until 1853 and was by no means universally enforced: as late as 1864, 9,425 persons were known to have died of small-pox in England and Wales.[4] Sanitary conditions were almost beyond belief to anyone who has perhaps not read the graphic description of Tom-all-Alone's in Dickens's *Bleak House* (1852–53); yet the first Public Health Act dates 1848, the year in which the second great cholera epidemic killed 54,000 in England and Wales.[5] It is not too much to say, then, that there was no such thing as "medical science" in the first half of the nineteenth century in England.

Now in 1829 the licensing powers of medical practitioners in England were vested principally in three corporations by Royal Charter. These were the Royal College of Physicians, which was chartered by Henry VIII in 1518 and granted exclusive licensing authority within a seven-mile radius of London; the Royal College of Surgeons, which shared its lowly status with the barbers until 1745 but did not become the Royal College of Surgeons until 1800; and the Society of Apothecaries, the lowliest of the three, which broke away from its union with the grocers in 1616 by a charter which was not, however, ratified by Act of Parliament until 1815. None of these were colleges in the current sense of the word: although lectures might be given at them, they were primarily examining and licensing bodies. They conferred no degree. Who then trained the practitioners? The answer is (a) the two universities, Oxford and Cambridge, which alone conferred the degrees of Bachelor of Medicine and Doctor of Medicine, (b) hospitals in London in which physicians and surgeons took pupils in return for a substantial fee, (c) Scottish, Irish, or foreign universities, and (d) numerous private schools in London, the most famous of which was the

---

2. *Middlemarch* (Edinburgh and London, 1871–72), II, 259.
3. Charles Newman, *The Evolution of Medical Education in the Nineteenth Century* (London, 1957), p. 56. This is the best general treatment of the subject that I have found, and I owe much to it.
4. Paul Vaughan, *Doctors' Commons: A Short History of the British Medical Association* (London, 1959), p. 6.
5. Ibid., pp. 5–6.

Great Windmill Street School of John Hunter, where Benjamin Rush went to learn surgery after taking his M.D. degree at Edinburgh.

There were two grades of physicians: the Fellows, usually graduates of Oxford or Cambridge, and Licentiates, who had been trained in hospitals or private schools or at universities other than Oxford and Cambridge. In addition there were Extra-Licentiates, whose training was usually inferior to that of the Licentiates and who were restricted to practice outside the seven-mile radius of London. In 1829 there were only 98 Fellows, 268 Licentiates, and 40 Extra-Licentiates.[6] As between the years 1842–44 only seven graduates of Oxford and nine from Cambridge were admitted to the College,[7] it is obvious that most of the members had their training elsewhere. Members who had not taken the M.D. degree at a university were thus not Doctors of Medicine but were (rarely) Fellows or more usually Licentiates of the Royal College of Physicians (F.R.C.P. or L.R.C.P.).

By Act of Parliament physicians were supposed to be "profound, discreet, groundedly learned and deeply studied in Physic."[8] As examinations were conducted orally in Latin, certainly the candidate had to be a man of some learning. The courses of study at Oxford and Cambridge required a minimum of seven years and a maximum of ten; hence it might be expected that Oxbridge graduates would be the most highly trained of all practitioners. Not so. Medical instruction at both universities, except for witnessing a couple of dissections, was wholly theoretical. At Cambridge, where regulation prescribed a course of lectures by the Regius Professor, the Regius Professor in 1817 had not lectured in a hundred years.[9] Further, a Cambridge M.A. could become an M.D. without attending any lectures, without hospital experience, and without examinations.[10] Training in Scottish and Continental universities varied in quality from the relatively superior of Paris, Leyden, and Edinburgh to the complete absence of any curriculum at Aberdeen and St. Andrews. The hospitals offered little organized instruction: students might attend lectures on anatomy during the winter and could attend "hospital practice" at restricted times but were largely left to build up their own programs. Private schools, on the other hand,

6. Sir George Clark, *A History of the Royal College of Physicians of London* (Oxford, 1966), II, 739.

7. A. M. Carr-Saunders and P. A. Wilson, *The Professions* (Oxford, 1933), p. 76n. Quoted from the *Report of the Select Committee on Medical Education* (1834).

8. Newman, p. 1. He notes that the word *physic*, "up to the end of the sixteenth century, meant 'natural science' rather than medicine, and even after that time it is often difficult to be sure in which sense the word is used."

9. Ibid., pp. 10, 124.    10. Ibid., p. 10.

were much better organized: they conducted lectures on anatomy through-out the year, and the best of them offered lectures on medicine, chemistry, and midwifery, as well.[11]

The Royal College of Surgeons had its own hierarchy, consisting of Members and Licentiates; in 1843 a third order, Fellows, was instituted.[12] Before 1813 the training of a surgeon consisted of a period of apprentice-ship that had been reduced from seven to five years by 1815 but was never rigidly enforced and one course of lectures on anatomy and another on surgery. In 1813 the College added the requirement of a certificate of at-tendance at a recognized hospital.[13] After 1815, however, the Apothe-caries' Act of 1815, to which we shall come in a moment, forced the College to make its requirements complementary to those of the Society.[14] Ac-cordingly it increased the number of lectures on anatomy and surgery, raised its standards, and required certificates of dissection. In those pre-radiology days the surgeon could operate only on morbid conditions that manifested themselves externally, but in order to operate successfully he had to know a great deal more of anatomy than physicians knew. This knowledge was primarily acquired in the hospitals, where the apprentice attended lectures, witnessed demonstrations, and followed the Master around the wards. Inasmuch as some 400 students attended (Sir) Astley Cooper's lectures and at least 100 followed him about the wards, however, it is evident that there was little personal instruction.[15]

Apothecaries before 1815 were not expected to be learned men; socially they still ranked as shopkeepers. Lady Chettam, we know, liked a medical man to be on the same footing as servants. The elder Pendennis, we are told, "was a gentleman of good education, and of as old a family as any in the whole county of Somerset." But circumstances forced him to serve an apprenticeship to an apothecary, and afterwards he kept "a very humble little shop in the city of Bath," with his name and a gilt pestle and mortar above the door. There he performed the duties of apothecary-surgeon and sold over the counter plasters, tooth-brushes, hair-powder, and perfumes as well. Finding favor with the gentry of the town, he was able to shut up his shop and keep a little surgery, and even to acquire a one-horse carriage in which to make his calls. His secret ambition, however, had always been to

11. Ibid., pp. 34–37.
12. Sir Zachary Cope, The Royal College of Surgeons of England (London, 1959), p. 70.
13. Newman, p. 18.                    14. Cope, p. 43.
15. R. C. Brock, The Life and Work of Astley Cooper (London, 1952), pp. 28–29. The date is c. 1811.

be a gentleman, and a fortunate investment in copper-shares enabled him to retire and become one. And "it was now his shame, as it formerly was his pride, to be called Doctor, and those who wished to please him always gave him the title of Squire." But such rises, we may guess, were uncommon. You will remember Mr. Perry, in Jane Austen's *Emma*, who is treated respectfully by Mr. Woodhouse, though not as an equal, and it is a matter for comment when he presumes to set up a carriage. Before 1815 the training of apothecaries amounted to little more than an apprenticeship of five or six years, but in 1815 the Society made an historic move—the most important one before 1858, when the State assumed charge of qualifications—that gave most medical, as opposed to surgical, training into its hands for the next fifty years. Under the Act the Royal College of Physicians still retained its ancient privileges within the seven-mile radius of London, but no one else who qualified thereafter could practice medicine without the license of the Society.[16] To be eligible for its examination, the candidate was required to have a good standard of general education, including a knowledge of Latin, to have served a five years' apprenticeship, to have attended two courses of lectures on anatomy and physiology, two on the theory and practice of medicine, one course on chemistry, one course on materia medica, and to have put in six months' attendance at a recognized hospital.[17] It was under these regulations that Keats served a four years' apprenticeship and was excused from the fifth in order to attend Guy's Hospital, where he remained for nine months before passing his examination and being licensed for a profession that he never followed.[18]

Socially and in prestige the physicians, as might be expected, ranked first, surgeons next, and apothecaries last. The prestige of the physicians rested partly upon history and partly upon the authority to license practitioners in medicine within a seven-mile radius of London, although it was really impossible to enforce this prerogative. In theory the three types of practice were mutually exclusive, but in 1829 a legal decision gave apothecaries the right to charge either for advice or drugs but not both.[19] This decision merely legalized an already existing state of affairs and was doubtless inevitable, for conditions in the late eighteenth and early nineteenth centuries were changing rapidly. One aspect of the change was an increase in population and a correspondingly greater need for medical service than the few physicians could furnish. To satisfy this need surgeons and apothe-

16. Cope, pp. 37–38.                    17. Newman, p. 74.
18. See Walter Jackson Bate, *John Keats* (Cambridge, Mass., 1963), pp. 30–67, passim.
19. Newman, p. 78.

caries began to take both qualifications, and thus sometime before 1830 the term "general practitioner" came into being.[20] In 1834 most of the 8000 Licentiates of the Royal College of.Surgeons held the second qualification of apothecary and functioned as general practitioners.[21]

Even so, quacks far outnumbered qualified practitioners. In the census of 1851 practitioners of all kinds were asked to state whether or not they held a medical diploma; only about a third claimed to have diplomas.[22] Other evidence, however, suggests that the proportion of unqualified to qualified was more nearly 9:1.[23] As it was almost impossible to prosecute quacks successfully, George Eliot is quite right in saying that quackery had "an excellent time of it." Such a state of affairs may have mattered less than we think today, for practice by even the best of physicians was empirical. The physician took the patient's history, inquired about symptoms, and prescribed treatment. What is astonishing is that except for tongue, pulse, general appearance, and occasionally blood or urine, there was no physical examination of the patient.[24] The first record of a physical examination at Guy's Hospital was 10 November 1824; another, that of one Timothy Leary, is recorded on 19 October 1825; but by 1831 physical examinations at Guy's became rarer.[25] What this shows, inasmuch as the stethoscope had been invented by Laënnec in 1819, is that there was no attempt at the best medical centers to take advantage of improved technology. Even in the 1830's there was no microscope at St. Bartholomew's Hospital.[26] But in the kingdom of the blind the one-eyed man (or woman) may be king (or queen), and the old woman who in 1775 taught Dr. William Withering of Birmingham the virtues of foxglove (digitalis) in the treatment of dropsy[27] surely did more for her dropsical patients than the most eminent medical man could have done.

We know a good deal about George Eliot's reading in the field of medicine preparatory to writing *Middlemarch*. In August-September 1869, she recorded in her Journal that she was reading Renouard's *History of Medi-*

20. Clark, II, 649; Cope, p. 35. The earliest use of the term found by Clark (p. 637n.) dates 1812.

21. Carr-Saunders and Wilson, p. 76.

22. Cecil Wall, *The History of the Worshipful Society of Apothecaries of London* (London, 1963), I, 193.

23. Newman, p. 59, quoting a report by Dr. Edward Harrison on medical practice in Lincolnshire in 1805. Presumably the proportion would have differed little twenty-odd years later.

24. Ibid., pp. 28–29.                          25. Ibid., pp. 87–92.

26. Ibid., p. 106.                              27. Clark, II, 604.

*cine*, an "Encyclopaedia about the Medical Colleges," the life of Dr. William Cullen, J. R. Russell's *History and Heroes of Medicine*, "etc."[28] The *Quarry* contains additional evidence of her wide reading of medical books and journals, especially *Lancet*, and even of an obscure American treatise by Dr. John Ware entitled "Remarks on the History and Treatment of Delirium Tremens."[29] Further, on 26 May 1870, she spent a morning with Professor Rolleston at Oxford and watched him dissect a brain.[30] She was thus well prepared to create a believable young practitioner and introduce him into a provincial town such as she knew from experience and an authentic professional environment.

We can now, I think, draw some valid conclusions about the practitioners of Middlemarch. There are four others with whom Lydgate has to compete for patients: Dr. Sprague, "the physician of most 'weight,' " whose reputation rests partly upon a treatise on meningitis written thirty years earlier; Dr. Minchin, whom we see diagnosing a cramp as a tumor but who can quote Pope's "Essay on Man"; Mr. Wrench, who diagnoses Fred Vincy's typhoid as a "slight derangement"; and Mr. Toller, who follows the "lowering system" of treatment, which meant bleeding, blistering, and starving. A fifth, named Gambit, is an ignorant man who calls the breathing apparatus "longs" and who is principally known as an accoucheur, although he has "a satisfactory practice among shopkeepers." All have the advantage of being already well established before the arrival of Lydgate. To the inhabitants of Middlemarch all are "doctors," and each has his staunch adherents. The distinction betwen the two physicians graced by George Eliot with the title of "doctor" and those without it should now be clear: unless the physicians were extra-licentiates with degrees from a non-English university—and such evidence as there is (Dr. Sprague's defense of the colleges, for instance) argues against the supposition—they were graduates of either Oxford or Cambridge. Mr. Wrench, Mr. Toller, and Mr. Lydgate are all surgeons and are so denominated by George Eliot. Since all three function as general practitioners, it is possible that all hold the additional qualification of apothecary, although if Mr. Wrench and Mr. Toller qualified before 1815, as is likely, they might have practised without it. By the time that Lydgate qualified, however, the dual qualifi-

28. *George Eliot's Life as Related in Her Letters and Journals*, Arranged and Edited by Her Husband J. W. Cross (Edinburgh and London, 1885), III, 97, 99.

29. *Quarry*, I (Kitchel, pp. 21–36), is almost altogether restricted to notes on medical subjects.

30. Cross, III, 111.

cation was customary, and I think that we may assume that he holds both qualifications and is entitled to subscribe himself L.R.C.S., L.S.A. About Gambit it is unsafe to hazard a guess.

If our assumption about Dr. Sprague and Dr. Minchin is valid, we know that their education was primarily classical and that the medical portion of it would have been almost altogether theoretical and that quite possibly they were not required to pass any examination at all. The intention of their curriculum was to produce educated gentlemen, not competent practitioners. Small wonder, then, that Dr. Minchin cannot distinguish a cramp from a tumor. The only surprising thing about the two physicians is that, with membership in the Royal College totalling 146 in 1795 and 213 in 1809[31]—to give a range of dates when they might have qualified—both should have settled in the same provincial town. However that may be, they fell into the local custom of charging for medicines rather than for advice. Local custom in this respect apparently varied: Dr. Thorne, a qualified physician, was criticized at about the same time for compounding his own prescriptions and charging for them.

Since we do not know the dates when Messrs. Wrench and Toller qualified, it is not possible to be very specific about their training. Before 1813, as we have seen, they might have done so by serving an apprenticeship and attending a single course of lectures on anatomy and another on surgery; between 1813 and 1815 attendance upon surgical practice in a hospital would have been required. About Lydgate's training, however, we know a good deal. We know that he has studied in London, Edinburgh (which was thought to provide training superior to that in England), and Paris. At the end he would have presented himself at the Royal College, with his certificates, which would have been entered in a registry. Promptly at six o'clock the President would have taken the chair, with nine other members of the Court of Examiners seated about him. He would then have asked one of the examiners to conduct the oral examination, which lasted about an hour. After the subjects of anatomy, physiology, surgery, and medicine had been covered, the examination would have been thrown open to other members. When the questions had ended, the candidate would have withdrawn while the Court deliberated. If five of the nine members were satisfied, the candidate would have been recalled, his certificates returned to him, and a diploma given him.[32]

Lydgate, we may assume, underwent such an examination by the Royal College of Surgeons and a similar one by the Society of Apothecaries. The

31. Clark, II, 738–39.                    32. Cope, pp. 136–37.

certificates that he would have presented to the College would have been from London and Edinburgh hospitals only since certificates from foreign hospitals were not then recognized.[33] Why, then, did George Eliot send him to Paris? There were several reasons. For one, most of the progress in medicine between 1800 and 1850 was made by the French.[34] Further, Paris did not offer the same difficulty in obtaining bodies for dissection as did England, where the only sources were the bodies of the executed, the few that could be purchased from survivors, and those supplied by "resurrectionists" like that respectable tradesman Jerry Cruncher in *A Tale of Two Cities* or the murders of Burke and Hare in Scotland in 1828 and Bishop and Williams in London in 1831. Finally, as we know from the novel, Lydgate was attracted to Paris by the work of certain eminent men and their successors—Bichat, who showed that organs have membranes and tissues and that diseases are in the tissues rather than in the organs as such; Broussais, whose publications in 1808 and 1816 stimulated research in pathological anatomy; Laënnec, the inventor of the stethoscope and the authority on auscultation; and above all Louis, a pioneer in the discrimination of various fevers.[35]

In Middlemarch we never see Lydgate performing an operation; rather he is engaged as a general practitioner whose special interest is fevers. The cases that we observe are those of Peter Featherstone, who is afflicted with asthma and an old man's cough and who, after gradually weakening and becoming bedridden, dies of natural causes that doubtless lay beyond the aid of medical science of any age; Fred Vincy, whom Lydgate correctly perceives to be in the pink-skinned stage of typhoid; Mr. Casaubon, who suffers from a "fatty degeneration of the heart," as it was first described by Laënnec and about which, as Lydgate admits, medical science of the day was insufficiently informed; the charwoman's cramp, which Lydgate easily diagnoses as a cramp, not a tumor; Mr. Trumbull's pneumonia, which Lydgate treats principally by watching the course of the disease and letting nature work upon a strong constitution; and, most important of all, the delirium tremens of Raffles.

As a product of the latest and best training available at the time, Lydgate is unquestionably superior to the other practitioners of Middlemarch—a

---

33. *Quarry*, I (Kitchel, p. 24), derived from an editorial in *Lancet*, 29 Jan. 1831, pp. 596–98.

34. Fielding H. Garrison, *An Introduction to the History of Medicine* (Philadelphia and London, 1914), p. 339; Richard Harrison Shryock, *The Development of Modern Medicine* (Philadelphia and London, 1936), p. 149.

35. Evidence is in both the novel and *Quarry*, I.

man ahead of his times in several respects. Aside from his innovation in charging for advice rather than for medicines (whereby he offends his fellow-practitioners), his use of the stethoscope and the microscope and his desire to conduct *post mortems* are not only in advance of Middlemarch practice but of London as well. His treatment of Trumbull would have been not only unprecedented in Middlemarch but especially offensive to the other practitioners. And finally his treatment of Raffles's delirium tremens, although thwarted by Bulstrode, is intended to make use of the very latest treatment—admittedly experimental—advanced by the American Dr. Ware.

Insofar as George Eliot's notes enlighten us, Lydgate's modernity, except in the case of Raffles, derives principally from his training in Paris. In fact, however, much of it seems to have been a return to the best of the practices of Thomas Sydenham (1624–89), sometimes called "the English Hippocrates." Sydenham tried to cure patients without resort to mystery and dogma and insisted upon clinical observation rather than theory. He was interested especially in fevers and gout, on both of which he wrote treatises. Although he popularized the use of cinchona bark (the source of quinine) in the treatment of fevers, whenever he considered that medicine could not materially affect the disease, he did nothing at all.[36] Nothing could have been more radical. When we remember that Lydgate really did nothing at all in treating Trumbull and that his later worldly success depends mainly upon his treatment of patients suffering from gout, on which he too wrote a treatise, we may see him as a follower of Sydenham.

Lydgate, George Eliot tells us, came to Middlemarch with the aim "to do good small work for Middlemarch, and great work for the world" (I, 265). As we know, he is defeated by a combination of local circumstances and certain deficiencies in his own character which cause him to form an unfortunate marriage that soon has him deeply in debt. Money obligations involve him with Bulstrode, and the downfall of Bulstrode carries Lydgate with him. Forced to leave Middlemarch, he "gained an excellent practice, alternating . . . between London and a Continental bathing-place," specializing in gout, "a disease which has a good deal of wealth on its side." But he himself is not fooled: "he always regarded himself as a failure; he had not done what he once meant to do" (III, 363).

The story of Lydgate, then, is the tragedy of a man made for better things. But as with all tragic heroes, the fatal flaw lies within himself: he

36. Gordon Wolstenholme, *The Royal College of Physicians of London* (London, 1964), pp. 396–97.

is quite insensitive to the feelings of others and therefore altogether tact-
less in his relations with his fellow-practitioners. His self-confidence takes
the form of arrogance, and the spots of commonness which George Eliot
attributes to him include the fact that "that distinction of mind which
belonged to his intellectual ardour, did not penetrate his feeling and
judgment about furniture, or women, or the desirability of its being known
(without his telling) that he was better born than other country surgeons"
(II, 268). More than anything else perhaps it is this lack of discrimination
in women that causes his downfall: he marries a beautiful but shallow
woman who has no interest in his profession, his scientific researches, or
his money problems—but who has a stronger will than he and conquers
him. Married to Dorothea, who "liked giving up" and who desired nothing
better than "voluntary submission to a guide who would take her along
the grandest path" (I, 41), he might have been the John Hunter, the Sir
Astley Cooper, or the Sir William Lawrence of Middlemarch. Dorothea
was clearly the right choice for him, and unless one sees more in that dilet-
tante Will Ladislaw than I do, the marriage would have been equally good
for her. But then we should not have had that great novel *Middlemarch*.

# Sensation Fiction in a Minor Key: THE

## ORDEAL OF RICHARD FEVEREL

Benjamin Franklin Fisher IV

*Hahnemann Medical College*

WHEN GEORGE MEREDITH began to write *The Ordeal of Richard Feverel* early in 1858, he had for several years been experimenting with various verse and prose forms, trying to find a medium suitable to his abilities and desires.[1] That he may not have been entirely at ease with the materials in his first genuine novel has been the thesis of many a critique from 1859, when the novel first appeared in June, to the present. The first reviewer of *Feverel*, writing in the *Leader* (2 July 1859), simultaneously complimented and chastised the youthful novelist: "George Meredith can write well and conceive grandly, but he has yet to learn to correct, or at any rate to conceal, his eccentricities."[2] Twentieth-century critics of *Feverel* have seen diverse centers of interest in the novel, but in this respect they are only the progeny of their anonymous Victorian ancestor quoted above in experiencing difficulty with the book. Joseph Warren Beach writes, "In this story nothing goes under its own name, and no one under his." He continues: "One of the distracting features of Meredith is his uncertainty of tone."[3] More recent critiques, following another of Beach's lines of thought, agree that a good deal of burlesque and parody lie just below the surface of the novel, and that the form is one of great experimentation, emphasizing "Meredith's intellectual exuberance and his desire to dazzle."[4]

---

1. Lionel Stevenson, *The Ordeal of George Meredith* (New York, 1953), pp. 47ff., 60. All references to *The Ordeal of Richard Feverel* are to Professor Stevenson's revised Modern Library Edition (New York, 1968), which reproduces the text of the original 1859 version. All other references to Meredith's novels are to the Memorial Edition, 29 vols. (New York, 1909–12).

2. This anonymous review is conveniently located in *Meredith: The Critical Heritage*, ed. Ioan Williams (London, 1971), pp. 61–62.

3. *The Twentieth-Century Novel* (New York, 1932), pp. 40–41.

4. Joseph Warren Beach, *The Comic Spirit in George Meredith* (New York, 1911), in a chapter treating *Feverel* entitled, significantly, "The Wiseacre" (pp. 34–55) mentions specifically the "invariably gay spirit of ridicule" accorded Sir Austin and his System in the first edition of the novel. See also Susanne Howe, *Wilhelm Meister and His English Kinsman* (New York, 1930), pp. 268–77; Stevenson, *The Ordeal of George Meredith*, p. 61; Walter F. Wright, *Art and Substance in George Meredith*

Shortly after the appearance of *Feverel*, Meredith himself wrote to
Samuel Lucas, editor of *Once A Week*, deprecating the book's weaknesses
and obscurities. He concluded his letter: "I would rather have Mudie and
the British Matron with me than the whole Army of the Press."[5] Such a
statement suggests, most obviously, that the fledgling novelist was eager
for sales and recognition. Like Edgar Allan Poe, with whom he shared a
paramount desire to create great poems, Meredith "wrote prose for bread
and fame."[6] To insure success in securing bread and fame, an author had
frequently to cater to public taste, and while "*The Ordeal of Richard
Feverel* has been read in many ways," to quote Gillian Beer,[7] I find that
no reading has taken as its thesis any account of the supernatural or melodramatic elements which Meredith incorporates into his text.

His crushing disdain for popular fictional taste in his time, moreover,
has often led critical attention away from his bids *for* popularity.[8] Though
fantastic and uneven in their bidding powers, *The Shaving of Shagpat* and
*Farina* betray a young man's familiarity with literary models of an exotic,
if timeworn, Gothic-melodramatic sort. While the term "sensation novel"
apparently was not coined until several years after *Feverel*, the founder
of that school, Wilkie Collins, had been at work for nearly a decade by

---

(Lincoln, Nebraska, 1953), pp. 42, 147ff.; Phyllis Bartlett, "Richard Feverel, Knight-
Errant," *BNYPL*, 63 (July 1959), 329–40; William H. Marshall, "Richard Feverel,
'The Original Man,'" *VN*, 18 (Fall, 1960), 15–18; Irving H. Buchen, "The Importance
of Minor Characters in 'The Ordeal of Richard Feverel,'" *BUSE*, 5 (Autumn 1961),
154–66; Donald Fanger, "George Meredith as Novelist," *NCF*, 16 (March 1962), 317–
28; John W. Morris, "Inherent Principles of Order in 'Richard Feverel,'" *PMLA*, 78
(Sept. 1963), 333–40; L. T. Hergenhan, "Meredith's Attempts to Win Popularity:
Contemporary Reactions," *SEL*, 4 (Fall 1964), 637–51; I. M. Williams, "The Organic
Structure of 'The Ordeal of Richard Feverel,'" *RES*, ns 18 (Fall 1964), 16–29;
Lawrence Poston, III, "Dramatic References and Structure in 'The Ordeal of Richard
Feverel,'" *SEL*, 6 (Autumn 1966), 743–52; J. Raban Bilder, "Meredith's Experiments
with Ideas," *VN*, 38 (Fall 1970), 18–21; Gillian Beer, *Meredith: A Change of Masks*
(London, 1970), p. 28. The quotation is from L. T. Hergenhan, "Meredith's Use of
Revision: A Consideration of the Revisions of 'Richard Feverel' and 'Evan Harring-
ton,'" *MLR*, 59 (Oct. 1964), 541.

5. *The Collected Letters of George Meredith*, ed. C. L. Cline (Oxford, 1970), pp.
39–40. For Mudie's influence upon Meredith's critical reception, see Guinevere L.
Griest, *Mudie's Circulating Library and the Victorian Novel* (Bloomington, Ind.,
1970), pp. 138–43.

6. The phrase is Thomas O. Mabbott's in "On Poe's 'Tales of the Folio Club,'" *SR*,
26 (April 1928), 171. Meredith's own divided aims are considered in Fanger, "George
Meredith as Novelist," p. 321.

7. *Meredith: A Change of Masks*, p. 11.

8. Hergenhan, "Meredith's Attempts to Win Popularity," p. 637. In reviewing Professor Stevenson's biography of Meredith, Clarence L. Cline mentions Meredith's
divergence from the methods of Dickens, Thackeray, and Trollope, i.e., from those
novelists whose works were readily accepted. See *JEGP*, 54 (July 1955), 443.

the time of Meredith's first novel, and *The Woman in White*, "the supreme sensation novel," as Gordon Ray calls it, rivalled *Evan Harrington* as magazine serial fare the next year.[9]

The terms "Gothic" and "Sensation" become interchangeable in surveying the diverse paths of terror fiction of the nineteenth century. In an introduction to Charlotte Brontë's *Villette*, which originally appeared in 1853, the late Geoffrey Tillotson points out that she employed techniques of "what would soon be called 'sensation'—such things as the nocturnal appearance of a mad woman, or the rescue of an employer from his blazing bed," and Lucy Snowe's confrontation with a "ghost" who is a human being in disguise.[10] Professor Stevenson says of Wilkie Collins: "In his hands the Gothic tale of terror was finally domesticated," and this domesticated Gothicism was rechristened Sensationalism during the later part of the century. Critical scrutiny perceived the ancestry of the Sensation Novel delineated as far back as Walpole, however, and saw its transmutation through Radcliffe, Lewis, Bulwer, and Ainsworth before coming to full flower in Collins, Miss Braddon, Mrs. Wood, and even Rhoda Broughton. The term "sensation novelists" apparently first appeared in *The London Review* for 16 February 1861, in relation to American writers, and it enjoyed special vogue during the sixties. But the term "'sensation'" had already been applied to Collins in an 1855 review of *Antonina* and *Basil*, and it would persist as a familiar coinage, in the very hands of Meredith himself, for one, till the nineties.[11] Writing to Edward Russell in 1891, Meredith informed him that "the present taste is for the direct, incisive, sensational" in fiction.[12] Stereotyped sensation features soon came into prominence: "a cruel father . . . a mysterious legend and a family doom . . . three broken hearts, leading respectively to immediate death, imbecility, and lunacy." Henry James mentions as Miss Braddon's stock-in-trade "a skilful combination of bigamy, arson, murder, and insanity."[13]

9. Stevenson, *The Ordeal of George Meredith*, pp. 76–77; Ray's comment appears in his preface to *The Woman In White*, ed. Kathleen Tillotson and Anthea Trodd (Boston, 1969), p. v.

10. *Villette*, ed. Geoffrey Tillotson and Donald Hawes (Boston, 1971), p. 6.

11. Stevenson's statement appears in his review of Nuel P. Davis's biography of Collins in *JEGP*, 56 (July 1957), 507. See also "Catchpenny Literature," *The London Review*, 16 Feb. 1861, 171. I am indebted to my colleague Randolph Woods Ivy for furnishing me this reference. The 1855 article is "Modern Novelists—Great and Small," *Blackwood's Edinburgh Magazine*, 77 (May 1855), 566. See also "Our Novels: The Sensation School," *Temple Bar*, 29 (June 1870), 410–12.

12. *Letters*, p. 1043.

13. See "Sensation Novels," *Quarterly Review*, 113 (April 1863), 504–5; James's remark is in "Miss Braddon," *Nation*, 1 (9 Nov. 1865), 593. See also Margaret O.

With some few alterations, these characteristics appear in certain portions of *Feverel*, which, so far as I am aware, has never even been mentioned in connection with sensationalism.

Meredith was indeed well aware of the eagerness for such "'Victorian Gothic" tales. Apropos of some Christmas stories he wrote to Lucas in December 1859: "There is no ghost-walking, and picturing of the season, as we are accustomed to see," and several days later he mentioned the improbabilities—and the popularity—of *The Woman in White*, which is considered a landmark among sensation novels. Still another letter condemned the excesses of a second giant among melodramatic best-sellers, Mrs. Wood's *East Lynne*, and deplores the execrable taste of its avid readers.[14] To look closely at *Feverel* in its first edition, however, suggests that at least one gesture of its young author was toward several of those familiar Gothic, melodramatic conventions which persisted in fiction through the century. Side by side with the desire to draw responses of chills and fright from avid readers was the ever ready impulse toward mockery of what might be ludicrous in such works. The gauntlet of burlesque and laughter confronting Gothic fiction numbered among its representatives Beckford's *Azemia*, Jane Austen's *Northanger Abbey*, Barrett's *The Heroine*, to name but a few, in its early days. Then came Poe, who in "How to Write a Blackwood Article" and other such tales, tumbled the entire preceding legions of Gothic horror stories up, down, and about with hilarious raillery. Given Meredith's own interest in the comic impulse, it is in no way doubtful that his awareness of the popular might all too easily veer off into paths where the frightful would confront his well known "silvery laughter" and come away turned inside out and upside down by means of burlesque, satire, and parody. In *Feverel* one may detect the young novelist's models being ranged subtly for the good-humored scrutiny of alert, sophisticated readers.

Sir Austin Feverel is presented to us in chapter I as "Baronet, of Raynham Abbey, in a certain Western County folding Thames: a man of wealth, and honour, and a somewhat lamentable history" (p. 4). This introductory description could very well come, with no great transpositions, from the pages of Mrs. Radcliffe or Monk Lewis or Maturin, or from Collins and his imitators. Sir Austin's mysterious past could be counted upon to win readers geared for heroes and heroines with strange backgrounds of guilt,

W. Oliphant, "Sensation Novels," *Blackwood's Edinburgh Magazine*, 91 (May 1862), 564–84.

14. *Letters*, pp. 49, 51–52, 146–47.

fear, and passion. His heritage of land wealth, the very name Raynham Abbey, suggest a stock situation. Sir Austin of the as yet unknown past hates women, as Gothic hero-villains frequently did, and the abbey seems ever on the verge of becoming one of those "haunted castles" so necessary for backdrops to frightening deeds in Gothic novels. Combining these "clues" with "a Mrs. Malediction" and the mention of "the Ordeal of the Feverels" (pp. 14, 16–17) further strengthens an unwary reader's impression that subsequent chapters will amplify these mere hints of family madness, for madness is what the neighboring gentry consider the Feverels' ordeal to be. The impression that Sir Austin's bent is toward madness, and that he will, in some future chapter, perpetrate some villainy as a result is intensified by this thought of his nephew Adrian, as he hears his uncle prowling through Raynham late at night: "A monomaniac at large, watching over sane people in slumber" (p. 64). The evil night prowler peoples the pages of Gothic and sensation fiction, and the presentation here is slanted toward cajoling readers to think about Sir Austin in that way. But no raving lunacy, no stagey, violent fits of raving ever occur in either Sir Austin or Richard, our two most important Feverels, to satisfy any Gothic enthusiasts. True, Richard's young wife Lucy is stricken with brain-fever and dies (pp. 589–90), but there is no great space devoted to detailing her sufferings, and her malady takes the form of silent withdrawal instead of the more characteristic terrifying, action-packed form of madness to be found in the works of Poe, Maturin, or *Blackwood's* writers. The importance of the inner turnings of psychology rather than outward, sensational manifestations are what Meredith wishes to stress. And this failure to fulfill, speaking sensationally, comes even after we read that Sir Austin had been earlier "shaken by one tremendous shock of Heaven's lightning," leaving him with "Stricken Pride, and a feverish blood" (p. 17). This rhetoric brings to mind Walpole's Manfred and a whole host of frightening personages branded by supernatural marks or afflicted with remorse for past crimes but still plotting epic diabolic schemes.

In the manner of Jane Austen's *Northanger Abbey* or of his own father-in-law's *Nightmare Abbey*, in which the traditional haunted castle proves indeed not to be haunted at all, Meredith takes occasion to dart mild ridicule at his own Sir Austin and perhaps, by way of that humor, at a reading audience too eager for the horrific. The Baronet takes a midnight peregrination through Raynham, in a chapter entitled "Arson," with all the forebodings that that word conjures in sensation fiction. In good stock fashion Sir Austin ends near the chamber "where his son was lying in the left wing of the Abbey" (p. 65). Traditional Gothic suspense is implied in the rhetoric of the ensuing passage: "At the end of the gallery which led to it, he discovered a dim light. Doubting it an illusion, Sir Austin accelerated his pace. This wing had aforetime a bad character. Notwithstanding what years had done to polish it into fair repute, the Raynham Kitchen stuck to the tradition still, and preserved certain stories of ghosts seen there, and thought to have been seen, that effectually blackened it in the susceptible minds of new-housemaids and under-cooks, whose fears would not allow the sinner to wash his sins. . . ." One immediately questions why young Richard, "the Hope of Raynham," is allowed by his strict, over-protective parent to sleep in such surroundings, but the seeker after thrills in fiction would never have wondered for an instant—because in Gothic novels innocents *always* slept in haunted or unsafe chambers. Such a reader would instead plunge on, with bated breath, to learn what might befall Sir Austin or young unprotected Richard. The narrative continues: "As the Baronet advanced, the fact of a light burning was clear to him. A slight descent brought him into the passage, and he beheld a poor human candle standing outside his son's chamber. At the same moment a door closed hastily. He entered Richard's room. The boy was absent. The bed was unpressed: no clothes about: nothing to show that he had been there that night. Sir Austin felt vaguely apprehensive." That this man, this arch priest of scientific rationalism, as he considers himself, should even for a moment think of ghosts or the suggestion thereof is a deflating shaft, in the manner of mock-heroic, aimed at his much loved "System." And, as with Jane Austen's Catherine Morland, any reader who has grown too enamored of traditional fictional chills and thrills is shortly doomed to disappointment in imagining dire circumstances coming Sir Austin's or Richard's way. Sir Austin is not beset by any evil, he falls through no trapdoor, he confronts no diabolical ghost, he finds no attacker besetting the absent Richard. Since the turn of this novel is psychological, the Baronet learns only that his son has been indulging in spiteful pranks, and readers learn perhaps that the all too inviting "Arson" is the mere firing of a neighboring farmer's rick instead of a colossal holocaust in Raynham itself. As in *Northanger Abbey* and *The Heroine*, the protagonist, and through him the reader, finds things not so bad as they initially seem to be.

Yet, as if to lure on a popular audience despite this letdown, Meredith dangles more sensationalism before those who might still hope for mystery and intrigue in the book. The sections concerning Richard's important fourteenth birthday fasten one's attention once more directly upon the

Feverel ordeal, the very use of which word in the title might lead some readers to anticipate something in the nature of the *Horrid Mysteries, The Mysterious Warning, The Fate of Smedley*, or *The Fatal Revenge* turned modern. Further eerie circumstances in the life of the young hero are introduced early on the morning of this signal day. Richard sees "the shadow of a solitary cypress, planted by some sad-minded Ancestress" (p. 43), and he quickly calls Rip's attention to this ominous shadow's pursuit of himself: "Look! do you see how that shadow follows me?—just look . . . . They say in our family that when we any of us come across it in this way— like this, look!—there's going to be mischief." His great-great grandfather had been similarly pursued by this shadow just prior to his engaging in a fatal duel. While this omen serves on the one hand to make *Feverel* appear like fairly conventional literary fare (there are similar ominous symbols in *The Bride of Lammermoor, Rookwood*, and *Bleak House*), and while Richard's own duel, far off as yet, with Lord Mountfalcon is foreshadowed here, the cumulative effect is something far different from the old-fashioned incident and physical violence of the shilling shocker. Instead the "death" which Richard's duel brings for him is mental death, i.e., death-in-life, loss of spontaneity accompanied by a plunge into gloom, which befalls him after losing Lucy. So psychological accuracy replaces the blood-and-thunder incident in turning the river that is the Gothic tradition through the locks of sensation fiction and thence out again toward the modern psychological novel of a James, a Faulkner, or a Joyce.

The ominous cypress tree appears twice again in connection with Richard, "O Richard of the Ordeal," as Adrian so tellingly dubs him. One night after he and Lucy have fallen in love they are on the lake, discussing her dream about the felling of the tree (p. 209); shortly thereafter we read: "The shadow of the Cypress was lessening on the lake," and this statement occurs, significantly, while the star of Richard's and Lucy's love is in the ascendant. Lucy notices particularly that the shadow "does point toward us," and, good though this *may* be at the time, the end of their happiness and the frightful consequences of the resultant grief are foreshadowed here, if offhandedly, even though the young lovers disregard the warning. The final mention of the tree, in which its portentousness is again disregarded, occurs just before Richard hastens off to duel with Mountfalcon (p. 585). He gazes from his son's bedroom window toward the lake and recalls the shadow which he had, significantly, ignored on the night he and Lucy rowed near it. He then rushes off to keep his appointment, is wounded, and catastrophe descends upon Raynham and its inhabitants

290 Benjamin Franklin Fisher IV

in consequence. And so the old familiar haunted castle, peopled with madness and rife with horrors, is domesticated into a more realistic fiction in that the madness and death are here made psychologically plausible. Their physical manifestations are once again played down in Meredith's hands, and the emotional consequences are emphasized instead.

Another familiar feature from traditional terror fiction, all too familiar to many, is the ghost who ever lurks close to the protagonist, at times for good, at times for evil, always for evoking terror from the reader. To be sure, a supernatural being would be one drawing card for popular recognition—a budding novelist would be quite likely to present his readers with one for that very reason—and so a ghost glides through the early portions of this 'prentice novel from time to time. Few readers in 1859 would have found peculiar the opening portions of chapter III (p. 21) where, on the night of Richard's seventh birthday, we learn that "Sir Austin sat in the presence of a phantom." Sure enough, later that night an apparently supernatural, beautiful lady appears at Richard's bedside, as if to discover to him, too, the presence of a phantom, although she kisses him instead of perpetrating foul deeds upon his person. Sir Austin immediately inquires if people have been talking about ghosts to the boy, "and then prophesies that this nocturnal midnight visitor bodes ill for Raynham: What he has seen, has been seen in this house before, and is not a good omen. I do not perhaps altogether believe in supernatural visitations. Call it an optical delusion. It is in the habit of coming upon us when something is about to happen" (pp. 225–26). In Sir Austin's very hesitancy to doubt the supernatural, Meredith furnishes just enough titillation to lure along a gullible reader through the stylistic intricacies of the early chapters of this rather baffling book.

Like the shadow of the cypress, this nocturnal appearance suggests the family ordeal or curse once more. Humor enters again, however, and quickly, for once more Sir Austin's scientific pretensions quail before the unknown, and instead of little Ricky's being restrained from walking near a cliff's precipitous drop, combatting quicksand, or battling fierce beasts, he is denied toys, ices, and cakes. Thus another mock heroic deflation of sensationalism may, but may not, provide sufficient warning against taking too seriously in this novel the supernatural for the supernatural's sake. Richard's Uncle Algernon is wounded during games later in the day, his leg is amputated, and Sir Austin, "not altogether dissatisfied," remarks that he had foretold a catastrophe. But Algernon's injury results from natural circumstance; it smacks little of the old-fashioned intervening evil spirit and much more of the type of fictional realism found, for example, in Thackeray's low-key, offhanded treatment of George Osborne's death in *Vanity Fair.* The ghost proves ultimately to be Richard's mother (p. 26), returned to spend some stealthy moments loving her boy, and Meredith provides us with an example of the explained supernatural akin to those of Mrs. Radcliffe and her imitators, in whose works corpses are really only wax figures, eerie music is discovered to come from a concealed eolian harp, and ghosts prove finally to be living human beings in disguise.

But, as in the case of the cypress tree and its shadow, almost as soon as readers begin to assume that *Feverel* may not indeed be primarily a thriller at all, we confront the ghost once more in a real sensation-novel circumstance. On the night of Richard's fourteenth birthday, as Sir Austin leaves off eavesdropping upon his son and Rip, and is about to depart stealthily, the chapter closes with the rhetoric of a genuine Collins sort of "cliff hanger": "As he did so, a cry was heard in the passage. He hurried out, closed the chamber, and came upon little Clare lying senseless along the floor." The next chapter begins on the next morning with a recounting of gossip concerning the fire at Farmer Blaize's home and the source of what had so terribly frightened little Clare. As if to taunt readers for the explained ghost of an earlier chapter, Meredith writes again in good sensational style: "Raynham counterbalanced Arson with an Authentic Ghost of a Lady, dressed in deep mourning, a scar on her forehead, and a bloody handkerchief at her breast, and frightful to behold! and no wonder the child was frightened out of her wits and lay in a desperate state awaiting the arrival of the London Doctors" (p. 70). Readily detected, even though no great space is allotted to detailing them, are the genuine sensational elements of fire, fright, and possible supernaturalism. The fact that they are kept in a low key probably results from Meredith's seeing an advantage in moving quickly from such hackneyed material toward greater plausibility, and perhaps he wished to throw out a crumb for the ordinary reader before moving quickly into his chief concern, the probing of egotistical human nature, i.e., the emotional ordeal of Richard.

This chief concern occupies the next six chapters, in which we see Richard's self develop another stage in growth, as the consequences of the rick burning begin to affect him psychologically. Chapter XV opens with the narrator's intruding to explain away the "ghost" once for all. The tone of this opening suggests an uncertain mockery, i.e., according surface solemnity to what is really laughable (p. 119): "Laying of Ghosts is a public duty, and as the mystery of the Apparition that had frightened little Clare was never solved on the stage of events at Raynham, where dread walked the Abbey, let us go behind the scenes a moment. Morally superstitious as the Baronet was, the character of his mind was opposed to anything like spiritual agency in the affairs of men, and when the matter was made clear to him, it shook off a weight of weakness and restored his mental balance. . . ." A letter has revealed to him that Lady Feverel had returned once more to see her son. Thus while those who are not in on the whole truth continue to wonder fearfully, to keep dread walking, readers possessed of a more alert, sophisticated knowledge naturally realize that a psychological novel, a History of Father and Son, as this book is subtitled, will contain no supernatural claptrap. Indeed from this point on to the end, there are no more of these half-hearted gestures toward the conventionally mysterious. In 1875 and 1896 Meredith revised *Feverel* and either cut the portions containing supernatural leanings altogether or altered them so that a reader's attention would grapple more quickly, and thence remain centered upon, the psychological slant of the novel—on the interest in character rather than a multitude of incidents which affect characters (and then only at the surface level of entertainment).[15]

In the first version of *Feverel* Meredith, like Collins but to a much less obvious extent, domesticated Gothicism in one way by modifying considerably what had been the incredible into plausible components of the newly developing realistic and psychological type of fiction. Although Meredith acknowledged his unsuccessfulness in using popular supernatural or horrific fare, clearly he could never wholly dissever himself from such materials. While he so often scathingly denounced the common entertainment fiction of his times, and while he is so often mentioned in terms of his divergence from the mainstream of Victorian fiction, he often betrays a suppressed desire, if ever so minor, to bridge the gap. Richard's wedding, for instance, is foreshadowed to Mrs. Berry in "a supernatural tendency in [her] fire to burn *all on one side*: which signifies that a Wedding approaches the house. Why—who shall say? Omens are as impassible as Heroes. It may be because in these affairs the fire is thought to be all on one side" (p. 292). Here is an additional example of Meredith's fleeting attention to supernaturalism, mixed with a humorous, cavalier escape clause. And both Richard's Uncle Algernon (p. 315) and the display of the wedding cake (p. 378) suggest that Meredith remodeled the timeworn

15. The revisions are given amplest study in Lillian Sacco's Ph.D. dissertation, "The Significance of George Meredith's Revisions of 'The Ordeal of Richard Feverel.'" University of Southern California, 1967.

"horrible" and "unaccountable" "apparition," as Algernon and the cake are
called by their beholders, into the more modern psychological, hence more
immediately believable, shock response resultant upon any such sudden
confrontation. And finally (pp. 390–91) we encounter Sir Austin "nursing
the devil," as Meredith terms it, while "he sat alone in the forlorn dead-
hush of his library." The phrasing is pure Gothic, but here is no medieval
devil with horns and pitchfork; instead the "devil" is the injured pride, the
egotism of Sir Austin himself that replaces the tiresome spectre of ghost
stories. Meredith had indeed presented to his readers just such a typical
supernatural devil, albeit with comic undertones, in *Farina* (XXI, 73–74),
that spoof on supernatural fictions, symbolically employing them, toward
portraiture of man's inner workings. As is typical of his techniques in
*Feverel*, he moves quickly away from the aspect of the devil as mere devil
to show, more importantly, the impact of darker human impulses on Sir
Austin's and Richard's minds.

Interest in and verging toward the supernatural were to recur in Meredith's subseqeunt ventures in novel writing. For example, the opening
chapter of *Sandra Belloni* might easily lead an unwitting reader into thinking that a supernatural being is singing. But a real Emilia, not a fading
spirit, soon captures one's attention. In *The Adventures of Harry Richmond*
occurs the famous scene of the statue "coming to life." Long years after
*Feverel*, in *Diana of the Crossways*, probably his most popular book,
Meredith showed that his heroine might all too easily have fallen into
inferior writing when she penned her own novels. She pondered portraying
"wicked princes, rogue noblemen, titled wantons, daisy and lily innocents,
traitorous marriages, murders, a gallows dangling a corpse dotted by a
moon, and a woman bowed beneath" (XVI, 359–60). Instead, however,
Diana, like her creator, preferred that species of novel in which there are
"no hair-breadth 'scapes, perils by sea and land, heroisms of the hero, fine
shrieks of the heroine. . . . She did not appeal to the senses nor to a superficial discernment" (XVI, 263). And in *Beauchamp's Career* appears an
authorial intrusion expressing envy of writers who succeed in writing
genuine supernatural thrillers:

> We will make no mystery about it. I would I could. Those happy
> tales of mystery are as much my envy as the popular narratives of
> the deeds of bread and cheese people, for they both create a tide-way
> in the attentive mind; the mysterious pricking our credulous flesh to
> creep, the familiar urging our obese imagination to constitutional

exercise. And oh, the refreshment there is in dealing with characters either contemptibly beneath us or supernaturally above. My way is like a Rhone island in the summer drought, stony, unattractive, and difficult between the two forceful streams of the unreal and the over-real, which delight mankind—honour to the conjurors! My people conquer nothing, win none; they are actual, yet uncommon. It is the clockwork of the brain that they are directed to set in motion and—poor actors to vacant benches! the conscience residing in thought-fulness which they would appeal to. . . . (XII, 236–37)

This theory is illustrative of Meredith's treatment of his materials in *Feverel,* for in that book the author and the reader zigzag at all times between the real and the romantic, between the natural and the super-natural. One critic succinctly phrases it: "The reader [is] asked to adapt himself quickly, and sometimes almost simultaneously to levels of cari-cature, burlesque, realistic comedy, irony, romantic idyl, serious explora-tion of man's darker motives, and finally to pathos and tragedy."[16] As
16. Hergenhan, "Meredith's Use of Revision," p. 541.
Professor Stevenson used to inform his classes, a subtle intellect is neces-sary to enjoy Meredith, and in *Feverel* the appeal to a reader's responses is at times uncertain. While Meredith's principal occupation in his first novel was with scrutinizing the workings of human character, he was never far from an awareness of how a novelist might capitalize on incredible beings and unreal situations, comic though they might be to those whose chief interest is plausibility and who are attuned to the ludicrous potential in supernatural or sensational works.